RIDING EAST

THE SS CAVALRY BRIGADE IN POLAND AND RUSSIA
1939-1942

Also by Mark Yerger
SS-STURMBANNFÜHRER ERNST AUGUST KRAG

RIDING EAST

THE SS CAVALRY BRIGADE
IN POLAND AND RUSSIA
1939-1942

MARK C. YERGER

Schiffer Military History
Atglen, PA

ACKNOWLEDGMENTS

Numerous institutions and individuals helped with the gathering of material needed for this volume. All were essential for its completeness and their various contributions deeply appreciated.

My special thanks to Zuzana Pivcova and the staff of the Vojensky historicky archiv in Prague for their constant help with massive research during several visits. Robin Cookson and the staff of the military records and photographic sections of the National Archives, Washington DC, helped in all ways possible during numerous visits. I also thank the Berlin Document Center for providing photographic material over the years.

Long time friends and newer associates, some of whom sadly died before completion of the book, helped with critical detail data or illustrations. For this my thanks go especially to Phil Nix for his knowledge, proofreading and advice as well as many photos. My appreciation for photo materials also extends to Walter Ott, Jakob Tiefenthäler, Jess Lukens, Jost Schneider and several private sources. Extraordinary thanks must go to James Lucas for support and inspiration during frequent periods when I wanted to abandon the research. All maps are by George Nipe and my fullest admiration of his cartographic skill is combined with my gratitude for the time he invested while busy working on his own manuscript. Four modest contributors chose to remain anonymous but I want to give my deepest acknowledgment to "Booty" who deserves to have his name on the cover for his work.

My family lived through all the frustrations typical of a researcher. My mother and sister, despite still not fully understanding exactly what I research, contributed with support and stress relief through a long period. In the final hectic and stress filled weeks, my cat, Fred, managed to keep my nerves under emotional control.

Henry Deemer taught me more than anyone else about numerous facets of the Third Reich. I have never forgotten his influence and credit him with my desire to learn. Otto Weidinger taught me to be an objective and neutral historian void of political opinion. He was my confidant, friend and the person I've admired most in my lifetime so his inspiration will never be forgotten. Finally, this lifetime of topic study was started by my grandmother, Katheryn Woelper, and I thank her for my beginning while never forgetting her early support.

Research is a collective effort. If this book makes a small contribution to recording history, then the above persons should to be thanked by those who gain from it.

Mark C. Yerger
1996

DEDICATION:
To the woman I hope to marry

Book Design by Robert Biondi.

Printed in the United States of America.
ISBN: 0-7643-0060-1

We are interested in hearing from authors with book ideas on related topics.

Published by Schiffer Publishing Ltd.
77 Lower Valley Road
Atglen, PA 19310
Please write for a free catalog.
This book may be purchased from the publisher.
Please include $2.95 postage.
Try your bookstore first.

CONTENTS

INTRODUCTION

With the end of the Second World War having passed its half century anniversary, the stream of books on the period seems never-ending. Few other topics have generated more interest than the numerous facets of the SS. An organization that created civil SS units, elite field troops, controlled the police (Polizei), handled security and intelligence of all types, created its own economic enterprises as well as establishing the concentration camps, the fascination with its numerous tangents seems insatiable.[1] The volume of surviving documents the organization produced is extraordinary and makes one wonder how such extensive record keeping was maintained prior to the computer era.

Undoubtedly the most written about SS topics are units, operations and personalities of the Armed SS (Waffen-SS). Some aspects of this portion of the SS have been examined in depth while others within this category have not, whether due to lack of notoriety or unavailable surviving documentation. Those units created which developed into front line combat units such as "Leibstandarte," "Das Reich," "Wiking" and "Totenkopf" have been written about extensively and hopefully will be examined in even greater detail.[2] They were elite combat field units and existed the longest with resulting lengthy battle histories. They are often referred to as the "classic" divisions. As such they are not only rightfully respected for their legendary accomplishments in battle but were also responsible for ushering in developments in warfare still in evidence today.

By the conclusion of hostilities, the number of Waffen-SS divisions had grown to 38 and included armored, infantry, mountain and cavalry divisions. Roughly half of these units were formed in the latter half of the war and had personnel compositions of less than established divisional manpower strength. Along with these, numerous smaller SS units, mostly of brigade or large combat group in size, were also deployed in addition to armed Police units, SS-Totenkopfverbände (Death's Head Units) as well as troops engaged in combat derived from the numerous SS schools and training units established. In many cases these non-divisional combat formations were disbanded, rebuilt, absorbed by other units or destroyed, especially in the final year of the conflict when ad-hoc formations were as numerous as they were short lived. Many of these and the individuals who served in them performed honorable service for their country and amazing feats of bravery in both offensive and defensive operations, especially in the case of armored units. Other units, due to a variety of circumstances, not the least of which was their operational assignment, had a less than honorable operational deployment history as far as any retrospective analysis of their record is concerned.

Cavalry units were still considered front-line elite troops in most countries during the decade prior to WWII. Not only was their mobility appreciated, but in the few years just prior to the war,

---

[1] See "Anatomy of the SS State" and "The Order of the Death's Head" for good overall views of the complexities of the SS organization and command structure. Numerous texts are available covering the more important Waffen-SS units including works by Stein, Koehl, Bender/Taylor and Klietmann (see bibliography) which give outline histories of numerous elements as well as volumes outside the scope of this work dealing with other facets of the SS and, to a much smaller extent, the Polizei. Unfortunately, few individual biographies of SS officers have been written. Though of no historical importance, a secondary deluge of publications deals with all aspects of collecting memorabilia of the period of which SS material is among the most sought after. The value of these items has grown to the point of a cottage industry producing reproductions having been created.

[2] Histories have been written for most of these classic units though many divisional formations have received scant attention. The same is the case with non-divisional sized elements and sub-divisional components.

these units accomplished their mission with no strain on factories already overextended trying to produce sufficient material to furnish new fully motorized units. Under certain terrain or climatic conditions, mounted formations could accomplish tasks unsuitable for motorized troops. However, with the obsession of most armies to re-equip with this technological advancement, the benefits of cavalry were seemingly lost to the major combatants by the eve of WWII except for Russia which utilized its Siberian cavalry in large numbers and with great effect. The obsession with mechanized units seems to have negated the value of mounted troops in a European conflict in the mind of Hitler's pre-war military planning, for both the Army and Waffen-SS.

Mounted units existed in the General SS (Allgemeine-SS) during the 1930s. The SS Cavalry Brigade (SS-Kavallerie-Brigade), whose history along with its precursor units forms this study, drew some of its early cadre from these Allgemeine-SS cavalry formations, most importantly the eventual brigade commander Hermann Fegelein. As such, the first chapter gives a background to these Allgemeine-SS cavalry troops to familiarize the reader with them when assimilating biographical data on various members of the primary topic.

Other cadre came from a variety of existing units of the SS and Police including the SS-Totenkopfverbände in which the initial cavalry regiment(s) were a component within the complex SS command hierarchy. Later, the restructure of the field units and higher echelons of the SS resulted in the SS-Kavallerie-Brigade being designated a component of the Waffen-SS. Allgemeine-SS officers serving with the Brigade simultaneously became reserve Waffen-SS officers, often at an initially lower rank. These ranks were designated with the suffix "d.R." (der Reserve).

In defense of the then forming and later much expanded front line Waffen-SS combat units, the technical grouping together of various SS components (including the concentration camps) as all being part of the Waffen-SS was made by Reichsführer-SS Heinrich Himmler at the stroke of a pen. Himmler's action was vehemently objected to by professional military SS leaders such as Paul Hausser who considered their units strictly military formations.[3] A career SS *military* officer who spent the pre-war period serving in the SS special purpose troops (SS-Verfügungstruppe), or later the vast majority of Waffen-SS front line units, pursued a career with totally different operational objectives, training, career goals and eventual accomplishments than those of other facets of the SS. Himmler's connecting of all these facets of the SS has affected the reputation of this group of soldiers even to this day, as the layman immediately thinks that every SS man was assigned to a concentration camp. This narrow-minded attitude is unfortunately present in many historians as well. During the final stages of manuscript preparation I contacted a well known authority of German *Army* armored units. A telephone conversation progressed normally on various aspects of archive research until I was asked what my sphere of interest was. When I replied the Waffen-SS the dry response was "oh, one of *those.*"

However, the *technical* connection existed between various SS elements, as evidenced by the collective judgment as a criminal organization against the entire SS organization at the Nuremberg trials, which should probably be re-evaluated in retrospect. To collectively judge guilty the *entire* Waffen-SS is, in the opinion of this author, displaying ignorance of historical facts. Given units and individuals performed differently at different tasks and should be judged from that perspective. Most units and individuals who fought in Waffen-SS front line units did so honorably and, despite this, they were denied post war veterans benefits given to other members of the Wehrmacht. This is but a single example of the harm produced by the consolidated condemnation issued at Nuremberg. The fact that these front line divisions were, in the majority, field combat soldiers is evidenced even today by the German government (extremely sensitive of and against pro-Nazi sentiments) which allows veteran associations of those units to exist. Some of this situation could have been addressed and corrected by senior German Army commanders in the post war period. However, many forgot

---

[3] The senior officer of the Waffen-SS and recognized as its developer and most influential commander. Hausser established the SS officer school in Braunschweig, was inspector of the pre-war Armed SS, led the first Waffen-SS division to be formed ("Das Reich"), commanded the first SS corps formed (II.SS-Panzer-Korps) and later commanded an Army Group. Decorated with the Knight's Cross with Oakleaves and Swords, he attained the highest SS rank (SS-Oberst-Gruppenführer) and authored the first post war history of the Waffen-SS. He was the senior member of the Waffen-SS veterans association and died in 1973.

their glowing accolades and requests for Waffen-SS field formations during the conflict when writing their memoirs, choosing instead to downplay their contribution and abilities. Even a superficial examination of period documentation confirms the *wartime* positive opinion of numerous well-known senior Army commanders with regard to the SS divisions under their command.

Some units and individuals did exceed normal battlefield conduct and war crimes were committed, but certainly not by all units or individuals. On the other side of the fence, no judgment was ever made against *any* allied units which exceeded normal military behavior in the field despite documentation proving such conduct occurred.

Although the later mid-1942 formed SS Cavalry Division (SS-Kavallerie-Division) had personnel from the earlier Brigade as a portion of its cadre, it was for all practical purposes a new unit which incorporated a second generation of officers, NCOs and men. This unit, with a final designation of 8.SS-Kavallerie-Division "Florian Geyer," was highly decorated and remained operational until destroyed in Budapest during February 1945. In the case of the Knight's Cross, which was awarded for single feats of bravery or combat leadership, this later division was the sixth most decorated unit of the 38 divisions and numerous other smaller armed units of the Waffen-SS and Police.[4] A totally separate award instituted in 1941, though often incorrectly considered a lower decoration, was the German Cross in Gold. It was only awarded for repeated acts of bravery in combat while the Knight's Cross could be given for a single combat engagement.[5] Numerous individuals serving with the later SS-Kavallerie-Division were awarded this decoration as well, some of whom served with the Brigade or its predecessor independent regiments. Information is provided for these individuals when available and relevant to the primary topic under examination.[6]

References to "the Division" or "SS-Kavallerie-Division" are for this later formed unit. Two other SS cavalry divisions, the 22.SS-Freiwilligen-Kavallerie-Division "Maria Theresia" and the 37.SS-Freiwilligen-Kavallerie-Division "Lützow" also were formed but the latter was of lesser strength than the original SS-Kavallerie-Division and "Maria Theresia."

From initial sub-element commands or staff positions in the SS-Kavallerie-Brigade, three officers later became divisional commanders, aside from Hermann Fegelein, who also led the subsequent SS-Kavallerie-Division.[7] The unheralded officers who served as first staff officers (1.Generalstabsoffizier or Ia) also ranged from good to excellent and were major contributors to the operational success of the Brigade as were some superb junior commanders.[8]

As will be seen in the text, the Brigade was subordinated or attached to a variety of senior SS area leaders and units as well as Army elements, sometimes simultaneously, on a temporary basis. The latter instances occurred mostly in Russia and the former during deployment in Poland, though the unit was under overall SS administrative control in both theaters. When engaged in combat on the front lines, SS troops were under Army tactical command.

The tasks assigned the SS-Kavallerie-Brigade and its predecessor independent regiments sometimes resulted in harsh action, especially in Poland, where excesses took place under direct orders on more than one occasion. These were among the duties in Poland that the unit was created to accomplish, partly to relieve German Army units initially assigned the task of occupational duty.

---

[4] Only "Das Reich," "Wiking," "Leibstandarte," "Totenkopf " and "Nordland" received more awards of the decoration. Krätschmer, "Die Ritterkreuzträger der Waffen-SS."

[5] The rare German Cross in Silver also existed for contributions of a non-combat nature and though several members of the Brigade or Division were awarded this decoration during later service, none were awarded to any individual for duties while assigned to the Brigade or its precursor formations.

[6] Only a few were awarded the German Cross in Gold for actions with the Brigade (or earlier component formations) due to the award only being instituted in 1941.

[7] See biographies for Karl Gesele, Gustav Lombard and August Zehender.

[8] All Ia are covered with known biographical information and/or photograph during the period they were assigned. These were Christian Reinhardt, Rudolf Maeker and Karl Gesele. See individual biographical synopsis as well for junior commanders with their photographs or as footnoted annotations.

The operational necessity of a second line formation for rear area security, the resettlement policies benefiting ethnic Germans adopted after the Polish campaign, the potential punishment for disobeying direct orders and the ferocity of combat with which the Russians and Germans, and to a lesser extent the Poles, engaged on the Eastern front must be considered when formulating a retrospective opinion of this unit or a specific individual. With regard to ideology, the eastern front fighting was a war between opposites viewing their opponents as the incarnation of their total enemy. Foremost of these factors, as far as the second line units were concerned, were the policies established and coordinated under Heinrich Himmler's direct control by way of units and senior area commanders under his authority. The somewhat complex command structure of the SS in Poland is explained within its own chapter.

As a front-line combat formation in 1942, the Brigade fought very, especially the reconnaissance element. The bravery and tenacity with which these troops engaged the enemy is documented as well as their value to superior level Army commanders.

The verdict at Nuremberg stated that *membership in the SS or one of its units did not necessarily constitute guilt, though the SS as a whole was judged a criminal organization.* This attitude is pertinent when examining an individual unit operational history or specific individual. Likewise, when forming opinions a human being is morally responsible for his actions, regardless of the potential consequences of disobedience.

Long overdue credit should be given to members of the Polish and Russian civilian populations, many of whom fought back during the occupation of their country and paid for that bravery with their lives. Also, though many texts often view the Russian soldier as less skilled than his German counterpart, those who served in that theater knew him as a tenacious and brave enemy to be respected and often feared. Partisan warfare was outlawed by the Geneva convention in defense of the creation of units to combat them, while the methods utilized by Himmler to control their activity was equally harsh. Both sides fought bitterly for their beliefs and country, with both sides being capable of extreme action against their respective opponent.

Studying this period without the emotional contacts of the generation who lived in the period allows only the assimilation of documentation. It will never be possible to understand fully the mind set of participants in a conflict that hopefully will never again manifest itself in a similar fashion among civilized peoples. However, at the time of this writing (1995) actions in Bosnia are ample proof that ideological opposites are capable of barbaric actions against their fellow man. The lesson seems to have been again lost with the passage of time, reason enough that such things be examined and remembered.

Mark C. Yerger

1

ALLGEMEINE-SS
CAVALRY UNITS

The Allgemeine-SS created cavalry units during the pre-war period and although the units themselves did not form a unit basis for the early regiments of the eventual SS-Kavallerie Brigade and still later SS-Kavallerie-Division, they should be examined for several reasons. Not the least of these relevant factors is that they did provide some of the cadre of officers and men when the SS Death's Head Mounted Regiment (SS-Totenkopf-Reiterstandarte) was formed in September 1939. Some later commanders, though not necessarily transferring directly from Allgemeine-SS units, served with these formations during the earlier phase of their SS careers. This is also the case with a number junior officers and, in some instances, NCOs and men as seen by their individual biographical data. When the SS-Totenkopf-Reiterstandarte was created, its composition was based on the structure adhered to by Allgemeine-SS mounted units. They were generally a higher status unit than the normal Foot Regiments (Fuß-Standarten) of the Allgemeine-SS and attracted an often better social class of recruit.

Allgemeine-SS cavalry regiments (SS-Reiterstandarten) were components of SS Districts (SS-Oberabschnitte) which came into being in mid-November 1933, starting with the original existing five SS Groups (SS-Gruppen). These encompassed the primary geographical areas of Germany: South (Süd), North (Nord), East (Ost), Southeast (Südost) and West.[1] Following these five, others were created both inside as well as outside Germany proper as the number of individual units and geographical areas to be covered grew. Each SS-Oberabschnitt had a cavalry leader (Reiterführer) assigned to its command staff.[2] The districts were further divided into sub districts (SS-Abschnitte). These districts are explained when connected to this period of SS-Reiterstandarten history. Both these command echelons underwent an almost constant change in structure, subordinated components and designations throughout their existence.

Unlike the normal SS-Fuß-Standarten, the SS-Reiterstandarten were for most of their existence directly subordinated to the SS-Oberabschnitt of their assigned district. Beginning in September 1933 some SS-Oberabschnitte contained a separate cavalry sub-district (SS-Reiterabschnitt) which controlled two or more Reiterstandarten.[3] However, these specialized sub-district level commands were dissolved at the end of October 1936 after which their Reiterstandarten were again directly subordinated to the SS-Oberabschnitt of their operational area.

Each SS-Reiterstandarte contained five or more cavalry troops or platoons (Reiterstürme) and were designated by Roman numerals, a medical detachment (Sanitäts-Staffel) and a bugler section

---

[1] The first of the original SS Gruppen was formed in July 1932 to control the growing number of Abschnitte and Standarten, some of the latter having a history prior to that as far back as the late 1920s. By the end of the war there were 23 SS-Oberabschnitte, 45 SS-Abschnitte and more than a hundred Fuß-Standarten, apart from the Reiterstandarte and smaller specialized units. By comparison, in July 1931 there were only eight SS-Abschnitte controlling 38 SS-Fuß-Standarten and no Reiterstandarten had yet been formed (eventually 24 existed at one time or other).

[2] Most of these staff position appears to have been assigned in mid-1934. At that time the known Reiterführer of the SS-Oberabschnitte were Hermann Fegelein (Süd), Hans Floto (Mitte), Karl Deinhardt (Nordost), Kurt Hass (Nord), Kaspar König (Rhein), Paul Brantenaar (Ost), Dr. Fritz Hausamen (Südwest) and Ewald Zapp (West). The position appears to have been eliminated when the SS-Reiterabschnitte were formed.

[3] SS-Reiterabschnitte are known to have existed for SS-Oberabschnitte Südwest, Elbe, West, Südost, Süd, Nordost and Nordwest during the period that command level existed. Most men assigned to this command position during its brief existence had previously been Chief Reiterführer of the SS-Oberabschnitte. Among later officers of the SS-Totenkopf-Reiterstandarte to hold this position were Hermann Fegelein (Reiterführer of Reiterabschnitt V and later commander of the SS-Kavallerie Brigade) and Josef Fritz (Reiterführer of Reiterabschnitte II and later a squadron commander).

(Trompeterkorps) with the various components spread throughout the area assigned the Reiterstandarte. They were normally abbreviated in documents (example: R.1 equaled SS-Reiterstandarte 1).

With a personnel strength comparable to a military regiment in the pre-war period, the wartime strength became considerably less as fit cadre were transferred to active duty. Assigned to the Allgemeine-SS units were war wounded or individuals of an age past normal combat suitability. As with all components of the SS, there was an almost constant reshuffling, transfer, dissolving, re-naming and rebuilding of units. Though the Allgemeine-SS Reiterstandarten existed throughout the war, the following data covers only superior units and commanders for the SS-Reiterstandarten *until the September 1939 start of WWII*. At that time the first formation was created that would, after expansion and further development, become the eventual SS-Kavallerie-Brigade. Allgemeine-SS ranks listed are the highest attained during that command period to keep confusion for the reader to a minimum.[4]

Cities listed for the units are the Reiterstandarte headquarters area (Standort). Officers who held an Allgemeine-SS command often held a lower rank while serving in a reserve or fully active capacity in the Waffen-SS, Polizei or one of the armed forces after the war began but simulta-neously retained their Allgemeine-SS rank.

SS-Reiterstandarte 1 (SS-Oberabschnitt "Nordost")[5] formed on January 15, 1934 in Intersburg (East Prussia).[6] Commanders:

SS-Obersturmführer Horst von Skepsgardh:	Formation to September 1936
SS-Sturmbannführer Philipp Hahn:	September 1936 to September 1939

SS-Reiterstandarte 2 (SS-Oberabschnitt "Nordost") formed on January 1, 1934 in Marienburg (West Prussia). Commanders:

SS-Obersturmführer Dr. Albert Sack:	Formation to May 1934
SS-Standartenführer Dr. Helmut Kluck:	May 1934 to June 1935
SS-Untersturmführer Klaus Lessing:[7]	June 1935 to January 1936
SS-Hauptsturmführer Karl Kasch:	January 1936 to April 1938
SS-Hauptsturmführer Rudolf Osterroth:	April 1938 to September 1939[8]

SS-Reiterstandarte 3 (SS-Oberabschnitt "Nordost") formed on January 1, 1934 in Lyck (East Prussia) and moved to Treuburg in February 1935. Commanders:

SS-Oberscharführer Wilhelm von Kulesza:	Formation to August 1934
SS-Standartenführer Fritz Jancke:	August 1934 to March 1936
SS-Untersturmführer Philipp Hoffmann:	March 1936 to November 1936
SS-Obersturmbannführer Erdmann Skudlarek:	November 1936 to August 1938
SS-Sturmbannführer Pelagius Herz:	August 1938 to May 1939
SS-Hauptsturmführer Otto Hampel:	May 1939 to September 1939[9]

---

[4] Many of the SS-Oberabschnitte were split into new districts (with resulting changes in the units assigned to them to include the SS-Reiterstandarten) or had designation changes when a new district with the same title was formed in 1939/40. Along with the numbered SS-Reiterstandarten, another was named for the inspector of Allgemeine-SS cavalry units for most of the pre-war period, Wilhelm von Woikowski-Biedau. The other senior cavalry position in the Allgemeine-SS during the pre-war years was the SS Chief Mounted Leader (Chef Reiterführer der SS) attached to Himmler's staff. The position was held by Georg Skowronski in February 1934. A history of the Allgemeine-SS units would be vast and outside the scope of this study and hence the limitation of information to September 1939 (month the SS-Totenkopf-Reiterstandarte was formed and war started).

[5] SS-Oberabschnitt "Nordost" (Northeast) was formed on December 15, 1933 in Königsburg.

[6] Formation dates for some Reiterstandarten are per an untitled compilation list produced by the SS-Personalkanzlei in Berlin on December 21, 1938.

[7] He held command as an officer candidate and was promoted to SS-Untersturmführer on April 20, 1937.

[8] He retained command until May 1945.

[9] Hampel served with the SS-Totenkopf-Reiterstandarte but retained this command as well until November 1, 1942.

SS-Obersturmbannführer Paul Brantenaar (left) and his adjutant SS-Untersturmführer Wolfgang Crass. Both wear the typical uniform of Allgemeine-SS mounted units and Crass displays the adjutant's corded accouterment designating his position. The crossed lances collar insignia indicated assignment to an independent mounted unit. In this case Brantenaar was Reiterführer of SS-Oberabschnitt "Ost." Members of numbered Standarten had the regimental number on their collar. Craas became one of the initial SS-Totenkopf-Reiterstandarte cadre and held several assignments within the first unit and the later Brigade. Brantenaar also commanded SS-Reiterstandarte 7. (Photo: Phil A. Nix)

SS-Reiterstandarte 4 (SS-Oberabschnitt "Nordwest")[10] formed on February 1, 1934 and headquartered in Hamburg until August 1934, then moved to Rhena until October 1935 and Lübeck until April 1936 when it returned to Hamburg. Commanders:

SS-Obersturmführer Wilhelm Jahn:	Formation to August 1934
SS-Hauptsturmführer Fritz Krüger:	August 1934 to March 1936
SS-Hauptsturmführer Hellmuth Otte:	March 1936 to March 1937
SS-Hauptsturmführer Reinhold Kleemann:	April 1937 to September 1939[11]

SS-Reiterstandarte 5 (SS-Oberabschnitt "Nord")[12] formed on March 1, 1934 in Pyritz and moved to Stetten in August 1936. Commanders:

SS-Scharführer von Heyden-Linden:	March 1934 to April 1934[13]
SS-Obersturmbannführer Wilhelm Messner:	April 1934 to November 1936

[10] Formed as SS-Oberabschnitt "Nord" from SS-Gruppe "Nord" in 1933. It was divided into SS-Oberabschnitt "Nord" and SS-Oberabschnitt "Nordwest" on April 1, 1936.

[11] He retained command until May, 1945.

[12] This SS-Oberabschnitt was in reality SS-Oberabschnitt "Ostsee" (East Sea) and was formed in April 1936 from a portion of the original "Nord." It did not receive its new title until April 1940 when a new SS-Oberabschnitt "Nord" formed in Oslo.

[13] Information kindly provided courtesy Phil A. Nix.

SS-Hauptsturmführer Karl Struve: November 1936 to February 1938
SS-Obersturmführer Walter Schadendorf: March 1938 to September 1939[14]

SS-Reiterstandarte 6 (SS-Oberabschnitt "West") formed on April 9, 1934 in Düsseldorf. Commanders:

SS-Sturmführer Hermann Müller:	April 1934 to October 1934
SS-Obersturmführer Peter Wexel:	October 1934 to January 1935
SS-Hauptsturmführer Ewald Zapp:	January 1935 to September 1935
SS-Obersturmführer Dr. Günther von Wolff:	September 1935 to August 1936
SS-Obersturmführer Heinz Offermann:	August 1936 to March 1938
SS-Standartenführer Johann Mörschel:	March 1938 to November 1938
SS-Obersturmführer Willi Plänk:	December 1938 to September 1939[15]

SS-Reiterstandarte 7 (SS-Oberabschnitt "Ost") formed on April 23, 1934 in Berlin. Commanders:

SS-Obersturmbannführer Paul Brantenaar:	April 1934 to March 1936
SS-Obersturmführer Dr. August Schwedler:	March 1936 to October 1936
SS-Standartenführer Paul Brantenaar:	November 1936 to September 1939[16]

SS-Reiterstandarte 8[17] (SS-Oberabschnitt West) formed on April 26, 1934 in Münster and in October 1936 moved to Paderborn. Commanders:

SS-Obersturmführer Carl von Bock und Polach:	April 1934 to February 1936
SS-Sturmbannführer Otto Dorne:	February 1936 to October 1936
SS-Hauptsturmführer Dr. Otto Fritzel:	October 1936 to October 1938
SS-Sturmbannführer Hans Baumgardt:	November 1938 to September 1939[18]

SS-Reiterstandarte 9 (SS-Oberabschnitt "Nordwest") formed on May 1, 1934 in Oldenburg and moved to Bremen in December 1936. Commanders:

SS-Oberscharführer Robert Hartwig:	May 1934 to September 1934
SS-Sturmbannführer Josef Fritz:	September 1934 to January 1935
SS-Sturmbannführer Carl Deinhard:	January 1935 to April 1935
SS-Untersturmführer Rudolf Osterroth:	April 1935 to October 1936
SS-Sturmbannführer Hans von Salviati:	October 1936 to February 1938
SS-Obersturmführer Bernhard Massury:	February 1938 to July 1938
SS-Standartenführer Wilhelm von Woikowski-Biedau:	July 1938 to September 1939[19]

SS-Reiterstandarte 10 (SS-Oberabschnitt "Fulda-Werra")[20] formed on March 4, 1934 in Koblenz and moved to Arolsen in February 1936. Commanders:

Dotharbus von Weyhe:[21]	May 1934 to May 1935

---

[14] He commanded until 1943 when leadership went to Willi Plänk (who served with the SS-Totenkopf-Reiterstandarte) until May, 1945. Rank for Schadendorf was his highest pre-war.

[15] Held command until May 1945 and was a reserve officer in the Waffen-SS (served with the SS-Totenkopf-Reiterstandarte).

[16] He held command until January 1942 (see photo).

[17] Absorbed the Stürme of 23.SS-Reiterstandarte in September 1936 when that Standarte was dissolved.

[18] He held command throughout the war until May 1945.

[19] Replaced as inspector of Allgemeine-SS mounted units by Friedrich-Wilhelm Krüger in May 1938 and held command of SS-Reiterstandarte 9 until May 1945.

[20] Formed on January 1, 1937 from elements of SS-Oberabschnitt "Rhein" (Rhine).

[21] Rank unknown, he would have been an NCO as commander.

SS-Hauptsturmführer Hermann Fegelein as Führer of Reiterabschnitt V and Reiterführer SS-Oberabschnitt Süd during late 1934. (Photo: BDC)

SS-Sturmbannführer Kaspar Koenig:	May 1935 to March 1936
SS-Obersturmbannführer Carl von Pichl:	March 1936 to April 1937
SS-Sturmbannführer Ludwig Lang:	April 1937 to December 1937
SS-Hauptsturmführer Rolf Becher:	December 1937 to September 1939[22]

SS-Reiterstandarte 11 (SS-Oberabschnitt "Südost") formed on April 1, 1934 in Breslau, moved to Trebnitz in September 1935 and back to Breslau in November 1935. Commanders:

SS-Untersturmführer Wilhelm von Woikowski-Biedau:	April 1934 to September 1934
SS-Sturmbannführer Walter Moreth:	September 1934 to early 1935[23]
SS-Untersturmführer Karl von Fircks:	early 1935 to August 1935
SS-Obersturmführer Rudolf Bösel:	August 1935 to September 1936
SS-Untersturmführer Wilhelm Gervers:	September 1936 to December 1936
SS-Obersturmbannführer Josef Fritz:	December 1936 to September 1939[24]

---

[22] Held command until May 1945 and served with the SS-Totenkopf-Reiterstandarte.

[23] Information kindly provided courtesy of Phil A. Nix.

[24] Held command until May 1945 and served as a reserve officer with the SS-Totenkopf-Reiterstandarte.

SS-Reiterstandarte 12 (SS-Oberabschnitt "Nord") formed on June 1, 1934 in Scherwin. Commanders:

SS-Obersturmführer Oswald Herde:	June 1934 to July 1935
SS-Sturmbannführer Hans Krüger:	July 1935 to October 1935
SS-Sturmbannführer Erdmann Skudlarek:	October 1935 to November 1936
SS-Obersturmführer Jakob Wein:	November 1936 to September 1938
SS-Hauptsturmführer Karl Struve:	September 1938 to December 1938
SS-Hauptsturmführer Herbert Gilhofer:	December 1938 to September 1939

SS-Reiterstandarte 13 (SS-Oberabschnitt "Rhein")[25] formed on July 1, 1934 in Mannheim and moved to Heidelburg in February 1937 before returning to Mannheim. Commanders:

SS-Untersturmführer Karl Schnerr:	July 1934 to January 1935
SS-Scharführer Dr. Otto Fritzel:[26]	January 1935 to April 1935
SS-Sturmbannführer Hans Floto:	April 1935 to September 1936
SS-Sturmbannführer Kaspar König:	September 1936 to November 1936
SS-Sturmbannführer Hans Floto:	November 1936 to June 1938
SS-Sturmbannführer Rudolf von Geyr:	July 1938 to September 1939[27]

SS-Reiterstandarte 14[28] (SS-Oberabschnitt "Südwest") formed on July 9, 1934 in Karlsruhe and moved to Stuttgart in February 1937. Commanders:

SS-Anwärter Freiherr von Rosen:	July 1934 to September 1934
SS-Anwärter Klaus Lessing:	September 1934 to May 1935
SS-Obersturmbannführer Hermann Florstedt:	May 1935 to March 1936
SS-Sturmbannführer Phillip Hahn:	March 1936 to October 1936
SS-Obersturmbannführer Kaspar König:	October 1936 to July 1939[29]

SS-Reiterstandarte 15 (SS-Oberabschnitt "Süd") formed on July 15, 1934 in Regensburg, moved in May 1936 to Landshut and finally to München (Munich) in November 1936. Commanders:

SS-Obersturmführer Hermann Fegelein:[30]	July 1934 to September 1934
SS-Obersturmführer Eberhard von Kunsberg:	September 1934 to April 1936
SS-Obersturmführer Max Linbrunner:	April 1936 to October 1936
SS-Sturmbannführer Franz Lang:	October 1936 to May 1937
SS-Obersturmbannführer Carl von Pichl:	June 1937 to September 1939[31]

SS-Reiterstandarte 16 (SS-Oberabschnitt "Elbe")[32] formed on August 28, 1934 in Dresden. Commanders:

SS-Sturmbannführer Hans Floto:	August 1934 to August 1935
SS-Sturmbannführer Carl Deinhard:	August 1935 to July 1936
SS-Obersturmbannführer Arthur Müller:	July 1936 to September 1939[33]

[25] SS-Oberabschnitt "Rhein" was formed on January 1, 1934, in Wiesbaden.

[26] He was commissioned September 15, 1935. See SS-Reiterstandarte 8.

[27] Retained command after start of the war until November 1942.

[28] It combined with 13.Reiterstandarte during November/December 1936 and then later again became a separate unit.

[29] Commanders unknown after this date.

[30] Commander of the SS-Totenkopf-Reiterstandarte and the SS-Kavallerie-Brigade. See Chapter 2 for biography.

[31] He retained command throughout the war until May 1945.

[32] Formed on November 16, 1933 from part of SS-Gruppe "Ost," it was titled "Mitte" from June 1934 to April 1936.

[33] He retained command until May 1945.

Günther Temme as an SS-Untersturmführer and staff officer with Reiterabschnitt IV in 1936 before moving to SS-Reiterstandarte 7. He later transferred to the SS-Totenkopf-Reiterstandarte from the SS Main Riding School in Munich and was among the most important staff officers and junior commanders. (Photo: BDC)

SS-Reiterstandarte 17 (SS-Oberabschnitt "Süd" and SS-Oberabschnitt "Main") formed on September 1, 1934 in Oberstdorf and moved to Bad Würrishofen in March 1935. During this time assigned to SS-Oberabschnitt Süd. Dissolved at the end of October 1936, its personnel were absorbed by SS-Reiterstandarte 15. SS-Reiterstandarte 24 (SS-Oberabschnitt "Main") was formed in April 1936 and existed until October 1936. It obtained the numerical designation 17 as of November 1936. Commanders:

SS-Sturmbannführer Ludwig Lang:	September 1934 to April 1936 (dissolved)
SS-Hauptsturmführer Franz Klebl:	April 1936 to November 1936 (R.24 renumbered) to September 1939[34]

SS-Reiterstandarte 18 (SS-Oberabschnitt unknown) formed in 1935 and dissolved in late 1936. It was reformed in Vienna in 1938 at which time it became a component of SS-Oberabschnitt "Donau."[35]

SS-Hauptsturmführer Hans von Treichel:	1935 to November 1936
Franz Rinner:[36]	November 1936 until dissolved
Pre-war commander in Vienna:	Walter Turza

---

[34] ibid.

[35] Formed as SS-Oberabschnitt "Osterreich" (Austria) in mid-February 1934 and retitled "Donau" in May 1938. It was considered an illegal organization in Austria until April 1938.

[36] He held command as an NCO and was promoted SS-Untersturmführer in May 1939.

SS-Reiterstandarte 19 (SS-Oberabschnitt unknown) formed in 1935 and dissolved during October 1936. Reformed in Graudenz after start of the war. Commanders:

SS-Hauptsturmführer Anton Stebani:	1935/1936
SS-Sturmbannführer Franz Lang:	1936 until dissolved in October 1936

SS-Reiterstandarte 20 (SS-Oberabschnitt "Nordost") formed in April 1939 in Tilsit. Commanders:

SS-Hauptsturmführer Gustav Mertsch:	April 1939 to June 1939
Ernst Rademacher (NCO):	June 1939 to September 1939

SS-Reiterstandarte 21 (SS-Oberabschnitt "Mitte") formed on April 11, 1935 in Braunschweig and moved in December 1938 to Hannover. Commanders:

Koch (first name and rank unknown):[37]	April 1935 to October 1936
SS-Sturmbannführer Hubert von Wuthenau:	October 1936 to May 1939
SS-Sturmbannführer Pelagius Herz:	May 1939 to September 1939

SS-Reiterstandarte 22 (SS-Oberabschnitt "Elbe") formed on April 1, 1935 in Halle. It was dissolved at the end of October 1936 and its units incorporated into SS-Reiterstandarte 16. It was reformed in Posen on November 10, 1942. Commanders:

SS-Sturmbannführer Peter Wexel:	April 1935 to February 1936
SS-Untersturmführer Friedrich Prager:	February 1936 to October 1936

SS-Reiterstandarte 23 (SS-Oberabschnitt "Rhein") formed in March 1935 in Freiburg and dissolved in September 1936. It was reformed in late 1939 in Pirmasens and assigned to SS-Oberabschnitt "Südwest." Commander:

SS-Obersturmführer Dr. Otto Fritzel:	March 1935 to September 1936

SS-Reiterstandarte 24 ((SS-Oberabschnitt "Main") formed in April 1936 and was redesignated SS-Reiterstandarte 17 in November 1936 (see SS-Reiterstandarte 17). Commander (when designated R.24):

SS-Obersturmbannführer Josef Fritz

---

[37] Last name and command is confirmed by the SS-Personalkanzlei, but no officer with that last name is listed as commanding the Reiterstandarte in the July 1935 SS Dienstalterliste, so probably an NCO holding the position.

2

HERMANN FEGELEIN

If a single name is synonymous with the cavalry units of the Waffen-SS it is Hermann Fegelein. He was the sole official commander and single Knight's Cross winner of the SS-Kavallerie-Brigade along with being the only Swords to the Knight's Cross holder awarded that decoration for actions while assigned to the 8.SS-Kavallerie-Division.

The oldest son of retired army Oberleutnant (first lieutenant) Hans Fegelein, Otto Hermann Fegelein was born to a Catholic family in Ansbach on October 30, 1906. He inherited an early love of riding from his father that continued to grow following his family moving to Munich in 1912 where his father was assigned to a military riding school. Fegelein completed his primary educa-

The welcome reception at Munich train station on June 28, 1937 after SS-Obersturmbannführer Hermann Fegelein won a tournament competition. Shaking hands are Christian Weber and SS-Gruppenführer Karl Freiherr von Eberstein (Führer SS-Oberabschnitt Süd) with Fegelein standing beside Eberstein. Next to Fegelein is SS-Brigadeführer Christian Diehm (Führer SS Abschnitt I). (Photo: Jost Schneider)

tion in 1917 followed by secondary education and two semesters of university studies in Munich until 1926. It would appear that six months in the army assigned to a machine gun unit with Cavalry Regiment 17 in 1925-1926 was his only formal military training. He may have also served briefly in a Free Corps (Freikorps) unit.[1]

After enlisting in Munich with the Bavarian Land Police (Landespolizei) on April 20, 1927, he served as an NCO and later became a police officer candidate at which rank he left the police on August 16, 1929. With his family still living in Munich, access to his father's riding school on Albrechtstraße allowed him to indulge his passion for riding and equestrian competition that would eventually lead to his service career choice in the SS. Riding competitions also allowed him to travel extensively throughout Europe in the inter-war period.

Joining the Allgemeine-SS on May 15, 1933, he was commissioned an SS-Untersturmführer effective June 12, 1933. His first assignment was adjutant to the Reiterführer of SS-Gruppe Süd which later became SS-Oberabschnitt Süd. Fegelein held this assignment and that of Special Duties Officer (Sonderführer) until July 1934 when he assumed command of 15.Reiterstandarte in Munich until September that year. Having been promoted to SS-Obersturmführer effective April 20, 1934, he next assumed command of Reiterabschnitt V (see Chapter 1) and held that position until the command was dissolved at the end of October 1936. In May 1934 he also became Reiterführer of SS-Oberabschnitt Süd. After being promoted to SS-Hauptsturmführer on November 9, 1934, and SS-Sturmbannführer on January 30, 1936, Fegelein was among the fastest rising young Allgemeine-SS cavalry officers.

On June 16, 1936 Himmler selected Fegelein to be commander of the SS Main Riding School (SS-Hauptreitschule) to be constructed in Munich.[2] The school was a popular stop for numerous

---

[1] Para-military formations formed in the chaotic inter-war period and commanded primarily by former WWI officers for whom the individual formation was usually named. The units were eventually disbanded and most usable troops absorbed by the Storm Troops (Sturmabteilung or SA). Fegelein's personal records indicate two years service in 1925-26 by which time the Freikorps had been disbanded for two years.

[2] Letter from Himmler to SS-Oberabschnitt Süd appointing Fegelein commander of the school (besides his command of SS-Reiterabschnitt V). He was given until July 1, 1936 to establish the functional needs of the facility. The school was a component of SS-Oberabschnitt Süd. It was subordinated and reported to the inspector of Allgemeine-SS cavalry (Inspekteur Allgemeine-SS Reiterei), SS-Obersturmbannführer von Wiokowski-Biedau who led that portion of the SS Main Office (SS-Hauptamt) and SS-Brigadeführer Weber who was inspector of SS riding schools (Inspekteur der SS Reitschulen). Designed by architect Karl Meitinger and built by the firm of Otto Schiedermaier in Munich, work on the main structure began October 20, 1936 with a planned completion date of July 1937. Fegelein selected SS-Obersturmführer Franz Friedrich as adjutant of the school. This school provided the SS riding instruction, permanent base for training and contestants for the numerous pre-war equestrian tournaments both in and outside Germany, with the first competition held in Munich from January 18-20, 1937. The school continued to supply competitors for tournaments as late as May 1941 and in the pre-war years Hermann Fegelein was often a very successful competitor. Many men who competed while assigned to the school would later have positions among the SS-Totenkopf-Reiterstandarte, Brigade or later Division when they formed. These included Waldemar

In these two photos Fegelein (here as an SS-Standartenführer in command of the Main Riding School in Munich) conducts SS-Oberführer Günther Claussen on a tour of the school in 1939. Fegelein wears an embroidered cufftitle with the name of the facility. (Yerger Archives)

visiting senior SS officers and this, along with his reputation as a rider, made Fegelein one of the best known junior SS officers. He competed well in numerous tournaments throughout the peace-time years and assisted in preparing the equestrian events for the 1936 Olympics in Berlin. Aside from being awarded the Riding Sports Badge (Reitersportabzeichen) in Gold, during his time as commander of the school he was promoted to SS-Obersturmbannführer on January 30, 1937, and again to SS-Standartenführer on July 25th the same year. Fegelein remained commander of the

Fegelein, Hans-Viktor von Zastrow, Karl Warth, Günther Temme, Otto Meisterknecht, Karl Fritsch, Sepp Syr and Herbert Schönfeldt (see command lists within the text for their early assignments or full biographies except for Syr and Warth who served with the later SS-Kavallerie-Division.). The school placed well in all its tournaments and continued as a source of training and replacements for the field units after the war began. Himmler considered it a showplace installation and invited numerous SS dignitaries to visit it when in Munich, which could only be indirectly advantageous to the career of the school commander. Established as an Allgemeine-SS facility, the Waffen-SS later created other schools for mounted troop training.

school, which he listed as his residence during the war years, until the first week of September 1939. He then prepared to assume command of the soon to be established SS-Totenkopf-Reiterstandarte.

As commander of the original regiment Fegelein was given the reserve rank of SS-Obersturmbannführer in the Waffen-SS in March 1940 but was allowed to wear his higher ranking Allgemeine-SS insignia (he became a Waffen-SS Standartenführer on February 1, 1942). Awarded the Iron Cross 2nd class on December 15, 1940 and the Iron Cross 1st class on June 28, 1941, he was the only full commander of the SS-Kavallerie-Brigade during its existence.[3] On March 2, 1942, he was awarded the Knight's Cross based on an official recommendation which reads as follows:[4]

"Since January 25, 1942 the SS-Kavallerie-Brigade was located on the southeast front of 23rd Army Corps in the sector north of Nikulino-Polowinino-Saizewo-Dmitrowo-Sokolomo. The Brigade was assigned the task of preventing the advance of strong enemy forces that had breached the gap west of Rshev, towards the south against the rear of the 206th Division.

'The Brigade foiled all attempts of the enemy with great dash accomplished in spite of heavy casualties. Not only did the SS-Kavallerie-Brigade defeat all efforts of the enemy, but they also led the main offensive attacks. In addition they led the encircling and annihilation attacks which lasted for days.

'During all the defensive and offensive fighting, the personal unshakability, exemplary bravery and constant desire to attack of the Brigade Commander was shown. He was able to complete his

One of a group of formal portraits taken by Heinrich Hoffmann of SS-Oberführer Fegelein after his award of the Oakleaves as commander of Kampfgruppe "Fegelein," prior to taking command of the SS-Kavallerie-Division. (Photo: Jess Lukens)

[3] He returned to Debica for reformation with some Brigade elements and after mid-March 1942 Gustav Lombard commanded those Brigade elements still in Russia until April, prior to the formation of Kampfgruppe (battle group) "Zehender."

[4] The award was recommended on March 2, 1942 by the commanding general of XXIII.Armeekorps, General der Infanterie Albrecht Schubert.

On the left (shown as an SS-Obersturmbannführer) is Emil Rehfeldt who commanded II./Polizei Regiment 3 of Kampfgruppe "Fegelein" and was awarded the German Cross in Gold on January 15, 1943 for leadership of that Bataillon. He became the first general staff officer (Ia) of the Estonian Brigade and ended the war as Ia of the 20.Waffen-Grenadier-Division der SS (estnische Nr.1). On the right in Polizei uniform is Karl Liecke who assumed command of II./Polizei Regiment 3 after Rehfeldt was wounded. He later commanded Kampfgruppe "Fegelein" following Fegelein's departure until it was dissolved in March 1943. As an SS-Sturmbannführer he won the German Cross in Gold on February 28, 1945 while commander of SS-Gebirgsjäger-Regiment 27 of the 13.Waffen-Grenadier-Division-SS "Handschar" (kroatische Nr.1). These two commanders were heavily involved with the battlefield success of Kampfgruppe "Fegelein." (Photos: BDC)

assignments with endless attack operations during which he rallied his men behind him.

'On February 5, 1942 the Brigade attacked a strong enemy group northwest of Tschertolino on the personal decision of the Brigade Commander. The attack was carried out under his personal leadership with a tremendous swing in a bold advance, in spite of the most difficult terrain and weather conditions, against a vastly superior enemy in possession of strongly fortified positions.

'Through taking of the useful street emergency point and important train station in Tschertolino, accomplished only after heavy fighting against tough enemy resistance, the ring around the stronger enemy forces was closed. The encircled enemy was only annihilated after hours of continuous night attacks. These were led by the Brigade Commander who personally commanded the strongpoint group.

'The enemy lost 1800 dead and tons of material while we suffered minimal casualties. The resulting shortening of the front freed stronger forces and the SS-Kavallerie-Brigade succeeded in tightening the ring around the encircled enemy southwest of Rshev in a bold attack. The route to the village of Jersowo, which was taken on February 14, 1942 after heavy fighting which teetered back and forth, completed the challenge for the destruction of the surrounded enemy group.

'SS-Standartenführer Fegelein was able to completely defeat these strong enemy forces with his enthusiastic decision making and full tempered leadership. His personal bravery and readiness for action enabled the cleansing of the situation southwest of Rshev."[5]

---

[5] "Kurze Begründung und Stellungnahme der Zwischen Vorgesetzten."

Fegelein at the Führer's headquarters just prior to departing to take command of the SS-Kavallerie-Division in 1943. (Photo: National Archives)

When the Brigade began expansion to become the SS-Kavallerie-Division in the spring of 1942, Fegelein left in May to assume a position in the SS Main Operational Office (SS-Führungshauptamt) as head of the inspectorate for cavalry and horse-drawn transportation (Inspekteur Reit-und Fahrwesen [Inspektion 3]).[6] He was promoted to SS-Oberführer on December 1, 1942.

Returning to a field command he was given command of SS-Battle Group (Kampfgruppe) "Fegelein" on December 1, 1942 for which he was awarded the Oakleaves to the Knight's Cross on December 21, 1942.[7] Wounded while leading the Kampfgruppe on December 23rd, after his recovery he was assigned to take command of the SS-Kavallerie-Division on April 20, 1943 and was promoted SS-Brigadeführer on May 1st.[8] An award of the German Cross in Gold came on November 1, 1943, following a recommendation by temporary divisional commander Bruno Streckenbach for Fegelein's leadership of the SS-Kavallerie-Division during the summer of 1943

---

[6] The SS-Führungshauptamt grew in complexity from its creation in 1940 till 1945. In 1940 Amt (office) II (Waffen Inspektion/weapon inspection) covered all weapon types. This later expanded to become Amtsgruppe (office group) C (arms inspection) with separate inspectorates for each weapons type of which Inspektion 3 was cavalry and horse drawn transportation. In addition a separate Amtsgruppe A covered weapons, equipment and vehicles of all types. Under this separate Amtsgruppe cavalry and horsed transportation was covered by Amt VI.

[7] The units composing this Kampfgruppe were already in combat when this battle group was ordered formed by the SS-Führungshauptamt: SS-FHA, Kdo. Amt. d. WSS, Org.Tgb.Nr. 8810/42 geh. "Aufstellung der SS-Kampfgruppe 'Fegelein,' dated December 21, 1942 with immediate effect. Not all units ordered for the Kampfgruppe were of the strength (or quality) envisioned by SS higher headquarters. The primary unit was II./SS-Polizei-Regiment 3 (4.SS-Polizei-Division) led by SS-Hauptsturmführer Emil Rehfeldt until wounded on December 20th when command went to SS-Hauptsturmführer Karl Liecke who also took command of the Kampfgruppe after Fegelein was wounded. In addition to a signals platoon, the Kampfgruppe contained a battery of foreign made artillery, an attached army artillery battery, an anti-aircraft detachment with light and heavy weapons and a small number of assault guns. It was not until command of the Kampfgruppe passed to Liecke that Polizei Regiment 15 (provided by the Ordnungspolizei having been formed as troops for a HSSPF command) arrived to become a component having been ordered assigned when the Kampfgruppe was formed. Fegelein's award recommendation text for the Oakleaves, for leading this small unit for less than a month, was not available for study. The Kampfgruppe was awarded several German Crosses in Gold and Fegelein utilized several former members of the Brigade in his staff that had reassigned to the SS-Führungshauptamt or other assignments in Germany. Some of these later served with the SS-Kavallerie-Division.

[8] In a message to the SS-Kavallerie-Division Fegelein gives the date as April 23rd, but although given the command in April, he did not arrive and assume leadership until May 1943. The divisional commander, Fritz Freitag, was ill and hospitalized so it was temporary commander August Zehender whom Fegelein relieved.

which was then approved by the commander of LVII.Armeekorps.[9] The document attests to Fegelein's personal bravery in the field and reads as follows.[10]

"December 23, 1942: Two Russian regiments supported by artillery attacked Golaja primarily from the east, but also from a northwesterly direction, with the intent of breaking through the wide front by attacking our forces there. Our troops were in need of rest and not yet organized so it can only be attributed to the personal bravery and cold-bloodedness of the commander, SS-Brigadeführer Fegelein, that this attack broke up against the unbending defense of our units. SS-Brigadeführer Fegelein rallied the battle groups through his display of energy while staying with his troops on the front lines. Here he was wounded, but despite this he fought on until mid-day, thus bringing the Russian attack to a standstill.

'May 17, 1943: During the extremely intense fighting with the militarily organized partisan groups under the leadership of Russian Lieutenant-General Kolpak, SS-Brigadeführer Fegelein was able to execute a severe blow to the main strength of the enemy during an attack that resulted in their defeat. During the fight SS-Brigadeführer Fegelein set an example for his officers and men by personally destroying a strongly fortified bunker.

'May 24, 1943: During the annihilation of a strongly armed partisan battalion armed with heavy grenade launchers and machine guns, SS-Brigadeführer Fegelein led his men from the front

Fegelein as commander of the SS-Kavallerie-Division in Russia during the summer of 1943. He wears the summer regulation white tunic most often worn by commanders. (Yerger Archives)

[9] Fegelein had already left command of the division as Streckenbach signed the recommendation as temporary divisional commander (Kommandeur SS-Kavallerie-Division i.V.) on October 7th. Bender/Taylor in "Uniforms, Organization and History of the Waffen-SS," volume 3 gives January 1, 1944, as the start of Streckenbach's command. This would have been the date he was officially given full command. At all times it is endeavored to give the actual commander at a given date, the subtle points of temporary, full or substitute being academic as the individual in command was the commander. As with all documents compiled away from the field, there are often inaccurate or misleading points, such as Fegelein's individual Berlin compiled records used by Bender/Taylor not giving him command on November 1 when Streckenbach already signed his award recommendation in October while commanding the division as Fegelein's substitute. This again points out the academic point of "full" verses "temporary" assignments.

[10] "Vorschlag für die Verleihung des Deutschen Kreuzes in Gold" dated October 7, 1943 and signed by SS-Standartenführer Bruno Streckenbach. The recommendation was approved the following day General der Panzertruppen Friedrich Kirchner, commander of LVII.Armeekorps.

In these two 1943 photos, Fegelein meets with SS-Obergruppenführer Hans-Adolf Prützmann. Prützmann was HSSPF for south Russia and the Ukraine at that time and utilized some elements of the SS-Kavallerie-Division Fegelein was then commanding for special operations. He became Höchster SS und Polizeiführer (a level higher than normal HSSPF). This command encompassed the areas of the HSSPF Schwarzes Meer and HSSPF Russland-Süd which combined in October 1943. Prützmann retained both those individual posts as well. He later became Himmler's liaison officer for the Oberkommando der Wehrmacht, inspector for the late war "Werewolf" units and in the final days was Himmler's representative at Admiral Karl Dönitz's headquarters. After being captured by the British, he committed suicide on May 21, 1945. (Yerger Archives)

Fegelein leaves a divisional staff meeting in the late summer of 1943 followed by SS-Obersturmbannführer Günther Temme. (Yerger Archives)

of the attack which proceeded through very difficult swamp terrain. During the attack, Brigadeführer Fegelein stormed the strongly fortified partisan strongpoint with such enthusiasm that his men finished the task by completely destroying the enemy in a very short period of time. The results of this attack were cited in the Armed Forces report on June 12, 1943.

'May 31, 1943: Based on statements from prisoners, SS-Brigadeführer Fegelein executed an attack with a patrol of his men against a partisan camp located in the swamps south of Poljaka. The opponent defended himself doggedly. The enemy, far superior in number, was able to fight for only 20 minutes. During that time the partisan camp was taken through the cold-blooded action of the commander. The enemy lost a large number of dead and wounded, of which only 11 dead and 22 wounded were left behind.

'August 26, 1943: The Russians managed a breakout near Bespalowka with the newly arriving 353rd, 394th and 409th Divisions along with the remaining portions of the 6th and 24th Security Divisions. The enemy was also supported with strong tank forces. Fegelein distinguished himself through his unequaled cold-bloodedness by always making appearances at the hotspots on the front with his men. He displayed tenacious defense and rallied his men to the task.

'August 28, 1943: After a very heavy artillery and grenade barrage on the thinly occupied lines of the 1st, 2nd and 3rd Squadrons of SS-Kavallerie Regiment 1, the Russians attacked with a 3:1 advantage in separate waves. The Russians were able to break through our lines deeply at four different points and then sent strong forces through the openings. With that, the danger of an immediate attack on Werchine-Bischkin was obvious. With the Regiment's reserves of 60 men under the leadership of an SS-Untersturmführer, the Regiment was able to break through and reach point 168.4 and put up a shield against Bol-Gomolscha to the south. The surrounded elements of the of the Squadron were freed by a patrol and a line connecting points 168.4 and 177.7 was established. During this 18-hour fight, SS-Brigadeführer Fegelein was found at the most important positions and, with his unshakability and his quick decisiveness, he was able to resolve even the most hopeless situations. With his influence the tactical intention of the opponent, the advance through the forest, was hindered.

Fegelein listens to a civilian during a pause in 1943. On the right is SS-Standartenführer Gustav Lombard and with back to camera SS-Obersturmbannführer Günther Temme. (Photo: National Archives)

'*September 8, 1943: The enemy attacked hill 199.0 with an immensely superior force and couldn't be repelled from his position. In spite of this, SS-Brigadeführer Fegelein ordered the weakened 4th and 5th Squadrons of SS-Kavallerie Regiment 1 to counterattack. Through his personal leadership the attack was successful despite extremely strong enemy defenses. Not only was the hill taken but high casualties were inflicted on the Soviets.*

'*September 13, 1943: The enemy opened a heavy artillery and grenade launcher barrage south of and on hill 208.5. The left neighboring unit was gone and the 1st Squadron was attacked from the rear. Hill 157.1 had to be held until assault guns and tanks were brought up. The commander had been following the fighting from one of the hills and reported the diminishing strength of his troops, which had certainly tired due to the continuous fighting that lasted for several days and nights. SS-Brigadeführer Fegelein stormed the hill and in spite of his heavily bleeding recent wound (the lower part of his arm had a bullet pass through it) positioned himself at the head of his right flank and held the hill until it was relieved. With his action the impending catastrophe was avoided.*"

Having been wounded once again on September 9, 1943, Fegelein was transferred to his final assignment following his recovery. On January 1, 1944, he became liaison officer between Himmler and Hitler at the latter's headquarters. His September 1943 wound also resulted in his award of the Wound Badge in Silver. Promoted to SS-Gruppenführer on June 21, 1944, Fegelein was awarded the 83rd Swords to the Knight's Cross given to a member of the German Armed Forces on July 30, 1944. The decoration was bestowed for the actions of his command during the late summer of the previous year following a recommendation by the commander of XLII.Armeekorps.[11] Along with the above decorations he was given the Close Combat Clasp in Silver and numerous Rumanian awards for bravery and leadership.

He married Gretl Braun (sister of Hitler's mistress Eva Braun) in June of 1944 but the close ties by marriage to Hitler did not prevent Fegelein's eventual demise. With confusion and intrigue

---

[11] "Aktenvermerk" dated August 6, 1944. The recommendation also was supported by the senior commanders of 8.Armee and 1.Panzer-Armee.

An early 1944 photo as an SS-Brigadeführer taken after Fegelein was awarded the German Cross in Gold. (Photo: National Archives)

rampant during the final days of the 3rd Reich, Hitler searched for a scapegoat for Reichsführer-SS Heinrich Himmler's disloyal conduct and had Fegelein shot for desertion on April 29, 1945.

Fegelein was a career SS officer well suited to the Allgemeine-SS period of his career, especially command of the Munich riding school. Although brave and highly decorated, some of his later awards (Oakleaves and Oakleaves with Swords) may reflect more the accomplishments of the men and units he commanded. Due to his lack of formal staff training one can dispute Fegelein's abilities as a tactician or staff qualified divisional level commander in comparison to some of the other SS cavalry leaders, such as the extremely qualified and gifted Wilhelm Bittrich.[12] In the field he was therefore more apt to depend, at least to some degree, on the skills of an able staff and experienced junior commanders when commanding at divisional level, though proof of his personal bravery under fire is documented. He fostered the careers of many of his subordinates and utilized numerous early cavalry officers within his later headquarters assignments. Fegelein was among the most decorated officers of the Waffen-SS, being one of only 24 SS officers awarded the Knight's Cross with Oakleaves and Swords, as well as attaining senior field rank. He appears to have been close with his most senior commanders and highly qualified staff while seeing to it that the bravery of his subordinates was acknowledged by awards or promotions.

---

[12] The Knight's Cross and its higher versions (Oakleaves and Oakleaves with Swords) could be awarded for personal bravery as well as significant contribution to the war effort in the case of senior commanders. Wilhelm Bittrich, who first commanded the SS-Kavallerie-Division when it was formed, was one of the most respected and highly decorated commanders of the Waffen-SS. Born in 1894 he served in WWI as a fighter pilot and joined the SS in 1932. During the pre-war period he led a company in Regiment "Germania" and a battalion in Regiment "Der Führer." In 1939 he became headquarters adjutant of the "Leibstandarte." He took command of Regiment "Deutschland" in December 1940 and remained in command until replacing a wounded Paul Hausser as commander of SS-Division "Reich" in October 1941. Bittrich commanded the SS-Kavallerie-Division throughout 1942 and in mid-February 1943 took leadership of the 9.SS-Panzer-Division "Hohenstaufen." During the Normandy campaign he again replaced Paul Hausser (who had been given command of 7.Armee) and led II.SS-Panzer-Korps for the remainder of the war. He was awarded the Knight's Cross with Oakleaves and Swords as well as the German Cross in Gold, ending the war as an SS-Obergruppenführer. He died in 1979.

3

THE OCCUPATION OF THE GENERAL GOVERNMENT OF POLAND AND THE HIGHER SS AND POLICE LEADER

The initial occupation and security forces of the SS and Police (Polizei) in Poland followed closely on the heels of the German Armed Forces (Wehrmacht) troops that concluded the first of the lightning campaigns. These troops consisted of the Action Groups (Einsatzgruppen), followed by the Death's Head Regiments (Totenkopfstandarten) and various elements of the Order Police (Ordnungspolizei or Orpo).[1] In addition Self Police (Selbschutz) units were organized from ethnic Germans (Volksdeutsche) living in Poland.[2] The Wehrmacht also contributed troops for this rearguard and occupational duties as the latter function came under their authority for the first two months after the campaign began.

Poland was to be divided following the completion of the campaign. Those portions of the country considered former German territories were incorporated into the Reich.[3] The area not incorporated or annexed to the Reich, geographically the largest, was designated the General Government of Poland (Generalgouvernement Poland). This area was under complete German control and authority, unlike the pre-war annexation of Czechoslovakia to the Reich whose citizens were allowed a greater day-to-day contribution in the routine operations of their country. Hitler appointed Reichsminister Dr. Hans Frank as Governor of the General Government and as head of the civil administration he was the senior official with, at least in theory, the most power and authority. As such he was to coordinate all activities (SS, civil and Wehrmacht) in the area. A second-level senior civil administrator was assigned to each of four districts initially composing the General Government as well.

All areas of Poland were to be used for the resettlement of ethnic Germans who obtained full German citizenship with this, including the General Government area as well as the annexed portions of pre-war Poland. Coming to the General Government from newly acquired areas, particularly the Baltic states, the Volksdeutsche, and the elevation to Reich citizen status of the German minorities already living in those areas conquered, gained prominence and control regarding land, business ownership and citizen rights. These resettlement policies were to a large degree an SS operated affair since Himmler was Reich Commissioner for the Strengthening of German Nation-

---

[1] For a detailed history of the Einsatzgruppen see Krausnick, "Hitlers Einstazgruppen, Die Truppe des Weltanschauungskrieges 1938-1942."

[2] The groundwork for creation of the Selbschutz units, especially brutal and vindictive against their former countrymen, was undertaken by units and personnel under Reinhard Heydrich's command. For creation of these units and the early phase of the Polish campaign (and events leading up to it) regarding RSHA (abbreviation for the Central Security Department of the Reich created in 1939) the best source is a thesis by Browder, "Sipo and SD, 1931-1940: Formation of an Instrument of Power." No complete history of the Sipo and SD has yet been published, but various aspects of it, primarily its early history, have been examined in detail.

[3] Portions of Poland were used to enlarge East Prussia and Upper and Lower Silesia, areas that had, at one time or other in history, been part of Germany. "Danzig-West Prussia" was established as well as the Posen district. The largest industrial city district in Poland (Lodz) was annexed as well. It was renamed Litzmannstadt and would become a primary early forced labor area with many Poles forced from their homes sent to labor camps in the area. These new districts (Gau in Party territory terminology) also were divided into new SS-Oberabschnitte ("Warthe" and "Weichsel"). The existing "Nordost" and "Südost" were expanded.

In this photo (center) with white coat and Government Officials peaked hat is Dr. Hans Frank. Beside him is SS-Obergruppen-führer Wilhelm Koppe, who replaced Friedrich-Wilhelm Krüger as HSSPF "Ost" in November 1943 and held that assignment until 1945. Frank was hanged in 1946 after the post-war Nuremberg trials and Koppe died in 1975. (Photo: Phil A. Nix)

alism (Reichskommissar für Festigung Deutschen Volkstums or RKFDV).[4] In the early stages following the campaign there was even an exchange between Russia and Germany of citizens belonging to each country whose location lay in the newly acquired areas obtained by both powers.[5] In addition, the General Government was the receiving area for Jews and other peoples deported from the Reich or the incorporated other areas formerly part of Poland.

Himmler had already envisioned the required special tasks in Poland. Among these were elimination of armed resistance, forced expulsion of Poles to make room for Volksdeutsche settlers, confiscation of property and possessions as well as utilization of slave labor. Units of the SS and Police undertook these assignments as well as control of the conquered areas. The eventual fate of the people within or sent to the General Government from other newly occupied areas became an SS responsibility. This command structure and the elements that would compose it were being established when the above earlier units were already quelling armed resistance and rounding up political and civil administrators. They also targeted any intelligentsia considered a security risk, while simultaneously commencing procedures to concentrate Poland's Jews into specific areas (ghettos) in cities with populations over 500.

---

[4] Himmler's office was responsible for the reception, movement and resettlement of the Volksdeutsche who were to live in the new areas. In addition, Himmler controlled the Central Office for Ethnic Germans (Volksdeutsche Mittelstelle or VOMI) under SS-Obergruppenführer Werner Lorenz that oversaw all needs of the areas created for these refugees while in transit to their new homes along with their actual placement in conjunction with teams of the RKFDV. See Lumans, "Himmlers Auxiliaries, The Volksdeutsche Mittelstelle and the German National Minorities of Europe 1933-1945" for an overview of this ambitious but doomed to failure plan for expansion of those newly designated German areas. Also see Krausnick, "Anatomy of the SS State," pages 274-291 for its structural development. When Russian forces advanced in the final years of the war these settlers abandoned the area and retreated to the Reich proper.

[5] This included both official exchanges of citizens as well as thousands of Jews who fled the German controlled areas and crossed over to Soviet areas of occupation.

Friedrich-Wilhelm Krüger, shown here (left) as an SS-Gruppenführer in the Allgemeine-SS and (right) as an SS-Obergruppen-führer in command of the 6.SS-Gebirgs-Division "Nord" (he was by then also a General der Polizei). Born May 8, 1894 in Strassburg, he served in WWI as an officer and joined the SS in 1930. Early in his career he left the SS and served with the SA, while retaining his SS rank, and reported to Himmler on the potential revolt of the SA. He attained General rank in the SA before returning to the SS in 1935. He was promoted to SS-Obergruppenführer on January 25, 1935 and was also a member of the Reichstag beginning in 1932. In 1935 he was posted to Himmler's personal staff and in March 1936 became inspector for border and watch guard units. As inspector of all mounted units he was assigned to the SS-Hauptamt from May 1938 until becoming HSSPF "Ost" in 1939. He stayed in Poland as HSSPF, surviving several attempts by the resistance on his life, until removed after losing his long standing fight with Dr. Hans Frank. Placed in reserve, he requested a front-line posting in October 1943. He was reassigned to Himmler's staff until a command was found for him and became a General der Waffen-SS in May 1944. As his first combat assignment he led the 6.SS-Gebirgs-Division "Nord" from late May 1944 to August 1944. For his leadership of "Nord" Himmler personally recommended him for the Knight's Cross which was awarded to him on September 30, 1944. Krüger then commanded the V.SS-Gebirgs-Korps which he led from August 26, 1944 to March 1945. He committed suicide on May 10, 1945. (Photos: Phil A. Nix and BDC)

In 1937 Heinrich Himmler had, as commander of both the SS and Polizei, outlined the use of Higher SS and Police Leaders (Höherer SS und Polizeiführer or HSSPF) upon mobilization in Germany as well occupied territories. These senior leaders were *directly subordinate to him*, for accomplishing SS and Police coordination as well as fulfilling *specific assignments determined by him*. Himmler made the first appointments in areas of Germany in 1938. While the existing civil or Party administrations limited the powers attained by those HSSPF in Germany,[6] those appointed in the occupied territories, especially in Poland and Russia, attained the far-reaching powers of command and authority Himmler had originally intended to assist in the implementation of his policies. They were among the most powerful and coveted posts in the SS or Polizei for senior officers.[7] In most, though not all cases, the HSSPF also were the leader of the SS-Oberabschnitte within their command area. The following are the units and senior officers involved in the SS/ Polizei occupation duties of the General Government during the period between October 1939 and June 1941. All were under direct authority or in association with the HSSPF during that period when the cavalry units of this study were stationed there before reassignment by Himmler at the

---

[6] In most, though not all cases, the HSSPF for areas within the Reich was also the SS-Oberabschnitt Führer of the Allgemeine-SS. Like the conflict between Frank and Krüger, those HSSPF within Germany found conflict with their Gauleiter counterparts in the civil administration and in some cases the Wehrmacht.

[7] Many of the HSSPF were very early career SS officers and were among the most influential, as well as powerful, SS or Polizei officers. In 1942 Krüger was the eighth ranking officer in all the SS. See Birn "Die Höhrer SS und Polizeiführer" for a detailed examination of the persons holding these positions throughout Germany and the occupied areas to include their duties and personalities.

start of the 1941 Russian campaign. The structure and elements attached to each HSSPF of the other areas of former Poland incorporated into the Reich were generally similar.

From its arrival in Poland until subordinated to Himmler's field headquarters staff (Kommandostab "Reichsführer-SS") in June of 1941, the SS-Totenkopf-Reiterstandarte, which became two regiments, was subordinated to the HSSPF "Ost"[8] (East), SS-Obergruppenführer Friedrich-Wilhelm Krüger. Krüger was appointed on October 4, 1939 with his headquarters located in Krakau. Hans Frank considered Krüger a subordinate and tried to have him officially subordinated to him but was unsuccessful. The resulting personal conflict and rivalry between the two was constant concerning control of the various units and tasks assigned within the General Government, as Frank was the designated senior Party official and Krüger assigned by the SS. Both individuals were, however, equally involved in the fate of the people deported to or from within the General Government as well as Poles removed from their pre-war homes or positions. While Frank's position was meant to extract all possible human and material resources possible from the area, Himmler's policy was more concerned with dominating the peoples of the area with little or no regard for lost resources of any type. Though Frank's purpose was more useful from a practical outlook, he was limited by a lack of troops under his direct authority. Krüger, as Himmler's direct subordinate, controlled these forces in the form of the SS and Police troops stationed within the General Government.

Directly under him, Krüger had *two* chains of command controlling the same subordinated units and, for purposes of explanation, one of the command chains existed in a "normal" (for routine matters) and "special" (for operational assignments) structure depending on situation. His direct subordinates in both chains of command received instructions from their command section in Berlin for *administrative* matters. Orders came directly from Himmler by way of Krüger for *operational* matters. Krüger's highest ranking and most important subordinates in the two command chains were as follows.

The Senior Commander of the Order Police (Befehlshaber der Ordnungspolizei) during the time the cavalry unit(s) were in Poland were Oberst der Schutzpolizei Emil Horing (October 1, 1939 to October 25, 1939), General der Polizei Herbert Becker (October 25, 1939 to October 31, 1940) and Generalleutnant der Polizei Paul Riege (October 31, 1940 to August 22, 1941).[9] This command consisted of the Protection Police (Schutzpolizei), Rural Police (Gendarmerie) and 13 armed police battalions (Polizei Bataillone) divided among the four districts of Warsaw, Lublin, Random and Krakau existing within the General Government.[10] Krakau had four Polizei Bataillone while the other districts contained three each. The commander assigned for the Ordnungspolizei units in each district also commanded the regimental staff that controlled the armed Polizei Bataillone within his district.[11] The district area commanders were Oberstleutnant der Schutzpolizei Karl Brenner[12] (Warsaw), Oberstleutnant der Schutzpolizei Gerrett Korsemann (Lublin), Oberstleutnant der Schutzpolizei Ferdinand Heske (Radom) and Oberst der Schutzpolizei Emil Horing (Krakau).

---

[8] The command started in September 1939 as a HSSPF for the rear area of Armeeoberkommando 8 and 10 (Theodor Eicke) and became HSSPF "Lodz" upon Krüger's appointment. Lodz (renamed Litzmannstadt after a WWI general) was annexed and the position was redesigned HSSPF "Ost" on October 31, 1939, still retaining its headquarters in Krakau. It is not to be confused with the earlier existing HSSPF "Ost" whose jurisdiction encompassed the Berlin area and was retitled HSSPF "Spree" on November 14, 1939.

[9] Several other men held the post in the years following the departure of the cavalry regiments for Russia. After Riege were Rudolf Müller-Bonigk (August 1941 to September 1941), Gerhard Winkler (September 1941 to May 1942), Herbert Becker (May 1942 to August 1943), Hans Grünwald (August 1943 to March 1944), Fritz Sendel (March 1944) and ending with the original man to hold the position, Emil Horing, from March 1944 until the area was abandoned in January 1945.

[10] Although after SS Kavallerie Regimenter of this study left the Generalgouvernement, a fifth district was added in August 1941 which had been Russian occupied since Poland was divided: District Lemberg, named after its primary city which had been Lvov before the occupation, was added under SS and Police Leader Fritz Katzmann whose previous post position in the Radom district was taken by Karl Oberg. It encompassed an area southeast of the original General Government and was previously designated district Galizien.

[11] These district Polizei Regimenter were later redesignated Polizei Regimenter 22, 23, 24 and 25.

[12] Some sources show Brenner not assuming his position until February 1940 so another officer possibly served in this capacity before him though no specific individual has been documented.

The Befehlshaber der Ordnungspolizei in the General Government, General der Polizei Herbert Becker (right) with the SS und Polizeiführer for Lublin, SS-Brigadeführer Odilio Globocnik. Becker, born March 13, 1887 and a Polizei officer since before WWI, held his post in the General Government from October 25, 1939 to October 31, 1940 and then became the inspector of Ordnungspolizei units in Hamburg. He returned to the General Government at his old position from May 1, 1942 to August 1, 1943, following which he became Generalinspektor of the Schutzpolizei in the Hauptamt Ordnungspolizei until May 1945. (Photo: Phil A. Nix)

As an Ordnungspolizei command, the Order Police Main Office (Hauptamt Ordnungspolizei) issued administration orders directly to the Befehlshaber der Ordnungspolizei and supplied his units. This post was subordinate to Krüger in the special chain of command when operations were directed to Krüger by Himmler, bypassing the Hauptamt Ordnungspolizei. Krüger could also bypass the Hauptamt Ordnungspolizei under the guise of "emergency situations." Cooperation between the Orpo and the HSSPF was good. The Befehlshaber der Ordnungspolizei controlled the normal routine activities of the commanders and units under their authority.

The Senior Commander of the Security Police (Befehlshaber der Sicherheitspolizei und SD) position consisted of controlling the Secret State Police (Gestapo), Criminal Police (Kripo) and Security Service (Sicherheitsdienst or SD). During the deployment of the cavalry units in Poland the position was held by SS-Brigadeführer Bruno Streckenbach (November 1, 1939 to January 14, 1941) then SS-Oberführer Eberhard Schöngarth.[13] The abbreviation for the elements of the Sicherheitspolizei was Sipo.[14] This command controlled the units, personnel and Sipo lower level commanders within each of the four districts.[15] The district Sipo commanders were SS-Obersturmbannführer Josef Meisinger (Warsaw), SS-Oberführer Lothar Beutel (until October 23, 1939) and then SS-Sturmbannführer Dr. Alfred Hasselburg (Lublin), SS-Hauptsturmführer Fritz Liphardt (Radom) and SS-Sturmbannführer Walther Huppenkothen (Krakau). The senior command control office in Berlin was the Central Security Department of the Reich (Reichssicherheitshauptamt or RSHA) commanded by Reinhard Heydrich. Heydrich's power structure and desire for direct control made cooperation between these units and Krüger often less than as with the Orpo. Himmler's intervention was occasionally required for settling differences arising from Heydrich's use of authority. As with the above Polizei, Streckenbach and his successors would have normally controlled the day-to-day activities of the units under his command. Himmler assigned these senior appointments or approved those made in the case of RSHA by Heydrich.

---

[13] Schöngarth held the position (until June 1943) after the cavalry units left for Russia when replaced by Dr. Wilhelm Bierkamp who then held the post until early February 1945.

[14] The title of Befehlshaber der Sicherheitspolizei und SD separated its two offices, the SD being a Party office and the Sicherheitspolizei a State office.

[15] The Gestapo and Kripo were considered separate as to general function from the tasks of the Security Service (SD).

The first Befehlshaber der Sipo und SD for the General Government of Poland, Bruno Streckenbach, shown here at left as an SS-Oberführer in dress uniform (note SD sleeve diamond) and on the right as an SS-Gruppenführer and divisional commander in the Waffen-SS. Born February 7, 1902 in Hamburg, Streckenbach joined the SS in August 1931 and became an SS-Untersturmführer on December 24, 1932. He served with 98. and 28.Standarten from December 1932 to early November 1933. Promoted to SS-Obersturmbannführer on November 9, 1933, the day he was assigned to the SD Hauptamt, he led the SD units in Hamburg. Promoted to SS-Standartenführer on April 20, 1934, he stayed with the SD (and later RSHA) during the pre-war years and was promoted SS-Oberführer on September 13, 1936. He was still with RSHA when posted to the General Government in October 1939 having been promoted to SS-Brigadeführer on April 20, 1939. He left that position in mid-January 1941 and was promoted SS-Gruppenführer und Generalleutnant der Polizei on November 9, 1941, serving as a bureau chief (Amtschef) in RUSA. After requesting a front line assignment he became a reserve (d.R.) Waffen-SS Obersturmführer in September 1943 and an SS-Hauptsturmführer d.R. on March 10, 1943 while being trained in anti-tank units. He went to the SS-Kavallerie-Division on March 11, 1943, after another promotion to SS-Sturmbannführer d.R., as commander of the anti-tank detachment (Panzerjäger Abteilung) and was promoted to SS-Standartenführer on August 28, 1943. For actions at this command he won the German Cross in Gold on December 15, 1943. He took temporary command of the Kavallerie-Division from Fegelein in September 1943 and became full commander in January 1944 when promoted SS-Oberführer. In mid-April 1944 he took command of the 19.Waffen-Grenadier-Division der SS (lettische Nr.2) and held command until May 1945 during which he was promoted to SS-Brigadeführer (Waffen-SS) on July 1, 1944 and to SS-Gruppenführer (equivalent to his highest Allgemeine-SS rank) on November 9, 1944. Streckenbach and his Latvian unit had more success than many of the foreign units and for his leadership of this division was awarded the Knight's Cross on August 17, 1944 and the Oakleaves on January 16, 1945. Unlike many pre-war non-combat career SS officers, he did well as a field commander and spoke French as well as English. After the war he spent 10 years as a prisoner of the Russians and died on October 28, 1977 in Hamburg. (Photos: BDC)

The Leader of SS and Self Police (Führer SS und Selbstschutz) assigned in mid-November 1939 was SS-Oberführer Kurt Hintze. His position appears to have been established to coordinate the dissolving of the Selbschütz units created during the Polish campaign. This senior position was eliminated at the end of January 1940 with the units placed more directly under Krüger's command through an SS und Selbstschutz Führer in each district. SS-Oberführer Karl Schuster (Warsaw), SS-Standartenführer Walter Gunst (Lublin), SS-Standartenführer Wilhelm Hiller (Radom) and SS-Oberführer Gustav Stolle (Krakau) were the district commanders while Hintze's post existed.[16]

---

[16] Walter Gunst moved to the Warsaw position at the end of January 1940 and was replaced by SS-Standartenführer Ludolf von Alvensleben as district Lublin commander. Both men then held these posts until they were eliminated in July 1940.

Herbert Schöngarth, here as an SS-Oberführer, was Befehlshaber der Sipo und SD from mid-January 1941 to June 1943. Previously holding the same assignment for the Dresden area, he later became Befehlshaber der Sipo und SD den Haag (Holland) from July 1944 to May 1945. He was hanged on May 15, 1946. (Photo: Phil A. Nix)

With the elimination of an SS und Selbstschutz Führer above district level, these commanders reported to their district level SS and Police Leader (SS und Polizeiführer) or direct to Krüger, as in the case of the SS-Totenkopf-Reiterstandarte. Among the units involved were the two SS-Totenkopfstandarten based in the General Government. The latter were the 8.SS-Totenkopfstandarte in Krakau (based in Radom after July 1940) led by SS-Oberführer Leo von Jena and the 11.SS-Totenkopfstandarte commanded by SS-Standartenführer Karl Diebitsch with its three Bataillone divided between Warsaw, Lublin and Random districts. Cooperation from the SS-Totenkopf-standarten was less than desired by Krüger. These unit commanders considered themselves directly subordinate to the Inspektorate of SS-Totenkopfstandarten in Berlin and were operating in Poland before being put under Krüger's direct authority. Both the Totenkopfstandarten and Selbschutz were eliminated as an occupation force by mid-1940.[17]

The above three primary posts represented one chain of command. The position of Police President (Polizeipräsident), normally a member of the above command line under a HSSPF, was eliminated in the first weeks in the case of Krüger's appointments.

The SS-Totenkopf-Reiterstandarte (and later both regiments) were directly under Krüger's command after the post of Führer SS und Selbstschutz was eliminated. As will be seen, it undertook operations independently or in conjunction with the various Polizei, Sipo and SD units of each district, as it was the largest armed unit under the HSSPF, was mobile and had squadrons dispersed within each of the four districts. The Berlin authority for the cavalry unit was initially the Inspektor der SS-Totenkopfstandarten (inspector of reinforced SS Death's Head regiments) as the unit was created as a component of the SS-Totenkopfverbände. After this post was eliminated in 1940, the administrative command element was the SS Main Operational Office (SS-Führungshauptamt) which absorbed and combined many of the previously existing command authorities.[18]

---

[17] The 11.SS-Totenkopfstandarte (formed in early 1940) moved to Holland in July 1940 and the 8.SS-Totenkopfstandarte (formed in Krakau in early 1940) moved to Radom to replace it. Both units later reformed as infantry regiments with 8.SS-Totenkopfstandarte becoming SS-Infanterie Regiment 8 of the 1.SS-Infanterie-Brigade (mot) in the summer of 1941 and 11.SS-Totenkopfstandarte becoming part of the SS-V.-Division as SS-Infanterie-Regiment 11 in November 1940. The men of the Selbschütz were absorbed, depending on skills and background, into various units of the SA, Polizei and SS after July/August 1940 at which time the district post of SS und Selbstschütz Führer was eliminated.

[18] See Krausnick, "Anatomy of the SS State," pages 291-301.

The Ordnungspolizei district commander for Warsaw, Karl Brenner, shown (left) as a Generalleutnant der Polizei and (right) as an SS-Gruppenführer in the Waffen-SS. Brenner won the German Cross in Gold on June 16, 1944 as Befehlshaber der Ordnungspolizei Ukraine and the Knight's Cross on December 31, 1944 as commander of the 6.SS-Gebirgs-Division "Nord" which he led from November 1944 to May 1945. He died on February 14, 1954. (Photo: BDC)

The other chain of command under Krüger were the four district SS and Police Leaders (SS und Polizeiführer or SSPF), also assigned in 1939, whose duties were similar to Krüger's but at a lower level. This position was created to relieve the HSSPF of some of the increasing number of tasks they were assigned. Their command authority, depending on situation and orders, also controlled the units of the Polizei (armed battalions), Sipo, SD, Selbstchutz and assigned portions of the SS-Totenkopf-Reiterstandarte. Krüger had total authority and control with these subordinate commanders and apart from routine matters would normally prefer them for "special operations and tasks." They were senior to the district commanders or leaders of the Orpo, Sipo, SS-Totenkopfstandarten and SS und Selbschutz. The SSPF and their districts were SS-Gruppenführer Paul Moder (Warsaw), SS-Brigadeführer Odilio Globocnik (Lublin), SS-Oberführer Fritz Katzmann (Radom) and SS-Gruppenführer Karl Zech (Krakau). Except for Zech, who was replaced in October 1940 by SS-Oberführer Hans Schwedler, all these individuals retained their SSPF post throughout the period the cavalry units being examined were in Poland.

After Krüger, the next senior authority for the SSPF was Himmler who often assigned the SSPF specific tasks directly. As was Himmler's habit, he divided rule, authority and command while retaining the prerogative to give specific orders to individuals or commands at all levels, as well as selecting or approving all the senior SS and Polizei appointments himself. The SSPF normally controlled the squadrons of the SS-Totenkopf-Reiterstandarte based within their district for routine operations as well.

An SS court was assigned to the HSSPF as all units and personnel under Krüger's command were immune to prosecution under Army or civil authority, unless in the former case they were

The SS and Police Leader Lublin, Odilo Globocnik, in civilian clothes (note Party and SS membership pins). He became HSSPF Adriatisches-Kustenland (Adriatic Coastland) in mid-September 1943 and held that assignment until May 1945 with the rank of SS-Gruppenführer und Generalleutnant der Polizei. He committed suicide after being captured by British forces in May 1945. (Photo: BDC)

The SS and Police Leader Krakau, Karl Zech, shown here as an SS-Brigadeführer. He was relieved of his post for refusing to confine Jews to the Krakau ghetto and later served on the staffs of several SS-Oberabschnitte. Tried by an SS court, he was dismissed from the SS in March 1944 and committed suicide on April 1, 1944 to avoid disgracing his family. (Photo: Phil A. Nix)

Paul Moder, shown here as an SS-Brigadeführer in command of SS-Abschnitt III of the Allgemeine-SS which he led from February 1934 to November 1938. He served as SS and Police Leader for Warsaw from November 14, 1939 to August 4, 1941. As an SS-Sturmbannführer d.R. he was killed on February 19, 1945 while commanding the I./Artillerie Regiment of the "Totenkopf" Division. In the right background is SS-Sturmbannführer Ernst Deutsch, commander of SS-Bataillon "N." (Photo: Phil A. Nix)

The Ordnungspolizei commander for the Lublin district, Gerrett Korsemann (here in a later photo as an SS-Gruppenführer and HSSPF Russland-Mitte). He was in the SA and Polizei before joining the SS. Himmler transferred him to the Waffen-SS as an SS-Hauptsturmführer where he served with "Leibstandarte" and later "Totenkopf" divisions on the front lines. He was over 50 years old when serving with a combat unit in 1945 due to his displeasing of Himmler at his HSSPF post. He survived the war and died on July 16, 1958. (Photo: Phil A. Nix)

serving in Army units at the time an offense took place. The senior appointments were of similar organization for the HSSPF in Russia though the number of auxiliary troops generally larger with an often higher number of SSPF due to geographical size of the command areas.[19]

The 1939 to mid-1941 period that the cavalry units under study were stationed in Poland was chaotic and in early months almost anarchic. At this phase of the German occupation, policies of resettlement, control, forced emigration, quelling of potential armed resistance, confiscation of property and use of valuable labor resources were the primary directives and operations undertaken by Frank and Krüger, and hence the forces under their jurisdiction.

---

[19] Specific HSSPF and commands for Russia are footnoted when encountered within the history of the Brigade. The later SS-Kavallerie-Division, when reforming at various times in its history, would also be occasionally under the authority of the HSSPF in its operational area.

4

1939-1940

The first units formed for the eventual SS-Kavallerie-Brigade were two mounted standards (Reiterstandarten) equal to cavalry regiments (Kavallerie Regimenter). Both units remained components of the Brigade as well as the later formed SS-Kavallerie-Division until 1945.[1] As will be seen, the development of these initial units was complicated and continuous during the early stages of their existence when variations of composition were tried, rejected and revised in an attempt to find the best Order of Battle for units of this type. This constant revision of components remained a characteristic throughout the existence of the eventual Brigade as well.

The initial formation was designated the SS-Totenkopf-Reiterstandarte. Formed as a Mounted Detachment (Berittene Abteilung) in Berlin during the second week of September 1939, the unit was created for operational deployment in Poland. A staff (Stab) and the first four squadrons (Schwardonen) numbered 1 to 4 came into existence at that time with the majority of recruits being SS personnel, along with a members of the Schutzpolizei which provided barracks during the week of formation for 2nd and 3rd Squadrons. During the first weeks following formation, the strength of 1st Squadron in personnel and mounts exceeded the other three by approximately 20%, with the four Squadrons divided into two mounted sections (Reitstaffeln) of two squadrons each. During the week in Berlin when these units were formed the primary officers assigned were as follows:

staff (Stab)
commander (Kommandeur):	SS-Standartenführer Hermann Fegelein
Ia (1st General Staff Officer):[2]	Hauptmann der Schutzpolizei Ludwig Lehner
IIa (adjutant):	SS-Hauptsturmführer Albert Faßbender
IVa (administration officer):	SS-Hauptsturmführer Otto Hampel
physician (Arzt):	SS-Untersturmführer Dr. Harald Strohschneider
veterinarian (Veterinär):	SS-Hauptsturmführer Dr. Hans Herling
vehicle superintendent (Fahrdienstleiter):	SS-Untersturmführer Kurt Zimmermann
replacement post (Nachersatzstelle):	SS-Sturmbannführer Günther Temme

1st Squadron was under the command of Squadron Leader (Schwardonschef) SS-Sturmbannführer Franz Magill.[3] His platoon leaders (Zugführer) were SS-Untersturmführer

---

[1] The terms Standarte and Regiment are synonymous with the former reflecting the para-military formation terms used in the pre-war period by the Allgemeine-SS mounted units as well as formations of the storm troops (Sturmabteilung or SA) created during Hitler's rise to power. Likewise, the word "Totenkopf" (Death's Head) is more related to pre-war formations and as will be seen the cavalry units later adopted terminology for their formations to reflect their primary status as military formations. The Brigade would contain two regiments while the later SS-Kavallerie-Division had 3, later 4 and, after German cavalry units were reformed, ended with 3 cavalry regiments when destroyed in Budapest.

[2] Taken from a period staff document, the term Ia (1.Generalstabsoffizier) is more associated with the senior staff member of a division versus a regimental sized unit, at which level the position would be more correctly Führer beim Stabe (staff leader) or Major beim Stabe. Lehner left the unit in 1940 and with the rank of SS-Sturmbannführer und Major der Schutzpolizei served on the staff of SS-Oberabschnitt "Süd."

[3] Born August 22, 1900 in Kleist, Magill served in the Army from 1918 to 1933 with several cavalry units. He joined the Allgemeine-SS with SS-Reiterstandarte 7 in April 1933 and moved to SS-Führerschule Braunschweig after being commissioned. There he served as a riding instructor and commander of the school mounted unit as an SS-Untersturmführer. Magill taught at the Braunschweig until September 1939 during which he was promoted to SS-Hauptsturmführer on September 15, 1935 and to SS-Sturmbannführer on April 20, 1938. Joining the SS-Totenkopf-Reiterstandarte when it formed, he led several squadrons, one of the later organized mounted detachments and also was commander of SS-Kavallerie-Regiment 2

Hermann Gadischke, shown here as an SS-Sturmbannführer. He was one of the initial platoon leaders of 3rd Squadron and then took command of a machine gun squadron in the period of half-regiments during late 1940. For much of 1941/42 he led 4th (machine gun) Squadron of Kavallerie-Regiment 1 in Russia and won the Iron Cross 1st class on January 15, 1942. When the SS-Kavallerie-Division formed he was a special duties and reserve officer on the divisional staff and later took command of the supply and transport sections of the Division. At this command he was killed in Budapest on February 6, 1945 with the rank of SS-Obersturmbannführer. (Yerger Archives)

Wilhelm Reichenwallner,[4] SS-Obersturmführer Hans-Viktor von Zastrow and SS-Untersturmführer Wolfgang Craas.

2nd Squadron was formed at the police barracks (Schutzpolizei Kaserne) at Berlin-Gneisenau-Straße and led by SS-Obersturmführer Herbert Schönfeldt.[5] His platoon leaders were SS-Obersturmführer Friedrich Butz, SS-Untersturmführer Thorvald Roloff and SS-Untersturmführer Walter Berndt.

(see text), wining the Iron Cross 2nd class on September 1, 1941. In November 1941 he went to the staff of the Higher SS and Police Leader for middle Russia (Russland-Mitte) and was promoted SS-Obersturmbannführer on January 30, 1942. Next, from late December 1942 to February 1943, he led the SS-Sonderbataillon "Dirlewanger" composed of ex-convicts and poachers (named for its first commander, Dr. Oskar Dirlewanger). After returning to his staff position with the HSSPF, in February 1944 he took command of the supply troops of the 14.Waffen-Grenadier-Division der SS (galizische Nr.1). He was one of the most important early leaders of the early units.

[4] After moving to command a squadron, he was commander of the Brigade Staff Quarters. Returning to a field command, he was killed on February 9, 1943 as an SS-Hauptsturmführer in command of 5th Squadron, Kavallerie-Regiment 1 in the SS-Kavallerie-Division.

[5] Like Franz Magill, Herbert Schönfeldt was an experienced and important early leader in the SS-Totenkopf-Reiterstandarte. Born on September 23, 1906 he served with 14.Reiterregiment of the Army as well as the Army cavalry school in Hannover from 1925 to 1938. He came to the SS in February 1938 as an SS-Untersturmführer assigned to the SS Main Riding School in Munich. He was also a member of the Police and was promoted Oberleutnant der Schutzpolizei on September 1, 1939. After joining the SS-Totenkopf-Reiterstandarte upon formation, he held several commands at squadron or higher level (see text). He became an SS-Hauptsturmführer d.R. in the Waffen-SS in March 1940 and briefly served with the Hauptamt Ordnungspolizei in 1941 before returning to the Brigade in November with full (active) SS rank. Schönfeldt won the Iron Cross 1st class on January 26, 1942 as commander of 5th Squadron, SS-Kavallerie Regiment 2. Promoted to SS-Sturmbannführer on April 20, 1942, when the SS-Kavallerie-Division was formed in May 1942 he went to the replacement unit for two months before serving as a staff officer in the SS Economic and Administration Main Office and SS Main Operational Office. He then transferred to the SS Remount Office in Cholm (which he eventually commanded) and served there until killed on April 28, 1945.

3rd Squadron had SS-Sturmbannführer Rudolf Ruge[6] as its commander when formed at the Spandau police barracks. Ruge's platoon leaders were SS-Obersturmführer Helmuth Guggolz, SS-Untersturmführer Kehren, SS-Untersturmführer Heinrich Dieckmann and SS-Untersturmführer Hermann Gadischke.

Finally, 4th Squadron was formed and led by SS-Hauptsturmführer Rolf Becher. He had SS-Obersturmführer Walter Dunsch, SS-Untersturmführer Hermann Lindemann and SS-Untersturmführer Rolf Bierter as platoon leaders.

Total strength of the staff and four squadrons at the end of formation week was 27 officers, 424 men and 399 horses. The forming of other units and continued expansion of the already existing elements would take place at their assigned areas in Poland. At first the staff and 1st Squadron went to Posen[7] which served as temporary base for what was referred to in documents simply as the SS-Totenkopf-Reiterstandarte without a numerical designation. The 2nd and 3rd Squadrons also went to Posen and took up quarters in the former Prussian Königs-Jägerkaserne, while the 4th Squadron had barracks 13 kilometers north of Lodz at Lucmierz. By command of Reichsführer-SS Heinrich Himmler, upon arrival in Poland the entire unit was under the auspices of the Higher SS and Police Leader "East," SS-Obergruppenführer Friedrich-Wilhelm Krüger. Krüger was responsible for supervision of its continued expansion and any needed assistance as well as decisions regarding its deployment in the field, which began almost immediately while the unit continued forming.

Field Operations in Poland

As previously stated, the SS-Totenkopf-Reiterstandarte was created for operational deployment in Poland. More specifically, it was to serve as a second-line unit performing mopping up actions as well as typical police duties. Mopping up actions consisted of the search for straggling Polish soldiers which were overrun by the German forces during the Blitzkrieg of September 1939. These troops posed a potential threat as they often formed groups of irregulars or recruited Polish civilians to fight as partisans against the occupying German forces. Typical second-line duties included the search for and seizure of all weapons in the possession of the Polish population. Other secondary missions assigned to the Reiterstandarte were varied in nature. They included the protection of the Volksdeutsche (ethnic Germans) from the resident Polish population and the deportation of Poles to work camps in Germany or within the General Government of Poland. The unit also enforced the German laws of the new General Government of Poland and approved laws of the former Polish nation. In addition the Regiments were responsible for hunting down criminals that had escaped from Polish prisons during the invasion.

Throughout the occupation the SS-Totenkopf-Reiterstandarte not only worked in conjunction with other second line German units, but also with the Polish Police. Here their task was to apprehend any criminals considered a menace to the remaining native population or immigrating Volksdeutsche. The rules that the SS-Totenkopf-Reiterstandarte and the members of the German Police followed were straightforward. Anyone who broke German or Polish law was deported to another area in the General Government (usually a work camp). Those who resisted or attempted to flee were often shot immediately.

When setting up a Volksdeutsche village, many of the resident Poles were removed from their homes and farms to be replaced by the immigrating Volksdeutsche. There was, in almost all cases, a remaining Polish population and it was not uncommon that the Polish police, as well as the local Polish government, remain intact and function under the supervision of the Germans. In some cases the mayor of a village would remain a Pole. The Poles that remained in the villages were

---

[6] Born January 31, 1895, Ruge served in WWI and with the Schutzpolizei as an officer in 1921-1922. He joined the Allgemeine-SS in June 1933 with 4.Standarte and became an SS-Untersturmführer on November 9, 1933. Ruge served as an instructor at SS-Führerschule Bad Tölz beginning in 1934 and was promoted to SS-Obersturmführer on April 20, 1935, to SS-Hauptsturmführer on September 15, 1935 and to SS-Sturmbannführer on September 12, 1937. After leaving the cavalry unit he returned to Bad Tölz and served briefly with the artillery replacement unit of the Polizei Division, a replacement battalion of the 6.SS-Gebirgs-Division "Nord" and the staff of SS-Abschnitte XXIII. Promoted to SS-Obersturmbannführer on January 30, 1942, from August 1942 he commanded the Police riding school in Rathenow and then became the Cavalry Inspector of the Ordnungspolizei.

[7] This Prussian city was one of many lost by Germany under the Versailles Treaty.

Albert Faßbender (left) as an SS-Hauptsturmführer with SS Abschnitt III just prior to joining the SS-Totenkopf-Reiterstandarte and right as an SS-Hauptsturmführer with "Totenkopf" collar insignia in an early 1940 photo. Born on June 30, 1897, in Saarbrücken, Faßbender was among the important early officers of the SS-Totenkopf-Reiterstandarte as well as the Brigade. A WWI combat veteran having served in a cavalry unit, he joined the SS in 1932 and became an SS-Untersturmführer on November 9, 1934. Faßbender served as a staff officer with SS Abschnitt III of the Allgemeine-SS until September 1939 during which he was promoted to SS-Obersturmführer on September 15, 1938 and SS-Hauptsturmführer on September 13, 1939. He was with the cavalry unit in Berlin during initial formation as adjutant and then became staff legal advisor as an SS-Hauptsturmführer d.R. in the Waffen-SS effective March 1, 1940. Faßbender commanded a detachment during the 1940/41 period of half regiments. Promoted to SS-Sturmbannführer on April 20, 1941, he was the Major beim Stabe of the Brigade during expansion then took command of 6./Kavallerie-Regiment 1. He later becoming commander of the important Reconnaissance Detachment in August 1941 and led it until the end of that year when reassigned to the Brigade staff. He won the clasp to the Iron Cross 2nd class on January 19, 1942. He left the Brigade in January 1942 and later went to SS-Truppenübungsplatz Debica in Poland for formation of the SS-Kavallerie-Division. In Debica he assisted with the initial rebuilding of the reconnaissance detachment and then took command of the new SS-Kavallerie-Regiment 3 when it formed in June of 1942, holding command until late August 1942 when Hans-Viktor von Zastrow was assigned command. He transferred to the SS-Führungshauptamt assigned to Inspektion 3 (cavalry and horse drawn transportation) of Amtsgruppe C (arms inspectorates) as a staff officer under Hermann Fegelein. From September 1943 to November 1944 he was commander of the supply/transport sections of the 13.Waffen-Grenadier-Division der SS "Handschar" (Kroatische Nr.1). His last known posting was with a unit refurbishment staff in December 1944. He was awarded clasps to both his WWI Iron Crosses while with the Brigade. (Photos: BDC)

instructed not to offer assistance in the form of food or shelter to the any of their now homeless countrymen. Citizens not abiding by these rules were arrested and deported to designated areas of the General Government.

The tasks given to the SS-Totenkopf-Reiterstandarte late in the month of September 1939 corresponded to plans set out by Himmler. While most units were still arriving and setting up barracks, the rest were in the field performing mopping up operations as well as searching for weapons and munitions. Since the Polish government was now defunct, the SS-Totenkopf-Reiterstandarte was also assigned to help uphold basic law and order (such as protecting local farmers from thieves when bringing their produce to market). The unit also suppressed the initial wave of anarchy in a land with no apparent government by arresting a large portion of the increasing number of criminals.

On September 27th the 1st and 4th Squadrons began an intensive series of search and seizure operations. On this day 1st Squadron began by securing the highway between Lodz and Zgierz and the towns of Kaly and Anderejow. These actions immediately produced three pistols, a field cannon, two grenades, a rifle and three swords. Two Poles were taken prisoner for possessing weapons. The 4th Squadron dispatched four patrols, each of half-platoon strength and searched the towns of Orla, Grodnici as well as the forest area between Krasnodeby and Grodnici. They then moved on to Bzura, Ruta, Alexandrow, Jastrzebia, Bruzyczka and Piaskowice. These units turned up three straggling Polish soldiers and a large amount of German munitions of various calibers in the forest area near Grodnici. On the 28th, the 4th Squadron sent a patrol to search from the forest southwest of Lucmierz to Sobien, during which they found three more Polish soldiers. The next day 1st Squadron was called upon by the mayor of Zgierz to search all houses within his town. A platoon was sent out to perform this operation while another platoon was sent to search the settlements north of the highway between Lodz and Mileszki and between Lodz and Brzeziny. They found three pistols, a rifle and a grenade. The 4th Squadron sent out a patrol in the area of Lucmierz to put an end to the increasing cases of armed robbery and took 43 people prisoner. On the 30th, the 1st Squadron continued the operations searching the settlements south of Lodz to the Wiskitno-Ruda line and the settlements along the main road between Lodz and Dabrowa.[8]

October continued in much the way that September had. However, as mopping up operations began to wind down, the search for weapons among the general population increased. The units got little rest and were dispatched daily to perform searches in towns situated in the large areas of the newly conquered countryside. In general, records report that the population behaved in a calm and submissive manner towards the German military and police units. Despite this, the Germans were worried about rumors of large bands of partisans fortified by hidden ammunition depots. Pursuit of these rumors was essentially fruitless and revealed nothing to support them.

While the 2nd and 3rd Squadrons were busy building and setting up barracks, the 1st and 4th Squadrons continued with the intensive operations they started in September. On October 2nd the two platoons of the 1st Squadron searched the farms north of the highway between Lodz-Mileszki and between Lodz and Brzcziny. Six Poles were taken prisoner for the possession of two rifles. The 4th Squadron departed on a two day patrol, first making a round trip from Lodz to Krosniewice and another to Strykow and back. Six thieves, four Polish criminals and four Polish soldiers as well as a four ton truck with Polish artillery ammunition were found. Further patrol operations by the 1.SS-Totenkopf-Reiterstandarte west of Lodz on the 3rd revealed an ammunition depot in the vicinity of Rydzyny complete with airplane bombs, grenades and detonators. On the 6th, the 4th Squadron was put into action carrying out a "special assignment" in the area of Kutno, the details of which were not reported.[9] On the 7th the 4th Squadron was dispatched to search the homes in the vicinity of Strykow. 60 rounds of carbine ammunition and seven gasmasks were captured.

---

[8] "Gefechtsberichte v. 20-24.9.1939"

[9] "Special Tasks" or "Special Assignment" were terms often used in written documents for execution procedures and similar operations. Although no documentation was found confirming it in this instance it is probably the case as these types of operations were not described in documentation at lower levels. "Special tasks" therefore, especially in Poland, most often involved implementation of policies against the Jewish population or individuals with the potential to be partisans.

Shown in 1943 with the SS-Kavallerie-Division are, from right, SS-Standartenführer Gustav Lombard (then commander of Kavallerie-Regiment 1), SS-Brigadeführer Hermann Fegelein (then commander of the SS-Kavallerie-Division) and SS-Obersturmbannführer Günther Temme. Born on August 29, 1900 in Botschin, West Prussia, Temme was a primary officer in the early unit period as well as with the eventual Brigade. His staff skills were appreciated by Fegelein who had him assigned to serve with him several times. He joined the SS in January 1934 after serving in the SA and was promoted to SS-Untersturmführer on July 1, 1935. As an officer he was posted to the staff of SS-Reiterabschnitt IV until October 1936 and promoted SS-Obersturmführer on January 30, 1936. Reassigned to the staff of SS-Reiterstandarte 7 on November 1, 1936, where he remained there until July 1937, he was promoted to SS-Hauptsturmführer on January 30, 1937. Temme was among the best riders in the pre-war SS and competed in the 1936 Olympics. From July 1937 to April 1939 he was assigned to the SS-Hauptamt with the Inspectorate of Allgemeine-SS Cavalry. Promoted to SS-Sturmbannführer on April 20, 1939, he was reassigned to the SS Main Riding School in Munich the same month and remained there until September 1939 when he went to the SS-Totenkopf-Reiterstandarte staff during formation. In January 1940 he became Major beim Stabe and held that post until March 1941. He next took command of a replacement squadron in Munich (3./Kavallerie-Ersatz-Abteilung) and later commanded the Kavallerie-Ersatz-Abteilung when Hans-Viktor von Zastrow returned to a squadron command at the front. By late December 1941 Temme also returned to the front, leading the Reconnaissance Detachment in Russia for which he won the Iron Cross 1st class on March 25, 1942. He continued as commander during refit until May, during which he was promoted to SS-Obersturmbannführer on March 16, 1942. He then returned to the Munich riding school (which he may have commanded for a short time) for the rest of the year. Temme went with Hermann Fegelein as a personal staff advisor when the latter was assigned command of the SS-Kavallerie-Division in April 1943 and stayed with Fegelein until August when reassigned to Amt VI (cavalry and horse transportation) of the SS-Führungshauptamt. He was involved during that period with various cavalry matters, separate responsibilities than those of the cavalry inspectorate, including the Munich school and the HSSPF "Ost" until late January 1944. Begining in February 1944 he took over leadership of the SS remount office of SS-Oberabschnitt Wartheland where he was promoted to SS-Standartenführer on December 21, 1944 and this is his last known assignment. (Photos: National Archives and BDC)

On the 11th, the men of the Reiterstandarte were given a brief rest from their continuous operations and were inspected by the commander of the Ordnungspolizei, General der Polizei Kurt Daluege. During his visit, Daluege took the opportunity to remind the men of the nature and importance of their duties in the newly-conquered areas of Poland.

On October 12th the operations continued as the 4th Squadron was called upon by the commander of the prison in Zgierz to search and pacify the inmates there. As the searches continued, symptoms of organized resistance began to surface. On October 14th, the 1st Squadron of SS-Reitstaffel I, under the order of the Ordnungspolizei and the Armeeoberkommando, managed to

Kurt Daluege as an SS-Oberst-Gruppenführer in command of the Order Police (Ordnungspolizei). He held that position through the early war years and then became Deputy Reichsprotector of Bohemia and Moravia. He was hanged in Prague by the allies in 1946. (Photo: Phil A. Nix)

find a Polish farmer who had collected a number of weapons including a hunting rifle, a Russian rifle, a German pistol, 105 rounds of German ammunition, 60 rounds of Polish ammunition, a truck with six cases of anti-tank ammunition and a team of horses with a carriage. Other gear found among his gatherings was a grouping of Polish and German military equipment including gasmasks, breadbags, blankets, pack frames and field packs. On the 19th the 4th Squadron was sent to the area north of Strykow and secured 14 cases of machine-gun ammunition, a case of machine gun parts, two packs of machine pistol ammunition, a Polish light machine gun and two limbers[10] with 40 cases of Polish artillery ammunition.

On October 20th, a platoon of the 1st Squadron found a cache of smuggled equipment during a search on the highway between Lodz and Brzeziny. Three days later the 1st Squadron set up a road block on the highway between Lodz and Konstantynow and managed to discover 400 kilograms of horseshoes and various Polish army goods. On the 26th, the 4th Squadron brought in four Polish criminals who were set free from the prison in the vicinity of Leczyzca when the war began. To finish the month of October, the 1st Squadron found various pieces of radio equipment being used by the Poles to listen to foreign broadcasts.

Aside from searching for weapons and munitions, the SS-Totenkopf-Reiterstandarte found itself pursuing crimes of a lesser nature such as theft. Stealing from local farmers while bringing their produce to market proved to be a significant problem. During one action between October 8th and the 14th, 26 Poles were taken prisoner for armed robbery or smuggling. Due to the aggressive manner in which the German forces pursued these thefts, reports of robberies decreased dramatically. There were also reports of Poles harassing the immigrating ethnic German population.

---

[10] The two-wheeled detachable front part of a gun carriage which usually supports an ammunition chest.

November 1939: First Reorganization

In mid-November the plan to organize the SS-Totenkopf-Reiterstandarte into 12 squadrons distributed throughout the General Government of Poland was initiated. An order for the formation of a replacement detachment at the Hauptreitschule (main riding school) Munich was also given.[11]

The staff, medical detachment and the 12 Squadrons were set up in the following cities:

Unit	Headquarters (Standort)
Staff :	Warsaw[12]
Medical Detachment :	Warsaw
1st Squadron :	Warsaw
2nd Squadron :	Garwolin[13]
3rd Squadron :	Seroczyn
4th Squadron :	Zamosc
5th Squadron :	Chelm
6th Squadron :	Tarnov
7th Squadron :	Krakau
8th Squadron :	Kielce
9th (replacement) Squadron :	Warsaw (later Lodz)[14]
10th (heavy) Squadron :	Kamiena
11th (technical) Squadron:	Lublin
12th (horsed battery) Squadron:	Krakau

After the 12 squadrons were assigned to their posts they went about setting up quarters for the care and feed of their horses. With the arrival of cold and snowfall, the road situation in the General Government became catastrophic. Due to the vast distances between the Standorte (up to 400 miles) communication became difficult. The few telephone connections that existed often broke down which added to the communications problem.

The cold weather experienced by the new formations proved the necessary cold-weather equipment was inadequate. The general lack of much needed blankets, gear and clothing forced the troops to send out units to gather the necessary equipment in the General Government. A special commando force, which acted independent of the twelve squadrons, was formed for the task of procuring rations and feed for the horses. Finding the necessary rations and feed proved difficult and the adequate supply of fuel was only accomplished through lengthy negotiations with the Wehrmacht.

Despite all of these operational problems, units were dispatched daily to fight against the increasingly strong Polish partisan resistance. Some squadrons, such as the 3rd Squadron in Seroczyn, found themselves engaged against partisans fighting uninterrupted for weeks at a time.

Other units, such as the 1st Squadron, were deployed as firing squads carrying out ordered executions,[15] while the 5th Squadron was given the task of transporting some 1000 prisoners from Chelm to Sokal. During this march, 440 prisoners were reported shot while trying to escape.[16]

---

[11] "Einsätze der 1.SS-Totenkopf-Reiterstandarte."

[12] Polish name "Warszawa," German "Warschau." It was the capital city of Poland.

[13] Small town in what was Russia before the formation of the Polish state under the Versailles treaty. Before the war began this city was the home of a Polish cavalry regiment whose barracks were intended to eventually house the Polish Cavalry School "Graudenz." This cavalry establishment consisted of housing for the men, a riding hall, several administration buildings and a movie theater. When the 2nd Squadron arrived they found the barracks in ruins. Not only were the barracks partly destroyed by bombs, but there was also no available water and sanitary conditions were unacceptable. Conditions were so poor that the Squadron required almost 60,000 RM for materials to make necessary repairs and improvements.

[14] The German name for the town was Lodsch. They later renamed it Litzmannstadt after a WWI general.

[15] "Einsätze der 1.SS-Totenkopf-Reiterstandarte."

[16] "Einsätze der Schwadronen nach dem 15. November 1939 nach der Aufstellung der 1.SS-Totenkopf-Reiterstandarte."

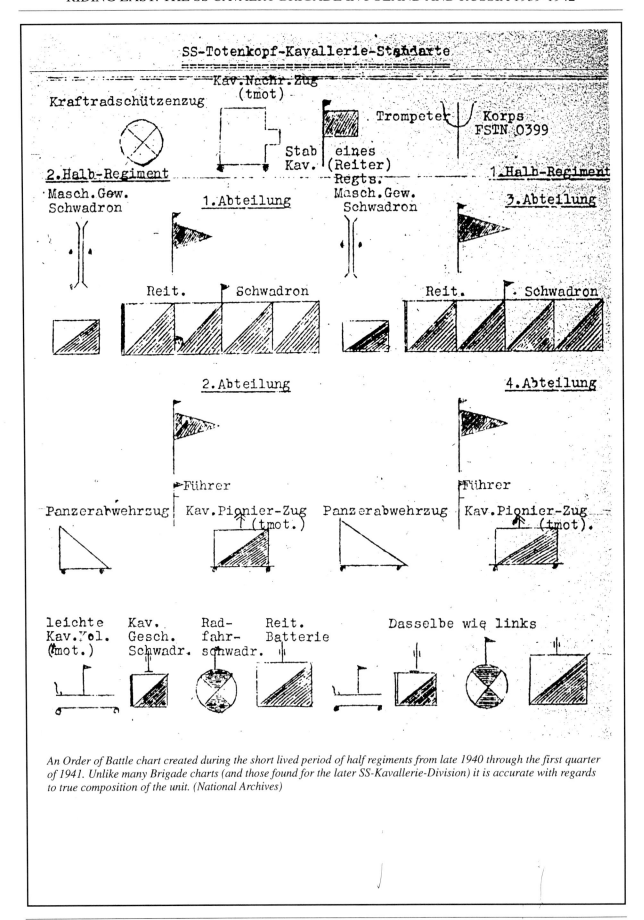

An Order of Battle chart created during the short lived period of half regiments from late 1940 through the first quarter of 1941. Unlike many Brigade charts (and those found for the later SS-Kavallerie-Division) it is accurate with regards to true composition of the unit. (National Archives)

It was decided within the reorganization plans that the operational headquarters would be situated in Warsaw and Fegelein along with the staff moved there from Lodz during the second week of December 1939. On December 15, 1939, Himmler issued an order that officially redesignated the unit the 1.SS-Totenkopf-Reiterstandarte.[17] This designation not only further differentiated the unit from similar titled mounted Allgemeine-SS units but indicated (by use of its numerical prefix) that further units were eventually planned. At this point strength of the Reiterstandarte had increased to 584 officers and men.

The planning for the final structure of the 12 squadrons began in late November. A list of preliminary selections for commanders dated November 24, 1939 shows that the eventual number of squadrons for the unit was at first to have been ten with a replacement element, two heavy units and a technical squadron. In addition, two riding batteries (Reitende Batterien) were to form the heavy fire support of the Standarte. However, as unit development progressed, the previously mentioned total of 12 squadrons were formed by the spring of the following year. This planned expansion, as well as the addition of the medical detachment, was accomplished during the first three months of 1940 with additional squadrons being created later. The new squadrons were composed of experienced cadre from existing units combined with replacements arriving from Germany. By the first week of April 1940 the basic formation and composition of the full unit was completed. Officer assignments and locations of the 1.SS-Totenkopf-Reiterstandarte at that time were as follows:[18]

Staff - Warsaw

commander:	SS-Standartenführer Hermann Fegelein
staff leader (Major beim Stabe):	SS-Sturmbannführer Günther Temme
adjutant (IIa):	SS-Hauptsturmführer Franz Friedrich
ordnance officer (OO):	SS-Untersturmführer Franz Rehbein[19]
physician (IVb):	SS-Obersturmführer Dr. Harald Strohschneider[20]
veterinarian:	SS-Hauptsturmführer Dr. Hans Herling
weapons and munitions officer:	SS-Untersturmführer Herbert Hänel
Army/SS liaison officer:	SS-Hauptsturmführer Otto Hampel
administration officer (IVa):	SS-Sturmbannführer Wilhelm Jeppe[21]

[17] SS-Totenkopf-Standarte, "Standartenbefehl Nr.5," dated December 27, 1939 and signed by Fegelein at his headquarters in Warsaw. The order stated to his men that Himmler issued the name change order on the 15th. The order gives specifics for writing various assignments and positions using the new title and implies that at some point the Allgemeine-SS term of Reitersturm had been used in place of Schwadron in the previous weeks while specifying that the latter term was to be used exclusively from that date on. However, in the case of all name or title changes, documents are seen both in the field and from higher echelons using the incorrect title at a given time. As an example of the confusion of conflicting data within period documents, a Stammtafel written by SS-Kavallerie-Regiment 1 in 1940 incorrectly gives the name change effective in November when all documents written at that time refer to the unit as simply SS-Totenkopf-Reiterstandarte or Berittene Abteilung.

[18] Although the squadrons had been established, not all platoons were fully formed or operational so at this point in time not all platoon leader positions had been assigned. The existing squadrons provided men for newly created units. Most squadrons were to eventually have four platoons (three mounted and a machine gun platoon) with the heavy weapon and technical units having a different composition. Most officers held Allgemeine-SS rank and in most cases of junior officers, retained that rank level as Waffen-SS reserve officers.

[19] Born September 28, 1912 in Rellingen, Rehbein joined the SS in September 1838 with an SS-Totenkopfstandarte. He became an SS-Untersturmführer on April 20, 1940 and served for most of the time the Brigade existed during which he was promoted to SS-Obersturmführer on June 21, 1941 and to SS-Hauptsturmführer on April 20, 1942. While with the Brigade, he also served as staff Ic (intelligence officer), IIa/IIb (adjutant for officers and enlisted men) and III (legal officer). He won the Iron Cross 1st class on February 25, 1942. In mid-1942 he transferred to the SS Remount Office in Cholm and in November moved to the cavalry inspectorate of the SS-Führungshauptamt. Recruited by Hermann Fegelein, he was awarded the German Cross in Gold on January 15, 1943 while assigned to SS-Kampfgruppe "Fegelein" and then served from April to October 1943 with the staff of the SS-Kavallerie-Division. He ended the war with the cavalry inspectorate and became an SS-Sturmbannführer on November 1, 1944.

[20] Also commanded the medical detachment.

[21] Born on February 28, 1900 in Berlin, he joined the Allgemeine-SS in July 1926 with 30.Standarte. Promoted to SS-Sturmbannführer on October 1, 1932, he served in an administration post with SS-Gruppe "Ost" until May 1935 when he moved to a similar position with SS-Oberabschnitt "Mitte." He was promoted to SS-Obersturmbannführer August 23, 1933, to SS-Standartenführer April 20, 1934, and to SS-Oberführer April 20, 1936. He served as a special duties officer with the Gestapo from August 1934 to April 1935 and then was senior administration officer of SS-Oberabschnitt "Nordost." Jeppe joined the SS-Totenkopf-Reiterstandarte in March 1940 as an SS-Sturmbannführer d.R. and served in both regiments before temporary assignment to the Einsatzstab RFSS (later Kommandostab "Reichsführer-SS") as a reserve officer from May to September 1941. Promoted to SS-Obersturmbannführer d.R. on September 1, 1940, he returned to the SS-Kavallerie-Brigade when it began expansion and

legal advisor: SS-Hauptsturmführer Albert Faßbender
vehicle department leader :   SS-Hauptsturmführer Hans Harder

Medical Detachment - Warsaw
1st Platoon: SS-Untersturmführer Dr. Karl Reinsch
2nd Platoon: SS-Untersturmführer Dr. Kurt Sickel
3rd Platoon: SS-Untersturmführer Dr. Walter Riehm
4th Platoon: SS-Untersturmführer Dr. Rudolf Hödel

1st Squadron - Warsaw
Squadron Leader: SS-Hauptsturmführer Waldemar Fegelein
1st Platoon Leader: SS-Untersturmführer Norbert Peters
2nd Platoon Leader: SS-Obersturmführer Friedrich Buntz
3rd Platoon Leader: SS-Untersturmführer Ernst Grabsch

2nd Squadron - Garwolin
Squadron Leader: SS-Sturmbannführer Rudolf Ruge
1st Platoon Leader: SS-Untersturmführer Heinrich Dieckmann

3rd Squadron - Seroczyn
Squadron Leader: SS-Hauptsturmführer Gustav Lombard
1st Platoon Leader: SS-Obersturmführer Willi Plänk
2nd Platoon Leader: SS-Obersturmführer Hermann Gadischke
3rd Platoon Leader: SS-Untersturmführer Ernst Imhoff[22]

4th Squadron - Jamolsk
Squadron Leader: SS-Sturmbannführer Josef Fritz[23]
1st Platoon Leader: SS-Obersturmführer Horst Lange
2nd Platoon Leader: SS-Untersturmführer Walter-Hubert Schmidt

5th Squadron - Chelm
Squadron Leader: SS-Hauptsturmführer Wilhelm Reichenwallner[24]
1st Platoon Leader: SS-Untersturmführer Helmuth Guggolz[25]
2nd Platoon Leader: SS-Untersturmführer Heinrich Poth

6th Squadron - Tarnov
Squadron Leader: SS-Hauptsturmführer Hans-Viktor von Zastrow[26]

stayed until reformation as a division was completed in 1942. From November 1942 to September 1943 he was assigned to the SS Economic and Administration Main Office (SS-Wirtschafts und Verwaltungs-Hauptamt) as head administrator for SS-Oberabschnitt "Weichsel" and was promoted to SS-Standartenführer d.R. on November 9, 1943. After serving on the staff of the Higher SS and Police Leader Russland-Mitte he went to XII.SS-Armee-Korps as corps administration officer and was awarded the German Cross in Silver on February 20, 1945.

[22] Born March 7, 1901 and in 1943 was commander of 1st Squadron, SS-Kavallerie-Regiment 1. Promoted to SS-Sturmbannführer on November 9, 1943 he was then serving with SS-Reiterstandarte 6 and ended war assigned to the 37.SS-Freiwilligen-Kavallerie-Division "Lützow." He died on August 31, 1982.

[23] Born May 25, 1899 he was an SS-Untersturmführer in the Allgemeine-SS since December 24, 1932. Promoted to SS-Obersturmführer November 9, 1933, SS-Hauptsturmführer on February 14, 1934, SS-Sturmbannführer on November 9, 1934, and SS-Obersturmbannführer on January 30, 1936, (all in the Allgemeine-SS) his rank as a squadron commander would have been his (lower) Waffen-SS reserve rank. He commanded SS-Reiterstandarte 9 (Allgemeine-SS) in 1934/35 and then became Reiterführer of SS-Reiterabschnitt II. He then led SS-Reiterstandarte 11 starting in December 1936. Fritz returned to that latter assignment for the duration of the war.

[24] Killed February 9, 1943 while commanding 5th Squadron, SS-Kavallerie-Regiment 1 (SS-Kavallerie-Division).

[25] In the autumn of 1943 took command of 2nd Squadron, SS-Kavallerie-Regiment 16 (SS-Kavallerie-Division) as an SS-Hauptsturmführer.

[26] Little is known about the career of this eventual regimental commander. Born on December 4, 1907, he was commissioned an SS-Untersturmführer

1st Platoon Leader:	SS-Untersturmführer Arthur Schlaefke
2nd Platoon Leader:	SS-Untersturmführer Wolfgang Craas

7th Squadron - Krakau
Squadron Leader:	SS-Hauptsturmführer Herbert Schönfeldt
1st Platoon Leader:	SS-Obersturmführer Viktor von Sessler-Herzinger
2nd Platoon Leader:	SS-Untersturmführer Thorvald Roloff

8th Squadron - Kielce
Squadron Leader:	SS-Hauptsturmführer Walter Dunsch[27]
1st Platoon Leader:	SS-Untersturmführer Heinrich von Truchsess[28]

9th Replacement Squadron - Warsaw (later Lodz)
Squadron Leader:	SS-Hauptsturmführer Rolf Becher
1st Platoon Leader:	SS-Untersturmführer Rolf Metz
2nd Platoon Leader:	SS-Untersturmführer Rolf Bierter

9th Replacement Squadron - SS Main Riding School (SS-Hauptreitschule)[29]
Squadron Leader:	SS-Obersturmführer Karl Fritsche[30]
Riding Instructor:	SS-Obersturmführer Otto Meisterknecht
Riding Instructor:	SS-Obersturmführer Karl Warth

10th (heavy) Squadron - Kamiena[31]
Squadron Leader:	SS-Obersturmführer Franz Rinner
1st Platoon Leader:	SS-Untersturmführer Heinrich Täger
2nd Platoon Leader:	SS-Untersturmführer Hans Berg

11th (technical) Squadron - Lublin
Squadron Leader:	SS-Sturmbannführer Franz Magill
1st Platoon Leader:	SS-Untersturmführer Johann Billerbeck[32]
Combat Engineer Platoon Leader:[33]	SS-Untersturmführer Friedrich Maletta

in the Allgemeine-SS on September 15, 1935. Serving with the SS-Reiterstandarte 7 in the pre-war period, he was a rider in numerous competitions for the SS Main Riding School in Munich before the war. He held several squadron commands between both of the two regimental units that were first formed before becoming the first commander of SS-Kavallerie-Regiment 3 when this unit was created during formation of the SS-Kavallerie-Division. He was killed while holding this command, with the rank of SS-Sturmbannführer, on December 10, 1942 and was posthumously awarded the German Cross in Gold on February 7, 1943.

[27] Born on February 12, 1905 Dunsch joined the SS in 1932 and when commissioned SS-Untersturmführer in November 1935 served with 6.Motorstandarte. He stayed with this unit until November 1936. Promoted to SS-Obersturmführer on November 9, 1936 and SS-Hauptsturmführer on April 20, 1938, he became adjutant of SS-Reiterstandarte 16 in November 1936 and remained there until joining the SS-Totenkopf-Reiterstandarte as an SS-Hauptsturmführer d.R. effective March 1, 1940. Reassigned to the Brigade staff in 1941 as VI (Indoctrination Officer) he went to the staff of the Higher SS and Police Leader "Nord" in March 1943. Moving to the SS Cavalry School in Zamosc during September 1943, this was his last wartime assignment.

[28] Killed on April 29, 1945 with SS-Flak Abteilung 9, 9.SS-Panzer-Division "Hohenstaufen."

[29] The replacement units were first divided between the SS-Hauptreitschule in Munich and a direct access replacement near the Standarte headquarters with the former being the official replacement depot per an order issued by Himmler on October 30, 1939 (RFSS, AR/180/39). The Munich school was also involved with initial riding training since they were obviously well equipped to do so. As will be seen this replacement pool expanded even before the elements of what became the SS-Kavallerie-Brigade were combined.

[30] Transferred to the Pionier (engineer) Kompanie of the Brigade when formed.

[31] As of April 1940 this unit consisted of a machine gun platoon, a mounted platoon and two mortar platoons.

[32] After leaving the Brigade (he later served with its artillery unit) he served as a battery and detachment commander in the Artillerie Regiment of the 17.SS-Panzer-Grenadier-Division "Götz von Berlichingen" during the Normandy campaign. He was killed on May 15, 1945 as an SS-Hauptsturmführer and detachment commander in Artillerie Regiment 37, 37.SS-Freiwilligen-Kavallerie-Division "Lützow."

[33] Formed and added to the Reiterstandarte in March 1940.

Hermann Fegelein in riding kit during 1940. He wears the Rider Sports Badge in Gold on his left breast. (Yerger Archives)

Signals Platoon Leader:[34]   SS-Untersturmführer Wilhelm Wiersch[35]

Anti-Tank Platoon Leader:[36]   SS-Hauptsturmführer Maximilian List

12th (horsed battery) Squadron- Krakau[37]

Squadron Leader (or Battery Leader):   Oberleutnant der Schutzpolizei Arno Paul[38]

1st Platoon Leader: SS-Obersturmführer Hermann Lindemann

2nd Platoon Leader: SS-Untersturmführer Walter Berndt

---

[34] 1.SS-Totenkopf-Reiterstandarte, "Gliederung und Ausrüstung der 1.SS-Totenkopf-Standarte," dated April 18, 1940 and signed by staff leader Günther Temme, shows assignments for both the engineer and signals platoons to 11th Squadron, the latter having been previously with the staff in Warsaw. 11th Squadron would also contain a 3.7cm anti-tank platoon and a heavy infantry gun platoon (Granatwerferzug). By the following month the signals platoon was again (more logically) reassigned to the staff area of the Reiterstandarte according to a strength report sent to the General Inspector of Death's Head units (Generalinspektor der SS-Totenkopfstandarten) dated May 16th, 1940. This inspectorate was dissolved on August 8, 1940 and the unit would report to the SS Main Operational Office (SS-Führungshauptamt) which was created and absorbed the old inspectorate and most duties of the original SS Main Office (SS-Hauptamt). The section of the SS-FHA dealing with Waffen-SS units was Amt I (Kommando der Waffen-SS).

[35] Commanded the signals company of the Brigade when formed.

[36] Probably not operational until June when List was assigned as platoon leader.

[37] Consisting of four, 8cm field guns with three light machine guns for close support, the term platoon leaders is from a period document listing the 3 primary officers as no unit size smaller than a battery was found in the German Kstn system of organization for artillery (each platoon controlled two weapons).

[38] Later became commander of the Brigade's artillery detachment.

1940 Operations

As 1940 began, assignments for the squadrons remained virtually unchanged. The units continued searching for weapons and trying to uphold law and order as defined by the governing Germans. From the 4th to the 7th of January 1940, the 3rd Squadron was deployed in the area of Stozek where they shot a partisan leader and took two other partisans prisoner for possession of firearms. Operations of this type continued for the 3rd Squadron and on the 9th they managed to capture four partisans during a raid in conjunction with the Polish Police. In Socki the unit discovered several firearms including two carbines, a pistol, a rifle and a hunting rifle. During the seizure of these weapons a Pole, who was reported to have resisted, was shot. His remaining five comrades were taken prisoner.

In January, the 5th Squadron was again assigned to transport operations and were responsible for guarding a transport of 600 prisoners on their way from Lublin to Chelm. This operation began during the evening of the 12th when SS-Hauptsturmführer Wilhelm Reichenwallner was requested by the leader of the Sipo in the district of Chelm to guard the transport upon its expected arrival at 0200. The Sipo commander ordered that the prisoners were to remain in the train cars from the time of arrival until the next morning. To perform this operation, SS-Hauptsturmführer Reichenwallner assigned 20 men to guard the train.

The next morning Reichenwallner received a call from the leader of the guards. Reichenwallner was informed that the train cars, mostly 2nd and 3rd class wagons, were overcrowded and that in their aisleways lay about 40 dead prisoners that had not survived the transport. Upon inspection of the cars, the guards had found excrement everywhere while the trains themselves were in shambles. When the doors to the trains were opened they determined that dysentery had broken out among the occupants. They decided that it would be wrong to send the infected train into the area of Chelm. Therefore, the train was to be taken into the forest area in the direction of Ruda where all the occupants were to be shot.

Since the 5th Squadron only had 500 rounds of ammunition in their possession and the Wehrmacht would not give them any of theirs, it was impossible to carry out this idea. Therefore, the acting District President (Landrat) was ordered to dispatch a group of eight men of the Field Police, who were equipped with the necessary machine guns, to take over the operation. Reichenwallner himself ordered one of his NCOs and ten men to assist in the executions. The plan was that the executions were to be undertaken in two formations. One formation was to perform the killings while the other guarded the remaining prisoners. The two groups were to switch at pre-determined intervals until the task was completed. Reichenwallner could not personally attend the executions because he had previously been requested to attend an inspection tour of the area with General Governor Dr. Hans Frank and SS-Brigadeführer Walter Schmitt.[39]

Upon meeting SS-Brigadeführer Schmitt, Reichenwallner was immediately informed that one of his men had been shot during the operation. He was told that during an escape attempt, a group of angry prisoners had surrounded one of the SS men and one of them took out an old revolver and shot him. The man was taken to an SS doctor, but died later.[40]

On January 14, 1940 a platoon from the 3rd Squadron was requested by the Polish police and the mayor of Stoczek to apprehend a group of criminals consisting of four people. They were well known thieves within the community and during their last robbery they badly wounded an innocent Polish bystander. The 3rd Squadron experienced no difficulties overtaking the criminals and gave them a summary execution. On the 15th and 18th, the 3rd Squadron was again put into action, this time searching for weapons in the villages of Rossa and Russastara. Here they found two loaded carbines and infantry ammunition. The owners of the weapons, three Poles, were shot while trying to escape. Searches continued on the 20th and a Pole was shot for possessing a weapon. On the 22nd, the Polish police requested the 3rd Squadron to apprehend a Pole who was known to be in

---

[39] Schmitt was head of the SS Personnel Main Office (SS-Personalhauptamt).

[40] The full incident described was related in "Einsatz am Sonnabend den 13.Januar 1940" written the following day.

Troops from one of the squadrons towing infantry guns. (Yerger Archives)

possession of a weapon. The man was shot immediately. On the 25th a rider battery was sent into the forest to search for thieves at the request of the Forest Service. The same day, a "rebel" pole was captured by the 3rd Squadron at the request of the Polish police and shot immediately.[41] On January 29th, a platoon of the 1st Squadron was sent to Prague to assist in a large SD planned raid.

No documentation for notable actions has been found for the month of February 1940. During this month, the units continued to build-up their new quarters as well as training new recruits, new horses and conducting continuing infantry and cavalry training for the troops. Despite the hard work, there were a number of problems. For example, as the units expanded, the original supply of horses had to be split up, leaving each unit with a deficiency of trained mounts.

Since there was no supply of replacements available in the Reich to make up for this deficiency, the Reiterstandarte had to buy horses from the Poles. These horses all had lice and most were sick, and so therefore could only be properly incorporated into the regiments beginning in early March. The horses received special attention and care from the veterinarians followed by rigorous training by the experienced cadre of the units. Things started to take shape in March and on the 19th, a series of inspections began with 1st Squadron being inspected by SS-Obergruppenführer August Heissmeyer, head of the SS Main Office, and SS-Oberführer Hans Schwedler who later became SS and Police Leader for Krakau.

On March 30th, the largest operation to date by the 1.SS-Totenkopf-Reiterstandarte began. The Regiment was put on full alert at 2200 hours and shortly thereafter the Higher SS and Police Leader of the General Government, Friedrich-Wilhelm Krüger, issued the order for all available units in Krakau to march to Kielce. In Kielce the Regiment received its final march orders sending all available units to Skarzysko-Kamienna (Standort of the 10th Squadron) where they are to arrive by 1900 hours the next day. The rumor was that a large band of irregular Polish soldiers with a strength of approximately 300 men and led by a Polish Captain were located in the forest areas of Kamienna.

For this action the 1st, 7th, 8th, 9th, 10th and the 12th Squadrons as well as the 51.Polizei Bataillon of the Ordnungspolizei were called in while all other available units were put on alert. The first units to arrive to the scene were situated on the roads connecting the villages surrounding the forested area of Kamienna. Before the operation began, several cannons were set up on the streets while the troops prepared to begin the search for the irregular soldiers, an action which was to start on the 1st of April. To commence the operation, several reconnaissance patrols were sent out to search for any sign of the Polish irregulars. The Poles, realizing that they were surrounded, immediately attempted a breakout against the 51.Polizei Bataillon. Their attempt became a heated battle which lasted for several hours. When the 10th Squadron arrived with its infantry cannons to relieve the Polizei Bataillon, the Poles, realizing they were suddenly outnumbered and out-gunned, retreated to the hilly, swampy areas of the forest. This break-out attempt gave away the location of the Poles and from then on a series of small battles began which were characterized by the Germans chasing the Poles while the Poles fought then quickly retreated.

Due to their inferior strength in comparison with the Germans, the Poles often used "hit and run" tactics which bought them extra time to find a better breakout point and maintain an element of surprise. Other similar tactics used by the Poles were also observed. To divert attention, the Poles would send out groups of three soldiers at a time to snipe the German units. This usually resulted in the Poles discarding their weapons and running back into the forest or the swampy areas to hide after the Germans pinpointed them.

Following the breakout attempt, the Germans regrouped and closed around the Poles even tighter. The Poles also regrouped elsewhere and plotted their next breakout attempt which took place on the 2nd.

This was the strongest breakout attempted by the Poles and for it they chose an area near the town of Lomzna and utilized a truck and a heavy machine gun. The German forces were again too

---

[41] The events of January 1940 were gleaned from "Einsätze der 1.SS-Totenkopf-Reiterstandarte" and "Einsätze der Schwadron 2.T.R. von ihren ersten Anfängen bis 1. Juni 1940."

Waldemar Fegelein (younger brother of Hermann Fegelein) shown (left) as an SS-Untersturmführer when assigned to the Hauptreitschule Munich in 1936/37 and (right) as an SS-Obersturmbannführer in command of SS-Kavallerie-Regiment 2 in 1944. Born January 9, 1912 in Ansbach, he joined the SS in April 1933. After being commissioned in June 1936 he was assigned to the staff of SS-Reiterabschnitt V until October 1936. He transferred to the Munich riding school as an instructor until March 1940 during which he was promoted to SS-Obersturmführer on July 25, 1937, and to SS-Hauptsturmführer on July 25, 1938. In March 1940 he took command of 1st Squadron of the SS-Totenkopf-Reiterstandarte (which became 1st Squadron, SS-Kavallerie-Regiment 1) and was promoted to SS-Sturmbannführer on April 20, 1941. As a squadron commander he won the Iron Cross 2nd class on December 15, 1940, and the Iron Cross 1st class on July 10, 1941. During the summer of 1941 he was temporary commander of SS-Kavallerie-Regiment 1 during part of the Pripet actions. He left the Brigade in late 1941 and was assigned to the SS-Führungshauptamt as Cavalry Inspector (Chef Inspektion 3) and was also temporarily head of Amt VI (cavalry and horse transportation). He returned to combat with the SS-Kavallerie-Division in June 1943 and commanded SS-Kavallerie-Regiment 2 until the end of March 1944, during which he was promoted to SS-Obersturmbannführer on January 1, 1944. For his regimental command he won the German Cross in Gold on December 2, 1943, and was personally awarded the Knight's Cross by Himmler on December 16, 1943. Assigned again to command Amt VI of the SS-Führungshauptamt effective April 1, 1944, he remained there briefly until becoming commander of SS-Kavallerie-Regiment 17 of the 22.SS-Freiwilligen-Kavallerie-Division "Maria Theresia" in mid-1944. He was promoted to SS-Standartenführer on December 21, 1944 and in 1945 briefly led the formation staff of the 37.SS-Freiwilligen-Kavallerie-Division "Lützow" (actually a large battle group) formed in 1945 from remnants of the two SS cavalry divisions engaged in Budapest. (Photos: BDC and Yerger Archives)

strong and realizing their failure, the Poles retreated again into the swampy and hilly areas to take cover.

Continuous reconnaissance operations by the Germans helped to track the movements of the band of irregular Polish forces. As the movements of the Poles were continuously monitored and charted by the Germans, the noose around them tightened even more. As the Germans patrolled and searched through neighboring towns, the male population was rounded up and shot or forcefully removed from the area, while the women and children were evacuated. This prevented the Poles from recruiting new partisans which would have strengthened the band of irregular soldiers considerably. Finally, on the 8th of April 1940, after almost eight days, the Germans managed to surround their enemy and overwhelm them with firepower. None of the Poles surrendered and none survived.[42]

The Polish irregular troops scared the Germans considerably and they greatly over-estimated their strength. Besides deploying the previously mentioned Squadrons, many others, most notably the 3rd Squadron under SS-Hauptsturmführer Gustav Lombard and the 1st Platoon of the 2nd Squadron under SS-Untersturmführer Heinrich Dieckmann (which was subordinated to Lomard) were deployed in the outlying areas, securing bridges and rounding up and evacuating the male population. The Germans were ready for the big fight that never took place and after the operation was over, general tensions increased with the Germans beginning larger scale deportations of the non-German male population.

More replacements, volunteers from members of the Allgemeine-SS and Political Leaders (Politische Leiter), arrived in April and their training was initiated immediately upon arrival. To keep up with the increasing demand the recruits imposed, horses continued to be bought from the Polish population. As before, the health of the horses was considerably poor and several weeks of care and training were required before the animals could be put into service.

Creation of the 2.SS-Totenkopf-Reiterstandarte

Further expansion of the 1.SS-Totenkopf-Reiterstandarte and changes followed during May. The 13th and 14th Squadrons began forming in the first two weeks that month to be based in Warsaw and Krasnystaw respectively.[43] It was further decided to base the 9th (replacement) Squadron in Lucmierz directly subordinated to the Standarte with the replacement unit in Munich reduced to a platoon.[44] By mid-May 1940 the 1.SS-Totenkopf-Reiterstandarte had increased to 1908 officers and men. At this point it was decided to split the existing unit into two separate elements starting on May 15, 1940 with completion of the separation accomplished during the remaining months of 1940.[45] The resulting units would be designated the 1. and 2.SS-Totenkopf-Reiterstandarten.[46] Using the existing squadrons of the original Reiterstandarte, the two newly reformed units each contained six squadrons and were formed as follows:

1.SS-Totenkopf-Reiterstandarte
commander : SS-Standartenführer Hermann Fegelein

The 1.SS-Totenkopf-Reiterstandarte consisted of a staff (existing staff in Warsaw), with a signals platoon, motorcycle dispatch platoon, engineer platoon[47] and trumpet corps. The unit squadrons and their locations were as follows:

1st Squadron at Seroczyn, after July Warsaw	(former 3rd Squadron)
2nd Squadron at Kielce	(former 8th Squadron)
3rd Squadron at Krakau	(former 7th Squadron)
4th Squadron at Tarnov	(former 6th Squadron)

[42] "Einsätz der Schwadron 2.T.R. von ihren ersten Anfängen bis 1. Juni 1940" and "Aus dem Kriegstagebuch der 3.Schwadron/ 1.T.R. St. v. 5.4.-11.4.1940 einschließlich" dated 17.4.1940.

[43] The 13th Squadron was partly motorized but the length of time these two squadrons existed was brief due to division of the 1.SS-Totenkopf-Reiterstandarte into two separate units the following month.

[44] Personnel from the replacement unit in Poland had been reassigned to an NCO school for specialized training during January.

[45] Kommando der Waffen-SS, Ia/Tgb-Nr. 38/40 g.Kdos./FiGa, "Gliederung der SS-Reiterstandarten," dated May 21, 1940. Strength lists returned to the Inspektion der SS-Totenkopf-Standarten throughout the summer and early autumn show the split took most of the remainder of 1940.

[46] From establishment of the two regiments until official name changes in early 1941 documents are found with both Reiterstandarte and Reiterregiment as name designation, although during this period the former is correct according to regulations in effect during that period.

[47] Newly formed under SS-Obersturmführer Karl Fritsche, the original existing engineer platoon was given to 2.SS-Totenkopf-Reiterstandarte.

5th (heavy) Squadron at Warsaw	(former 1st Squadron)
6th (horsed battery) Squadron at Krakau	(former 12th Squadron)

2.SS-Totenkopf-Reiterstandarte
commander : SS-Sturmbannführer Franz Magill

The 2.SS-Totenkopf-Reiterstandarte consisted of a staff located at Lublin with a newly created with signals platoon, motorcycle dispatch platoon, engineer platoon and a trumpet corps, the latter created from the original trumpet corps of 1.SS-Totenkopf-Reiterstandarte. The unit squadrons and their locations were as follows:

1st Squadron at Garowlin   (former 2nd Squadron)
2nd Squadron at Chelm   (former 5th Squadron)
3rd Squadron at Zamosc   (former 4th Squadron)
4th Squadron at Krasnystaw, transferred to Jablon in mid-September (former 13th Squadron)
5th (heavy) Squadron at Kamienna, transferred to Lukov after September (former 10th Squadron)
6th (horsed battery) Squadron at Lublin   (former 11th Squadron)

The other squadrons, not transferred in total, were disbanded and used to strengthen existing units as part of the expansion program. Effective June 1, 1940 the 9th (replacement) Squadron lost its numerical designation and was retitled "Replacement Squadron" (Ersatzschwadron) and was now responsible for replacements for both Standarten along with the smaller replacement portion at the SS-Hauptreitschule in Munich.

In a report written by the commander of the 1.SS-Totenkopf-Reiterstandarte, a brief summary of the events in May were reviewed. Overall, the general population in the western districts of Poland was reported as calm whereas partisan activity in the eastern and southern districts (Helm, Sumacs, Kasnistaw, Tarnov) presented a number of problems for the occupying German forces. The cavalry squadrons, however, maintained an excellent success rate against the partisans and lost only one man, while 37 partisans were taken prisoner and 12 were killed.

At the same time the mood of the working population was reported to be somewhat apathetic and non-motivated. While the Germans had plans to develop the local villages into progressive farming communities, the residents had no desire to take part in such endeavors. To motivate the workers, the squadrons warned residents and officials of the towns that failure to work was viewed by the German authorities as sabotage against the German Reich and would be henceforth dealt with accordingly.[48]

In general, the Germans were pleased as operations to procure food for the troops and horses, protect Volksdeutche immigrants and the seizures of weapons and munitions were relatively successful. The morale of the troops was reported as good. Training of officers and men arriving in the area was on schedule. A number of actions began after the first week of May. In general, these actions continued to be pacification or search operations. Again the Germans managed to discover a considerable amount of ammunition and supplies, while at the same time the search for known criminals and the investigation of any signs of partisan resistance continued.

Between May 9th and 17th the 4th Squadron of the 1.SS-Totenkopf-Reiterstandarte was deployed searching the vicinity of Culece for ammunition and weapons. The search revealed 30 full wagons of artillery ammunition as well as a rifle and a case of infantry ammunition.

On May 10th, the 2nd Squadron of the 1.SS-Totenkopf-Reiterstandarte spent the day pursuing criminals in Radkow without success. A report not yet investigated was a robbery that took place on the 24th of September the previous year. The investigators questioned the local population and

---

[48] "Einsätze der 1.SS-Totenkopf-Reiterstandarte."

Gustav Lombard (left) as an SS-Sturmbannführer with Wilhelm Bittrich and the SS-Kavallerie-Division in Russia during late 1942 and (right) as an SS-Standartenführer in command of Kavallerie-Regiment 1 during 1944. Born April 10, 1895 in Spielburg, Lombard joined the SS in May 1933 with SS-Reiterstandarte 6 and quickly moved to SS-Reiterstandarte 7 as a platoon leader (Truppführer) where he was commissioned an SS-Untersturmführer on May 15, 1935. He remained with this unit during the pre-war years and was promoted to SS-Obersturmführer on September 13, 1936 and SS-Hauptsturmführer on September 11, 1938. Promoted to SS-Hauptsturmführer d.R. (Waffen-SS) on March 1, 1940, he joined the SS-Totenkopf-Reiterstandarte as commander of 3rd Squadron in February 1940. Taking command of the mounted detachment (Reitende Abteilung) of SS-Kavallerie-Regiment 1 in March 1941, he was promoted to SS-Sturmbannführer on June 21, 1941 and assumed command of SS-Kavallerie-Regiment 1 on August 18, 1941. He was temporary commander of the SS-Totenkopf-Reiterstandarte and the Brigade when Fegelein was absent and commanded the Brigade remnants in the field after mid-March 1942 which then totaled some 700 men. Promoted to SS-Obersturmbannführer on March 16, 1942, he remained with the SS-Kavallerie-Division commanding Kavallerie-Regiment 1 and was temporary divisional commander serving between Wilhelm Bittrich and Fritz Freitag in the winter of 1942/ 43. Promoted to SS-Standartenführer on January 30, 1943, he won the German Cross in Gold on February 11, 1943, and the Knight's Cross on March 10, 1943. After April 1943 he was assigned to the HSSPF Russland-Mitte (Erich von dem Bach) for anti-partisan operations. He headed the formation staff of the 29.Waffen-Grenadier-Division der SS (italienische Nr.1) from October to December 1943. Lombard was temporary chief of the Kommandostab "Reichsführer-SS" in late December 1943 and then led an independent Kampfgruppe for the HSSPF Russland-Mitte. Promoted to SS-Oberführer on March 12, 1944, he commanded the 31.SS-Freiwilligen-Grenadier-Division from October 1944 to May 1945 during which he was promoted to SS-Brigadeführer on January 30, 1945. Captured by the Russians he spent 10 years as a POW and died in Germany on September 18, 1992. Fluent in English, he was among the important early cavalry leaders with regard to unit development and field operations. For a period before the war he worked in the United States for Chrysler in Missouri. (Photos: Jess Lukens and Yerger Archives)

managed to identify the robbers by circulating pictures of the known criminals, who were unknown in this particular region. The day was not a total loss however, as the squadron leaders were informed of possible ammunition hidden in the forest east of the town. Here they found a tank still intact, as well as a truck that was missing its wheels.

On May 11th, signs of organized resistance surfaced once again. The day began as usual with the 2nd Squadron of the 1.SS-Totenkopf-Reiterstandarte searching the villages of Telatyn and Kmiczyn and the forest south of Zulice. They also managed to search some of the Ukrainian population, but turned up nothing.

However, the Ukrainians reported that there was a gathering where Polish nationalist songs were sung several days before on the 3rd of May in Nabroz, a village seven kilometers from Zulice. A man in a Polish uniform, riding horseback with a Polish flag attached to the back of his hat, supposedly rode through the village spreading a rumor that the Germans were soon leaving Poland. The unit immediately dispatched bicycle reconnaissance units to search for the man, but no new information on his whereabouts was found.

On May 12th, the search for the man in Polish uniform continued. The Germans collected 50 Ukrainians and interrogated them about the Polish rider. The Ukrainians, who hated the Poles, provided far-fetched statements about the Poles which the Germans did not take them seriously. Further patrols revealed nothing other than an unloaded infantry rifle.

On May 14th, the 2nd Squadron went to Nabroz to search for the Polish rider. He was found, along with four others who were also taken into custody. The Polish rider's uniform as well as a sidearm were confiscated. The 2nd Squadron then rode further to Good Stara Vies, where the leader of the Squadron warned the mayor of the village about the work policies. Apparently, the inhabitants there were not working in accordance to the order of the Landrat (district president). The Squadron rode to Wisznow where the commander again warned the mayor about the unacceptable work ethic of his residents.

During the previous few days, the Ukrainians were reported to be causing a number of problems for the Germans. They allegedly wanted revenge on the Poles for the all the robberies, kidnappings and murders inflicted upon them during the Russian occupation.

On the 15th, the combat group "Seipel" rode to Steniatyn to capture a supposed murderer that shot a Ukrainian during the Russian occupation. The man was apprehended and sent to a work camp in Germany.

On the same day, the 2nd Squadron received a report that there was a supply of ammunition in the forest area east of Radkow. The report proved to be accurate and the Squadron managed to recover 30 horse wagons and some artillery munitions. In Radkow the Squadron took the opportunity to warn the mayor of the German work policies and, upon returning to Posadow, the unit found that the warnings were taking good effect.[49]

Action in Lykoszyn resulted in the taking of 16 prisoners. Among them was a man whom the Germans had been seeking for some time. This individual had apparently fired a gun into a retreating group of German soldiers on the 12th of September the previous year. Also, the Ukrainian police managed to find some weapons. The police had set up a routine roadblock to perform random checks on passers-by and a few members of a well-known partisan group were stopped. The search revealed various weapons and the Ukrainians promised the Germans that they would pursue the case further with all available resources. From mid-May to mid-June various units were sent to protect immigrating Wohlhynien Germans from the resident Poles. A platoon of the 1st Squadron was assigned to the area of Kutno, while three platoons of the 9th Replacement Squadron in Lodz were assigned to the areas of Lem, Lemschütz and Lodz.

At 1500 hours on Saturday, the 25th of May the acting Sipo commander in Chelm informed the 5th Squadron that a Polish Captain by the name of Niezolowski had rallied the youths of Czarnolozy, Ostruv, Majdan-Ostrowski and Wierzbica to start a fight with 5th Squadron. This information had apparently been reported to the SD by a Pole.

The 5th Squadron departed in march formation at about 1900 hours with four platoons (three mounted and one motorized) which consisted of three officers and 169 men. In addition, the Sipo commander and six men accompanied the formation. The Pole who had reported the gathering to the SD was also brought along to show the supposed gathering place. The meeting was to take place at 2200 hours in the northern part of the forest in Czarnolozy near the village of Wojslawice.

When the troops arrived at 2200 hours they quickly surrounded the area and began searching for the Polish Captain and the meeting. The informant showed SS-Hauptsturmführer Reichenwallner the gathering place. At the meeting place the officers found an old fire place as well as evidence of

---

[49] Ibid.

horses. The officers were convinced this was indeed a meeting place, although it had been some time since it was used. Due to the sounds of approaching storms and a light rain, the officers assumed that the gathering moved to another unknown location.

At dawn the next day (the 26th) Reichenwallner departed with the mounted platoons and moved further south towards Czarnolozy. The motorized platoon was assigned to perform a search and apprehended seven Poles who were known to be members of the partisan organization in Wierzbica.

Reichenwallner gathered his troops on the hills of Czarnolozy to discuss plans for the rest of the day with his platoon leaders. As they were about to leave for another village, they heard machine gun fire from the north and saw a smoke cloud rise. Soon after they saw a column of smoke, indicating something was burning. Reichenwallner sent a rider platoon in the direction of the smoke columns and the heavy machine gun platoon to follow them as a back-up unit. During a ride through a clearing, two fleeing Polish riders were seen from a distance on a hill that was about 800 meters away. The group took off to pursue the Poles and as the Poles noticed them, they let their horses run and hid themselves in a building. They were quickly taken prisoner and taken away. It was later determined that the smoke columns were coming from two burning houses.

The leader of the 3rd Platoon later reported to Reichenwallner that he had received machine gun fire from a distance of about 500 to 600 meters while riding through a forest enroute to another village. The unit immediately searched for the machine gunners but couldn't even determine the location the Poles had been shooting from. When a messenger was dispatched to bring up the machine gun platoon he received rifle fire on the way. A group from the platoon set up in the western part of the village also received machine gun fire. After being noticed, the Poles fled over the northern hills. The platoon quickly sent a few riders after them and managed to take them prisoner. The rest were shot from a distance of 400 to 500 meters.

The village was then searched for any remaining weapons or munitions. During a search, a few soldiers had just discovered a rifle and a cleaning kit when the house they were searching suddenly broke into flames. The others watched as a Pole ran out of the house with the fleeing SS men following shortly behind. Just as the two SS men had reached safety, the house blew up, thus proving that there were more munitions still in the houses.

The immediate danger gone, the search operation was turned over to the Sipo which managed to retrieve the remaining members of the organization as well as considerable amounts of weapons and munitions. During the course of the operation, 12 Poles were shot fleeing and 23 were taken prisoner while no casualties were reported for the 5th Squadron.[50]

Between the 29th of May and the 6th of June, the 6th Squadron, along with other elements under the command of the SS and Police Leader of Lublin, were assigned to procure food for the men and feed for the animals. On the 30th of May Polish police once again summoned SS cavalry units to help them track down criminals. This time the 3rd Squadron of the 1.SS-Totenkopf-Reiterstandarte undertook the search for an escaped convict. After the man was discovered, he fought back with hand grenades and a rifle. His escape attempt was fruitless, however, and he was shot during the struggle. Elsewhere on the 30th of May, the 4th Squadron of the 2.SS-Totenkopf-Reiterstandarte was called in by the Field Police (Feldgendarmerie) to search for partisans who had stolen some goods in the town of Mogilnicki.

The Squadron arrived too late however, and the Field Police determined that the partisan group had split up, with one part boarding a train and another retreating into the forest. Since the units of the Feldgendarmerie were scheduled to take part in a large "special action," the 4th Squadron remained in the area as a support unit for them.[51]

While the health of the troops was reported good during the month of June 1940, the horses were ill with chest colds. This posed several problems for the units and kept the veterinarians occupied. Reports for the month of June included only light actions, such as rounding up Jews and

---

[50] "Gefechtsbericht für die 5.Schwadron der 1.SS-Totenkopf-Reiterstandarte" dated 26.5.1940.

[51] "Raubüberfall am 29.5.1940 im Kreise Krasnystaw, an die 4.Schwadron 2.SS-Totenkopf-Reiterregiment" dated 4.6.1940.

transferring them to labor camps. The units were also involved in operations to protect the immigrating Volksdeutsche. Besides routine duties, training for all units continued as recruits arrived replacing the older SS men.

On June 9th, the 2nd Platoon of the 4th Squadron (Krasnystaw) was called in by the Feldgendarmerie. They had received reports on the whereabouts of a number of partisans from the Polish police in Zabroczev. The unit departed and upon arrival were directed by the police to the residences of the partisans, who lived about 9 kilometers from the city. After surrounding the houses, they realized that the partisans had already fled.

On June 13th the 1.SS-Totenkopf-Reiterstandarte was given orders to send elements to Turek to protect the immigrating Volksdeutsche. For this operation the Reiterstandarte dispatched a heavy machine gun half-platoon which consisted of an officer, 27 men and 31 horses. On June 14th the 3rd Squadron was assigned to take over the transport of 156 Jews that were to be transferred from Janowice to a forced-labor camp in Zamoce. During the march, one of the prisoners was shot trying to escape.[52]

Also on the 14th SS-Sturmbannführer Franz Magill took official command of the recently created 2.SS-Totenkopf-Reiterstandarte. In commemoration of this occasion, the new commander inspected the barracks of the 1st Squadron. During his visit Magill promised to do his best to support the unit.

The 1st Squadron of the 2.SS-Totenkopf-Reiterstandarte spent June 15th to the 17th in preparation of an upcoming combat training exercise that took place on the 18th in a forest clearing near Podsamczc (several kilometers south of Garwolin). This exercise took place in the presence of SS-Standartenführer Fegelein with the troops using live rounds and cardboard cut-outs in the shape of enemy soldiers to make the exercise as realistic as possible. The exercise took place with a platoon leader and three groups of ten men each, each with a group leader. During the drill, the leader of the exercise, SS-Untersturmführer Heinrich Dieckmann, issued orders to each platoon as the action proceeded. All the while, each group leader was observed to see how he completed his task.

After the exercise was completed, the results were discussed by SS-Standartenführer Fegelein in the presence of the men and deemed successful. The exercise served as the concluding phase of the unit's infantry training.

During the evening of the 21st a festive occasion, known as the "Sommersonnwendfeier" (midsummer festival) took place. In the vicinity of Garwolin the 1st Squadron of the 2.SS-Totenkopf-Reiterstandarte set up a large bon-fire and opened the festivities with singing. After the first song was concluded and the fire was raging, SS-Untersturmführer Heinrich Dieckmann gave a speech welcoming the guests, many of whom were Volksdeutsche immigrants from Garwolin. After his speech everyone started singing "Flamme empor" and the traditional wreath was thrown in the fire. The festivities concluded with the singing of the SS-Treuelied (SS loyalty song) and a salute to the Führer.

On the 22nd, the 9th Replacement Squadron from Lucmierz was sent to Turek to assist the many cases of arson reported. Besides performing large scale protection operations for the immigrating Volksdeutsche and Wolhynien German population, the 1st Platoon of the 1.SS-Totenkopf-Reiterstandarte shot a Polish convict who tried to escape while the 2nd Platoon captured various members of a Polish secret organization in conjunction with the SD.[53] Elsewhere in Poland, men of the 1st Squadron of the 2.SS-Totenkopf-Reiterstandarte were invited to a "Sonnwendfeier" in Neu Podely by the ethnic Germans who resided there.

On June 23rd, at the request of the Kreishauptmann in Garwolin, the 1st Squadron of the 2.SS-Totenkopf-Reiterstandarte marched to Parysow and a platoon of 27 NCOs searched the surrounding area. Several items of interest were found and handed over to the police. No one was killed or arrested during this action.

---

[52] "Einsätze der 1.SS-Totenkopf-Reiterstandarte."

[53] "Lage und Tätigkeitsbericht des 1. und 2. SS-Totenkopf-Reiter-Regiments" dated 10.10.1940.

It was common for the Polish families who lost their homes and possessions to the German evacuation policies to return to their homes and harass the ethnic Germans that were given their houses by the German resettlement authorities. On June 29th the 1.SS-Totenkopf-Reiterstandarte received a report about a Polish family that returned home after being evacuated. The Standarte then dispatched a patrol to pick them up to be re-evacuated.

In July 1940, the units mainly took part in evacuation and pacification operations. Many of the Poles had already been transported off to eastern areas of the General Government while others were sent to forced-labor camps in Germany. As the occupation progressed, the rules that governed the dwindling Polish population became increasingly harsh.

On July 1st new laws were put into effect concerning the carrying of identification papers for the general population. At first the Germans only issued these identification papers, which were to be carried by all residents. This, however, allowed the residents to roam freely throughout the country and travel from town to town. As the instances of arson and other acts of sabotage increased, the Germans realized that this system was unsuitable. The new laws mandated that residents not only carry their papers, but they also had to be stamped upon arrival or departure from each village. This allowed the Germans to track the whereabouts and the traffic of the population. To understand the atmosphere of General Government in July 1940 as well as the attitude of the occupying German forces at this point, it is best to read a section of the war diary of the 1.SS-Totenkopf-Reiterstandarte translated verbatim:

"There are many days when we must send out small patrols to pick up Poles that make shelter in chicken coops and wander around. Complaints from the Ethnic Germans and the Wohlhynien Germans are common and upon investigation reveal nothing. There are also increasing cases of the Ethnic Germans and the Wohlhynien Germans taking in Poles to be their servants for egotistical reasons. They even give them shelter and a place to stay. The enthusiasm to work and the enterprising spirit here are generally non-existent. The Ethnic Germans and the Wohlhynien Germans seem to be of the opinion that 'now we are in the Reich and everything is in order!' They ignore the fact that they are supposed to be building and working.

'Even here, after the Warthe district has been declared a Reich area, there are still towns in which Germans live and the mayors are Polish. Is this not more than a favorable situation for the Poles ? Also, with regards to the law, the Poles and Germans have equal rights. What is a punishment for the Germans is a reward for the Poles! The Poles are not used to the relatively mild punishments and they can't stand them. It is impossible, however, to bring law and order to these poor towns without contradicting the laws themselves.

'After a village is occupied, the first searches are performed at night. Every Polish residence and farmstead is searched. When we search them, the Poles hide themselves in sheds and barns and defend themselves adamantly with pitch-forks. Sometimes there are homeless wanderers who hide themselves in these barns without the owner's knowing or without his wanting to know. Sometimes they are the farmer's neighbors who are trying to avoid being taken away by the evacuation. Sometimes they are people that say that it was the farmer who forced them to stay there, although they don't appear to have any signs of oppression or starvation. It is often difficult to decide who to let stay and who to send away, and more often than not it is those that are dependents that are spared the evacuation, but only in as much as there are enough people left over to be put to work.

'No legal grounds exist to take prisoner those Poles who provide food and shelter for others. Each particular case is difficult to judge and when no decision can be made, those in question are handed over to the SD. If the occupants of a farm are evacuated, then the ownership of the farm is declared forfeited and the farm is handed over to the immigration service, which usually fills the farm with Ethnic Germans or Wohlhynien Germans on the same day."[54]

---

[54] "Kriegstagebuch der 1.SS-Totenkopf-Reiterstandarte".

On the 4th of July a night patrol from the 1.SS-Totenkopf-Reiterstandarte consisting of an officer and 19 men surround the village of Flicianow and performed a search of the farm situated there. Thirteen homeless wanderers were taken prisoner and handed over to the SD. The remaining residents were instructed to report to the moving commission for immediate evacuation.[55]

On the 7th of July a patrol from the 1.SS-Totenkopf-Reiterstandarte consisting of an officer and eighteen men was sent to Wiescice and Spiemierz. In Wiescice several women and children that were left behind by emigrating Polish families posed a problem for the settling Wolhynien Germans. The four children and seven women are picked up and sent to Czepow. Along with the women and children, the unit apprehended a Polish family that gave another Polish family shelter. They were also sent to Czepov. On the 8th of July the 1st Platoon of the 3rd Squadron of 1.SS-Totenkopf-Reiterstandarte performed a routine execution of a criminal.[56]

During the next week members of the 1.SS-Totenkopf-Reiterstandarte apprehended 23 men, 18 women and seven children that either avoided the emigration policies enforced by the German authorities or gave shelter to emigrating Poles. These people were brought to Uniejov and handed over to the SD for further transport to Lodz.

On the July 9th the German agencies decided that the remaining Polish authorities had to leave. All Polish mayors were apprehended and replaced by Germans. Reports from this action indicate that the resident immigrant German farmers as well as the new German mayors were not concerned with the welfare of the departing Polish authorities and made no pleas for their well-being. They also noted the remaining Poles offered no resistance. The apprehended Polish authorities were scheduled for evacuation to Dobra on the 11th, but the train that was supposed to transport them was overcrowded, so they were set free.

On the 17th the recruiting period for the 1st Squadron of the 2.SS-Totenkopf-Reiterstandarte (Garwolin), which began early in the year, was concluded with a final combat exercise in conjunction with the 1st and 5th Squadron of the 1.SS-Totenkopf-Reiterstandarte (Seroczyn). The combat exercise was designed to test the squadrons in their riding as well as infantry abilities and was observed by such notables as the later SS and Police Leader for Krakau district SS-Oberführer Hans Schwedler,[57] SS-Standartenführer Hermann Fegelein and SS-Sturmbannführer Franz Magill as well as their staffs. For entertainment, the 1st and 5th Squadrons performed training exercises while the 1st Squadron of the 2.SS-Totenkopf-Reiterstandarte demonstrated a river crossing. After the exercise several speeches were given and SS-Hauptsturmführer Gustav Lombard was thanked for arranging the exercise which was deemed successful. Afterwards the first "Camaraderie-Evening" for the new recruits took place which several high officers of the Police and the Wehrmacht from the surrounding areas attended.

On July 25th the 2nd Squadron of the 1.SS-Totenkopf-Reiterstandarte executed two professional criminals at the order of the government appointed lawyer upon judgment in Kilce. Four people where also apprehended by 2nd Squadron on the order of the SD. After being captured they were handed over to the SD.[58]

In July 1940 one casualty was reported when a man from the 5th Squadron of 1.SS-Totenkopf-Reiterstandarte drowned during a routine bridge crossing. The health of the troops was reported as being good while that of the horses was noted as improved in comparison with the previous month.[59]

In late July SS-Oberführer Hans Schwedler paid the 1.SS-Totenkopf-Reiterstandarte a visit. At this special occasion, Schwedler was given the opportunity to inspect a squadron of the Regiment. Also in late July the Higher SS and Police Leader, SS-Obergruppenführer Friedrich-Wilhelm Krüger,

[55] Ibid.

[56] "Lage und Tätigkeit des 1. und 2. SS-Totenkopf-Reiter-Regiments" dated 12.8.1940.

[57] Officially assumed the post in October 1940.

[58] "Lage und Tätgkeit des 1. und 2. SS-Totenkopf-Reiter-Regiments" dated 12.8.1940.

[59] Ibid.

arranged for the filming of the Warsaw units of the Standarte.[60] The month ended with the 4th Squadron of the 1.SS-Totenkopf-Reiterstandarte from Tarnov came to Krakau to take part in a parade before General Governor Dr. Hans Frank. 3rd Squadron personnel of 2.SS-Totenkopf-Reiterstandarte were guests at the reception held for Frank.

The actions undertaken by the squadrons in the month of August 1940 continued to further the German resettlement programs and general law enforcement according to German policies. A status report written for the month of August indicated that the behavior of the general population continued to remain calm and subdued. This is attributed to the fact that the entire male Jewish population had been put to work by an action undertaken by the 2nd, 3rd and 5th Squadrons of the 2.SS-Totenkopf-Reiterstandarte and the 2nd Squadron of the 1.SS-Totenkopf-Reiterstandarte. Also a contributing factor was the rounding up of 1500 Poles by 1.SS-Totenkopf-Reiterstandarte who were sent to Dachau concentration camp.[61]

On August 4th and 5th the 2.SS-Totenkopf-Reiterstandarte along with the Fuß-SS (foot SS) and the Order Police took part in a "special action" ordered by the SS and Police Leader for the district of Lublin, Odilio Globocnik. On the 14th of August the 2nd Squadron of the 1.SS-Totenkopf-Reiterstandarte executed four dangerous criminals by order of the SD, while on August 30th the 1st Squadron of the 1.SS-Totenkopf-Reiterstandarte executed 87 Poles in Warsaw by the order of the SD.[62] Protection of the Wolhynien Germans from the remaining Polish population continued to be a necessity and a rider platoon as well as a heavy machine gun half platoon of the Replacement Squadron based in Lucmierz were assigned for these duties for the entire month. On a lighter note, both the 1. and 2. SS-Totenkopf-Reiterstandarten took part in the filming of a movie for the homefront titled "Kampfgeschwader Lützow" (Fighting Regiment Lützow).

In September 1940 the policies of the German occupation continued to be implemented. Reports indicate that the Polish population continued to behave in a calm and reserved manner since there was nothing special to report. While there were no casualties for the units during this month, the general health of the troops was reported as only satisfactory due to several cases of a virus, which reports refer to as the "Polish Sickness." The condition of the horses was noted as improved although the cases of chest colds were still high in number. Food supplies received through the new supply depots of the Waffen-SS were satisfactory, while the lack of trucks and hauling equipment for the motorized platoon as well as the lack of equipment for the signals and the engineer platoons slowed down general operations. Several moves also took place during the month of September. The men of the 4th Squadron started moving their barracks and headquarters from Krasnysteav to Jablon early in the month with the men and horses making the final move on the 15th. The 5th Heavy Squadron moved from Kamienna in the district of Radom to their new barracks in Lukov in the Lublin district on the 18th.

Also during the month of September 1940, 200 new men arrived as replacements from Munich and both regiments conducted a large oath-taking ceremony for these men as well as a farewell party for the men over the age of 35 who were relieved and sent back to Germany for reassignment. Other recreational activities for the men included a three-day horse riding and jumping tourney in Krakau for members of the SS and Police.

The nature of specific actions remained unchanged during September. Noted actions included the 2nd Squadron of 1.SS-Totenkopf-Reiterstandarte escorting farmers which enabled them to safely bring in their harvest, while border duties were performed by the Engineer (Pionier) Platoon of the 2.SS-Totenkopf-Reiterstandarte in Balcez. On the 19th and 20th of September 1600 Poles of the Warsaw population were taken prisoner by the 1st and 5th Squadrons of the 1.SS-Totenkopf-Reiterstandarte after the shooting of an SD member by a Pole. During this same period, troops of

---

[60] Ibid.

[61] "Lage und Tätigkeit des 1. und 2. SS-Totenkopf-Reiter-Regiments" dated 7.9.1940, consisting of two different reports with the same title and date.

[62] Ibid.

the same unit took 700 Jews prisoner in Otwock and handed them over to the SD, while other troops of the Standarte were given the task of executing 200 people by the order of the SD.[63] On the 22nd a search was performed by 80 riders each of the 2nd and 3rd Squadrons and 40 riders of the 4th Squadron of the 2.SS-Totenkopf-Reiterstandarte at the request of the SS and Police Leader in Lublin. The action involved the villages of Sitno, Horyszow, Polski and Janowka. During this action several Poles were apprehended for the possession of numerous pieces of army equipment and ammunition.

The month of October 1940 was a festive month for the men of the SS-Totenkopf-Reiterstandarten. On the 6th the regiments took part in a parade in Warsaw before the General Governor, Reichsminister Dr. Hans Frank and General Field Marshal Wilhelm List.[64] The parade marked the one year anniversary of the "Führer Parade" which was held the year before in commemoration of the conquest of Poland. On the 26th units of the 1.SS-Totenkopf-Reiterstandarte took place in another parade, this time in Krakau before the General Governor and Reichsführer-SS Heinrich Himmler. That parade marked the one year anniversary of the establishment of the General Government of Poland. Several other high-ranking Generals of the SS, including SS-Bridageführer Hans Jüttner, SS-Gruppenführer Ortwin Pohl and SS-Bridageführer August Frank also paid visits to the Standarten and had the opportunity to inspect their barracks and headquarters.[65]

Nothing out of the ordinary was reported for October 1940. The general population was reported as continuing their calm behavior, while the men and horses experienced no casualties and were reported as healthy. Several training exercises were held in accordance with a general order received from the command office of the Waffen-SS.

The month of November 1940 was a festive month for the men of the SS-Reiterstandarten and aside from normal duties, there were a number of notable parties and ceremonies that they attended.

On the 2nd the festivities for a large German hunting holiday named the "Hubertusjagd" began. The events surrounding this festive occasion are described in great detail in the war diary of the 1st Squadron of the 2.SS-Totenkopf-Reiterstandarte, a translation of which is presented here for the reader's interest:

"In spite of the terrible storm a few days before, preparations for the 'Hubertusjagd' were completed. This time the Jadgreiten (mounted hunt) took place in the afternoon. Some of the officers of the Wehrmacht also took part in the hunt. As before, the 'Jagdreiten' took place in two fields. The 'Jagdreiten' in the first field was led by SS-Obersturmführer Dieckmann while the other 'Jagdreiten' in the second field was led by SS-Oberscharführer Friebe, who was chosen to be Master of the hunt. The stretch was 40 kilometers long and consisted of both sandy and hilly land which passed through a forest. The course was diverse. The built-up hurdles, ditches, hedges and the 'Oxer,' that were appropriately positioned, made for a beautiful view. A high sandhill with a deep jump was especially noticeable. The beautiful warm weather made for a great day without any problems. The demands of this 'Jagdreiten,' in contrast to previous 'Jagdreiten,' were especially stressful due to the length of the course.

'Because of this, special recognition must be given both to the riders as well as the horses for their brave performance and their durability. The 'Jagdherr,' SS-Sturmbannführer Ruge, expressed his amazement of the performance of the entire Squadron. A Reich-German lady held out a small branch from an oak tree (Eichenbruch) to each rider, from which they took a small bite. Also, there

---

[63] "Lage und Tätigkeit des 1. und 2. SS-Totenkopf-Reiter-Regiments" dated 10.10.1940.

[64] Awarded the Knight's Cross as a Colonel General in command of 14.Armee on September 30, 1939.

[65] Jüttner headed the SS Main Operational Office (SS-Führungshauptamt) and Pohl at that time led the SS Main Office for Budget and Buildings (Hauptamt Haushalt-und Bauten) which was a heavy user of forced labor. Frank was a member of Pohl's command while all three men were awarded the German Cross in Silver for their contributions to the war effort.

was no lack of friendly conversation. At 1700 hours the entire Squadron returned to the barracks. Every SS rider was proud to have participated in the hunt. The excitement of the event gave the troops a fresh attitude towards their everyday duties. Everyone expressed their desire to participate in any future 'Jagdreiten.'

'To conclude the magnificent 'Hubertusjagd,' the 1st Squadron organized a 'comrade's evening' in the Wehrmacht district, in which high officers of the Wehrmacht and the Police as well as their guests took part. The Wehrmacht building was decorated with hunting memorabilia for this occasion. The decorations consisted of obstacles set up in the staircase that were very tastefully decorated with spruce branches. These obstacles gave every visitor the opportunity to prove his jumping abilities once again. The hurdles made fun for every visitor. The evening was opened by the Chef (commander) of the 1st Squadron, SS-Sturmbannführer Ruge. Above all he called to the most senior Wehrmacht officer, bid him a hearty welcome and thanked him for allowing the preparations for the evening's festivities to commence. It was only through this officer's permission that the men of the 1st Squadron could make the necessary preparations for the 'comrade's evening.' Continuing on, he greeted the members of the Wehrmacht and Police and their honored guests with a hearty welcome. SS-Sturmbannführer Ruge then reflected on the meaning of the 'Hubertusfest.' He also expressed his hopes that in the future there would be many opportunities for the SS and the Wehrmacht to celebrate such occasions together. In conclusion he thanked SS-Oberscharführer Hilgers for the excellently prepared course which had met every expectation and gave him special praise for his work. He concluded his speech with thought of the Führer.

'The main table had just been decorated with spruce branches and the higher officers of the Wehrmacht, along with their honored guests, took their places in the middle section of the table. The table looked beautiful. After dinner, the senior officer of the Wehrmacht gave a short speech and thanked SS-Sturmbannführer Ruge for his kind words. He also expressed his regret that he himself could not take part in the hunt. While concluding, he promised to remain in contact with the SS and expressed his hope that the coming winter weather would still allow a few more rides.

'The serious part of the evening finished and the atmosphere of the fest quickly relaxed. The evening was enhanced by conversation and soldier's songs and all the participants experienced hours of friendly comradeship that unfortunately ended all too quickly."

On the 8th preparations began for a large oath-taking ceremony that was to take place that evening. As before, an entry in the war diary of the 1st Squadron of the 2.SS-Totenkopf-Reiterstandarte gives the reader a good indication as to the nature of such an event:

"On the eve of the 9th of November, the anniversary of the Hitler's Putsch, the new recruits of the rider Squadrons, along with others in the greater German Reich, took their oath. SS-Obersturmführer Heinrich Dieckmann and SS-Untersturmführer Heinrich Held conducted our swearing-in ceremonies. The ceremony took place at midnight between the 8th and the 9th on an estate outside the city of Lublin.

'The bleachers as well as the entire area were covered with flags of the German Reich and the SS, at both sides of the bleachers stood an anti-tank gun. The recruits marched in at all four corners and at each corner stood a torch bearer. Close to the podium, which was decorated with flags and spruce leaves, stood an honor platoon of older SS-men which enclosed the open side of the square. At exactly midnight, the Squadron leader stepped forward and reported the strength of his Squadron to SS-Sturmbannführer Josef Fritz. SS-Sturmbannführer Franz Magill, who was to conduct the oath-taking ceremony, stepped up to the podium as the honor platoon presented itself. Then SS-Sturmbannführer Fritz reported the strength of his sworn-in men. With brief but appropriate words, SS-Sturmbannführer Magill spoke about the meaning of this moment and reminded the men not to take their oaths lightly. He also requested that those who were not able to uphold their oath not to take it. None said a word. These were loud, young men who were ready to fight for their Führer and their people.

'Now the oath taking ceremony was ready to begin. From each Squadron a recruit stepped forward and overtook the vow for his comrades. The honor platoon presented itself once again. The recruits stood still, raised their right hand to take the oath and SS-Sturmbannführer Magill read the oath aloud and, following a short pause, was repeated by the recruits. Then the sounds of the 'Treuelied' (loyalty song) sounded and the hour of the consecration came to an end. Every recruit realized that he had given the Führer his word and had overtaken the duty for the German people as well as for greater Germany. The Squadrons then returned to their barracks."

On the 10th of November 1940 SS-Obersturmführer Heinrich Dieckmann issued the order for his entire 1st Squadron to report in full march equipment for a promotion ceremony. The promotions were officially made on the 9th of November.[66] Ceremonies began with a speech by Dieckmann during which he expressed his satisfaction of the his troops and his happiness that the majority of the men had reached a higher rank. The names of those promoted were read aloud and those promoted stepped forward and formed a formation. Two SS-Rottenführer were promoted to SS-Unterscharführer, two Sturmmänner were promoted to SS-Rottenführer and 20 SS-Reiter were promoted to SS-Sturmmann. After each man was handed his promotion certificate and SS-Obersturmführer Dieckmann expressed his best wishes, he gave a short speech about the meaning of the promotions. *"Every promotion was well-earned and represents a commitment for every man, and therefore he has been formally recognized. Every comrade should emulate those promoted."* He ended the ceremonies with a triple "Sieg-heil."

On the 11th, ten SS cavalrymen were ordered to take part in a "special action." On the 16th, the leaders of the 1st Squadron of the 2.SS-Totenkopf-Reiterstandarte went to Warsaw to take part in a squadron and platoon leaders course. Several talks were conducted for leaders of both regiments. The newly recruited leaders arrived on Sunday in Warsaw followed by lectures given in Warsaw, Garwolin and Lukov. These lectures covered tactical plans for units of battalion strength. Visual aids such as sandboxes and maps were utilized with several exercises taking place in the field. To conclude these short courses, an inspection of the battlefield around Modlin took place on Tuesday. Here course instructors reconstructed the battle of III./"Deutschland" from September 28, 1939.

On November 20th the commander of 1st Squadron of 2.SS-Totenkopf-Reiterstandarte, SS-Sturmbannführer Rudolf Ruge, received orders to transfer to SS-Junkerschule Bad Tölz.[67] A large farewell party was organized and attended by all members of the Squadron. Ruge gave a short speech and afterwards SS-Obersturmführer Heinrich Dieckmann presented him with three large pictures of the Squadron.

On the 24th, more promotions arrived for the men of the 1st Squadron/2.SS-Totenkopf-Reiterstandarte. 60 SS-Reiter were promoted to SS-Oberreiter. On the 28th, SS-Standartenführer Hermann Fegelein and SS-Hauptsturmführer Gustav Lombard arrived in Garwolin to inspect the barracks. Ruge's replacement, SS-Hauptsturmführer Ulrich Görtz, arrived on December 29th to assume his duties as the new commander of 1st Squadron/2.SS-Totenkopf-Reiterstandarte.[68]

On December 1, 1940, some of the men were given leave and took the train to Warsaw where a theater showed the film "Jud Süß."[69] A formal barracks inspection of the 2nd Squadron of 1.SS-Totenkopf-Reiterstandarte took place the following day in anticipation of a visit from SS-Brigadeführer Carl-Maria Demelhuber. SS-Obersturmführer Paul Hoppe inspected the clothing, saddles and weapons as well as all equipment. Everything was found to be in order and no disciplinary actions were required.

---

[66] Most, though not all, SS promotions were made on January 30th (date Hitler assumed power) or November 9th (anniversary of the failed 1923 Munich putsch by the then infant Nazi party).

[67] The two primary officer training schools for the SS were in Bad Tölz (established in 1934) and Braunschweig (formed in 1935). Many graduating cadets were highly decorated and several eventually attained divisional commands. Experienced older field officers often served as instructors as did combat veterans while recovering from wounds or injury.

[68] "Abschrift des Kriegstagebuches der 1.Schwadron des SS-Totenkopf-Reiterregiments 2."

[69] A famous anti-Jewish propaganda film of the period.

SS-Gruppenführer Carl-Maria Demelhuber, one of several high ranking officers to inspect the cavalry units while they were stationed in Poland. At the time of his December 1940 visit Demelhuber was an SS-Brigadeführer and senior Waffen-SS commander "East" (Befehlshaber der Waffen-SS "Ost"). He held the position until it was eliminated in April 1941. In this later photo as an SS-Gruppenführer he is the senior Waffen-SS commander for the Netherlands and with him on the left is the captain of the battleship "Scharnhorst," Kurt Ceasar Hoffmann. On the right is SS-Brigadeführer Otto Bene in government officials uniform. The senior Waffen-SS commander assigned to an area was subordinated to the Higher SS and Police Leader for that sector. Demelhuber ended the war as commander of XVI.SS-Armeekorps and died in 1988. (Yerger Archives)

SS-Obersturmführer Heinrich Dieckmann then presented the barracks to SS-Hauptsturmführer Ulrich Görtz. SS-Brigadeführer Demelhuber arrived on December 4th along with SS-Standartenführer Fegelein, Detachment Commander Gustav Lombard and other squadron leaders of 1.SS-Totenkopf-Reiterstandarte. The program for the day included a combat exercise complete with a demonstration of a frontal attack conducted by a platoon under the leadership of SS-Obersturmführer Dieckmann which was supported by a heavy machine gun half-platoon. After the combat exercise, Brigadeführer Demelhuber took the opportunity to inspect the riding hall and the barracks as well as the new recruits. The day ended with a formal lunch where all the members of the visiting parties and the 2nd Squadron attended.

On the 5th, SS-Obersturmführer Heinrich Dieckmann, who had been with the Squadron stationed in Garwolin since its formation, received his orders to transfer to 3rd Squadron. The 2nd Squadron held a large farewell party for him during which Dieckmann gave his farewell speech:

"My old men, who built the Squadron together with me know my bond to the Squadron. I was satisfied with every officer, NCO and man, and I know that each of you stood on my side. I hope that you will give my successor, SS-Hauptsturmführer Görtz the same bonding and that you will be always ready to fight in battle."

SS-Obersturmführer Dieckmann shook everyone's hand and then handed over the Squadron to SS-Hauptsturmführer Ulrich Görtz. Görtz thanked Dieckmann and replied:

"I know that it is difficult for you to bid us farewell, because I know that you have grown with every member of the Squadron. May you settle in with your new unit quickly and I wish you the best from the bottom of my heart."

Görtz then turned to the men and expressed his wish that under his leadership they be ready to carry out any order given to him by the Führer.

During the following weeks, most of the men went on leave to Germany to visit their families for the holidays. On the 14th, a large German festival, the "Wintersonnenwende," marked the shortest day of the year. During the festival, speeches were made and some promotions were handed out. On the 15th, SS-Untersturmführer Heinrich Held was called to Warsaw where he was awarded the War Service Cross with Swords (Kriegsverdienstkreuz mit Schwerten). On the 24th, the remaining men who did not get to go on Christmas leave threw a large Christmas party. There was a large bonfire and the men were treated to festive meal where SS-Untersturmführer Held gave a speech and handed out various promotions. The men that were home for Christmas came back, those men that were in Poland for Christmas were granted leave to visit their families for the New Year's festivities. Another festival was thrown in Poland, similar to the Christmas festival, and the men had the opportunity to listen to Reichsminister Dr. Joseph Goebbels give a speech commemorating the new year.

Reorganization

During the autumn of 1940 the prospect of an eventual Brigade was being planned with a composition which was as yet undetermined. As early as the first week of November 1940 Fegelein was in verbal communication with the SS-Führungshauptamt to discuss the expansion. Being the first mounted SS field unit, it should be remembered that all units were conducting assigned operations while at the same time being restructured, expanded, trained and equipped with the inevitable difficulties encountered undertaking these tasks in the field during wartime. Also a degree of experimentation with various unit configurations was tried in order to find the most operationally suitable for the operations envisioned for the units.

Increased mobility and firepower were the primary needs of the eventual SS-Kavallerie-Brigade, along with efficient tactical deployment in the field. It was decided to combine the two existing Reiterstandarten into one Reiterstandarte divided into two half-regiments (Halb-Regimenter) with each half-regiment composed of two detachments (Abteilungen). Each half-regiment would have a detachment consisting of four horse equipped squadrons and a heavy machine gun squadron while the second detachment would contain the motorized and heavy weapons units.[70] These plans and the required units were laid down and ordered to be formed in early November 1940.[71] A Mounted Detachment (Reitende Abteilung) with an eventual staff squadron would be formed to oversee the mounted squadrons. Light motorized cavalry columns were added to each half-regiment and cyclist reconnaissance squadrons created. Increased firepower support of artillery and infantry guns were added as well.

By the first week of December 1940 the two units had been combined and placed under Hermann Fegelein's overall command. Unofficially redesignated SS-Totenkopf-Kavallerie-Regiment 1, formal notice of a change in title would come in January 1941. At this time the regiment had the following sub-units, locations and commanders:[72]

Regimental staff (Warsaw): A signals platoon (now fully motorized) led by SS-Untersturmführer Wilhelm Wiersch, motorcycle dispatch platoon led by SS-Oberscharführer Wilhelm Senne and the

---

[70] Fegelein stated in an order to the detachment commanders that for the horse squadrons the 4th Squadron was to be used as the replacement unit.

[71] SS-Führungshauptamt, Ia/Tgb.Nr.155/40 g. Kdos, "Umgliederung der SS-T-Reiterstandarten," dated November 12, 1940.

[72] Commanders list compiled from command documents, transfer orders, Dienstalterliste and Berlin Document Center files. Movement within the regiment of various officers was constant but became more stabilized once the Brigade was formed and its final composition was established. Locations are per letters from Fegelein to the SS-Führungshauptamt and the regimental Stammtafel.

regimental trumpet corps were the primary staff elements. Although staff list documents for confirmation have not been found it would be assumed the staffs of the two Reiterstandarten became the staffs of each half regiment with Fegelein retaining his staff for the overall regimental command duties.

First Half-Regiment (Warsaw)
Commander: SS-Standartenführer Hermann Fegelein
(in addition to regimental command)

I. Detachment (Abteilung) (Warsaw):
SS-Hauptsturmführer Gustav Lombard

1st Squadron (Warsaw):	SS-Hauptsturmführer Waldemar Fegelein
2nd Squadron (Garwolin):	SS-Hauptsturmführer Ulrich Görtz[73]
3rd Squadron (Warsaw):	SS-Obersturmführer Ernst Imhoff
4th Squadron (Jablon):	SS-Hauptsturmführer Otto Meisterknecht
5th (machine gun) Squadron (Lapiguz):	SS-Obersturmführer Hermann Gadischke

II. Abteilung (Warsaw):
SS-Hauptsturmführer Albert Faßbender

6th (technical) Squadron[74] (Warsaw):	SS-Obersturmführer Karl Fritsche
7th (horsed artillery battery) Squadron (Krakau):	SS-Hauptsturmführer Arno Paul[75]
8th (cycle reconnaissance) Squadron (Warsaw):	SS-Obersturmführer Willi Plänk[76]
9th (cavalry gun) Squadron (Warsaw):	SS-Obersturmführer Siegfried Kotthaus[77]
light cavalry column (Seroczyn):	SS-Obersturmführer Kurt Peters

---

[73] Born December 28, 1910, he joined the SS with a mounted unit of SS-Oberabschnitt "Nordost" in June 1933. Görtz transferred to the "Leibstandarte" in October 1934 and attended SS-Junkerschule Braunschweig starting in April 1935. Commissioned SS-Untersturmführer on April 20, 1936, he was assigned to the staff of SS-Oberabschnitt "Nordost." In May 1937 he transferred to the staff of the SS-Race and Settlement Main Office and later became staff adjutant as well as being promoted to SS-Obersturmführer on September 9, 1937. When the war began he moved to 5.SS-Totenkopfstandarte and later served as a platoon leader with 12.SS-Totenkopfstandarte. Promoted to SS-Hauptsturmführer on April 20, 1939 he was killed in command of his Squadron on March 18, 1942.

[74] Contained the signals, engineer and anti-tank platoons.

[75] Born in Girbirgsdorf on November 10, 1913, Paul served in the Army with II./Artillerie Regiment 4 from 1934 to 1937 and was also an Oberleutnant in the Polizei. Promoted to SS-Obersturmführer on April 20, 1940 and to SS-Hauptsturmführer on October 29th the same year, he became commander of the artillery component of the SS-Kavallerie-Brigade. After leaving the Brigade he went to the SS Remount Office in Rejowice from November 1942 to July 1944 when he transferred to the 13.Waffen-Gebirgs-Division der SS "Handschar" (kroatische Nr.1) for two months. His last posting was with the SS Remount Office in Kischbeck.

[76] Born January 16, 1911, he joined the Allgemeine-SS in February 1933. Commissioned an SS-Untersturmführer on April 30, 1936 he served as adjutant to SS-Reiterabschnitt VII until it dissolved and then moved to the staff of the Allgemeine-SS Reiterinspektorate as adjutant. Promoted to SS-Obersturmführer on September 12, 1937, and to SS-Hauptsturmführer on September 10, 1939, he held command of two different Allgemeine-SS Reiterstandarten (see Chapter 1). He joined the 1.SS-Totenkopf-Reiterstandarte in March 1940 as an SS-Obersturmführer d.R. and platoon leader and was promoted SS-Hauptsturmführer d.R. on September 1, 1941. Later holding several squadron commands in the Regimenter and eventually the reconnaissance detachment, he left the Brigade in March 1942 and served the rest of the war with the SS Cavalry Training and Replacement Detachment (SS-Kavallerie-Ausbildungs und Ersatz Abteilung). Promoted to SS-Sturmbannführer on June 21, 1943 and SS-Obersturmbannführer on November 11, 1944 he was awarded the German Cross in Gold on January 27, 1945 as commander of SS-Kavallerie-Ausbildungs und Ersatz Abteilung 8.

[77] Born April 11, 1900, he stayed with the Brigade as a squadron commander and when the SS-Kavallerie-Division formed served in 1943 as commander of 6th Squadron, SS-Kavallerie-Regiment 2, until at least July 1943. Transferred to the 17.SS-Panzer-Grenadier-Division "Götz von Berlichingen," he served at divisional adjutant (IIa) with the rank of SS-Sturmbannführer during the Normandy campaign.

Second Half-Regiment (Lublin):
Commander: SS-Sturmbannführer Franz Magill

III. Abteilung (Krakau):
SS-Hauptsturmführer Herbert Schönfeldt

1st Squadron (Krakau):	SS-Obersturmführer Karl Zilling
2nd Squadron (Kielce):	SS-Hauptsturmführer Walter Dunsch
3rd Squadron (Tarnov):	SS-Hauptsturmführer Hans-Viktor von Zastrow
4th Squadron (Chelm):	SS-Hauptsturmführer Wilhelm Reichenwallner
5th (machine gun) Squadron (Zamosc):	SS-Obersturmführer Kurt Wegener

IV. Abteilung (Lublin):
SS-Sturmbannführer Franz Magill
(dual command along with that of second half regiment)

6th (technical) Squadron (Lublin):	SS-Untersturmführer Friedrich Maletta[78]
7th (horsed artillery battery) Squadron (Lublin):	SS-Obersturmführer Paul Hoppe[79]
8th (cycle reconnaissance) Squadron (Lublin):	SS-Hauptsturmführer Hermann Lindemann
9th (cavalry gun) Squadron (Lublin):	SS-Untersturmführer Fritz Hohenberger[80]
light cavalry column (Lublin):	SS-Obersturmführer Horst-Günther Lange

As seen by the Order of Battle chart, the expansion and addition of units was not fully complete by mid-December 1940. With this expansion the first increase of the replacement unit took place. Two squadrons would now be maintained for replacements with a full squadron at the SS-Unterführerschule in Lucmierz and a second squadron established in Munich at the SS-Hauptreitschule.[81]

---

[78] A native of Neutitschein born on January 30, 1907, Maletta saw Army service from March 1932 to early 1940 during which he received technical and engineer training. His Army service ended with the 2.Pionierregiment based in Kremsier. He transferred to the engineer base in Dresden, after which the cavalry assignment followed in March 1940 and promotion to SS-Untersturmführer on April 20, 1940. He served later in the engineer company of the Brigade and received good evaluations from his superiors. He stayed with the SS-Kavallerie-Division when it formed and suffered a nervous breakdown for which Himmler had him brought up on charges of cowardice. Demoted to SS-Unterscharführer and transferred to the "Totenkopf" Division, he was killed in Russia on July 31, 1943.

[79] Killed on June 9, 1944 while an SS-Hauptsturmführer commanding the 19th company of SS-Gebirgsjäger Regiment 28, Kroatische SS-Freiwillige-Division.

[80] In 1944 he commanded the reconnaissance detachment of the SS-Kavallerie-Division.

[81] Notification sent by Fegelein to all commanders in both half regiments dated December 8, 1940. It also stated the depot and animal hospital to be used by the regiment.

5

1941

The first quarter of 1941 was relatively calm and uneventful in comparison with previous months. All squadrons of the two Half Regiments continued with routine patrols and search operations but by this time they resulted in little worth mentioning. Instead the troops mainly concentrated on honing their riding and fighting skills while the officers spent time training the continuous flow of newly arriving recruits. Also, many new horses had required training to meet the demands of newly arriving SS Riders.

Events in January set the tone for the early months of 1941 preceding Operation "BARBAROSSA," the German invasion of Russia. Sorties were relatively uneventful and seldom mentioned in unit records. The troops had settled down and patrol operations decreased considerably. The majority of the time was spent tending the horses and conducting routine barracks duties. The men were even afforded the opportunity to take a few leaves to Warsaw where several dance parties were given.[1]

Occasional festivities continued, however. During the third week of the January a large-scale riding exercise led by SS-Hauptsturmführer Gustav Lombard took place. Upon conclusion of the riding drills a large festive banquet was held. Following the main course and after dinner coffee was served, select officers and men gave speeches they had prepared especially for the occasion. SS-Hauptsturmführer Lombard was the first to speak and he gave a long speech in which he assessed the day's riding exercise and then continued lecturing further on the history of German cavalry. He mentioned such notables as the Huns, Avaren, Adolf Gustav, Friedrich II, Seydlitz, Ziethen, Schill, and his own ancestors who had a history with the cavalry. Lombard emphasized to the men that even though methods of war were modernizing with technically advanced tanks and airplanes, the cavalry remained an integral and important part of the German armed forces. The evening continued with officers giving the men political speeches followed by some of the men and NCOs presenting history reports with topics such as the history of National Socialist Germany, Adolf Hitler's rise to power, Frederick the Great and Bismarck.[2]

Aside from riding exercises, the recruits were continually trained by the more experienced cadre of the rider units. Several courses covering heavy infantry weapons were conducted by SS-Obersturmführer Friedrich Kotthaus, 9th Squadron commander in the 1st Half Regiment.

On January 25, 1941, a special order circular notified all personnel that effective immediately the 1.SS-Totenkopf-Reiterstandarte was to be referred to as "SS-Kavallerie-Regiment 1," indicating its military status by eliminating the pre-war para-military terminology used by Allgemeine-SS cavalry units reflected in the older designation.[3] This unit designation change, retaining a numerical specification, foreshadowed the further expansions that were not to take place until the end of March.

---

[1] "Abschrift des Kriegstagebuches der 2. Schwadron des SS-Kavallerie Rgt. 1 für die Zeit v. 1. Januar bis 31. Januar 1941."

[2] ibid.

[3] Bender/Taylor in "Uniforms, Organization and History of the Waffen-SS," volume 3, page 27, give this designation as officially being later but this earlier date is accepted as it originates within the unit and so illustrates what was actually being done in the field.

Any ceremonies with assembled members of the regiments were complete with the most impressive gray horse used to carry the kettle drummer of the band. Note that the SS designed panels around the drum with alternating Reich eagle and Death's Head emblems. (Yerger Archives)

January 30th marked the 8th anniversary of what was referred to as the "German Revolution," and another large assembly took place where many political and history speeches were given.[4] SS-Hauptsturmführer Ulrich Görtz (commander of 2nd Squadron/1st Half Regiment) held a talk about the founding of the Third Reich. The limitations placed on the German armed forces and the loss of German land in accordance with the Treaty of Versailles were other topics discussed. The evening ended as did all festivities for the SS cavalry units, with the singing of the "Treueleid" and a triple "Sieg-Heil."[5]

The squadrons spent February continuing with needed training exercises. Platoons would rotate through the various classrooms set up for instructional purposes. Important subjects included single and group attack methods, group defense tactics, terrain evaluation, sharpshooting and quick attack techniques for unfavorable terrain. Shooting exercises also continued with machine gun and other heavy infantry weapon courses.

On the 19th a war game exercise was conducted by the 2nd Squadron of the 1st Half Regiment with the 2nd and 3rd Platoons attacking 1st Platoon which was given the task of defending a hill. The 2nd and 3rd Platoons had to march 50 kilometers and then engage their opposition. After the hill had been secured, the 2nd and 3rd Platoons were expected to set up headquarters and establish wire communications with headquarters. This war game lasted uninterrupted for approximately 11 hours.

The supply of replacements continued to stream in and on February 22nd an additional 23 riders arrived at 2nd Squadron. To initiate the recruits they were sent on a march to Minsk where they participated in a parade held for General von Schenkendorf. Immediately afterwards the recruits had to march back to their base. Upon their arrival the training NCO, SS-Unterscharführer Ernst Lehnert, was waiting to inspect their rifles and pistols. Their first day maneuver experience as SS riders proved to be difficult at best.[6]

For the individuals in the 2nd Squadron of the 2nd Half Regiment, March began with a visit by SS-Standartenführer Fegelein and SS-Sturmbannführer Franz Magill, the commander of 2nd Half Regiment. Several exercises were conducted for the entertainment of the commanders. The squadrons spent the rest of the month conducting normal duties and additional exercises. The arrival of new riders and training regime of the units continued as in the previous months. The troops also spent much time learning to care for the new horses that were required by the recruits arriving from Germany.

On March 23, 1941, the 2nd Squadron of 1st Half Regiment took part in its first riding tournament, which was led by Squadron Commander SS-Hauptsturmführer Ulrich Görtz. It was quite an event and officials of the Wehrmacht, Police, the German Post Office (Postschutz) and the Railway Service (Reichsbahn) were invited. It was an intense day of riding competition with the riders being judged on the obstacle course, jumping exercises (group and single) as well as a dress inspection. The day ended with the usual "comrade's evening" in which all the invited guests took part.

March 1941 ended with the troops being put on full alert at midnight on the 31st. At 0130 hours the troops of the 2nd Squadron/1st Half Regiment were sent on a march to Tarnov. There the 1st and 2nd Platoons attacked the 3rd Platoon, which was waiting to defend positions that were set up the previous day. This exercise was observed by the commander of the First Detachment (1st Half Regiment), SS-Hauptsturmführer Gustav Lombard, and concluded at 1115 hours on April 1st.[7]

By the second half of March 1941 the elimination of the short lived structural concept of Half Regiments was in process. SS-Kavallerie-Regiment 2 was ordered again established as an independent unit from the 2nd Half Regiment of SS-Kavallerie-Regiment 1 (2.Halbregiment, SS-Kavallerie-Regiment 1). An order with immediate effect establishing this change and expansion was issued by

---

[4] Anniversary date of Hitler's assuming power: January 30, 1933.

[5] "Abschrift des Kriegstagebuches der 2. Schwadron des SS-Kavallerie Rgt. 1 für die Zeit v. 1. Januar bis 31. Januar 1941."

[6] "Abschrift des Kriegstagebuches der 2. Schwadron des SS-Kav. Rgt. 1 für die Zeit v. 1. February. bis 28. Februar 1941."

[7] "Abschrift des Kriegstagebuches der 2. Schwadron des SS-Kav. Rgt. 1 für die Zeit v. 1. März bis 31. März 1941."

The barracks entrance of 5th Squadron, SS-Kavallerie-Regiment 1 in the spring of 1941. (Photo: Private U.S. collection)

Hermann Fegelein on March 21st with the re-established SS-Kavallerie Regiment 2 to be operational by April 1st.[8] The former 1st Half Regiment (1.Halbregiment) was to compose SS-Kavallerie-Regiment 1. Detachment (Abteilung) level commands evenly dividing each Half Regiment into two components were replaced by a Mounted Detachment (Reitende Abteilung). This command element controlled the three mounted squadrons (numbers 1-3) and 4th (machine gun) Squadron of each regiment. By the third week of March the two regiments appeared as follows and as seen in the following list, not all commanders, units or staff assignments had yet been selected or completed for SS-Kavallerie-Regiment 2.[9]

SS-Kavallerie-Regiment 1
commander: SS-Standartenführer Hermann Fegelein

staff:	
adjutant:	SS-Hauptsturmführer Christian Reinhardt
ordnance officer:	SS-Untersturmführer Günther Boigs
food/rationed supplies officer:	SS-Untersturmführer Franz Conrad
regimental physician:	SS-Hauptsturmführer Dr. Fritz Baader
assistant physician:	SS-Untersturmführer Dr. Helmut Urbainski
veterinarian:	SS-Untersturmführer Dr. Otto Hubacek
administration officer:	SS-Hauptsturmführer Dietrich Bernhardt
1st technical officer for vehicles:	SS-Hauptsturmführer Hans Harder
2nd technical officer for vehicles:	SS-Untersturmführer Kurt Zimmermann
combat supplies officer:	SS-Obersturmführer Karl Richter
signals platoon:	SS-Untersturmführer Wilhelm Wiersch
motorcycle dispatch platoon:	SS-Obersturmführer Martin Braune[10]
trumpet corps[11] (band):	SS-Hauptscharführer Albert Hellmann

[8] SS-Kav.Rgt. 1, Tgb.Nr.29/41, "Aufstellung SS-Kav.Rgt. 2," dated March 21, 1941, SS-Kav.Rgt. 1, Tgb.Nr. 30/41, "Umbenennung," dated March 21, 1941 and SS-Kav.Rgt.1, Tgb.Nr. 33/41, "Aufstellung SS-Kav-Rgt. 2," dated March 28th. All orders were issued by Fegelein in Warsaw while all the commanders listed come from the regimental commander's reports, Dienstalterliste, lists composed by Fegelein during the week of the reformation order and miscellaneous regimental orders. In the case of many reformations and unit establishments, the official orders were often issued after the changes or creations had already completed the initial stages.

[9] Most squadrons for the 2nd regiment had only one or two platoon leaders at this time compared to the normal three in SS-Kavallerie Regiment 1. Each squadron also contained a car platoon (Spähtruppe). Staff officer positions not listed for the SS-Kavallerie Regiment 2 were unassigned at this date compared to Fegelein's command which was complete. Obviously care was taken to distribute a balance of experienced personnel to each regiment (see earlier lists of staff and commanders).

[10] Ended the war as an SS-Sturmbannführer in command of Flak Abteilung 17, 17.SS-Panzer-Grenadier-Division "Götz von Berlichingen." He died on April 28, 1967.

[11] The original band of the SS-Totenkopf-Reiterstandarte (or parts) would have been utilized when needed versus creation of a second full music detachment for SS-Kavallerie-Regiment 2.

Mounted Detachment (Reitende Abteilung)
commander: SS-Hauptsturmführer Gustav Lombard

staff:	
adjutant:	SS-Obersturmführer Wolfgang Craas
ordnance officer:	SS-Untersturmführer Walter von Scholz
food/rationed supplies officer:	SS-Untersturmführer Wilhelm Mevis
detachment physician:	SS-Untersturmführer Dr. Kurt Riehn
assistant physician:	SS-Untersturmführer Dr. Sepp Spitzy
veterinarian:	SS-Untersturmführer Dr. Hans Schiefer
administration officer:	SS-Obersturmführer Albert Krüger
anti-tank platoon:[12]	SS-Untersturmführer Arthur Kessler
1st Squadron:	SS-Hauptsturmführer Waldemar Fegelein
2nd Squadron:	SS-Hauptsturmführer Ulrich Görtz
3rd Squadron:	SS-Obersturmführer Johann Schmid
4th Squadron (machine gun):	SS-Obersturmführer Hermann Gadischke
5th Squadron (mortar/infantry gun):	SS-Obersturmführer Siegfried Kotthaus
6th Squadron (technical):	SS-Hauptsturmführer Albert Faßbender
7th Squadron (bicycle reconnaissance):	SS-Obersturmführer Wilhelm Plänk
8th Squadron (horsed artillery):	SS-Hauptsturmführer Arno Paul
light cavalry column:	SS-Hauptsturmführer Franz Rinner

SS-Kavallerie-Regiment 2
commanders: SS-Sturmbannführer Franz Magill
after April 10, 1941 SS-Standartenführer Heino Hierthes

staff (to eventually include a signals platoon and motorcycle dispatch platoon):[13]	
adjutant:	SS-Untersturmführer Dr. Walter Brück
physician:	SS-Untersturmführer Dr. Rudolf Hadlich
veterinarian:	SS-Untersturmführer Dr. Georg Leitner
administration officer:	SS-Obersturmbannführer Wilhelm Jeppe
food/rationed supplies officer:	SS-Obersturmführer Fritz Meyer-Schmidt
combat supplies officer:	SS-Hauptsturmführer Hermann Lindemann

Mounted Detachment (Reitende Abteilung)
commanders: SS-Hauptsturmführer Herbert Schönfeldt (temporary)
after April 10, 1941 SS-Sturmbannführer Franz Magill

staff:	
adjutant:	SS-Untersturmführer Werner Geissler
ordnance officer:	SS-Untersturmführer Ulrich Schulz
regimental physician:	SS-Untersturmführer Dr. Dominik Romani
assistant physician:	SS-Untersturmführer Dr. Franz Fischer
food/rationed supplies officer:	SS-Obersturmführer Joachim Kahleyss
veterinarian:	SS-Untersturmführer Dr. Erich Butt
administration officer:	SS-Untersturmführer Günther Queckenstedt
1st Squadron:	SS-Hauptsturmführer Otto Meisterknecht
2nd Squadron:	SS-Hauptsturmführer Walter Dunsch

---

[12] At various times in this period listed with a technical squadron or the regimental staff.

[13] These assignments were not yet manned for SS-Kavallerie-Regiment 2 and the platoons still in the process of formation at this time.

3rd Squadron: SS-Hauptsturmführer Wilhelm Reichenwallner
4th Squadron (machine gun):   SS-Obersturmführer Kurt Weber
5th Squadron (mortar/infantry gun):   SS-Hauptsturmführer Herbert Schönfeldt
6th Squadron (technical):   SS-Untersturmführer Friedrich Maletta
7th Squadron (bicycle reconnaissance):   SS-Hauptsturmführer Otto Hampel
8th Squadron (horsed artillery):   SS-Hauptsturmführer Friedrich Meyer
1 light cavalry column: SS-Obersturmführer Paul Hoppe

A cavalry replacement detachment (SS-Kavallerie-Ersatzabteilung) for the two regiments was also ordered to be expanded from the existing replacement units during the third week of March 1941.[14] Placed under the command of SS-Hauptsturmführer Hans-Viktor von Zastrow, the detachment contained a staff initially ordered stationed in Tarnov (later Warsaw) and three replacement squadrons at the time of its formation. 1st Replacement Squadron (1.Ersatz-Schwadron) was the former 4th Squadron, 1st Half Regiment of SS-Kavallerie-Regiment 1 (4./1.Halbregiment, SS-Kavallerie-Regiment 1) and was formed in Kielce to include the single machine gun platoon incorporated into the replacement detachment. It was later moved to Warsaw. 2nd Replacement Squadron was the former 4th Squadron of SS-Kavallerie-Regiment 2 (4./SS-Kavallerie-Regiment 2) and would be situated in Cholm and later Warsaw.[15]

The 3rd Replacement Squadron was newly formed and its troops primarily at the SS-Hauptreitschule (Main Riding School) in Munich with some troops in Laufenburg and Vienna.[16] At the middle of March 1941 the replacement units, locations and primary officers assigned were as follows:

SS-Kavallerie-Ersatzabteilung
(cavalry replacement detachment)
commander: SS-Hauptsturmführer Hans-Viktor von Zastrow

1st Replacement Squadron (Warsaw):   SS-Obersturmführer Ernst Imhoff
car platoon (Spähtrupp):   SS-Untersturmführer Franz Rehbein
1st Platoon: SS-Obersturmführer Norbert Peters
2nd Platoon: SS-Obersturmführer Friedrich Peters
Machine Gun Platoon: SS-Untersturmführer Hans Essel

2nd Replacement Squadron (Warsaw):   SS-Hauptsturmführer Stephan Charwat
1st Platoon: SS-Obersturmführer Viktor Sessler-Herzinger
2nd Platoon: SS-Untersturmführer Heinz Wowerat
3rd Platoon: SS-Untersturmführer Karl Hermann

[14] SS-Kav.Rgt.1, Tgb.Nr. 28/41.g.Kdos, "Aufstellung einer SS-Kavallerie-Ersatzabteilung" dated March 21, 1941 and signed by Fegelein. This was the regimental level order issued by Fegelein in response to the directive sent to him by the Kommandoamt der Waffen-SS of the SS-Führungshauptamt. It was in effect simply an expansion of the two existing Ersatzsquadronen.

[15] As related above, simultaneously there was a change in unit status with SS-Kavallerie-Regiment 2 becoming an independent unit. The older unit terms used for explaining the unit used as a basis for the 1st Squadron are from Fegelein's initial directives issued to SS-Kavallerie-Regiment 1. Within the same week are documents changing the old and new designations, thus explaining the mixture of terms used in explaining the basis of the 2 units. The cadre for 2nd replacement company was changed in a supplemental order dated a week after the initial formation directive: SS-Kav.Rgt.1 "Aufstellung und Umgliederung der Ersatzabteilung und SS-Kav.Rgt. 2," dated March 28, 1941. In this order Cholm was selected as the base for 2nd Squadron after an initial choice of Tarnov and, with the concept of Half Regiments no longer in effect, the new designation for the Squadron of SS-Kavallerie-Regiment 2 is used. The eventual permanent base of Warsaw for the staff and two squadrons of the SS-Kavallerie-Ersatzabteilung was selected at this time as well with a single squadron in Munich at the SS-Hauptreitschule. When the SS-Kavallerie-Division was formed from the remnants of the Brigade, the replacement formation expanded to regimental size.

[16] Due to various events, probably most important Himmler's thoughts for commanders in the eventual Brigade, this Squadron was the last formed and aside from the elements at Munich Himmler seemed unable to decide where the auxiliary portions of the Squadron would be based.

The commander of SS-Kavallerie-Regiment 2 from April to September 1941, Heino Hierthes, shown in 1937 as an SS-Sturmbannführer with SS-Totenkopfstandarte 2 "Brandenburg." Born July 25, 1897 in Neuburg, he was an Army officer in WWI and Munich Landespolizei officer before joined the SS in July 1937 as an SS-Sturmbannführer assigned to V./SS-Totenkopfstandarte 2 "Brandenburg." In August that year he moved to SS-Totenkopfstandarte 3 "Thüringen" in which he led VII.Sturmbann and later briefly commanded the entire Standarte. Promoted SS-Obersturmbannführer on April 20, 1939 he was awarded the clasp to the Iron Cross 2nd class in May 1940 while serving with the reconnaissance detachment of the "Totenkopf" Division. Hierthes commanded II./7.SS-Totenkopfstandarte in 1940 from September to November then led the "Totenkopf" infantry replacement battalion in Radolfzell until early January 1941. From January 10, 1941 he commanded 8.SS-Totenkopfstandarte and took command of SS-Kavallerie-Regiment 2 on April 10, 1941 following which he was promoted SS-Standartenführer on June 21, 1941. Fegelein considered him not aggressive enough and had him replaced in early September 1941. Hierthes took command of SS-Infanterie-Regiment 8 (1.SS-Infanterie-Brigade (mot) from September 1941 to the end of January 1942 when he was moved to the replacement unit of the Kommandostab "Reichsführer-SS," SS-Infanterie-Ersatz-Bataillon "Ost" (Infantry Replacement Battalion "East"). In October 1942 he moved to the SS-Hauptamt with Replacement Command "East" until February 1944. From March to May 1944 he was assigned to the replacement units of the 20.Estnische SS-Freiwilligen-Division and then moved in May 1944 to the command staff of the HSSPF Schwarzes Meer (Richard Hildebrandt) where he was assigned to the staff of the Befehlshaber der Waffen-SS "Ostland" (SS-Oberführer Dr. Gustav Kruckenberg). His last unit assignment began in September 1944, starting with assisting with the formation of the infantry regiments of the 15.Waffen-Grenadier-Division der SS (lettische Nr.1). From October 1944 to April 1945 he commanded that division's Waffen-Grenadier-Regiment 33 (lettisches Nr.44) and died as a Russian prisoner of war in 1953. (Photo: BDC)

3rd Replacement Squadron (Munich):	SS-Sturmbannführer Günther Temme
1st Platoon:	SS-Untersturmführer Franz Friedrich
2nd Platoon:	SS-Hauptsturmführer Egon Birkigt
3rd Platoon:	SS-Hauptsturmführer Rolf Becher

Almost all of the replacement unit officers listed above would return to the SS-Kavallerie-Brigade and combat unit commands or staff assignments during 1941 due to their experience.

The late spring and early summer of 1941 continued in much the same fashion as the early months of 1941 with new recruits arriving continually with many training exercises taking place for all members of the rider units. The war in the east was brewing and its approach sensed by the men of the SS-Kavallerie-Regimenter.

Members of the SS-Kavallerie-Regimenter during the final riding competition in Warsaw during May, 1941. (Yerger Archives)

Fegelein at the podium of the May 1941 meet surrounded by guests of the Army and other dignitaries. (Yerger Archives)

An opening ceremony riding demonstration at the meet. Within a short time the troops were in Russia assigned to the Kommandostab "Reichsführer-SS." (Yerger Archives)

The mounted band (Muzikzug) at the opening ceremony of the competition. (Yerger Archives)

SS-Standartenführer Fegelein competing during the final meet in Poland. (Yerger Archives)

The German Invasion of Russia: Operation "BARBAROSSA"

By the time Hitler had chosen a timetable to invade Russia his armed forces were fully prepared and, in his mind, capable of defeating what he viewed as his largest enemy in a matter of weeks. The creation and development of those units to be involved had progressed smoothly under the protection of the German-Russian non-aggression pact signed more than two years previously by Stalin and Germany's Foreign Minister, Joachim von Ribbentrop. The German forces preparing to invade Russia had the latest in equipment and also battle experience from the Polish and Western campaigns.

The invasion in the early morning of June 22, 1941, would be the largest operation in military history and involve Wehrmacht forces totaling more than 3,000,000 men. With more than 3,500 armored fighting vehicles, over 7,000 artillery pieces, 2,000 aircraft, half a million supporting vehicles and more than three quarter of a million horses. The success of the attack counted on the German technical and tactical superiority to defeat the massive Russian forces they opposed. Despite available intelligence the Russians were to prove totally unable to initially halt the German offensive.

Three primary units composed the invading forces stretched out along a massive 930 mile front from the Baltic to the Black Sea on June 21, 1941. Army Groups "North," "Center" and "South" contained the cream of Germany's forces and were led by her best and most experienced commanders.

Army Group "North" was led by Field Marshal Wilhelm Ritter von Leeb.[17] His units contained two Armies: 18th Army under Colonel General Georg von Küchler[18] and 16th Army led by Colonel General Ernst Busch.[19] His armored force, 4th Panzer Group, was ably commanded by Colonel General Erich Hoepner.[20] Leeb's forces were to attack from their launch points in East Prussia, cross the Memel river and destroy the Russian forces in the Baltic with the capture Leningrad as their primary initial objective. The Group's air support was to be provided by 1st Air Fleet commanded by Colonel General Alfred Keller.[21]

Army Group "Center" was the strongest of the three main groups and was to be the main attack force. Led by Field Marshal Fedor von Bock,[22] its operational front line stretched more than 250 miles. Equipped with two armored groups, 2nd Panzer Group under Colonel General Heinz Guderian[23] and 3rd Panzer Group commanded by Colonel General Hermann Hoth,[24] these combined forces were assigned to destroy the bulk of anticipated Russian infantry, motorized and armored units. Besides the strongest armored component of the three Groups, von Bock had 9th

---

[17] As a Colonel General he was awarded the Knight's Cross on June 24, 1940 as commander of Army Group "C."

[18] Awarded the Knight's Cross as commander of 3.Armee with the rank of General der Artillerie on September 30, 1939. He later became a Field Marshal and won the Oakleaves to the Knight's Cross on August 21, 1943 while commanding Army Group "North."

[19] Busch held command of 16.Armee in the 1940 Western Campaign and was awarded the Knight's Cross on May, 26, 1940 for his leadership. While still in command of 16.Armee he won the Oakleaves to the Knight's Cross as a General Field Marshal on August 21, 1943 and ended the war commanding Army Group "Northwest."

[20] As a General der Kavallerie he won the Knight's Cross as commander of 16.Armeekorps on October 27, 1939. While still commanding 4th Panzer Group he was arrested and hanged on August 8, 1944 for complicity in the July 20th plot to assassinate Hitler.

[21] Awarded the Pour le merite ("Blue Max") as a pilot in WWI, he led 4th Air Corps in the 1940 campaign and won the Knight's Cross on June 24, 1940.

[22] Awarded the Knight's Cross on September 30, 1939 as a Colonel General in command of Army Group "North." He was killed during a May 1945 air raid in Hamburg.

[23] Probably the most famous German Army commander, he was the visionary that made the armored forces a reality. As a General der Panzertruppen he won the Knight's Cross as commander of 19th Army Corps on October 27, 1939 and the Oakleaves for his command of 2nd Panzer Group on July 17, 1941. Twice dismissed and recalled by Hitler, he was Inspector of German Army armored forces in 1943 and became Chief of the Army General Staff in 1944.

[24] One of the best armored commanders who retained his position after the reversals of the first Russian campaign. He won the Knight's Cross as commander of 15th Army Corps on October 27, 1939 and for his leadership of 3rd Panzer Group was awarded Oakleaves to the Knight's Cross on July, 17, 1941. He later took command of 4th Panzer Group and was awarded the Swords to the Knight's Cross as its commander on September 15, 1943.

Army under Colonel General Albert Strauss[25] and 4th Army led by Field Marshal Günther von Kluge.[26] The infantry based Army units were to support the Group's armored thrust assigned to destroy the majority of Russia's armored and motorized units before targeting Moscow. 2nd Air Fleet would assist with massive air support commanded by Albert Kesselring.[27]

Field Marshal Gerd von Rundstedt commanded Army Group "South."[28] His command would actually oppose the largest number of Russian units with its three Armies and single armored group, 1st Panzer Group led by Colonel General Ewald von Kleist.[29] Their target was the crossing of the Dnjeper river after destroying Russian forces in their path and attack toward Kiev. Motorized and regular infantry consisted of 17th Army of Colonel General Carl von Stülpnagel[30] and 6th Army of Field Marshal Walter von Reichenau.[31] Considerable reserves were available in the form of the German 11th Army as well as the Rumanian 3rd and 4th Armies. 4th Air Fleet under Colonel General Alexander Löhr[32] provided the offensive air support for Group "South" in their drive to cross the Dnjeper and target Kiev.

Front line forces during the invasion of Waffen-SS formations were limited to some 110,000 combat troops of the six divisions in existence at that time. These divisions and their commanders were the "Leibstandarte" (Sepp Dietrich) and "Wiking" (Felix Steiner) attached to Group "South," "Totenkopf" (Theodor Eicke), and "Polizei" (Arthur Mülverstedt) both initially in reserve with Group "North," "Reich" (Paul Hausser) with Group "Center" that would eventually be one of the farthest advancing divisions in the drive to Moscow and "Nord" (Carl-Maria Demelhuber) to the north of the main attack line in Finland under the Norwegian Army Command.[33]

Each Army Group had a Higher SS and Police Leader assigned by Himmler for rear area operations.[34] For their operational assignments each HSSPF had an Ordnungspolizei Regiment subordinated to them consisting of a regimental staff with two armored car platoons, two anti-tank pla-

---

[25] Became ill at the start of the 1942 Russian winter offensive and replaced by Walter Model (see photo) under whose command the SS-Kavallerie Brigade would be subordinated.

[26] As a Colonel General and commander of 4th Army he won the Knight's Cross on September 30, 1939. He won the Oakleaves to the Knight's Cross as commander of Army Group "Center" on January 18, 1943, and the Swords for the same command on October 20, 1943. Kluge committed suicide in August 1944 to avoid arrest for complicity in the July 20th plot against Hitler.

[27] He would have the most successful career of the Luftwaffe generals assigned to the start of the invasion and already won the Knight's Cross as a General der Fleiger on September 30, 1939. As a Field Marshal he won the Oakleaves on February 25, 1942, and the Swords on July 18th that same year. In command of Army Group "C" he won the Diamonds to the Knight's Cross (one of only 27 awarded) on July 19, 1944. His final command was of German units in Italy.

[28] Awarded the Knight's Cross as commander of Army Group "South" on September 30, 1939. As commander of German forces in the west he won the Oakleaves on July 1, 1944 and the Swords while holding the same command on February 18, 1945.

[29] One of the most underrated German commanders, he won the Knight's Cross in the Western Campaign as commander of 22nd Army Corps on May 15, 1940. His command of 1st Panzer Group in Russia won him the Oakleaves on February 17, 1942 and as a Field Marshal in command of Army Group "A" won the Swords to the Knight's Cross on March 30, 1944. He died as a Russian prisoner of war in 1954.

[30] His command of 17th Army won him the Knight's Cross on August 21, 1941. He was hanged for complicity in the July 20th plot on August 30, 1944.

[31] As commander of 10th Army in the Polish campaign he won the Knight's Cross on September 30, 1939. He was killed on January 18, 1942 while in command of Army Group "South."

[32] Awarded the Knight's Cross after the Polish campaign on September 30, 1939. Later assigned to Army Group "E", he won the Oakleaves on January 20, 1945.

[33] As previously stated, histories of all these divisions have been written for examining details of the actions of these commanders during the invasion. In particular see Rudolf Lehmann, "Die Leibstandarte" and Otto Weidinger, "Division 'Das Reich'" for details of those divisions and their commanders in the campaign. In addition, separate biographies have been written on Hausser and Dietrich. All except Mülverstedt (killed in 1941) and Demelhuber won the Knight's Cross. Eicke won the Oakleaves before being killed in command of his division in 1943 while Steiner and Hausser won the Swords. Dietrich won the Diamonds to the Knight's Cross (one of only two awarded to men of the Waffen-SS) and like Hausser ended the war an SS-Oberst-Gruppenführer. Steiner and Dietrich died in 1966, Hausser in 1973 and Demelhuber in 1988.

[34] The Higher SS and Police Leaders for each Army Group's rear area were Hans-Adolf Prützmann (Army Group "North"), Erich von dem Bach (Army Group "Center") and Friedrich Jeckeln (Army Group "South"). These HSSPF were designated "A," "B" and "C" in relation to the Army Groups and their titles, as well as areas of operation, changed and expanded after the early months of the invasion. As seen later in the text, the cavalry units under examination, when attached to a HSSPF, fought in conjunction with von dem Bach.

toons, a signals company and a technical company. Three armed police battalions of four companies each were the main components of each regiment.[35] Four additional battalions and a police cavalry detachment were held in reserve for special use by all three HSSPF as well.[36]

The largest, most mobile and best equipped rear area SS troops controlled by Himmler were those units attached to his Headquarters Staff (Kommandostab "Reichsführer SS"). This staff consisted of a number of motorized or mobile units, to include the SS-Kavallerie-Regimenter that would comprise the soon to be formed SS-Kavallerie-Brigade.

Creation of the SS-Kavallerie-Brigade and
Assignamt to the Kommandostab "Reichsführer-SS" (1941)

Having functioned well in their assigned tasks, the two regiments were next assigned more extensive operations. Both regiments were officially reassigned to the Headquarters Staff (Kommandostab) "Reichsführer-SS" on June 21, 1941.[37]

Along with the other elements of this command staff led by the Chief of the Kommandostab SS-Brigadeführer Kurt Knoblauch and his First Staff Officer (Ia) SS-Obersturmbannführer Fritz Freitag, the Kommandostab "Reichsführer-SS" was created to conduct anti-partisan operations and assist in the rounding up of bypassed Russian army units for the remainder of 1941. The Kommandostab "Reichsführer-SS" operated in the area occupied by 9th Army, Army Group "Center" (9.Armee, Heeresgruppe "Mitte"). Elements of the Kommandostab began their journey to the rear combat areas in Russia almost immediately and were assigned to the area of XXXXII. Armeekorps starting on June 20. SS-Kavallerie Regiment 1 arrived before her sister regiment and was put in the area of the 87.Infanterie-Division (a component of XXXXII.Armeekorps) three days later for moping up operations with SS-Sturmbannführer Albert Faßbender serving as liaison officer between the regiments and the Army.

Himmler began to send official orders concerning the structure and composition of the Kommandostab "Reichsführer-SS" on June 20. These orders specified the staff would be composed of the following three primary combat elements along with SS-Kavallerie-Regimenter 1 and 2.[38]

The 1.SS-Brigade (motorized) was led by SS-Brigadeführer Richard Hermann when the cavalry regiments were assigned to the Kommandostab "Reichsführer-SS." It was created in April 1941 from existing SS-Totenkopfverbände. Retitled the 1.SS-Infanterie-Brigade (mot) in September 1941, it consisted of SS-Infanterie-Regimenter 8 and 10 (formerly SS-Totenkopfstandarten 8 and 10). The unit would later be expanded and become the cadre for the 18.SS-Freiwilligen-Panzer-Grenadier-Division "Horst Wessel."

---

[35] The Polizei Regimenter were designated "Süd," "Nord" and "Mitte" after the area of their assignment while the individual Ordnungspolizei Bataillone (designated by numbers only) for the three HSSPF were 314, 45 and 303 (for Group "South"), 53, 319 and 321 (for Group "Center") and 307, 316 and 322 (for Group "North"). Kommandostab "RFSS" addendum of units listing dated June 30, 1941.

[36] Polizei Bataillone 254, 320, 304, 315 and the Police Mounted Detachment (Polizei Reitende Abteilung) with a staff and three squadrons.

[37] Der "Reichsführer-SS," Tgb.Nr. 2359/41 dated June 17, 1941 and the Kriegstagebuch (KTB) Nr. 1 of the Kommandostab (entry for June 20, 1941). The Kommandostab (Headquarters Staff) "Reichsführer-SS" was the highest field command headquarters of the Waffen-SS. Under the supervision of the SS-Führungshauptamt this staff was created on April 7,1941, as the Action Staff (Einsatzstab) "Reichsführer-SS" for conducting operations and assignments under Himmler's direct authority, though its elements were subordinated to Army control when needed. Eventually the war situation disallowed Himmler's direct control of such combat troops and they were absorbed by various units of the Waffen-SS which were in turn operationally controlled by the Army. It was retitled the Kommandostab "Reichsführer-SS" on May 6, 1941 (SS-FHA, Org.Tbg. Nr. 1621/41 dated May 6, 1941). The units under its command varied as some were destroyed or used in the formation of larger units. For example it later was assigned the SS-Sonderkommando "Dirlewanger" and various foreign volunteer Standarten, all of which became higher formations (SS divisions or attached to them) and were detached from direct control of the Kommandostab. Its sub-elements were never larger than brigade strength and all three primary combat units during the period the SS-Kavallerie-Brigade was attached later formed the basis for full divisions (see text). In the first Russian campaign it had a force equal in strength to a division (approximately 18,000 personnel). Its replacements came from the SS-Ersatz-Bataillon "Ost" in Breslau and as has been seen it supplied several elements to the SS-Kavallerie-Brigade during its expansion and development. The Kommandostab existed until the end of the war though of less strength than in the early Russian campaign period. By the summer of 1944 its primary armed units were Flak Abteilung Kommandostab I and II along with the (re-established) Begleit Bataillon "Reichsführer-SS."

[38] "Kriegstagebuch des Kommandostabs 'Reichsführer-SS,' " dated 16.6.41-31.12.41.

The Chief of the Kommandostab "Reichsführer-SS," SS-Brigadeführer Kurt Knoblauch (above) with SS-Standartenführer Matthias Kleinheisterkamp (while both were assigned to the "Totenkopf" Division) in 1940 and (right) in the foreground Knoblauch is next to Theodor Eicke (commander of the "Totenkopf" Division). Born in Marienwerder on December 10, 1895, Knoblauch won both Iron Crosses in WWI and joined the SS in April 1935 as an SS-Sturmbannführer on Himmler's personal staff. He served in the SS-Hauptamt from May 1935 to September 1937 as a detachment ordnance officer and Ia. Promoted to SS-Obersturmbannführer on September 15, 1935, SS-Standartenführer on September 15, 1936 and SS-Oberführer on September 12, 1937, he returned to Himmler's personal staff in September 1937. Promoted to SS-Brigadeführer on September 30, 1939, he then commanded the replacement troops of the "Totenkopf" Division until June 1940 when he became divisional first staff officer (Ia) under Theodor Eicke. From December 1940 to April 1941 he commanded the 2.SS-Infanterie-Brigade and became Chef des Kommandostabs "Reichsführer-SS" in April 1941 when its elements began forming. As a Generalmajor der Waffen-SS effective March 30, 1941, he held command of the Kommandostab until the end of January 1943 during which he was also promoted to SS-Gruppenführer on January 30, 1942. He spent the rest of the war on Himmler's personal staff, where he was promoted to SS-Obergruppenführer on June 21, 1944, and died on November 10, 1952. (Photos: Phil A. Nix and Jost Schneider)

Toni Ameiser in a famous photo as an SS-Sturmbannführer assigned to the 22.SS-Freiwilligen-Kavallerie-Division "Maria Theresia" wearing the unique collar insignia utilized by that division. Born August 1, 1907, he joined the SS in March 1933 with SS-Reiterstandarte 17. Commissioned an SS-Untersturmführer on September 13, 1936, he was next assigned to SS-Reiterstandarte 15. He attended SS-Junkerschule Braunschweig from February to May 1940 and became a Waffen-SS Untersturmführer d.R. on August 1, 1940. Posted to the 16.SS-Totenkopfstandarte in August 1940, he moved to 14.SS-Totenkopfstandarte in September. From September 1940 to March 1941 he served as adjutant of 15.SS-Totenkopfstandarte. Reassigned to SS-Kavallerie-Regiment 1 on March 25, 1941, he led a light cavalry column, later becoming a Regiment and Brigade staff officer. Awarded the Iron Cross 1st class on February 25, 1942 with 3rd Squadron, SS-Kavallerie Regiment 1, he was promoted SS-Hauptsturmführer d.R. on March 16, 1942 and SS-Sturmbannführer on October 4, 1944. When the SS-Kavallerie-Division formed he led 1st Squadron, SS-Kavallerie-Regiment 2 and held temporary command of SS-Kavallerie-Regiment 1 in December 1942 when Gustav Lombard was temporary divisional commander. He was wounded in 1942 and 1943 and twice returned to the SS-Kavallerie-Division and then led Kampfgruppe "Ameiser" (Kavallerie-Regiment 17 remnants) in the Kowel pocket. His leadership of this 103 man group won him the Knight's Cross on November 1, 1944 for their 23 days of bitter combat. He commanded SS-Kavallerie-Regiment 17 as a component of the 22.SS-Freiwilligen-Kavallerie-Division "Maria Theresia." After Budapest he led SS-Kavallerie-Regiment 94 of the 37.SS-Freiwilligen-Kavallerie-Division "Lützow." He died on February 20, 1976. (Photo: BDC)

The 2.SS-Brigade (mot) was formed in May 1941 from two SS-Totenkopfstandarten reformed into infantry regiments and became the 2.SS-Infanterie-Brigade (mot) in September 1941. Consisting of SS-Infanterie-Regimenter 4 and 14, it was commanded during all of 1941 by SS-Brigadeführer Karl von Treuenfeld. It was later expanded and used as cadre to form one of the best Waffen-SS divisions composed of foreign personnel, the 19.Waffen-Grenadier-Division der SS (lettische Nr.2).

The SS-Begleit (escort) Bataillon "Reichsführer-SS" was formed as Himmler's personal escort battalion in mid-May 1941 under the command of SS-Sturmbannführer Ernst Schützek. Expanded in February 1943, it became the Sturmbrigade "Reichsführer-SS" and fought well in Corsica for which the then former Ia of the SS-Kavallerie-Brigade, Karl Gesele, was awarded the Knight's Cross as its commander. In October 1943 it was the cadre for formation of the 16.SS-Panzer-Grenadier-Division "Reichsführer-SS." A new escort battalion formed and remained a component of the Kommandostab "Reichsführer-SS" for the balance of its existence. Along with these three primary units the following support elements were also added to the Kommandostab "Reichsführer-SS" when it initially formed.

1) One signals company (Nachrichten Kompanie) for the Kommandostab "Reichsführer-SS" and each of its primary component Brigades

2) A military geologists company (Wehrgeologen Kompanie)

3) Supply troops (Nachschubdienste) drawn from Wohlau

4) An administration service (Verwaltungsdienste) including a food rations office (Verpflegungsamt) with a butcher platoon (Schlächterei-Zug) and a baking company (Bäckerie-Kompanie)

5) One German Red Cross (Deutsches Rotes Kreuz or DRK) unit including a medical depot (Sänitäts-Park), and an ambulance platoon (Krankenkraftwagenzug)

6) A veterinary company (Veterinär Kompanie) including a horse hospital and veterinarian depot

7) A field post office service (Feldpostdienste)

Even though SS-Kavallerie-Regiment 1 and 2 were officially referred to separately, the two were still considered to be the primary components of what was already unofficially being referred to as the SS-Kavallerie-Brigade. Lacking from the official composition of a Brigade level formation was a formal staff. The following list of officers and assignments shows some signs of the expansion to Brigade groundwork such as the horsed batteries losing their numerical squadron designation. Both regiments were at full strength and had all officer assignments posted. Junior officers would become more familiar to historians as the later regiment, detachment, company and squadron leaders within the Brigade and later the SS-Kavallerie-Division. Many younger junior officers eventually were decorated with the Knight's Cross or German Cross in Gold.[39]

Although this listing clearly outlines the structure of the Brigade, this composition was by no means strictly adhered to. Upon special orders by the Army or the Kommandostab "Reichsführer-SS," specific parts of the Brigade could be deployed in the form of a special detachment as situations warranted. This is primarily evident in the formation of the Vorausabteilung (advance [reconnaissance] detachment) which will be discussed later. Nonetheless, the two regiments *officially* appeared as follows on July 30, 1941:

SS-Kavallerie-Regiment 1
Commander: SS-Standartenführer Hermann Fegelein

adjutant:	SS-Hauptsturmführer Christian Reinhardt
ordnance officer:	SS-Obersturmführer Rudolf Maeker
food/rationed supplies officer:	SS-Obersturmführer Franz Conrad
regimental physician:	SS-Hauptsturmführer Dr. Fritz Baader[40]
assistant physician:	SS-Untersturmführer Dr. Helmuth Urbainski
dentist:	SS-Obersturmführer Dr. Siegfried Bock
veterinarian:	SS-Hauptsturmführer Dr. Gerhart Held
administration officer:	SS-Hauptsturmführer Michael Schottes
armorer:	SS-Hauptscharführer Karl Hilgardt
1st technical officer for vehicles:	SS-Hauptsturmführer Hans Harder
2nd technical officer for vehicles:	SS-Oberscharführer Alexander Grothe
combat supplies officer:	SS-Obersturmführer Karl Richter
signals platoon:	SS-Obersturmführer Wilhelm Wiersch
motorcycle dispatch platoon:	SS-Oberscharführer Wolfgang Reinhardt
band:	SS-Untersturmführer Albert Hellmann

[39] Not only did age become a factor in replacing some of the earlier commanders but there was, at this early stage of the war, a continuous influx of graduates from the SS officer training schools at Bad Tölz and Braunschweig as well as the other specialized training facilities now becoming available.

[40] Became chief medical officer of the Brigade when formed.

Mounted Detachment (Reitende Abteilung)
commander: SS-Sturmbannführer Gustav Lombard

staff:	
adjutant:	SS-Obersturmführer Franz Rehbein
ordnance officer:	SS-Untersturmführer Hermann Ahlborn
food/rationed supplies officer:	SS-Untersturmführer Wilhelm Mevis
detachment physician:	SS-Obersturmführer Dr. Willi Nieswandt
assistant physician:	SS-Untersturmführer Dr. Sepp Spitzy
dentist:	SS-Obersturmführer Dr. Arthur Götz[41]
veterinarian:	SS-Untersturmführer Dr. Hans Schiefer
administration officer:	SS-Obersturmführer Albert Krieger
1st Squadron:	SS-Hauptsturmführer Waldemar Fegelein
car platoon (Spähtrupp):[42]	SS-Standartenoberjunker Wilhelm Bingel
1st Platoon:	SS-Untersturmführer Willi Brutkuhl
2nd Platoon:	SS-Obersturmführer Anton Bug
3rd Platoon:	SS-Untersturmführer Kurt Becher[43]
2nd Squadron:	SS-Hauptsturmführer Ulrich Görtz
car platoon:	SS-Oberscharführer Wilhelm Heyd
1st Platoon:	SS-Obersturmführer Erich Krell
2nd Platoon:	SS-Untersturmführer Georg Vieth
3rd Platoon:	SS-Untersturmführer Otto Held
3rd Squadron:	SS-Hauptsturmführer Johann Schmid
car platoon:	SS-Oberscharführer Hans-Georg von Charpentier
1st Platoon:	SS-Obersturmführer Heinrich Diekmann
2nd Platoon:	SS-Untersturmführer Johannes Göhler
3rd Platoon:	SS-Obersturmführer Wilhelm-Hubert Schmidt
4th (machine gun) Squadron:	SS-Obersturmführer Hermann Gadischke
1st Platoon:	SS-Obersturmführer Erich Brockmann
2nd Platoon:	SS-Untersturmführer Willi Geier
3rd Platoon:	SS-Oberscharführer Richard Nakat
5th (heavy) Squadron:	SS-Obersturmführer Siegfried Kotthaus
1st Platoon:	SS-Untersturmführer Fritz Höhenberger
2nd Platoon:	SS-Untersturmführer Hermann Schneider
3rd Platoon:	SS-Oberscharführer Anton Vandieken

---

[41] Later assigned to the Reconnaissance Detachment, he was listed as missing in action during the January 1942 Peno battles.

[42] Only a component of the horse squadrons under the Mounted Detachment and the Reconnaissance Squadron.

[43] Born September 12, 1909 and joined the SS in 1934 with SS-Reiterstandarte 4. He served as an enlisted man and NCO with the SS-Totenkopf-Reiterstandarte starting in February 1940 before attending SS-Junkerschule Bad Tölz from April to July 1940. Commissioned an SS-Untersturmführer on January 30, 1941, he served as a platoon leader before becoming an ordnance officer on the Brigade staff in August 1941. He was also temporary Ia for a brief period. Promoted to SS-Obersturmführer on November 9, 1941 he also served as Army/Waffen-SS liaison officer. After being wounded, he went to the SS-Kavallerie-Ersatz-Abteilung in Warsaw following which he returned to the Brigade as an ordnance officer and, in early 1942, as Ic on the Brigade staff. Awarded the Iron Cross 1st class on February 25, 1942 he was wounded again in early 1942. Promoted to SS-Hauptsturmführer on March 16, 1942, after recovery he went to the SS-Führungshauptamt as a staff officer in Inspektion 3 (inspectorate for cavalry and horse drawn transportation) under Hermann Fegelein. He returned with Fegelein to Russia in December 1942 and was assigned to SS-Kampfgruppe "Fegelein" where he was promoted SS-Sturmbannführer on December 17, 1942 and earned the German Cross in Gold on January 15, 1943. He left the Kampfgruppe in late February 1943 and returned to the now restructured SS-Führungshauptamt assigned to Amt VI (office for mounted and horse drawn transportation) and served there for the remainder of the war, often as substitute office chief and inspector when Hermann Fegelein or his successors were temporarily assigned elsewhere. He was promoted SS-Obersturmbannführer on January 30, 1944 and finally SS-Standartenführer on January 1, 1945. He was well liked by Fegelein who fostered his career.

6th (technical) Squadron:	SS-Sturmbannführer Albert Faßbender
anti-tank platoon:	SS-Untersturmführer Werner Seelig
engineer platoon:	SS-Obersturmführer Karl Fritsche
7th (cycle reconnaissance) Squadron:	SS-Obersturmführer Willi Plänk
car platoon:	SS-Untersturmführer Walter Schädler
1st Platoon:	SS-Untersturmführer Hans Christoph
2nd Platoon:	SS-Untersturmführer Erich Streubel[44]
3rd Platoon:	SS-Untersturmführer Karl Weeke
horsed artillery battery:	SS-Hauptsturmführer Arno Paul
battery officer:	SS-Untersturmführer Franz Spichern
weapons section:	SS-Obersturmführer Walter Berndt
munitions section:	SS-Oberscharführer Karl Henning
light cavalry column:	SS-Hauptsturmführer Franz Rinner

SS-Kavallerie-Regiment 2
commander: SS-Standartenführer Heino Hierthes

adjutant:	SS-Obersturmführer Walter Bornscheuer
ordnance officer:	SS-Untersturmführer Kurt Peters
food/rationed supplies officer:	SS-Untersturmführer Hermann Lindemann
armorer:	unknown
detachment physician:	SS-Obersturmführer Dr. Dominik Romani
assistant physician:	SS-Obersturmführer Dr. Rudolf Hadlich
veterinarian:	SS-Hauptsturmführer Johann Kramer
technical officer for vehicles:	SS-Untersturmführer Kurt Zimmermann
combat supplies officer:	SS-Untersturmführer Hermann Hoffmeister
signals platoon:	SS-Untersturmführer Johann Stahl
motorcycle dispatch platoon:	SS-Untersturmführer Hans Kleinlogel[45]

Mounted Detachment (Reitende Abteilung)

staff:	
commander:	SS-Sturmbannführer Franz Magill
adjutant:	unknown
food/rationed supplies officer:	SS-Obersturmführer Veith Truchsess
detachment physician:	SS-Untersturmführer Dr. Kurt Richter
assistant physician:	SS-Untersturmführer Franz Fischer
veterinarian:	SS-Untersturmführer Dr. Erich Butt
1st Squadron:	SS-Hauptsturmführer Stefan Charwat
car platoon:	SS-Oberscharführer Willi Hammann
1st Platoon:	SS-Obersturmführer Richard Findeisen
2nd Platoon:	SS-Untersturmführer Rudolf Wappler
3rd Platoon:	SS-Oberscharführer Hein Weisspflock

[44] He moved to the staff of the Kommandostab "Reichsführer-SS" in 1941 but returned to the Brigade with the Reconnaissance Detachment in January 1942. As the commander of 1st Squadron he was awarded the Iron Cross 1st class on March 21, 1942.

[45] During the fierce January 1942 combats of the Reconnaissance Detachment he moved to that unit's 2nd Squadron as commander.

2nd Squadron:	SS-Hauptsturmführer Walter Dunsch
car platoon:	SS-Oberscharführer Hans Zech-Nentwig
1st Platoon:	SS-Obersturmführer Fritz Butz
2nd Platoon:	SS-Obersturmführer Helmuth Guggolz
3rd Platoon:	SS-Untersturmführer Felix Jahn
3rd Squadron:	SS-Hauptsturmführer Hans-Viktor von Zastrow
car platoon:	SS-Oberscharführer Karl Saffert
1st Platoon:	SS-Obersturmführer Horst Lange
2nd Platoon	SS-Untersturmführer Heinz Wowert
3rd Platoon:	SS-Untersturmführer Ulrich Schulz
4th (machine gun) Squadron:	SS-Obersturmführer Kurt Wegener
1st Platoon:	SS-Untersturmführer Hans Essl
2nd Platoon:	SS-Untersturmführer Ernst Lehnert
3rd Platoon:	SS-Oberscharführer Wilhelm Schmidt
5th (heavy) Squadron:	SS-Hauptsturmführer Herbert Schönfeldt
1st Platoon:	SS-Obersturmführer Heinrich von Kurz[46]
2nd Platoon:	SS-Untersturmführer Bodo Radmann
3rd Platoon:	SS-Oberscharführer Ulrich Schönberg
6th (technical) Squadron:	SS-Untersturmführer Friedrich Maletta
engineer platoon:	(squadron commander)
anti-tank platoon:[47]	SS-Untersturmführer Arthur Kessler
7th (cyclist reconnaissance) Squadron:	SS-Obersturmführer Anton Koppenwallner
car platoon (not a component in SS-Kavallerie Regiment 2)	
1st Platoon:	SS-Untersturmführer Walter von Scholz
2nd Platoon:	SS-Untersturmführer Werner Geissler
3rd Platoon:	SS-Untersturmführer Hans Loy
horsed artillery battery:	SS-Hauptsturmführer Friedrich Meyer
forward observer officer:	SS-Untersturmführer Gustav Etzler[48]
munitions officer:	SS-Untersturmführer Johann Billerbeck
battery officer:	unknown
light cavalry column:	SS-Obersturmführer Paul Hoppe

On August 2, 1941, Himmler sent communications to Baranowicze announcing the official creation of the SS-Kavallerie-Brigade using the two existing regiments as cadre along with other units that would form in the coming months.[49] After its expansion the Brigade was to remain

---

[46] Commander of the reconnaissance detachment of the SS-Kavallerie-Division for much of 1943 and killed on October 21, 1943.

[47] In addition to the weapons already held by the platoon, six additional 3.7cm weapons were given to the Brigade on August 8th by SS-Brigade 2 and divided between the two cavalry regiments.

[48] Awarded the Iron Cross 1st class on February 12, 1942. When the Division formed he took command of 2.Batterie and was awarded the German Cross in Gold on January 16, 1944 as commander of I./Artillerie Regiment 8 of the SS-Kavallerie-Division. He later commanded I./Artillerie Regiment 22, 22.SS-Freiwilligen-Kavallerie-Division "Maria Theresia." As an SS-Sturmbannführer he ended the war as the commander of Artillerie-Regiment 37, 37.SS-Freiwilligen-Kavallerie-Division "Lützow."

[49] The Chief of the Kommandostab and the HSSPF appear to have been among the last to be informed of the expansion and primary staff assignments. Fegelein announced the staff assignments on August 1st, saying they were effective July 28, 1941, and signing the document as "SS-Kav.Brigade Kommandeur." Throughout his career Fegelein made a concerted effort to stay in the good graces of and in direct contact with Heinrich Himmler.

Hermann Fegelein visits a colt born during transfer of the cavalry regiments to Russia with the elements of the Kommandostab "Reichsführer-SS." (Yerger Archives)

under the authority of the Kommandostab "Reichsführer-SS." The primary Brigade level assignments Himmler recommended at that time were:

Brigade Commander:	SS-Standartenführer Hermann Fegelein
Major beim Stabe:	SS-Sturmbannführer Albert Faßbender
Ia (1.Generalstabsoffizier):	SS-Hauptsturmführer Christian Reinhardt[50]
adjutant:	SS-Obersturmführer Karl Richter
ordnance officer:	SS-Untersturmführer Kurt Becher

Along with the above staff assignments, the replacement for Fegelein's command of SS-Kavallerie-Regiment 1 was assigned to SS-Sturmbannführer Gustav Lombard on August 18th. The commander of SS-Kavallerie-Regiment 2, SS-Standartenführer Heino Hierthes, was given command of SS-Infanterie-Regiment 8 (1.SS-Infanterie-Brigade) and command of the 2nd regiment was given to his replacement, SS-Standartenführer Hermann Schleifenbaum. This command transfer took place on September 5, 1941.

The time schedule and exact composition as ordered by the SS-Führungshauptamt would not become a reality for a variety of reasons, not the least of which were expanding and reforming an operational unit in the field.[51] Besides the two existing Kavallerie Regimenter (which would be

---

[50] Held the assignment until wounded in mid-August 1941 and replaced by SS-Obersturmführer Rudolf Maeker. Reinhardt also commanded the first reconnaissance unit of the Brigade immediately after it formed.

[51] Abt. Org./Tgb.Nr. 3751/41 geh. "Umgliederung der SS-Kav.Regimenter 1 und 2" dated September 6, 1941 with effect from September 1st. The command level of Reitende Abteilung Stab would no longer exist after late summer with the reduced number of squadrons controlled by the regimental staff. Many units would be less than ordered as far as strength and time allowed to become operational less than desired. No staff batteries or light artillery columns would exist (as originally ordered by the SS-Führungshauptamt) for the artillery detachment in 1941, the technical squad-

reduced to five squadrons each by the end of reformation) the following were created:

An engineer company (Pionier Kompanie) was created by combining the engineer platoon (Pionierzug) from the 6th Squadron of each regiment. Kompanie Chef was SS-Obersturmführer Karl Fritsche (he led a platoon as well) and 2nd Platoon leader was SS-Untersturmführer Karl Maletta.

The artillery detachment (Artillerie Abteilung) was formed by combining the two horsed batteries (Reitende Batterien) of the regiments although from operational unit assignments and strength availability charts they appear to each have mostly remained under their respective regiments instead of operating as an independent unit.[52] Detachment commander was SS-Hauptsturmführer Arno Paul and in addition he commanded 1st Battery. SS-Hauptsturmführer Friedrich Meyer commanded 2nd battery.

The most significant addition was the creation of a bicycle reconnaissance detachment (Radfahr-Aufklärungsabteilung). It formed from the 7th Squadrons of both regiments and the anti-tank platoon of the dissolved 6th Squadron of SS-Kavallerie-Regiment 1.[53] In period documents it was often referred to as the Brigade Advance Detachment (Vorausabteilung) during the first weeks when it was a temporary unit performing advance reconnaissance missions.[54] SS-Obersturmführer Christian Reinhardt was commander during the first week of August after which SS-Sturmbannführer Albert Faßbender assumed command until late December 1941. The unit contained three companies with an initial strength of well over 500 men. All former squadron commanders retained their commands after the unit formed. This component was equipped with as many vehicles as could be requisitioned as well as any other transport available including numerous bicycles. With the use of existing squadrons for formation of the reconnaissance unit and independent support units, the two cavalry regiments were reduced to five numbered squadrons each along with the artillery batteries.

The signals company remained under strength during 1941 and consisted of the existing regimental signal platoons as cadre with a small number of additional personnel and equipment subordinated from the Kommandostab "Reichsführer-SS." The unit also incorporated the signals platoon of the dissolved SS-Infanterie-Regiment 5 in September, 1941. Due to the nature of the Brigade's operations the signals unit was constantly trying to expand and obtain more equipment since its type of warfare required it to be in communication with a variety of controlling commands. The signals commander was SS-Obersturmführer Wilhelm Wiersch and his platoon leader SS-Untersturmführer Herbert Wende. Apart from this separate company there were signals platoons in both the cavalry regiments and the reconnaissance detachment. Additional signaling equipment was obtained whenever possible throughout 1941.

A medical company (SS-Hauptsturmführer Otto Mittelberger) and veterinary company (SS-Obersturmführer Fritz Eichin) was added from existing elements of the Kommandostab "Reichsführer-SS" as was an ambulance platoon. Both these units were bolstered with additional personnel from the Kommandostab's support units that contributed a second ambulance platoon in the autumn of 1941. A repair platoon (Werkstattzug) was added to the Brigade staff.

---

rons (6th) from both regiments dissolved to provide cadre for new units, the desired number of anti-tank platoons was never realized and various other small units took most of 1941 to be incorporated. Those units added in most cases were supplied from existing units within the Kommandostab "Reichsführer-SS" instead of being newly equipped units specifically for the Brigade. Franz Magill left the Brigade in early September which may coincide with the elimination of the Reitende Abteilung Stab for both regiments as they were then reduced to five squadrons each and controlled directly by the regimental staff though still referred to as the Mounted Detachment due to their higher mobility. References to the Reitende Abteilung would have been for 1-3 horsed squadrons and the machine gun unit (4th Squadron).

[52] Daily situation and strength reports for the Brigade do not list the artillery detachment (Artillerie Abteilung) separately and they are most often referenced with each battery named after its commander. It is assumed their personnel are within the statistics for the Kavallerie Regimenter since available strength reports for the Brigade do not list the detachment separately.

[53] SS-Kavallerie Brigade, Ia report dated August 31, 1941. SS-Kavallerie-Regiment 2 was ordered to retain its anti-tank platoon.

[54] Its sub elements at this time are referred to by their original squadron numbers. In daily situation reports it is first referred to as the bicycle reconnaissance detachment (Radfahr-Aufklärungsabteilung) during the first week of September 1941.

Fritz Freitag (left) as a Polizei officer and (right) as an SS-Standartenführer. The first Ia of the Kommandostab "Reichsführer SS" and later commander of the SS-Kavallerie-Division was born on April 28, 1894 in Allenstein. A WWI officer decorated with both Iron Crosses, he became an officer in the Schutzpolizei in February 1920. He was a tactical instructor at the Polizei-Offizierschule in Berlin-Köpenick and Chief of Staff of the Senior Police Officer attached to 14.Armee in the 1939 Polish campaign. Freitag became an SS-Obersturmbannführer on September 1, 1940 (he held equivalent Polizei rank). He served as the first Ia of the Kommandostab "Reichsführer-SS" and then the same position with the 1.SS-Infanterie-Brigade (mot) until October 1941. In November 1941 he was Ia to the Hauptamt Ordnungspolizei. He then moved to the SS-Polizei-Division as commander of SS-Polizei-Grenadier-Regiment 2 and later commanded a Kampfgruppe, during which he became an SS-Standartenführer on April 20, 1942. Freitag was commander of the SS-Kavallerie-Division from January 1943 to April 1943, won the German Cross in Gold on April 30, 1943 and was promoted to SS-Oberführer on August 6, 1943. In October 1943 he took command of the 14.Waffen-Grenadier-Division der SS (galizische Nr. 1) and held command until the end of the war. At his last command he was promoted to SS-Brigadeführer on April 20, 1944. He won the Knight's Cross on September 30, 1944, by recommendation of Himmler and committed suicide in 1945. (Photos: BDC and Jess Lukens)

Apart from the units ordered by the SS-Führungshauptamt, the Kommandostab "Reichsführer-SS" also later provided a light anti-aircraft battery.[55] Battery commander was SS-Obersturmführer Ewald Keyk. Other non combat support elements or facilities were also later attached from the Kommandostab, especially additions for the medical and veterinary units. Although combat ready strength of the SS-Kavallerie-Brigade depended on illness (both men and horses), wounds and other factors, the average operational strength after all units were formed or attached was approximately 3,300-3,500 men, 2900 horses and 375 vehicles of various types. An appreciable percentage of the Brigade troops were ill at a given time due to dysentery and the host of other illnesses encountered in Russia.

---

[55] The first Flak Abteilung for the Kommandostab "Reichsführer-SS" was established in Breslau during May 1941 in Breslau, consisting of four light (2 cm) and one medium batteries (3.7 cm) batteries. The light batteries were divided among the three Brigades under the Kommandostab "Reichsführer-SS" with the medium battery going to the Begleit Bataillon "Reichsführer-SS." Thus the SS-Kavallerie-Brigade had a 2 cm equipped battery attached to it upon formation and, although not considered at that time a permanent part of the SS-Kavallerie-Brigade, it was eventually one of the basis units for the Flak Abteilung of the SS-Kavallerie-Division in 1942.

Operation "Barbarossa"
Rear Area Operations of the SS-Kavallerie-Brigade

Even though Himmler did not formally order the formation of the Kommandostab "Reichsführer-SS" until June 21, 1941, the decision to go ahead with the formation began with the creation of its components during March and April 1941. The initial mention of the formations can be found in the war diary of the Kommandostab "Reichsführer-SS" which begins on June 16th. The entry for that day records that the Kommandostab "Reichsführer-SS" was ordered to Treskau (13 kilometers north of Posen) and was to be ready for action on the 18th. On the 19th the Kommandostab received a radio message from the SS Main Operational Office (SS-Führungshauptamt) to make contact with Army Group (Heeresgruppe) B, and was shortly thereafter sent to Arys (East Prussia). At this time the Kommandostab was subordinated to the staff of armored fortress (Festungsstab) "Blaurock."[56]

As ordered, some of the existing units assigned to the Kommandostab went to Arys on June 20th to link-up with the newly formed operational staff of Kommandostab. At the order of the Fortress Command Blaurock, the Kommandostab "Reichsführer-SS" was subordinated to the General Kommando of XXXXII.Armeekorps (42nd Army Corps). Later, the XXXXII.Armeekorps reiterated this order. Upon receipt of these orders, the Kommandostab left for Strassburg.[57]

On June 22, 1941 Operation "Barbarossa" commenced. A message from Hitler was given to all soldiers as well as a daily order from the senior commander (Oberbefehlshaber) of the 9.Armee, General der Infanterie Adolf Strauss.[58] Far away from the front, the Kommandostab "Reichsführer-SS" took quarter with other units awaiting orders in Grabnick. The next day SS-Kavallerie-Regiment 1 received a radio message from XXXXII.Armeekorps that it was to be subordinated to the 87.Infanterie Division. This was made formal according to the written Korps order which elaborated that the Regiment was to receive its orders through this division.[59]

"On June 26, 1941, SS-Obersturmführer Rudolf Maeker and men of an advance unit reached Narev by executing dashing advances over the Narev Crossing near Viczna. Maeker made the attack on Strekova-Gora possible by taking the crossraods located four kilometers east of Narev. Through his dashing leadership, SS-Kavallerie-Regiment 1 was able to successfully complete its task on the flank of 87.Infanterie Division."[60]

During the next few days most units of the Kommandostab "Reichsführer-SS," with the exception of the SS-Kavallerie-Regimenter 1 and 2, were deployed behind the front lines of the advancing offensive and were assigned to mopping-up operations alongside the army units to which they were subordinated. On the 26th of June these active SS units were put on alert and ordered to march to Wilna by order of the Chief of Staff XXXXII.Armeekorps.

On the 27th, however, Heinrich Himmler issued an order which was passed on to the troops by an officer of Himmler's personal staff, SS-Hauptsturmführer Werner Grothmann.[61] The order read as follows:

---

[56] "Kriegstagebuch des Kommandostabs 'Reichsführer-SS' Nr. 1," dated June 16, - December 31, 1941. The fortress commander was later Army Major General Edmund Blaurock, awarded the Knight's Cross on July 27, 1944 and the Oakleaves on February 19, 1945. When given the latter award he commanded 56.Infanterie-Division.

[57] "Kriegstagebuch des Kommandostabs 'Reichsführer-SS' Nr. 1," dated June 16, - December 31, 1941.

[58] Awarded the Knight's Cross for leadership of II.Armeekorps in the Polish campaign on October 27, 1939.

[59] "Kriegstagebuch des Kommandostabs 'Reichsführer-SS' Nr. 1," dated June 16, - December 31, 1941.

[60] "Begrüdung und Stellungnahme der Zwischen-Vorgesetzten" for Maeker's German Cross in Gold. See photo for biographical data.

[61] ibid.

"The march orders for parts of the Kommandostab 'Reichsführer-SS' are forbidden since this contradicts the general agreement. The Reichsführer-SS does not wish the troops of the Kommandostab 'Reichsführer-SS' to be assigned to occupations or similar assignments since he needs it for other tasks. Certain cases, for which parts of the troops find themselves fighting, constitute an exception. The Reichsführer-SS will speak with the Chief of Staff and is expected to arrive this afternoon."

On the 26th and 27th, the XXXXII.Armeekorps was informed that the Kommandostab "Reichsführer-SS" would no longer be under its operational command. The commanding officers of the XXXXII.Armeekorps did not agree with this decision, but after several discussions with members of Himmler's staff, General Strauss formally bid the farewell to the SS units he assumed would be part of the available order of battle for his 9.Armee.[62] His parting comment to those troops conflicts with many post-war Army oriented memoirs which minimize the value of SS troops by the Army in Russia.

"Without the units of the SS we wouldn't have known where to even begin during the past few days. Since we were able to employ many different parts of the SS troops at different points, our greatest worries were solved."

During the next few days, Himmler formed his operational plan for the units of the Kommandostab "Reichsführer-SS." At that time the units collected themselves and their gear and departed from their army units for new headquarters in various villages. Never having a chance to operate under army command, all the squadrons of SS-Kavallerie-Regiment 2 began to arrive in the area of Sonnau on June 29th with the final units arriving on July 1st.[63]

During this time the Reichsführer-SS issued an order for more awards of the Iron Cross 1st Class for the SS troops that had fought second line operations during the first week of the Russian campaign. Although Iron Crosses were awarded to the troops of the 87.Infanterie Division by the XXXXII.Armeekorps for these actions, none were awarded to men of the SS troops.[64] The award of Iron Crosses for the SS rear area troops was to be the subject of numerous disputes between the Army and the SS.

On the evening of July 1st, SS-Gruppenführer Hans Jüttner arrived for a meeting that was to take place the next day with the staff of the Kommandostab "Reichsführer-SS." The meeting the following day revealed that the recruit depot for the first battalion of the SS-Infanterie-Regiment 8 had been subordinated to the Kommandostab "Reichsführer-SS."[65]

Himmler visited his field command post during the first week of July and along with the newly-named Chief of the Kommandostab, SS-Brigadeführer Kurt Knoblauch, watched a parade formation presented by SS-Kavallerie-Regiment 1 on July 5th. The next day the leaders of the Kommandostab "Reichsführer-SS" received indications that their units would be used for mopping-up operations in the rear areas and put to special tasks by the political administrations in these areas.[66]

During the next week, exercises for the units were planned. These were to consist of forest and village actions encompassing typical engagements of a rear area occupation unit. Aside from all components of the Kommandostab "Reichsführer-SS," several newly forming units arrived and

---

[62] ibid.

[63] ibid.

[64] ibid.

[65] ibid.

[66] ibid.

were to take part in the exercises: the Freiwilligen Standarte "Nordwest" [67] consisting of the Freiwilligen Verband "Niederlande," Freiwilligen Verband "Flandern," and an SS-Infantrie Regiment previously based in Radom, Poland. On July 14th, SS-Kavallerie-Regimenter 1 and 2 reported ready for the exercises. On the 17th, Kommandostab "Reichsführer-SS" Chief SS-Brigadeführer Kurt Knoblauch arrived from Debica[68] and a special infantry regiment was assigned to accompany Knoblauch and the staff officers of the Kommandostab during the exercises. The next day, Knoblauch commenced the exercises by ordering an alert action for SS-Kavallerie-Regiment 2 which Knoblauch personally observed and later criticized.[69]

The Pripet Marshes

During the midst of the collective exercise, both SS-Kavallerie-Regimenter 1 and 2 were suddenly removed and given march orders to depart on the 21st for Baranowicze, the headquarters area for the Higher SS and Police Leader for the area of Army Group "Center," SS-Brigadeführer Erich von dem Bach. The regiments were immediately subordinated to von dem Bach for an operation in the Pripet marshes to be conducted against a band of partisans led by regular Soviet soldiers reported to be operating in the area. This operation, which would ultimately take place in two phases, resulted in a high cost in Russian casualties, both civilian and partisan, with low casualties for the regiments.

The enemy units, later reported to be two Russian cavalry divisions and a Russian rifle division,[70] broke through on Highway 1 during the nights of July 25th/26th and July 26th/27th between the villages of Sluzk and Bobruisk. Intelligence information reported them to be situated in the swamps in the area east of Nyshin.[71] In reaction to this potentially serious development, the commander of the rear area of Army Group "Center," General of the Infantry von Schenckendorff,[72] ordered the SS-Kavallerie-Brigade to immediately put together a special fire-brigade, termed a Vorausabteilung (Advance Detachment). Abbreviated in reports as the VA, it functioned as and later became the reconnaissance detachment of the Brigade and had the task of establishing a connection between the newly surrounded 1st Battalion of the 461.Infanterie Regiment in Budenitschi and the Rittmeisters Öhme Detachment in Osewiec.[73] After establishing the connection, the bicycle units of the Advance Detachment were to turn back south to comb through the marshes and find whatever enemy personnel they could. For this operation the SS troops making up this special unit were removed from the command of the SS-Kavallerie-Brigade and subordinated to the 162.Infanterie Division. After these initial operations were completed, the command of these units were to be returned to the SS-Kavallerie-Brigade (then in the initial phase of reformation and expansion) while the units themselves were to await further orders from Higher SS and Police Leader Erich von dem Bach.[74]

---

[67] Created in early April 1941 it eventually became the Freiwilligen-Legion Flandern in November 1941 and was composed of volunteers from Norway, Denmark and Holland when formed. Commanded throughout the first Russian campaign by SS-Sturmbannführer Michael Lippert, it was broken up in late June 1943 with its remaining troops used as cadre for the SS-Freiwilligen-Sturmbrigade "Langemarck."

[68] Debica, Poland was the site of the SS Troop Training and Replacement Center (SS-Truppenübungsplatz) ordered established in December 1939 and actually started in this area of the General Government in June 1940. The center was destroyed in 1944.

[69] "Kriegstagebuch des Kommandostabs 'Reichsführer-SS' Nr. 1," dated June 16, - December 31, 1941.

[70] "Die Kavallerie Divisionen der Waffen-SS," by Hans Bayer, page 28.

[71] "Kriegstagebuch des Kommandostabs 'Reichsführer-SS' Nr. 1," dated June 16, - December 31, 1941.

[72] Schenckendorff commanded troops assigned to the rear area of 9.Armee while Adolf Strauss commanded the front-line troops.

[73] "Die Kavallerie Divisionen der Waffen-SS," by Hans Bayer, page 28.

[74] "Kriegstagebuch des Kommandostabs 'Reichsführer-SS' Nr. 1," dated June 16, - December 31, 1941.

The order was issued at 1300 hours and at 1500 hours the quickly thrown together Advance Detachment,[75] under the leadership of SS-Hauptsturmführer Christian Reinhardt, was ready to depart. The following day the road was cut and the Advance Detachment, still subordinated to the 162.Infanterie-Division, was sent to intercept the enemy breakthrough while the regular mounted units intended for the operation were located in the Lachowicze area.[76]

Meanwhile, Hermann Fegelein, Kurt Knoblauch and Erich von dem Bach met in Baranowicze on the July 27th to plan the operation that was created to put an end to the Russian cavalry divisions as well as pacify all possible partisan resistance.[77] On the 28th, the Reichsführer-SS issued the following order to the Kommandostab "Reichsführer-SS" concerning the planned actions in the Pripet marshes:[78]

Kommandostab "Reichsführer-SS"   Headquarters, the 28th of July, 1941
Detachment Ia
War Diary No. Ia 18/0/41 secret.

<u>Special Order for the Kommandostab "Reichsführer-SS"</u>

<u>Subject:</u> Instructions for the combing-through operations of the Pripet swamps for the rider units.

I. <u>Performance Abilities of the Rider Units.</u>

1.) It is to be considered that the infantry units will have a difficult time keeping up with the rider units. Therefore, the rider units will be held to a marching distance of between 40 and 60 kilometers.

2.) Due to this, no useless wandering around is allowed.

3.) On days when fighting and local searches are initiated the units are to be held to a marching distance of between 20 and 30 kilometers.

II. <u>Participation of the Police.</u>

1.) The Security Police (SIPO) is to participate in the actions and operations of the other units. The Police are responsible for the reports and the messages of the units.

2.) As long as they are properly equipped and can spare their men, the Ordnungspolizei (ORPO) is also to participate in the actions and operations of the other units.

---

[75] This unit, officially referred to as VA/SS-KB-Kav.Rgt. 1 in documents, consisted of the 6th (technical) Squadron/SS-Kavallerie-Regiment 1, 7th (bicycle reconnaissance) Squadrons of SS-Kavallerie-Regimenter 1 and 2, one horse-drawn light artillery platoon (under the leadership of SS-Untersturmführer Fritz Höhenberger, at this time platoon leader of the 1st Platoon 5th (heavy) Squadron of SS-Kavallerie-Regiment 1), one anti-tank gun platoon (under the leadership of SS-Untersturmführer Rudi Schweinberger) and one signals truck.

[76] "Kriegstagebuch des Kommandostabs 'Reichsführer-SS' Nr. 1," dated June 16 to December 31, 1941.

[77] ibid.

[78] "Kommandosonderbefehl - Richtlinien für die Durchkämmung und Durchstreifen von Sumpfgebieten durch Reitereinheiten," dated June 28, 1941 and signed by Reichsführer-SS Heinrich Himmler.

3.) Motorized forces of the ORPO will advance at an equal pace along with the other units into the interior of the marsh areas and be responsible for the capture of railways and highways. With this it is to be considered that an opponent who wants to break out over the highways will not immediately come from the side, but will flee for a short distance towards the front and then, just before he reaches an area which he can someday break out from, he will make his move.

Patrol troops serving on the streets and roads are responsible for securing the entire stretch. These operations can perhaps be concluded in four days. In the mean time, stronger forces are to be dispatched for two day operations (which would cover about 60 km) only.

III. Descriptions of the Actions

1.) Every mopping-up action is to be carefully prepared. Continuous reconnaissance and reporting is to be conducted by patrol troops and air reconnaissance operations (conducted with Fieseler Storches) must precede them.

The population is to be warned by the use of fliers to be dropped by airplanes not to loot and pillage the areas.

2.) The troops should strive to comb through certain bordered areas, otherwise the ability to observe the general situation will be lost.

3.) Conducting a patrol operation without first securing the furthermost line would be foolish.

4.) The securing and capture of the borderline will be conducted by the motorized detachments of the rider regiments.

The securing operations must take the form of small all-around defenses since the line must be secured in the direction of the patrolled areas as well as towards the back. Furthermore, the trails that come out of the marsh areas must also be secured.

5.) Living and dead booty (cattle) must be secured.

6.) Stubborn resistance in the villages must be eliminated by the Luftwaffe in order to avoid casualties.

7.) In order for leadership to be able to maintain its direction and not get lost, excellent communication connections using devices of all types must be maintained during action. The danger that the troops will split up and lose their way in the swamps must be avoided at all costs.

IV. In Regards to the Population

1.) We must all understand it clearly that the villages in the swamp areas are either strongpoints for us or strongpoints for the enemy. Strongpoints for us can only be positions that have a population not only free of criminals, but also consisting of Ukrainian or other minority populations that view us as good and view the

Russians and Poles as bad. If this is the case, then we must see to it that these villages can defend themselves against pillagers and are developed completely as strongpoints for us. There are mayors to be brought in and appointed. The SIPO, which will be responsible for these operations, will be responsible for bringing in the people who will be entrusted with these operations. Also, the population must, in a limited fashion, be armed, since otherwise they will be run over by the enemy who will use their villages as strongpoints.

The population is to be informed that their village is occupied by posters hung in and around the villages. The rules of occupation are also to be stated to the population through the use of these posters. Furthermore, booty (food and horses) recovered from pillagers and partisans that is not needed by the troops is to be shared with the population.

2.) If the population serves as the enemy of Germany, is racially or humanly inferior, or indeed, as it often is in the marsh areas, made up of fleeing criminals, then all people that are suspected of helping the partisans are to be shot, while females and children are to evacuated and cattle and food are to be apprehended and secured. These villages are then to be burned to the ground.

3.) Either the villages and settlements are a network of strongpoints, whose residents kill partisans and pillagers and inform us of them, or they cease to exist. No enemy will be allowed to find support, food or shelter in these areas.

Signed H. Himmler

On the 29th of July the Brigade initiated the operation from launch points between Ratno, Dywin and Kobryn. The active units from SS-Kavallerie-Regiment 2 were situated on the right (south) while those from SS-Kavallerie-Regiment 1 were on the left (north) on the starting line connecting the cities of Lachowicze, Hancewicze and Luminiec. The Brigade staff was situated in Lachowicze. The regiments conducted their sweeps moving to the east and undertook pacification operations in the entire area. Fighting was reported in the first section against regular units of the Soviet army strengthened by partisan groups. The mixed group of Russian soldiers and partisans which fought against the Brigade troops in the area northeast of the Jasiolda river were completely annihilated.[79]

During the night of July 28th/29th the 6th Squadron engaged Russian cavalry six kilometers west of Budenitschi while the 7th Squadron engaged other Russian cavalry scouting units in Pasieka at 0300 hours on the 29th. Later that day the command post of the Advance Detachment was moved to the main road between Glusk and Budenitschi. At 1400 hours Patrol Platoon "Weeke" (named after 1st Platoon leader SS-Untersturmführer Karl Weeke of 7th Squadron, SS-Kavallerie-Regiment 2), patrolled a 50 kilometer area through the towns of Markaretsche, Shislin, Meshilaege, and Dudenitschi, all villages located in the area of Karamasy. During this time the Russian units attempted a break-out but were intercepted by Army troops in the sector neighboring Weeke's patrol. The men of the patrol could hear fighting and artillery fire during the entire night. Weeke's patrol returned to the command post of the Detachment at 0300 hours on the 30th.[80]

---

[79] "Abschlussmeldung der SS-Kavallerie-Brigade über Befriedung der Prypec-Sümpfe." Dated September 18, 1941 and signed by SS-Standartenführer Hermann Fegelein.

[80] Hans Bayer, "Die Kavallerie Divisionen der Waffen-SS," page 29.

At 1400 hours on July 30th Patrol Platoon "Weeke" cut the Russian cavalry troops in two. They then proceeded to pursue the Russians that made the split in a southeasterly direction, passing through Budentischi, Meshilesje, Olniza and finally to Glusk as their furthest advance point. The troops then spread out to cover a wider area and followed the Russians in west-northwesterly direction passing through Lutschki, Oksjabr and Novo Andrejewka. Weeke and his men followed the tracks left by the Russians in the sand, grass and hay, until they finally came upon one of their rest areas. Near Nowo Andrejewksa they finally met up with the Russians. The bicycles, which were at the lead of the Advance Detachment patrols, rode into a village when suddenly a Cossack cavalryman rode by. The bicycles took chase but couldn't catch him. Shortly thereafter, the remaining elements of the Advance Detachment patrol arrived. Suddenly, a battle erupted as the Cossack squadrons opened fire with their artillery and grenade launchers on the German units and managed to take out the signals unit's truck.

The German troops immediately set up their heavy machine guns and mortars and put them into action with good effect. The Cossack units then tried to surround the Advance Detachment troops by utilizing the neighboring forest as camouflage.

Even though they had nowhere to take cover, the German mortar and machine gun fire took a heavy toll and the Cossacks fled. The Germans were able to inflict further casualties on the Cossacks by adjusting their mortar fire to follow the retreating troops. After they had escaped deep enough into the forest, the Cossacks set up their mortars and returned fire. Their guns were poorly aimed, however, and the Germans suffered no casualties.[81]

Weeke's patrol returned to the Advance Detachment command post at 0700 hours on July 31st. Since the Cossack units were following some distance behind, the Detachment command post broke camp and paired up with Weeke's patrol. They then they moved onto the command post of the 162.Infanterie Division where they set up a bivouac.[82]

Another patrol, coded "Fritsche," (named for SS-Obersturmführer Karl Fritsche from the engineer platoon of 6th Squadron, SS-Kavallerie-Regiment 2) covered the areas southeast of Pasieka and around Ruchowo between July 28th and July 31st. Fritsche and his patrol came into contact with some of the Russian troops, both strong and weak, but no heated battles erupted. During his long trek, which covered between 230 and 260 kilometers of swampy terrain, Fritsche made constant reports on his thoughts about the Russian position. On August 1st, the 162.Infanterie Division launched an attack on the Russian units based on this information, the results of which confirmed Fritsche's assumptions.[83]

The Advance Detachment was put on alert at 0200 hours on Friday, August 1st. Shortly thereafter they received the task of taking part in an encircling action with the 162.Infanterie Division and a police unit that was to contain an entire Russian cavalry corps as well as a Russian infantry division. These units were now reported to be situated in the area of the highway between Glusk-Porjetschi. For this operation the Advance Detachment was put into position occupying the southern border of the town of Troitschany while the 162.Infanterie Division was in the northeast flanked by a police unit to the east. Due to the very difficult conditions imposed by the swamps, the patrols of the Advance Detachment abandoned their vehicles and departed on foot. The Russians then turned back to the northeast while the Germans continued to shell them with artillery fire well into the night. At this time the Advance Detachment assumed the Russians must run out of ammunition soon because they did not use it conservatively and had no supply lines. While the men of the Advance Detachment slept outside the town, the Russians were receiving food and shelter from the local population.[84]

[81] ibid.

[82] Hans Bayer, "Die Kavallerie Divisionen der Waffen-SS," page 30.

[83] ibid.

[84] ibid.

On August 2nd the Russians continued their movement within the pocket that the Germans had established. They continually tried to break out but always met with German units that denied them any success. On the 3rd, patrol troop "Geissler" (named after 2nd Platoon leader SS-Untersturmführer Werner Geissler of 7th Squadron, SS-Kavallerie-Regiment 2) located a Cossack squadron near Shiwun which they later engaged. On the 4th the command of the Advance Detachment was transferred to SS-Sturmbannführer Albert Faßbender.[85]

On August 4th, the Advance Detachment was assigned to reconnoiter the road to Ljaskowicze. After struggling through 11 kilometers of swamps the engineers were forced to build a 500 meter long bridge made of logs in order for the march to proceed. In Shiwun the Advance Detachment received fire from the village and the bordering forest. A battle erupted during which the Advance Detachment concentrated a barrage in the form of cavalry mortars and heavy machine guns. The Germans won the battle and counted 11 enemy soldiers dead. Patrol "Koppenwallner" (named for SS-Obersturmführer Anton Koppenwallner, commander of 7th Squadron, SS-Kavallerie-Regiment 2) mopped up the forest area near Shiwun and established contact with the Army 134.Infanterie Regiment. When the Advance Detachment finally reached the outskirts of Ljaskowicze that night, they confronted a well emplaced enemy. The Russians put up a good fight for two hours after which they retreated from the village. The battle was not over, however, as the Soviets counterattacked three times during the next one and a half hours using all their available heavy weapons in efforts to retake the town. After the battle the Germans counted 57 Russian dead while their casualties amounted to three wounded.[86]

On August 5th the Advance Detachment received the order to quickly approach the town of Sabolotje with the purpose of blocking a possible breakout attempt by the Russians to the west. At 2120 hours, the order was made more specific and instructed the troops to move eastwards and approach a predetermined section designated "Creek section #3" by passing through the town of Reppin. The Russians unsuccessfully proceeded to attack the Advance Detachment units and the fighting lasted until dawn the next day. Shortly thereafter the Advance Detachment of SS troops met up with the Advance Detachment of the Army 45.Infanterie Regiment. At 0900 hours this Army unit attacked Sabolotje from the south while the Advance Detachment of SS troops attacked from the west. The Russians retreated and left behind one complete artillery battery, four anti-tank cannons and various heavy machine guns. In the forest areas north and northeast of the Hof Buda and the Hof Reppelt the German units took 400 prisoners and counted another 200 enemy dead. They also came across more material: seven anti-tank guns, twelve machine guns, a large quantity of ammunition of various calibers and types as well as 600 horses. On August 8th the SS Advance Detachment had completed their objectives for the first operation of the Pripet marshes. Since the unit was no longer required by the Army for action, formal command of the unit was returned during the following week to the Kommandostab "Reichsführer-SS" and the SS-Kavallerie-Brigade. A few days later the Army notified the Kommandostab that the Advance Detachment would be placed under the command of the 252.Infanterie Division, should the need arrive.[87]

The last recorded action of the first combing-through operation in the Pripet marshes took place on August 13th. According to statements of residents in the town of Wieliczkowicze-Nowe taken by the anti-tank platoon of SS-Kavallerie-Regiment 2, there were supposedly 40 to 60 Russian officers in the area, armed with grenades, pistols and machine pistols.[88]

---

[85] "Zusammenfassende Meldung über die Kampfhandlungen der Vorausabteilung der SS-Kav.Brigade," to the Higher SS and Police Leader for the Commander of the Rear Area of Army Group "Center," dated August 11, 1941.

[86] Information from various sources including: "Zusammenfassende Meldung über die Kampfhandlungen der Vorausabteilung der SS-Kav.Brigade" and Bayer, pages 30 and 31.

[87] Information from various sources including "Tätigkeitsbericht für die Zeit vom 6. - 10. 8. 1941," to the Kommandostab "Reichsführer-SS" Abt. Ia in Arys, dated August 11, 1941 and signed by SS-Standartenführer Hermann Fegelein and Bayer, page 31.

[88] The details of this engagement are from "Bericht über den Einsatz des Pak-Zuges am 13.8.41 in Wieliczkowicze Nowe," dated August 15, 1941 and signed by SS-Untersturmführer Arthur Kessler.

Arthur Kessler as an SS-Sturmbannführer. The longtime anti-tank platoon commander and later reconnaissance platoon commander was born in Hamburg on August 12, 1912. He served with an Army anti-tank unit from 1935 to 1939 and joined the SS in August 1934 with an Allgemeine-SS engineer unit. Assigned to 1.SS-Totenkopf-Reiterstandarte after becoming an officer, he was commissioned an SS-Untersturmführer on July 1, 1940. Kessler served with both regiments in their 6th squadrons as well as the 3rd Squadron of the Reconnaissance Detachment where he won the Iron Cross 1st class on February 25, 1942. Promoted to SS-Obersturmführer on January 30, 1942, to SS-Hauptsturmführer on January 30, 1943 and to SS-Sturmbannführer June 21, 1944 he remained with the later SS-Kavallerie-Division throughout the war. When the SS-Kavallerie-Division formed he took command of 3./Panzerjäger Abteilung and in September 1943 took command of the Panzerjäger Abteilung when Bruno Streckenbach became divisional commander. As commander of the Panzerjäger Kompanie in the second (1943) Kampfgruppe "Z" he won the German Cross in Gold on April 17, 1943 and was killed in Budapest on February 11, 1945 as commander of the Panzerjäger Abteilung, 8.SS-Kavallerie-Division "Florian Geyer." (Photo: Jess Lukens)

The leader of the anti-tank platoon, SS-Untersturmführer Arthur Kessler, assumed that these Russian troops may have been related to the troops that had engaged the anti-tank and engineer units earlier in Hawrylizie. He then drove his platoon to the town of Miesin, located on the Polish-Russian border. Due to poor driving conditions in this area, Kessler had to leave the truck guarded by six of his men in order to continue the trip on foot. The path he chose led through the swamps for about two kilometers and a further two kilometers before the town of Wieliczkowicze. Then the troops encountered an impressive fort on the border with well-built defenses extending throughout the swamp area.

Kessler dispatched a patrol to reconnoiter the fort which determined it had been abandoned. His unit then burned the fort to the ground with the resulting large explosions revealing the fort was also used as a munitions dump.

Kessler next split his platoon into two groups. Kessler himself led a patrol and assigned the leadership of the rest of his platoon to SS-Unterscharführer Walter Wendt. The two units trudged through ten kilometers of swamps and thick forests. Residents stated that the Russians had set up double posts to protect themselves from any suprises. They also reported that there was a large Russian factory in Kiszcze flying the Russian flag. The two groups immediately set out to reconnoiter the concern. Kessler determined that the structure housed some 60 to 80 Russian officers. In front of the building was a look-out tower which stood approximately fifteen meters high with two guards who rotated as lookouts.

As the troops approached the building, SS-Unterscharführer Wendt gave the signal to his platoon: one group to the left of the path, one group to the right of the path. The men stood up to their knees in the swamp and there was only one thing left for them to do: attack the building from two sides.

Kessler ordered one group to fan left and another right. Kessler then approached the front of the structure in order to draw fire on himself, allowing the other groups to approach undetected. The guards in the towers must have noticed them because they started to give excited hand signals in the direction of the building. They then attempted to abandon the watchtower. Kessler's group was within 200 meters of the objective when they suddenly received strong fire. Due to the swampy terrain, they slowly came up to a distance of some 100 meters from the guard tower. At that point Kessler gave the order to attack. With enthusiasm and without regard for their lives, Kessler's men stormed forward. That was too much for the Russians and they started to flee. Kessler decided not to pursue them because it was getting late, they were too distant from the strongpoint of SS-Kavallerie-Regiment 2 as well as consideration of the unfavorable terrain.

Nonetheless, the Russians left behind five dead of which two were women, while some 18 to 20 wounded were evacuated by the Russians as evidenced by the considerable amount of blood trails exiting the battle area. The Germans also recovered considerable materials. The targeted structure as well as all of the neighboring buildings were then burned to the ground. Large explosions revealed munitions which was not located during the search. The men of the anti-tank platoon, having suffered no casualties, arrived back at the regimental strongpoint at 2345 hours that night.

With the taking of the Russian fort on August 13th, the first operation of the Pripet marshes had concluded. The Russian units engaged were completely destroyed. According to statements from prisoners, the Germans ascertained they had been fighting the 36th and 37th Russian Cavalry Divisions as well as the 121st Russian Rifle Division. The Germans were very successful in these operations as the statistics for this operation amply demonstrate. A report made on August 16th reveals the staggering results of the battles. Enemy casualties were placed at 15,878 killed and 830 taken prisoner.[89] Casualties were very light on the side of the SS-Kavallerie-Brigade. Reports state that they only suffered 17 dead and 36 wounded. Although no numerical figures were given, reports refer to high casualties for the 162.Infanterie Division of the Army (the Advance Detachment was subordinated to this unit for the operation) for the fighting in the Pripet marshes. The Germans lost 200 horses and some equipment in the operation but more than managed to compensate with replacement material recovered from the partisan units. Spoils consisted of approximately 20 artillery pieces of all types, some 30 machine guns and over 500 rifles with more than enough ammunition to supply these weapons for several battles. The 200 horses killed in action were replaced with the 800 to 900 enemy mounts captured.[90]

In a report made to Higher SS and Police Leader von dem Bach, Hermann Fegelein felt good about the performance of the SS-Kavallerie-Brigade. In his report the excellent performance of the unit leaders of the SS-Kavallerie-Brigade was credited with the success of the operation. There were no complaints about the performance of the SS cavalrymen as Fegelein paid tribute to their excellent marching performance: in 8 days the units marched as much as 400 kilometers in the difficult terrain posed by the swamps. Also praised for what were referred to as the "Suicide Patrols" of the Advance Detachment for the accurate information they retrieved during their numerous reconnaissance missions. Comparing the Brigade to the Army, Fegelein also noted the rela-

[89] This figure includes both regular Soviet soldiers and partisans and represents a collective total for the SS elements as well as the Army units for this operation. "Abschlussmeldung der SS-Kav.Brigade über der Prypec-Sümpfe" dated September 18, 1941. The figures vary at different times in various reports but even the lowest, 10,844 enemy reported killed in an August 11 report to the HSSPF, shows the one-sided losses of the operation.

[90] Information from various sources including: Bayer, page 31 and "Zu Abschlussmeldung für den 'Reichsführer-SS,'" to the HSSPF to the Commander of the rearward Army area "Center," dated August 13, 1941 and signed by SS-Standartenführer Hermann Fegelein.

tively high number of casualties the Army units suffered. Fegelein attributed the excellent performance of the SS men to the continuous training they underwent during the early months of 1941.[91]

To conclude his report Fegelein bitterly complained about the fact that although the Army units were awarded many decorations, his units were not awarded a single Iron Cross. These complaints took only minimal effect and on the August 16th General von Schenckendorff paid a visit to the Rider Detachment of SS-Kavallerie-Regiment 1 during which he awarded two clasps to the Iron Cross 2nd class (for those who had won the Iron Cross 2nd class in the First World War) and ten awards of the Iron Cross 2nd class.

On the 17th the Commander of the 162.Infanterie Division, Generalleutnant Dr. Franke, issued one award of the clasp to the Iron Cross 1st class, two awards of the Iron Cross 1st class and a further 15 awards of the Iron Cross 2nd class.[92]

Fegelein also found time to characterize the fighting abilities of his opponents. In a report filed nearly a month after the conclusion of the operation, he noted the "excellent defensive techniques" of the mixed Soviet Army and partisan units. Upon being attacked by the Germans, the partisan units would dig-in after which the Germans found it very difficult to throw them out of their positions. Fegelein also praised the willingness of the partisans to hold their posts and continue fighting despite their eminent doom.[93]

During the next four days, the units were allowed to recover from the operation, clean their gear and prepare for the next operation.[94] After concluding the first operation in the Pripet marshes, plans were quickly initiated for the second combing through operation in the rear area of Army Group "Center."

The SS-Kavallerie Regimenter and the
Second Combing-Through Operation of the Pripet Marshes

According to Brigade Order No. 1 (Brigadebefehl Nr.1), dated August 13, 1941, the SS-Kavallerie-Brigade was to annihilate the remaining enemy partisans between the Pripet marshes and Highway 1. For this operation, SS-Kavallerie-Regiment 2 was assigned to the right (south) with borders of David-Gorodec and Mosyr and SS-Kavallerie-Regiment 1 to the left (north) on Highway 1. SS-Kavallerie-Regiment 2 was to commence the operation on August 15th while SS-Kavallerie-Regiment 1 was not to depart until the 17th.[95] Both units operated independently from one another for this operation and their stories are covered separately.

SS-Kavallerie-Regiment 1 in and around Starobin
August 15 to September 2, 1941

As SS-Kavallerie-Regiment 1 began the second phase of the mopping-up and pacification operations within the Pripet marshes, the commander of the Brigade sent both regimental commanders in the field a message. This communication informed them that the upcoming final pacification operation in the area of Starobin held special priority. Despite recent actions in this area, small bands of well-equipped partisans were reported still roaming aimlessly and terrorizing the local population almost daily.[96]

SS-Kavallerie-Regiment 1, now under the temporary command of SS-Hauptsturmführer

[91] "Zu Abschlussmeldung für den 'Reichsführer-SS,'" dated August 13, 1941.

[92] "Tätigkeitsbericht für die Zeit vom 18. - 21. 8. 1941," dated August 21, 1941.

[93] "Abschlussmeldung der SS-Kav.Brigade über Befriedung der Prypec-Sümpfe," to the Ia of the SS-Kavallerie-Brigade dated September 18, 1941 and signed SS-Standartenführer Hermann Fegelein.

[94] "Abschlussmeldung der SS-Kav.Brigade über Befriedung der Prypec-Sümpfe," dated September 18, 1941.

[95] "Brigadebefehl Nr. 1" for the SS-Kav.-Brig. dated August 13, 1941 and signed by SS-Standartenführer Hermann Fegelein.

[96] Information for the actions of SS-Kavallerie-Regiment 1 in and around Starobin from various situation and tactical reports including: "Bericht über die Befriedung des Raumes Starobin," dated Sept. 4, 1941 and signed by SS-Sturmbannführer Gustav Lombard and "Abschlussmeldung der SS-Kav.Brigade über Befriedung der Prypec-Sümpfe," dated September 18, 1941.

Hermann Fegelein (center) with Rudolf Maeker (right) and another officer (possibly Franz Rehbein) during the summer of 1941. A native of Oels/Silesia, Maeker was born on May 19, 1916, and joined the SS in November 1933 with SS-Reiterstandarte 11. Moving to the Pioniersturmbann (engineer battalion) of the SS/VT in 1935, he attended SS-Junkerschule Bad Tölz in 1937/38. After graduation he went to Regiment "Germania" and became an SS-Untersturmführer on November 9, 1938. He was with "Germania" in Poland and the Western campaigns, winning both Iron Crosses, and left the unit in November 1940. Promoted to SS-Obersturmführer on July 1, 1940 he next served as 01 (Ordnance Officer) to the Befehlshaber der Waffen-SS "Ost" (Carl-Maria Demelhuber) in Poland until the spring of 1941 when he moved to SS-Kavallerie-Regiment 1. Later during 1941 he served as 01 and regimental adjutant of SS-Kavallerie-Regiment 2 as well as Ib (Quartermaster) and temporary Ia of the Brigade. He led portions of the initial reconnaissance unit and ended his Brigade service as a squadron commander in SS-Kavallerie-Regiment 1 for which he won the German Cross in Gold on May 24, 1942. Promoted to SS-Hauptsturmführer on March 6, 1942, he served as Ib on the staff of Kampfgruppe "Fegelein" from December 1942 to March 1943. He then commanded 3./SS-Kavallerie-Erstaz-Abteilung until February 1944 when attached to the staff of Heeresgruppe "Nord" (Army Group "North") as an aide to Field Marshal Walter Model at which position he was promoted to SS-Sturmbannführer on April 20, 1944. (Photo: National Archives)

Waldemar Fegelein,[97] set out on August 15th from the line connecting Hancewieze and Highway 1. The unit was in position to commence the operation on the 17th. The following day the lead group of the 2nd Squadron intercepted a group of partisans while coming through the forest southwest of Budza. These partisans immediately opened fire but were no match for the German units. The fight resulted in 34 regular Russian soldiers being captured (several were wounded) as well as various captured material in the form of several rifles, grenades and ammunition. No German casualties were suffered during this small skirmish.

Early in the morning of the 19th, the Russians destroyed the bridge near Lutowicze as the lead group of the vanguard (1st Squadron) reached the Volga river. Despite the difficult terrain, SS-Obersturmführer Anton Bug charged through the river with the lead group and surrounded Lutowicze so fast that the partisans residing in the town were unable to escape. Shortly afterwards a fight broke out between the platoon and a partisan group at the southern exit of the town. Nine Russian

[97] SS-Standartenführer Lombard was ordered to Brigade headquarters to temporarily replace SS-Standartenführer Hermann Fegelein who was attending to matters elsewhere.

From left are SS-Standartenführer Hermann Fegelein, SS-Gruppenführer Karl Wolff (Himmler's adjutant), Reichsführer-SS Heinrich Himmler and SS-Gruppenführer Erich von dem Bach (HSSPF Russland-Mitte) during Himmler's early July 1941 visit to the Kommandostab "Reichsführer-SS." (Photo: National Archives)

soldiers were killed during this battle. While the village was being mopped up, hand-to-hand combat broke out in one of the barns in the village. Four Russian soldiers, two of which were officers, were captured during the fight. Statements by the prisoners revealed that they had been given the task of blowing the bridge by the partisan commander. During the evening of the 21st the Regiment reached the area of Pywaszce.

On August 22nd the 3rd Squadron reached the town of Starobin at 0900 hours and was ordered to reconnoiter the town, the surrounding forests and swamp areas. That evening 3rd Squadron Chef SS-Hauptsturmführer Johann Schmid arrived at regimental headquarters to report to SS-Hauptsturmführer Waldemar Fegelein. His report about the conditions in and around Starobin was very negative. The German appointed mayor and members of his Hilfspolizei[98] had been murdered and the city was no longer under German control. 3rd Squadron then appointed a new mayor while members of the Squadron did their best to put the Hilfspolizei back together. There was evidence that the Jewish population was terrorizing the German sympathizers and that they had made Starobin a strongpoint for the partisans. Statements by residents of the town revealed that there were three partisan groups, one of which was well-equipped. The combined strength of the partisans was estimated at between 500 and 600 men.

In response to these reports SS-Hauptsturmführer Waldemar Fegelein set out for Starobin on August 23rd with all elements of the regiment except 1st Squadron. Arriving at noon, Fegelein was greeted with bad news. The new mayor was reported to have been murdered by three Jews the previous day and during the previous night the partisan groups made an attempt to burn the city to the ground. In response to the murder of the mayor, an order was issued to shoot the entire male

---

[98] German-sympathizing locals that volunteered to serve as policemen for the local German government.

Jewish population residing within the city. Fegelein explained the current situation to the Russian population and told them that the Reichsführer-SS had ordered the regiment to assist the pro-German non-partisan portion of the population while rebellious elements of the population were to be executed. The town was again searched by members of SS-Kavallerie-Regiment 1 as well as the Hilfspolizei and a number of suspicious people were apprehended. Of those apprehended, 21 were executed and 15 were released due to lack of evidence against them.[99]

Meanwhile the areas that were held by the partisans were systematically combed through. For this action the 2nd and 3rd as well as available portions of the 4th (heavy) Squadron were dispatched. During the afternoon of August 23rd, portions of the 4th Squadron under the leadership of SS-Obersturmführer d.R. Willi Geier, came upon a group of 19 partisans and engaged them in battle. This clash produced twelve prisoners, seven of which were badly wounded while the remaining seven partisans were killed in action. Several rifles and grenades were taken. In the combat report for this operation, SS-Oberreiter Gloth and SS-Sturmmann Moldenhauer were commended for multiple acts of bravery during the engagement. Later that day a fight erupted in Kopaciewicze between partisans and a reconnaissance patrol led by SS-Untersturmführer Johannes Göhler (2nd Platoon leader, 3rd Squadron, SS-Kavallerie-Regiment 1). The fight took place in terrain which made the most simple maneuver arduous. Due to these conditions a 20 meter log bridge had to be constructed. The battle was decided by several hand-to-hand combats with the 60 man strong band of partisans losing. 15 partisans were taken prisoner and the patrol captured a light machine gun and several carbines. These weapons were utilized in arming the Hilfspolizei. Combat reports for this action commended SS-Unterscharführer Hillmann and SS-Sturmmann Vitzen for multiple instances of bravery in action.

During the early hours of the morning on August 24th, the 2nd, 3rd and the balance of 4th Squadron reinforced with a platoon of the 1st Squadron in addition to several members of the Hilfspolizei (who were very familiar with the geography in this area) attacked the island in the marshes located west of Powarczyze. The Russian troops were well emplaced on the island and ready for battle. Their troops were equipped with weapons of all types and sufficient supplies to last for several weeks. In order to attack the island, the German cavalry troops had to wade waist-high through the swamp. The ensuing battle resulted in 28 Russians killed and two taken prisoner with no casualties for the Germans. Combat reports for this action commended SS-Hauptscharführer Stumpe and SS-Sturmmann Hemmerling as well as light machine gunners SS-Oberscharführer Wohlschlaegel and SS-Rottenführer Löchter for multiple acts of bravery. Also, the leaders of the unit were commended for concluding the operation without casualties, which was in part credited to the well-aimed fire of SS-Obersturmführer d.R. Willi Geier's heavy machine gun.

An attempt by the partisans to blow the bridge constructed by 3rd Squadron east of Starobin during the night of August 23/24 was foiled by SS-Rottenführer Tichei and SS-Oberreiter Ebner. This pair went alone to fight the three man partisan patrol and managed to kill them with their bayonets. During the same night, after the partisans realized that the Regiment had abandoned Starobin, twelve Russians tried to start fires in the town. A small group of SS men consisting of SS-Sturmmänner Schüsser, Breu, Oberweger, Martin and Eigner, which was left behind to patrol the village, caught the Russians during their attempt and shot them.

During the afternoon of August 24th SS-Kavallerie-Regiment 1 continued its march in the direction of Pohost and later reached Luban the evening of the 25th. The units were involved in several skirmishes with partisan units on the advance route.

On the 24th a platoon under SS-Untersturmführer Willi Brutkuhl managed to surround an area in a forest where two Russian paratroopers had landed. Brutkuhl received this information by questioning residents in the vicinity. Despite efforts to capture them alive, the paratroopers would not surrender and were killed while defending themselves. During the night of the 24th/25th a patrol

---

[99] "Bericht über die Befriedung des Starobin," dated September 4, 1941. This complete report was used for relating the rest of the Starobin combats undertaken by SS-Kavallerie-Regiment 1.

came upon a group of 38 partisans. A fight erupted and 17 of the enemy were taken prisoner.

Shortly afterwards the Regiment set up camp for the night in Luban. That night command received a radio message from SS-Sturmbannführer Gustav Lombard. Lombard stated that he was still substituting for SS-Standartenführer Hermann Fegelein and remained at Brigade Headquarters and thus was not able to join up with the Regiment at this time. He also reported that the reconnaissance actions of SS-Kavallerie-Regiment 2 had uncovered 500 armed partisans equipped with two artillery pieces in the area of Morocz. Based on these recent occurrences he ordered SS-Kavallerie-Regiment 1 to turn around and pass through Starobin and continue marching to Morocz to help encircle the enemy from the east. The riding batteries of SS-Kavallerie-Regiment 1 were returning from Turov, where they had been temporarily subordinated to SS-Kavallerie-Regiment 2 for the battles there, traveling north toward Highway 1. A messenger intercepted them and informed them that they were again subordinated to SS-Kavallerie-Regiment 2 and gave them the order to travel through Starobin in the general direction of Morocz. Their primary responsibility was to seal off the southwestern sector of Morocz.

At 0330 hours on August 26th a patrol of the 2nd Squadron under the leadership of SS-Oberscharführer Dr. Wilhelm Heyd took off for Morocz. While passing through the sector located 6 kilometers northeast of Starobin the patrol intercepted a well equipped group of partisans and it took the unit two hours to finally claim victory. During the fight SS-Sturmmann Schwimmer was killed and SS-Oberreiter Welsch wounded.

At 0900 hours SS-Sturmbannführer Lombard arrived in Pohost to obtain status reports from his officers. He informed the men that Brigade headquarters was in agreement with the plan devised by SS-Kavallerie-Regiment 1. He then ordered one platoon of the 2nd Squadron under the leadership of SS-Untersturmführer Georg Vieth to go ahead of the other squadron units and secure the northern exit of Starobin while the rest of the Regiment was marching through Starobin. The securing of this exit was vital to the operation as the path there led to Morocz through a swamped forest area.

No skirmishes erupted during the march but the reconnaissance patrol reported partisan activity in the area encompassing the entire area south of Starobin. The men of SS-Kavallerie-Regiment 1 were sure that the partisan leader was eager to attack the cavalry unit and the pro-German population in Starobin to avenge his recent losses.

Reports of attacks on mounted and motorcycle messengers increased. During one of these attacks SS-Rottenführer Löchter took four armed Russians prisoner after he shot and killed two others. The day's tally included 26 Russians killed and nine captured. Interrogations of those captured led the Germans to believe the partisan command post was located on a collective farm in the swamp area east of Morocz. The leader of the partisan units for the entire area of the Pripet marshes was reportedly one Danilo Zeika who was supposedly located at the partisan headquarters in Morocz.

Before noon on August 27th SS-Kavallerie Regiment 1 (minus the 2nd and 3rd Squadrons) reached Morocz despite the difficulties posed by the terrain during their transport. The population in Morocz consisted mainly of Poles who were very willing to help the Germans. Statements from the residents there revealed that the citizens had suffered badly under the partisan government of Zaika. Further statements by the townspeople confirmed that Zaika had his command post on a collective farm twelve kilometers east of Morocz.

While the rest of the Regiment was on its way to Morocz, the 2nd and 3rd Squadrons had their own agenda. 2nd Squadron was sent out in a northerly direction to secure the line between Starobin and Sakowicze. Several fights between the German patrols and partisan units were fought during their effort to seal off the assigned sectors. 3rd Squadron was sent to Domanowicze. As the Squadron approached this town, the partisans there demolished the bridge. The bridge was not completely destroyed, however, and the partisans as well as the entire male population immediately fled into the swamps in fear of the approaching German units. The population of Domanowicze was in full support of the partisans. The bakery and mill located there were at full capacity to supply the partisan units. Besides the bakery and the mill, the Squadron also discovered a partisan supply dump. After taking the town the Squadron sealed all three exits according to orders.

SS-Obergruppenführer und General der Polizei Erich von dem Bach, the Higher SS and Police Leader for the area of Russia the SS-Kavallerie Brigade operated in during 1941. He is shown in his headquarters and in the field with an unidentified Army general and Oakleaves winner. Born in Lauenburg on March 1, 1899, he served as an officer in WWI and was awarded both Iron Crosses. Joining the SS in 1931 he commanded 27.Standarte from February 1931 to July 1932 and was promoted SS-Sturmbannführer on December 6, 1931. He next commanded SS-Abschnitt XII until the end of January 1934 and was promoted to SS-Standartenführer 10, 1932, SS-Oberführer October 6, 1932 and SS-Brigadeführer December 15, 1933. While commander of SS-Oberabschnitt "Nordost" from February 1934 to February 1936 he was promoted SS-Gruppenführer on July 11, 1934. He was HSSPF "Sudost" (southeast) from June 1938 to May 1941 when he became HSSPF for the rear area of Army Group "Center." This was redesignated HSSPF Russland-Mitte (mid-Russia) in February 1942 and von dem Bach held the position from May 1941 to April 1943 though substitute commanders undertook the post after November 1942. Promoted to Generalleutnant der Polizei on April 10, 1941 and to SS-Obergruppenführer on November 9, 1941, he headed Himmler's anti-partisan command and units for that purpose from October 1942 to November 1944. Given the rank of General in the Waffen-SS in July 1944, he commanded XIV.SS-Armee-Korps from November 1944 to early February 1945. He then led X.SS-Armee-Korps for a week before taking command of the Oderkorps, composed of any units found in his command area, which he led until May 1945. Awarded the German Cross in Gold on February 23, 1943 and the Knight's Cross on September 30, 1944, he was brutal in Russia and suffered physical ailments as a result of his actions. He testified for the prosecution at Nuremberg where other defendants branded him a traitor. He was tried three times for his actions as HSSPF in Russia and died in a Munich prison during his third sentence on March 8, 1972. (Photos: Jess Lukens and Jost Schneider)

At 0315 hours on August 28th a platoon under the leadership of NCO Karl Hermann found itself fighting a partisan unit equipped with machine guns. The partisans retreated with the Germans following, but a plan to surround the enemy did not prove feasible because the routes the German unit selected were too swampy to keep pace with the partisans. The fight was not a total loss, however, as the Germans claimed nine partisans killed while suffering no casualties. 2nd Squadron reached their assigned positions around Morocz a short time later. Their task was to seal off all routes leading from Morocz to the north. 4th Squadron was assigned to the marsh regions to the west. At 0500 hours the officers of SS-Kavallerie-Regiment 1 were convinced that the partisans were surrounded. SS-Sturmbannführer Gustav Lombard arrived at Regiment headquarters shortly thereafter but temporary command remained with SS-Hauptsturmführer Waldemar Fegelein. Sev-

Willi Geier, platoon leader in 4th Squadron, SS-Kavallerie-Regiment 1, shown here on the left with SS-Totenkopfstandarte "Brandenburg" before the war and on the right as a soon to be commissioned SS-Standartenoberjunker. Born in the Rhineland on October 25, 1909, he served with an Army Flak unit from November 1929 to July 1935. He joined the SS in August 1935 serving with SS-Totenkopfstandarte "Brandenburg," SS.Reiterstandarte 7 and the SD. Commissioned an SS-Untersturmführer d.R. on July 1, 1940, he came to SS-Kavallerie-Regiment 1 in January 1941 as a platoon leader in 4th Squadron and was promoted to SS-Obersturmführer d.R. on April 20, 1941. He held that post until the end of 1941 after which he was assigned to SS-Junkerschule Braunschweig until the end of April 1942. Rejoining the new SS-Kavallerie-Division in May 1942, he took command of 3rd Squadron, SS-Kavallerie-Regiment 1. He was assigned to the new SS-Kavallerie-Regiment 3 (later renumbered 17) in March 1943 followed by promotion to SS-Hauptsturmführer d.R. on April 20, 1943. He took command of 1st Squadron in January 1944 and went to the 22.SS-Freiwilligen-Kavallerie-Division "Maria Theresia" when his regiment was used as cadre and won the German Cross in Gold on May 11, 1944 for his actions in the Kowel pocket. He survived the war and died in 1983. (Photos: BDC and Private U.S. collection)

eral patrols were sent out to reconnoiter the areas until the afternoon with some of these encountering enemy resistance.

In one instance a 30 man partisan unit attempted a breakthrough against 4th Squadron. This attempt was repulsed and the partisans left behind 21 dead. Another patrol, under the leadership of SS-Oberscharführer August Schulte-Uffelage, reported that the majority of the partisans had gathered on an island in the swamps northwest of Kochos. 3rd Squadron confirmed this report based on statements from local residents who reported that a group of 200 to 300 partisans led by Danilo Zaika himself had marched there the previous night.

Based on this information, a two-phase attack plan was developed by the regimental staff. The assault was planned for August 29th with the first phase involving two operations commencing in parallel. The first operation served to soften up the partisan units located on the island northwest of Kochos and any other partisans possibly located in western portions of the swamp area.

This was to be accomplished by positioning the artillery battery near Grabov where it was to bombard the island and by centralizing 5th Squadron near Analcycze so that the western portions of the swamp area could be effectively shelled. While these units were shelling the concealed partisans, 1st Squadron (strengthened by a grenade launcher platoon of the 4th Squadron) and 3rd Squadron were to mop up all of the buildings and farms on their way to attack Kochos. After the shelling had taken its toll and the city of Kochos was in German hands, the second phase of the attack was to begin. For this stage, 1st and 3rd Squadron as well as patrols from the regimental staff (Regimentsstab) were to attack the island while 2nd Squadron and parts of 3rd Squadron were to remain in the city. The remaining elements of the Regiment were to remain on alert.

The commander of SS-Kavallerie-Regiment 2 during most of the Russia period, Hermann Schleifenbaum is shown as an SS-Obersturmführer in the autumn of 1938 when assigned to SS-Totenkopfstandarte 2 "Brandenburg." Born May 8, 1908 in Siegen, Schleifenbaum served in the Army from October 1926 to August 1938 with Cavalry Regiments 8 and 13, ending his service as an Oberleutnant. Transferring to the SS in September 1938 as a staff officer, he served with SS-Totenkopfstandarte 2 "Brandenburg" and was promoted SS-Hauptsturmführer on January 30, 1939. When the unit became a component of the "Totenkopf" Division he led III.Bataillon and was promoted SS-Sturmbannführer on November 20, 1939. After the Western campaigns, where he won both Iron Crosses with "Totenkopf," he took command of I./SS-Infanterie-Regiment 8 on August 8, 1940. He replaced Heino Hierthes as commander of SS-Kavallerie-Regiment 2 in the first week of September 1941 and led the regiment until the end of March 1942. Fegelein recommended him for the German Cross in Gold but the award was refused at a higher level. For unknown reasons (Fegelein gave him very positive evaluations) he was moved from the cavalry unit (his career specialty) and transferred to the "Prinz Eugen" Division as commander of II./Gebirgs-Jäger Regiment 1 in May 1942. He considered this a step backwards in his career (having commanded a regiment) and filed a formal complaint requesting transfer back to the Army since "Prinz Eugen" commander Arthur Phleps considered him too inexperienced to command a mountain regiment. This transfer was approved and he returned to the Army in January 1943. (Photo: BDC)

The night before the attack 2nd Squadron reported vigorous partisan activity. The enemy was sending out patrols of their own, searching for escape routes to the north. One of these patrols was intercepted by 2nd Squadron. This reportedly strong patrol, consisting of 18 partisans, was annihilated. 3rd Squadron also reported lively partisan activity as they intercepted another patrol of 23 Russians, all of whom were captured. Radio contact between the units in the field and regimental headquarters remained disrupted as the partisans were in possession of a Russian radio noise generator.

On August 29th the Regiment departed at 0700 hours as ordered. The regiment commander, SS-Hauptsturmführer Waldemar Fegelein, accompanied the lead platoon of strengthened 1st Squadron after approval from SS-Sturmbannführer Lombard. The 1st Squadron, accompanied by the available troops of the 3rd Squadron, reached Kolchos without encountering any resistance and managed to capture four partisans on route. During an artillery barrage, SS-Sturmbannführer Lombard, SS-Hauptsturmführer Fegelein and SS-Hauptsturmführer Johann Schmid discussed the situation in Kolchos. SS-Sturmbannführer Lombard ordered the units to attempt to destroy the partisan's communication equipment, since it would prove a valuable asset should they attempt escape. The terrain in this area was also noted to be favorable for any escape plan the partisans could develop. During the attack the recent harvest was to be secured in and around Kolchos. This harvest was to returned to the general population after the attack was completed.

At 1200 hours the troops arrived on the island where they met up with partisan units that were quite shaken by the previous artillery barrage. SS-Kavallerie Regiment 1 along with the regimental staff units took 37 prisoners. 2nd Squadron beat off a breakout attempt and counted 72 enemy dead. Six Russian soldiers, one of whom was an officer, were engaged in hand-to-hand combat and were eventually taken prisoner. 4th and 5th Squadrons served as support units and took in 32 prisoners. At 2015 hours the units had reached the furthest exit on the island, thus sealing off the area and completing the operation.

The total enemy losses during the operation were 154 dead and 117 wounded. It was determined that the partisan leader Zaika and the rest of the partisans had managed to escape. These units were fighting against the Hilfspolizei stationed there who determined that the partisans had escaped to the east and had probably transferred their strongpoint to Domanowicze or Sosny.

The Germans were disappointed as both of these towns were islands in the swamps and there was no practical route to reach them. They were also wary of the excellent messenger system the partisans had developed.

On August 30th SS-Kavallerie Regiment 1 (except 3rd Squadron) returned to where they had started on the 25th near Luban. 2nd Squadron returned to the Starobin area where the Regiment was located and several transport wagons were pulled up. 3rd Squadron marched to the right side of the Regiment in the area of Zahalje-Marsh securing it from an attack on the flank. They were also given a special assignment to launch a surprise attack against Sosny. For this attack the Squadron was strengthened with a cavalry mortar platoon.

The commander of 3rd Squadron, SS-Hauptsturmführer Johann Schmid, took the planning of this attack into his own hands with good results. Entering the city and alerting the partisan messenger service of his presence there, his intentions were to give the enemy the impression that the units were simply going to pass through the city. Much further back and out of enemy view was a platoon under the leadership of SS-Obersturmführer Heinrich Dieckmann and a cavalry mortar platoon under the leadership of SS-Untersturmführer Johannes Göhler. Using a heavy thunderstorm to confuse the partisan units, the rearward units sealed the entrance of Sosny while the forward elements attacked the entry access. The surprise element of the attack, however, was not effective as the partisans were well prepared for an assault and had placed several machine guns outside of the city which immediately began to fire on the German units. One of the cavalry mortar crews instantly directed their fire on the machine-guns outside of the city while the other continued to fire on Sosny itself. The attack developed quickly and the partisans soon became demoralized as they watched many of their comrades fall under the superior German firepower. Some 60 partisans, several of whom were regular Russian officers, were killed in the fight. Statements taken from those captured confirmed that Sosny served as a central communications center for the partisan units. 3rd Squadron managed to recover much of this communication equipment. The town was then set on fire and several explosions revealed that Sosny also served as an ammunitions dump. Disappointingly, the partisan commander Zaika was not found.

Several members of the cavalry mortar platoon were recognized for their excellent work during this engagement and cited for valor in the battle report. The most notable were SS-Oberscharführer Anton Vandieken and his cannoners, SS-Unterscharführer Klaine and SS-Unterscharführer Nowak. A variety of booty was recovered and destroyed.

2nd Squadron was assigned to attack the town of Sawerchlessje, approximately 30 kilometers northwest of Sosny, before noon on the 2nd of September. SS-Obersturmführer Erich Krell and his platoon led SS-Kavallerie-Regiment 1 into the town and immediately received fire. This unit, instead of retreating, immediately went over into attack formation and took the offensive. Krell and his men immediately located a farm as the source of the fire and ran towards it. They were met by four partisans in the garden which was located in front of the barn and engaged them in hand-to-hand combat. The partisans fell quickly and the men at once showered the building with grenades. The explosions were huge, alerting the men that this was no ordinary barn and they later determined that Russian officers had kept quarters here and that it also served as a supply dump for a previously unknown Russian cavalry squadron.

After the battle several villagers were questioned regarding the whereabouts of the Russian cavalry squadron. They reported that they were hiding just a few kilometers away in a wooded area. While Krell's platoon searched the village for weapons, SS-Untersturmführer Georg Veith set out to try and track down the cavalry unit. Approaching the forest area, Veith's unit received fire and quickly moved into position. After they returned fire, the cavalry unit unleashed their heavy firepower. The rest of the unit, hearing this firefight, quickly departed to help Veith and his men. A heavy machine platoon under the leadership of SS-Oberscharführer Richard Nakat quickly showed up and under their protection, Veith and his men broke into the forest and engaged the Russians. The troops counted 18 Russian soldiers, some dressed in bandit outfits, fleeing into the swamp. No prisoners were taken, but 31 excellent horses were captured. Local residents stated that the Russian cavalry squadron had come from the forested area of Bobruisk and were on their way south. Based

The commander of the Brigade's attached anti-aircraft battery, Ewald Keyk, shown here as an Allgemeine-SS NCO. Born May 25, 1911, in Iötzen, he entered the SS with 25.Standarte in 1932 and was commissioned an SS-Untersturmführer in the Allgemeine-SS on November 9, 1934 followed by promotion to SS-Obersturmführer on January 30, 1939. He served in numerous units, coming to the Waffen-SS in January 1940 as an SS-Untersturmführer d.R. after serving with an Army anti-tank unit and was initially assigned to the SS anti-tank replacement company. Promoted to SS-Obersturmführer d.R. on October 29, 1940 he came to the SS-Totenkopf-Reiterstandarte in June 1940 and in early 1941 served as a platoon leader. In May 1941 he moved to the anti-aircraft replacement unit in Unna and when the first Flak unit was formed for the Kommandostab "Reichsführer-SS," he became a battery chief. He led this unit subordinated to the SS-Kavallerie-Brigade and when the SS-Kavallerie-Division was formed his unit served as partial cadre. He led this newly expanded Flak Abteilung from November 1942 to April 1943. Promoted to SS-Hauptsturmführer d.R. on March 16, 1942 he taught at several Flak schools from November 1943 to March 1944. In March 1944 he took command of the Flak Abteilung of the 19.Waffen-Grenadier-Division der SS (lettische Nr.2). His final command was Flak Abteilung 550 which was a component of V.SS-Gebirgs-Korps attached to the 32.SS-Freiwilligen-Grenadier-Division "30. Januar." He led this detachment from March 1945 until the end of the war and died in 1973. (Photo: BDC)

Walking in front from left are Kurt Knoblauch, Heinrich Himmler and Hermann Fegelein during an inspection by Himmler of the Kommandostab "Reichsführer-SS." (Photo: Jost Schneider)

on the positioning of the enemy cavalry squadron and the events of the last month, the officers of the Regiment were sure that the Russian cavalry formation had been in contact with the partisan elements located in Turov and Sosny.

In his report SS-Standartenführer Lombard praised the leadership abilities of Waldemar Fegelein and the commander of 4th Squadron, SS-Kavallerie-Regiment 1, SS-Obersturmführer Hermann Gadischke. Gadischke was noted as an excellent teacher who trained his troops well in Poland. The low casualties and the high success rate of the operations of the Regiment were credited to these training operations.

SS-Hauptsturmführer Waldemar Fegelein, commander of 1st Squadron, SS-Kavallerie-Regiment 1 and temporary commander of that regiment for the latter phase of the Pripet marshes actions for which he won the Iron Cross 1st class. (Photo: National Archives)

SS-Kavallerie-Regiment 2 and Operation "Turov"
August 15 to 21, 1941

As stated previously, SS-Kavallerie-Regiment 2 began the second combing-through operation of the Pripet marshes on August 15th. Situated on the southern flank of the SS-Kavallerie-Brigade, SS-Kavallerie-Regiment 2 began its eastward trek from David-Gorodec and Mosyr. What was to be a routine operation for the Regiment quickly threw them off-guard and briefly forced a radical change in planning.

To begin this second operation, 3rd Squadron of SS-Kavallerie-Regiment 2 was positioned furthest right and ordered to depart in an easterly direction from David-Gorodek during the evening of August 15th. As they approached the outskirts of Zapiesocze and Turov early in the morning on the 16th, the unit came upon a group of partisans which immediately engaged them in heated street fighting. During the opening phases of the battle, 3rd Squadron suffered one killed and two wounded. As the fighting continued, the partisan groups in the surrounding areas brought in massive reinforcements. Before noon arrived, the enemy was shelling the Squadron with several pieces of artillery and mortars as well as forcing them to take cover with heavy machine gun fire. During the fight, the Germans suffered another man killed, two missing in action and another seven wounded, while the partisan losses were estimated at 107 men killed. Despite their relative success, the Squadron leaders decided to retreat to Marjanpole and call for reinforcements citing a lack of ammunition and the fact that they were greatly out-numbered.

Estimates of the strength of the partisan units varied. One report cited the strength of the partisans to be between 400 and 600 men. Another estimated their number to be 700 men, two-thirds of which were civilians and the remaining one-third uniformed Russian soldiers.[100]

The commander of the Mounted Detachment (Reitende Abteilung) of SS-Kavallerie-Regiment 2, SS-Sturmbannführer Franz Magill, who was in charge of the rider squadrons (Squadrons 1-3) and the 4th Machine Gun Squadron, was up to this time busy training horses with his men in Lachwa.[101] After receiving reports about the engagement which occurred earlier that day, he reacted immediately by ordering a platoon of 1st Squadron and two platoons of the 4th Squadron to reinforce the 3rd Squadron in Marjanpole so that squadron could resume the fight. The two platoons of the 4th Squadron did not reach Marjanpole, however, as they became bogged down in the swamps on route. Shortly afterwards SS-Sturmbannführer Magill himself went to Marjanpole so he could receive first-hand reports from the returning 3rd Squadron. In Marjanpole, Magill met up with the commander of SS-Kavallerie-Regiment 2, SS-Standartenführer Heino Hierthes, who was busy assessing the situation. Upon the return of the 3rd Squadron, he immediately ordered the 3rd Squadron commander, SS-Hauptsturmführer Hans-Viktor von Zastrow, back to the eastern edge of Marjanpole to defend against a possible pursuit by the partisans. He also sent reconnaissance patrols towards the south up to the line between Chilozyce and Jozek.[102] Regimental commander Hierthes assessed the situation as follows.

Since the enemy was in possession of heavy infantry weapons (heavy machine guns, grenade launchers and possibly a few light field cannons), Hierthes thought it best to postpone an attack until heavier weapons arrived. He immediately ordered three anti-tank guns and all available ammunition for these weapons to be sent to Marjanpole. At this time all mortars were in transport to another location, so they could not be supplied to his units. Hierthes also determined that since Russian fighter planes had shown up over the towns of Luniniec, Zcuczewicze and Lachva, lighting the sky with flares during the previous two nights, the 400 to 600 man strong band of partisans must be in communication with Russian units located further east. In a report that he made on

[100] Information from various situation and tactical reports including: "Tätigkeitsbericht für die Zeit vom 14.-17.8.1941." to the Kommandostab "Reichsführer-SS" Abt. Ia, dated August 18, 1941 and signed by SS-Sturmbannführer Hermann Fegelein, "Aufklärungsergebnis bei SS-Kav.-Rgt. 2" to the SS-Kav.-Brig., dated August 19, 1941 and "Tätigkeitsbericht für die Zeit vom 18.-21.8.1941." to the Kommandostab "Reichsführer-SS" Abt. Ia in Arys, signed by SS-Obersturmführer Rudolf Maeker and dated August 21, 1941.

[101] Magill's units were not engaged at this time nor was it initially foreseen that they would take part in the second operation in the Pripet marshes.

[102] "Lagebericht beim SS-Kav.-Regiment 2 vom 15./16.8.41," dated August 16, 1941 and signed SS-Standartenführer Heino Hierthes.

The main road through Bobruisk, September 8, 1941. (Yerger Archives)

August 16th, Hierthes considered the band of partisans a major threat to the supply lines that reached XXXV.Armeekorps and recommended an immediate attack by the Luftwaffe to destroy the city. Hierthes himself postponed any further operations by his units until the situation could be discussed with either the Higher SS and Police Leader or the Ia of the Army Group "Center" rear area command.[103]

On August 17th, SS-Standartenführer Hermann Fegelein met with Higher SS and Police Leader Erich von dem Bach and his Ia at regimental headquarters in Lachva to discuss the circumstances surrounding the events of the previous day. Shortly following the meeting Fegelein regrouped the units of SS-Kavallerie-Regiment 2 in response to the situation. The 2nd, 3rd, 5th and 6th Squadrons, one platoon of the 1st Squadron, two platoons of the 4th Squadron, the regiment's assigned artillery battery and the Bicycle Reconnaissance Detachment were all sent to Marjanpole while 1st Squadron (with the exception of one platoon) was sent to Lachva and the remaining platoons of 4th Squadron sent to Mokroc.[104]

The Pripet marshes posed many problems for any transport operations, especially those of motorized units. Hard dirt roads were virtually non-existent in those areas and the troops found themselves trudging through the mud on narrow paths that appeared as major highways on their maps. These poor conditions caused numerous delays and relatively short distances required hours to travel. Also, the large number of river crossings undertaken by the units slowed down operational progress even further. Ferries were small and could only transport a minimal amount of men and munitions in one trip. In one case it took 20 hours for the artillery batteries of the regiments to complete a single crossing.[105]

As the troops were busy moving to their assigned positions, plans for the attack were developing. SS-Standartenführer Hermann Fegelein showed up at SS-Kavallerie Regiment 2 headquarters on the 19th to observe the planning as well as the coming battle itself. It was decided that the attack would take place on August 21st. The primary objectives were cited as the capture of Zapiesocze and Turov along with the "complete annihilation" of the enemy units located there.[106] It was also

---

[103] ibid.

[104] "Tätigkeitsbericht für die Zeit vom 14.-17.8.1941," dated August 18, 1941.

[105] "Gefechtsbericht über Unternehmen Turow," dated August 22, 1941 and signed by SS-Standartenführer Heino Hierthes.

[106] This quoted wording of the order was elaborated upon in many reports. The regimental commander of SS-Kavallerie-Regiment 2 made it very clear to the troops that they were to "completely annihilate" the partisans as opposed to simply attacking them and forcing them to retreat. This required the units to completely surround and seal-off all neighboring areas.

decided that the towns of Czernice and Pohost, which were located further east would also be taken as well. The following units were initially chosen to conduct the operation: [107]

1) The Reitende Abteilung of SS-Kavallerie-Regiment 2 (consisting of its 1st through 4th Squadrons)

2) One platoon from the 5th Squadron of SS-Kavallerie-Regiment 2

3) 6th Squadron of SS-Kavallerie-Regiment 2

4) The artillery batteries of SS-Kavallerie-Regimenter 1 and 2

5) Engineer units (it was not yet decided which) with cannon boats armed with deck mounted anti-tank guns

6) Motorized portions of the Reconnaissance Detachment consisting of eight officers and 134 men equipped with twelve light machine guns, four heavy machine guns and one anti-tank gun platoon

The Germans had every intention of carrying out their goal of "completely annihilating" the partisan units and set forth to construct a complete as well as precise plan which would result in a very successful operation. The partisans remained active by continually shelling Mariampol and Wieresnica with light artillery fire from August 16th to the 19th. At that time the available German units continually reconnoitered the surrounding area without results. On the evening of the 19th several units began to arrive in Mariampol starting with the anti-tank gun platoon led by SS-Untersturmführer Arthur Kessler. Next to arrive was a much needed shipment of heavy grenade launchers which were transported by truck from Grabov. Several units of 5th Squadron started arriving at 0100 hours on the 20th while the artillery battery of SS-Kavallerie-Regiment 1 did not arrive until 2000 hours after an 18 hour march.[108] Since the attack was to begin at 0400 hours the next day, that gave the men only six hours to rest and then prepare for a major attack that would last the entire next day.

During the morning hours of August 20th, the staff of SS-Kavallerie-Regiment 2 prepared its new command post in Mariampol. The actual move from Lachva proceeded that afternoon with the regimental commander, SS-Standartenführer Heino Hierthes, arriving at 1500 hours.[109]

That afternoon Hierthes issued orders outlining the operation.[110] He designated the majority of his regiment as components of the operation which would commence on August 21, 1941. The orders clearly stated the objective of the operation as the annihilation of the partisan forces in Turov and Zapiesocze. 1st Squadron, strengthened by a heavy machine gun and two anti-tank weapons, was to assume a pre-attack position in the area of Hill 133 (one kilometer west of Jozek) until 0300 hours during which it prepared for its attack on the southern edge of Turov. A recently identified partisan artillery piece in the wooded area east of Jozek was to be taken in a surprise attack at 0400 hours in conjunction with securing the secondary road leading from Turov to Storozowce. Holding this line would prevent any enemy withdrawal while allowing the unit to protect the flank of the regiment's troops from Choczen to Storozowce. 2nd Squadron was to be located in Wieresnicz after 0300 hours, serving as the operational reserve and reinforced with a heavy machine gun platoon and an anti-tank gun.

3rd Squadron was strengthened with a mortar platoon, an anti-tank gun, a heavy machine gun platoon and an infantry gun platoon. Assuming its attack launch point at 0300 hours on the outermost perimeter of the operational sector, it was given the assignment of leading the assault on the

---

[107] "Gefechtsbericht über die Kampfhandlungen in und um Turow," dated August 29, 1941 and signed by SS-Standartenführer Hermann Fegelein.

[108] Information from various situation and tactical reports including: "Gefechtsbericht über die Kampfhandlungen in und um Turow" and "Gefechtsbericht über Unternehmen Turow."

[109] ibid.

[110] The details of the order outlined in this and following paragraphs were recorded in "Regimentsbefehl," SS-Kav.-Rgt. 2, Ia Hi./Sch., dated August 20, 1941 and signed by SS-Standartenführer Heino Hierthes.

Shown during early formation of the SS-Kavallerie-Division after May 1942 are, from right, Albert Faßbender, Karl Gesele (with German Cross in Gold), Franz Rehbein (background), Dr. Edwin Jung and Hermann Fegelein (background). Gesele is also shown as an SS-Obersturmbann-führer with Knight's Cross won for command of the Sturmbrigade "Reichsführer-SS." Born August 15, 1912, in Riedlingen, Gesele joined the SS in August 1931 with 13.Standarte. Two years later he moved to the Political Readiness Detachment "Wurttemburg," which became part of Regiment "Deutschland," and was commissioned an SS-Untersturmführer on March 25, 1934. He served with 9., 10. and 17./Deutschland until early December 1936. After next being posted as adjutant of IV./"Deutschland" he was promoted to SS-Obersturmführer on January 30, 1937. Gesele then commanded 10./"Deutschland" from May 1938 to August 1940 and was promoted to SS-Hauptsturmführer on June 30, 1939. He won both Iron Crosses in the Polish campaign. Moving next to SS-Junkerschule Bad Tölz he served as a tactics instructor until May 1941 when he took command of a teaching group at the facility. He was assigned Ia to the Brigade in September 1941 and continued in that position with the later division as well until replaced due to illness in August 1942. Promoted to SS-Sturmbannführer on January 30, 1942, he won the German Cross in Gold on May 25, 1942, undoubtedly for his service as Brigade Ia. From February 1943 to October 1943 he commanded the Sturmbrigade "Reichsführer-SS" and was promoted to SS-Obersturmbannführer on June 21, 1943. For his leadership of the Sturmbrigade in Corsica he was awarded the Knight's Cross on July 4, 1944 and probably led the reformed Begleit Bataillon "Reichsführer-SS" during 1944. He then led SS-Panzer-Grenadier-Regiment 35 of the 16.SS-Panzer-Grenadier-Division "Reichsführer-SS" until the end of 1944. In early 1945 he took command of the 37.SS-Freiwilligen-Kavallerie-Division "Lützow." He also commanded the SS-Kavallerie Schule Göttingen for a short period in 1945. Gesele had a natural gift for tactics and was liked by all superiors throughout his career. He survived the war and died in 1968. (Photos: Jost Schneider and Jess Lukens)

outskirts of Zapiesocze following a preparatory artillery barrage by the cavalry artillery batteries. The bombardment was to begin at 0400 hours and continue until enemy artillery fire was suppressed. After reaching this initial objective, the Squadron, along with the other regimental components, were to continue their attack into the town proper under cover of their infantry support weapons. The artillery batteries were to then redirect their combined firepower on Turov.

A support element of anti-tank guns, designated as Group "Pripet," was ordered to add heavy support from motorized pontoons on the river bordering the marshes. Using the start of the artillery barrage as their signal to open fire, these guns were to direct their barrage against pre-designated targets and then provide additional support within their gun range to the individual attack squadrons. A second tactical support unit consisting of Group "Rosenfeldt"[111] and the anti-tank unit under SS-Obersturmführer Peter van Vessen were to prevent the enemy from making a river crossing on the northern bank of the Pripet river.

The engineer platoon was to load two anti-tank guns on a high-speed armored boat (Schnellboot) along with a motorized pontoon and quickly cross the Pripet river in front of the hill before Pohost. After the surprise attack took effect, the platoon was to land and take Pohost, denying the partisans a path to the east.

Group "Fritsche"[112] was assigned to reach Zytkowicze before 1200 hours. Then, under the protection of other units, Fritsche and his men were to march to the east and northeast of Zytkowicze and then on to Kolno. There they were to secure the bridge from Borki to Kolno over the Skrepicza river. Following this, reconnoitering operations were to be conducted in Borki. Should these operations reveal weak partisan forces, the group was to immediately engage and destroy them. In the event that the partisan forces were strong, the group was to hold them at their current position. In any case, the units were to prevent any escape by the partisans into the forests north of the Pripet by concentrating heavy fire from the flank formed before the forest's edge towards the west.

Armored patrol cars (Panzerspähwagen) under the leadership of SS-Untersturmführer Rudolf Wappler were to be driven to the 3rd Squadron after Zapiesocze had been successfully penetrated. After the city was taken the armored cars were to be used for reconnoitering the vicinity of Storozowcze.

Regimental headquarters for the operation were to be situated in Wieresnica until 0300 hours on August 21st when they were to be moved into the city of Mariampol. The field dressing station was to remain in Wieresnica while a hospital ship was located in David-Gorodek for collecting the wounded.

As elaborated upon earlier and as clearly stated in summary of the regimental orders, the main goal of the attack was not only to secure the city of Turov, but also to "completely annihilate" the partisans gathered there. In order to insure their destruction, the door was shut to every possible escape route which boxed-in the partisans.

In this respect, careful preparation by the leader of the Army special engineer unit (Pionier Sonder Kommando), Oberfeldwebel (staff sergeant) Rosenfeldt, insured the success of the engineers. For their part of the operation, Rosenfeldt and his men were to remain on the bank of the Pripet river and utilize their anti-tank gun in an artillery mode, shelling the towns east of Turov. Simultaneously, his presence on the Pripet river was to prevent the escape of partisans to the north. However, to the east of the suburb of Pohost an escape route was left open. To seal off this section, it was later decided that a special "shock" troop under the leadership of SS-Untersturmführer Friedrich Maletta would be formed from men of his engineer platoon. Maletta's assignment was to quickly capture the south coast of the Pripet from the north and secure the suburb of Pohost. These moves were to prevent the partisans from escaping to the east. Available for this assignment were two motorized boats, each equipped with an anti-tank gun.[113]

---

[111] Under the command of Army Oberfeldwebel Rosenfeldt, this unit mounted anti-tank guns to some of their pontoon boats.

[112] In other reports referred to as a mixed motorized unit of the SS-Advance Detachment or SS-VA.

[113] Information from various situation and tactical reports including: "Gefechtsbericht über die Kampfhandlungen in und um Turow" and "Gefechtsbericht über Unternehmen Turow."

Staff headquarters of the Brigade in Bobruisk, September 8, 1941. (Yerger Archives)

Other operations to prohibit the escape of the partisans were also outlined to avert a retreat to the north in the direction of Zytkowicze. This would be accomplished by closing off the area south of Kolno, know as the Skrepicza sector, by a special motorized unit of SS-Kavallerie-Regiment 1. Under the leadership of SS-Obersturmführer Karl Fritsche, it is also referred to as Group "Fritsche" in regimental orders. This make-shift unit consisted of some 150 men the artillery battery of SS-Kavallerie-Regiment 1 and several components of the Advance Detachment.[114]

Even before all of the units arrived or the final orders for the attack had been issued, the forward battery commanders reached their positions at dawn on August 20th so that they could continue reconnoitering the surrounding area. Until that time all reconnaissance reports had been negative with no enemy movements noticed. Unfortunately, last minute patrols managed to reveal several partisan groups which caused Hierthes to slightly alter his plans. The cities of Jozek and Choczen, which were reported on August 16th to be partisan-free, were now occupied. The most accurate

Units of the Brigade using barges to cross the Pripet river in September 1941. (Yerger Archives)

---

[114] "Gefechtsbericht über die Kampfhandlungen in und um Turow."

report noted a cannon and 20 men in a forest just outside of Jozek. Conducting further reconnaissance operations in the towns of Storozowce, Siemuradoze, Slepce and Ozierany proved impossible due to prohibitive road conditions. In view of this, the commander could only assume that the partisans, in anticipation of an attack by the Germans, had occupied these towns as well. Such an action would have provided them with the option of retreating southwards into the wooded areas in the direction of Ozierany.[115]

Continuing with the theme of "encircle and annihilate," modifications to Hierthe's original attack plans were initiated immediately with all escape routes having to be sealed off. It was decided that as the attack opened, a fast assault unit would speed south through Turov and capture the escape route leading south. Further actions to the south (such as a swinging encirclement) could not be planned because the land south of Jozek was reported as completely impassable. There was no chance that heavy weapons could be brought up in this sector.[116]

The Attack

The operation opened as planned on the morning of August 21st. At 0400 hours the artillery batteries of SS-Kavallerie-Regimenter 1 and 2 opened heavy fire on Zapiesocze from their assigned positions on either side of the road between Mariampol and Turov. Meanwhile, as the shelling of Zapiesocze proceeded, 3rd Squadron advanced towards the town. As they approached, the Squadron shot off red flares, signaling that the artillery fire was to be directed further towards Turov. At precisely 0420 hours the Squadron opened the attack on the town with the armored cars supporting the lead platoon. At the outskirts of Zapiesocze the group encountered strong partisan forces and only after a heated fight did they manage to break into the town. It was there that the Squadron engaged in brutal street fighting and forced to take cover to avoid the partisan's solidly effective rifle fire, grenade throwers and anti-tank guns.[117]

1st Squadron reached their assigned goals. Their first movement took them from their starting position on Hill 133 (one kilometer west of Jozek) at 0400 hours through Jozek and on to Choczen and Storozowce. They met virtually no resistance and proceeded to mop up both towns, set them ablaze and move on. Shortly after they received the signal to cease firing on Turov, the artillery batteries had switched their positions to the southern edge of Zapiesocze and opened fire on Choczen, Storozoce, Siemuradce, Czernicze and Slepce.

The 3rd Squadron continued fighting in Zapiesocze and took the town shortly before 0500 hours. The fight for Turov then began. In a daring swinging movement, the left group under the command of SS-Hauptsturmführer Hans-Viktor von Zastrow, in spite of encountering very well prepared enemy fortifications, reached the eastern exit of Turov at 0650 hours.

From the beginning of the attack, Group "Pripet" supported the other units from the banks of the Pripet river which lay on the northern side of Turov by firing the anti-tank guns they had mounted on their pontoon boats. They also had various other armed vehicles but these were quickly put out of action by well-aimed fire from enemy infantry, partially equipped with machine guns and several anti-tank guns. The partisans had built up good fortifications which they armed with their relatively weak guns. From above, the pontoon boats were strafed by machine gun fire coming from a Russian airplane. Although the boats were hit several times, no casualties were taken.

Following the 3rd Squadron through Zapiesocze was the Brigade's Staff Reconnaissance Platoon. After towns were taken, this group searched all the houses and shortly thereafter set them on fire. During their rampage, they were attacked by a group of approximately 100 poorly armed partisans which had been overrun by 3rd Squadron. The platoon wiped out this remaining band of

---

[115] Information from various situation and tactical reports including: "Gefechtsbericht über die Kampfhandlungen in und um Turow" and "Gefechtsbericht über Unternehmen Turow."

[116] "Gefechtsbericht über Unternehmen Turow."

[117] All information regarding the fighting in and around Turow on August 21st from: "Gefechtsbericht über die Kampfhandlungen in und um Turow" and "Gefechtsbericht über Unternehmen Turow."

A bridge over the Dnjepr river destroyed by retreating Russian troops in September 1941. (Yerger Archives)

Hermann Fegelein (left) with Rudolf Maeker during the summer of 1942. (Photo: Jost Schneider)

partisans and afterwards destroyed all their weapons. At 0650 hours the eastern exit of Turov was reached.

Regimental Headquarters had been moved to Zapiesocze at 0505 hours from where the commanders watched the three white signal flares brighten the dawn lit sky. Turov and Zapiesocze were now in German hands.

After the most forward troops had reached the eastern exit of Turov, all available men in the surrounding areas were loaded onto Kübelwagen and brought forward to form new fighting groups and continue the fighting further east of Turov.

The engineer platoon reached Pohost at 0730 hours and pushed into the town. As they arrived, a partisan cavalry group, led by a Russian officer, was waiting for them. Fighting ensued and many of the cavalrymen fled. The officer was later found dead. Later, at about 0900 hours, the engineers was attacked by strong infantry fire and grenade throwers on the northern edge of Pohost. They were subsequently forced to retreat to the bank of the Pripet river. During the battle, two men of the platoon were seriously wounded and later died.

Meanwhile, the Staff Reconnaissance Platoon had proceeded to Dworzec, a suburb bordering the eastern edge of Turov, and burned it to the ground. While the town was in flames, one of the houses blew up. It had been used by the partisans to store large amounts of artillery munitions. It was then assumed that in the area in and around Dworzec an enemy artillery group had taken position. Group "von Zastrow" (led by SS-Hauptsturmführer Hans-Viktor von Zastrow) raced ahead and reached Czernicze at 0830 hours, Slepce at 0900 hours, Ozierany at 0930 hours and Pohost at 1130 hours. With the exception of Slepce, von Zastrow's group was forced to engage in brief but difficult fighting, especially at the river crossing between Slepce and Ozierany. In Ozierany, von

Zastrow and his men threw the partisans back towards the south and the remaining 80 to 100 of the enemy managed to escape into the forests there.

Back on the northern bank of the Pripet river, the men of the engineer unit were waiting to renew their attack on Pohost. Since they were beaten back across the river, they had kept busy preparing their anti-tank gun equipped pontoon boats for the next attack. The new plan was to again engage the enemy from the river bank in a frontal assault. This time, however, Group "von Zastrow," which had turned back from Ozierany for the fight in Pohost, would attack from the rear. After hard fighting, Pohost was finally taken at 1500 hours.

With the taking of Pohost, Operation "Turov" was over. Apart from the 80 to 100 partisans that managed to escape in Ozierany, the goal of "complete annihilation" of the partisans had been reached. The enemy suffered between 600 and 700 dead with only ten taken prisoner. SS-Kavallerie-Regiment 2 listed the highest number of casualties inflicted on the enemy: some 400 with the loss of only four men killed and 12 wounded.[118] The total German cavalry casualties were minimal with only six dead and 18 wounded.[119] Despite their numbers, fully adequate equipment and well-built and well-camouflaged bunkers, the irregular Russian units were no match for the mobility and firepower of the SS-Kavallerie-Brigade.

On August 29th, SS-Kavallerie-Regiment 1 was transferred to Morocz and immediately began engaging partisan groups located east of this village. During these engagements, the Regiment noted that as they would approach the partisans, they dispersed into small groups of two or three men and fled southeast. The enemy found it relatively easy to escape, and because of this, the operations here could not be registered as a complete success. Local residents reported that the majority of the remaining partisans could be found in the area north of the Lake Kniaz and the Regiment immediately set out in pursuit. Upon reaching this area, the Regiment located a partisan occupied farm situated in a forest. The Regiment immediately engaged it and as a result 100 of the enemy were killed. Three partisan officers captured were later executed.[120] Material recovered included several heavy machine guns and various communication equipment. After this battle the Regiment reported that there was nothing left of the partisan occupied areas southeast and east of Morocz.[121]

On August 30th, SS-Kavallerie-Regiment 1 departed east once again and during the following evening joined with those portions of the Kommandostab "Reichsführer-SS" that had advanced furthest east. All the bridges in this area were destroyed by partisans and it took 24 hours to effect repairs. On September 3rd, 2nd Squadron of SS-Kavallerie-Regiment 1 captured 54 Russian cavalry horses and turned them over to the veterinary company. The Regiment then resumed its eastwards march and reached the road between Bobruisk and Mosyr on September 6th.[122]

On August 28th, SS-Kavallerie-Regiment 2 received reports from local residents that the city of Petrikow was occupied by partisans. The Regiment was then sent marching on the road running between the Pripet river and Witezny while their forward most detachment was stationed in Dorchi. On September 2nd at 1300 hours, 3rd Squadron of SS-Kavallerie-Regiment 2 reached the small village of Petrikow without encountering any resistance. Statements by residents revealed that the partisans recognized the approaching cavalry squadron and fled to the south. Meanwhile, on August 29th, the remaining troops of the Regiment encountered an enemy band wearing German uniforms and equipped with German weapons. This partisan unit was completely destroyed during the encounter. On September 1st, the mounted troops reached Kopatkewitschi where the motorized

---

[118] SS-Kavallerie-Regiment 2, "Unternehmen Turow am 21.8.1941" signed by Regimentskommandeur Heino Hierthes.

[119] "Beute und Verlustmeldung," dated August 22, 1941 and signed by SS-Standartenführer Heino Hierthes.

[120] "Tätigkeitsbericht für die Zeit v. 30.8. - 5.9.1941," to the Abteilung Ia of the Kommandostab "Reichsführer-SS," dated September 5, 1941 and signed by SS-Obersturmführer Rudolf Maeker.

[121] "Kriegstagebuch Nr. 1 des Kommandostabs 'Reichsführer-SS.'"

[122] "Tätigkeitsbericht für die Zeit v. 30.8. - 5.9.1941."

The SS-Kavallerie-Brigade staff quarters in Mosyr, September 1941. (Yerger Archives)

portions of the Regiment were situated and remained there as terrain conditions were too poor to continue. On September 2nd the Regiment reported that Mosyr was occupied by guerrilla forces. During the early hours of the next day the reinforced 3rd Squadron was sent to the city with the task of occupying it. The results of this engagement were not recorded in any available document but the war diary of the Kommandostab "Reichsführer-SS" indicates that Mosyr was occupied by parts of the Brigade on September 4th.

During this week SS-Standartenführer Heino Hierthes was ordered back to Berlin and SS-Sturmbannführer Hermann Schleifenbaum assumed command of SS-Kavallerie-Regiment Regiment 2.[123] He retained official command for the remaining period the regiment was in Russia.

Between the August 28th and September 5th the Advance Detachment dispatched patrols daily which departed from Dorohi Stare and reconnoitered the areas north and south of the main road (Highway 1). The results of the probes revealed considerably weakening partisan forces. In some areas patrols penetrated enemy occupied areas south of Highway 1 as far as 25 kilometers without incident.

On August 31st orders arrived that the Advance Detachment which had originally been formed as a temporary unit would be made the Brigade's permanent reconnaissance unit. From that date it was restructured and officially redesignated while retaining its previous components, becoming the Bicycle Reconnaissance Detachment (Radfahr-Aufklärungsabteilung). SS-Sturmbannführer Albert Faßbender, previously commander of the Advance Detachment, was given permanent command of the unit and led it for the remainder of 1941. On September 1st the Detachment was sent marching to Bobruisk and two days later on to Mosyr.[124]

On September 1st the Brigade staff reached Ptitsch and met up with most of the forward components. Two ambulance platoons comprised of one officer with 40 NCOs and enlisted men were subordinated to the Brigade by staff order of the Kommandostab "Reichsführer-SS." On September 5th the Brigade reached the eastern line between the cities of Mosyr and Bobruisk. The dual operations in the Pripet marshes were reported by the Brigade to headquarters as completed.[125]

[123] "Tätigkeitsbericht für die Zeit v. 30.8. - 5.9.1941" and "Kriegstagebuch Nr. 1 des Kommandostabs 'Reichsführer-SS.'"

[124] "Tätigkeitsbericht für die Zeit v. 30.8. - 5.9.1941."

[125] "Kriegstagebuch Nr. 1 des Kommandostabs 'Reichsführer-SS'" and "Abschlußmeldung der SS-Kav.Brigade über die Befriedung der Pripet-Sümpfe," dated September 18, 1941 and signed by SS-Standartenführer Hermann Fegelein.

In a report summarizing the conclusion of the operations in the Pripet marshes written by SS-Standartenführer Hermann Fegelein it is interesting to note how he describes the fighting characteristics of the Russian partisans:[126]

"Enemy forces were always annihilated when they consisted of regular Russian Army troops. The greatest difficulties were posed by the partisans. They are militarily the most dangerous threat that there could be behind a fighting army. Cold-blooded, brave until annihilated and asiatically cruel. The opponent forces our units to constantly be alert due to their wide stretching organization and their excellent communication network. Their knowledge of the terrain, their continuous obstruction of all paths through the laying of mines and the blowing of bridges, their ability to quickly dig-in and form machine gun nests at strategically advantageous locations and their calmness during difficult fighting in the swamps characterize their fighting abilities."

On September 5th, the men of the Brigade were awarded 36 Iron Crosses of the 2nd class as well as one Iron Cross 1st class which was given to the commander of SS-Kavallerie-Regiment 1, SS-Sturmbannführer Gustav Lombard.[127]

East Towards Rshev and 9.Armee

After the conclusion of the pacification operations in the Pripet marshes the Brigade was given it's next task on September 7th. This assignment called for the Brigade to conduct pacification operations in the area between the Dnjepr and Pripet rivers and the line between Retschiza and Ptitsch. Specifics of this plan instructed the Brigade to deploy SS-Kavallerie-Regiment 1 together with the Reconnaissance Detachment on the left flank and the SS-Kavallerie-Regiment 2 on the right flank. This operation was to be conducted by the Brigade without support from other elements of the Kommandostab "Reichsführer-SS."[128]

To initiate these operations, the reconnaissance elements were dispatched immediately to their assigned villages. The reconnaissance group of SS-Kavallerie-Regiment 1 was sent to Rjetschita and the group belonging to SS-Kavallerie-Regiment 2 went to Mosyr. On September 7th SS-Standartenführer Hermann Fegelein departed for Mosyr. During reconnaissance actions, SS-Kavallerie-Regiment 1 reported the residents from the area of Krassnyi Ostroff gave statements about a partisan group with a strength of between 400 and 500 men. This group, supposedly led by Russian army officers, was equipped with heavy weapons and maintained an ammunition dump. To pursue this group the Reconnaissance Detachment was sent to Choiniki on the 8th. The next day they departed from the south heading north to Krassnyi Ostroff while two battle groups (Kampfgruppen) from SS-Kavallerie-Regiment 1 were sent from the north.[129] On September 10th the five separate fighting components had surrounded the partisans in Krassnyi Ostroff and were ready to destroy them. Combat began that night and ended quickly. After the engagement 38 regular Russian soldiers were taken prisoner while 384 partisans were confirmed dead. The Germans suffered no troop casualties but two horses were killed and 19 more wounded.[130] It is interesting to note that SS-Gruppenführer Erich von dem Bach, the Higher SS and Police leader of the

---

[126] "Abschlußmeldung der SS-Kav.Brigade über die Befriedung der Pripet-Sümpfe."

[127] "Tätigkeitsbericht für die Zeit v. 6. - 12. 9. 1941," an den Kommandostab "Reichsführer-SS" Abt. Ia in Arys, dated September 12, 1941 and signed by SS-Obersturmführer Rudolf Maeker.

[128] "Tätigkeitsbericht für die Zeit v. 6. - 12. 9. 1941" and "Kriegstagebuch Nr. 1 des Kommandostabs 'Reichsführer-SS.'"

[129] The use of Battle Groups (Kampfgruppen) was a standard practice in all German WWII ground units. Composed of specialized (or readily available) equipment and personnel, their flexibility added considerably to success in countless smaller or emergency operations. Larger Kampfgruppen were often formed from remnants of divisions after heavy losses or when the primary elements left the front for rest and refit. See James Lucas, "Battle Group!, German Kampfgruppen Action of World War Two" for detailed histories of some of these units.

[130] "Tätigkeitsbericht für die Zeit v. 6. - 12. 9. 1941."

Staff conference in Russia during the autumn of 1941. From right are Karl Gesele (Ia) (unfolding map), with cigar in hand Gustav Lomnard (commander SS-Kavallerie-Regiment 1) and Hermann Fegelein (commander SS-Kavallerie-Brigade). (Photo: National Archives)

area, participated in the fighting from September 8th to the 12th and even led several air reconnaissance missions with his Fieseler-Storch.[131]

On September 9th the Brigade moved its headquarters to Choiniki while the staff of SS-Kavallerie-Regiment 1 with the Bicycle Reconnaissance Detachment were located in Retschiza and SS-Kavallerie-Regiment 2 in Jurewitschi.[132] A presentation of the Iron Cross 1st class by the rear area commander for Army Group "Center" was made to SS-Hauptsturmführer Waldemar Fegelein (commander of 1st Squadron, SS-Kavallerie-Regiment 1) on September 11th.[133]

On September 12th the area securing operations continued. SS-Kavallerie-Regiment 1 and SS-Kavallerie-Regiment 2 set out for a sector south of the line between Choiniki and Rurewitschi. During transport over the Pripet river, four men from 3rd Squadron, SS-Kavallerie-Regiment 2 drowned. During the continued advance, skirmishes with partisans revealed their fighting technique once again. As larger groups were encountered by the German units, the partisans would disperse into smaller units, lay mines and demolish bridges. They were also successful in disrupting supply lines. Other larger actions, such as attacking villages, became less frequent for the Brigade.[134]

[131] Ibid. Von den Bach's command encompassed the area behind Army Group "Center." That HSSPF position was later redesignated to reflect its geographical area and became HSSPF Russland-Mitte (mid-Russia).

[132] "Kriegstagebuch Nr. 1 des Kommandostabs 'Reichsführer-SS.'"

[133] "Tätigkeitsbericht für die Zeit v. 6. - 12. 9. 1941."

[134] ibid.

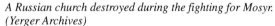

A Russian church destroyed during the fighting for Mosyr.
(Yerger Archives)

Aerial view of the Brigade headquarters at Choiniki, September 1941. (Yerger Archives)

After the annihilation of the mixed partisan/Russian army group around Krassnyi Ostroff the Regiments continued the pacification operations in designated areas.[135] During the evening of September 13th a general line connecting the towns of Krunki, Sawitschi, Tjatki, Rutschajewka, Cholmytsch, all the way to Rjetschitza was reached.

On September 15th SS-Brigadeführer Kurt Knoblauch held a discussion with Reichsführer-SS Heinrich Himmler about the actions of the SS-Kavallerie-Brigade. Himmler stated that the Brigades[136] were the only forces of the SS that were still available for mopping up operations in the rear areas. He therefore ordered that there would be no discussion about actions on the front. Higher SS and Police Leader Erich von dem Bach was informed of this decision.[137]

On September 16th the Flak Abteilung (Anti-Aircraft Detachment) "Ost" was subordinated to the Kommandostab "Reichsführer-SS" and sent to Truppenübungsplatz Arys-Süd (Troop Training Area in South Arys) by order of the SS-Führungshauptamt. On September 17th the Kommandostab's 2nd Ambulance Platoon (without its 3rd Group) was assigned to the SS-Kavallerie-Brigade.[138]

A now rare fight for a town erupted during the night of September 16th/17th after SS-Kavallerie-Regiment 2 had withdrawn west of Mosyr. The fight started when the city was fired on by partisan machine gunners in the hilly city outskirts but results of this skirmish were not recorded in the weekly tactical and situational report.[139]

On September 16th parts of the Reconnaissance Detachment were with SS-Kavallerie-Regiment 1 in Rjetschitza, portions with SS-Kavallerie-Regiment 2 in Jurewitschi while the remaining groups were in Choiniki. While situated in these towns plans were made based on partisan troop location intelligence ascertained by reconnaissance patrols. Pacification actions began on the 17th and successfully concluded the following day. The taking of two partisan camps that served as staff quarters for the partisan leaders (reportedly regular Russian army officers) were reported as a major coup. The first camp was located and taken by 2nd Squadron of SS-Kavallerie-Regiment 1 on the 17th. This camp was located on the so-called "Red Island" (a center of partisan activity) in the vicinity of Wischkoff -Buritzkaja. It was well camouflaged, strongly fortified and well equipped. 3rd Squadron of SS-Kavallerie-Regiment 1 found the second partisan camp on the 18th and took it

---

[135] "Tätigkeitsbericht für die Zeit vom 13. - 19. 9. 1941," an den Kommandostab "Reichsführer-SS" Abt. Ia in Arys, dated September 19, 1941 and signed by SS-Obersturmführer Rudolf Maeker.

[136] That is the 1st and 2nd SS-Infanterie-Brigade as well as the SS-Kavallerie-Brigade. Though not mentioning it, the Kommandostab also had the Begleit Bataillon "Reichsführer-SS" for operational deployment.

[137] "Kriegstagebuch Nr. 1 des Kommandostabs 'Reichsführer-SS.'" It is assumed Himmler's objections were a result of requests for "his" units by front line Army commanders.

[138] ibid.

[139] "Tätigkeitsbericht für die Zeit vom 13. - 19. 9. 1941."

the same day. This base was located on the road between Mosyr and Rjetschitza. Reports from this action indicate that much material was recovered after the operation.[140]

Elsewhere during the night of the 17th/18th the bridge crossing over the Usa river between Gomel and Rjetschitza was destroyed. The bridge served as a supply line for the Brigade from Gomel. During the night of the 18th/19th a collective farm leader, who had been appointed by the German occupying government, was murdered by partisans. This happened in a village occupied by an entire German regiment and smaller units of the Wehrmacht. The Germans were shocked at the audacity of the partisans to undertake such a coup and their ability to execute it.[141] On September 19th, 96 recruits arrived for the Brigade from the SS-Kavallerie-Ersatz-Abteilung (SS cavalry replacement detachment) on order of the SS-Führungshauptamt.[142]

On September 22nd the Brigade ended its most recent mopping-up operations and was assigned to pacification operations in the Dnjepr-Szos area. It was reported to the Kommandostab "Reichsführer-SS" that 42 Partisans had been shot, while 16 were taken prisoner including a special prize: the capture of Russian General Michael Rumanof.[143]

After the final sector pacification and annihilation of all partisan groups in the regions of Mosyr and where the Pripet, Dnjepr and the Lojew rivers meet, SS-Kavallerie-Regiment 1 gathered around Rjetschitza and SS-Kavallerie-Regiment 2 in the Lojew area. The Reconnaissance Detachment was transferred from Choiniki to Rjetschitza. The vehicle repair company (Werkstattkompanie) and the veterinary unit were sent to Gomel. Retreating partisan groups had reportedly gathered in the triangular area formed by connecting the towns of Gomel, Rjetschitza and Lojew. On September 24th the Brigade began its crossing of the Dnjepr river in the area west and south of Gomel. The next day the Brigade reported pacifying the local area and the advance units have completed crossing the river. They then continued their march in the direction of Gomel while conducting operations on both sides of their march route. On September 26th the most advanced troops of the Brigade were 20 kilometers west and south of Gomel performing securing operations. During these operations they encountered several small partisan groups which they fought and destroyed. They also managed to uncover several hidden ammunition and equipment dumps which they destroyed. The Brigade reported shooting 280 partisans and 87 criminals during these two actions and on September 27th they continued to conduct intrusions in occupied areas where they managed to capture a further eleven regular Russian soldiers and thirteen partisans. On September 28th, the main forces of the Brigade gathered around Gomel while the Brigade headquarters were transferred to Rjetschitza. The gathering in Gomel was completed on September 30th and after receiving their orders SS-Kavallerie-Regimenter 1 and 2 moved on to their assigned positions.[144]

On September 28th the Bicycle Reconnaissance Detachment began river crossing operations over the Dnjepr. While waiting to ford the river, the Detachment put their time to good use with training exercises in close-combat, sharp shooting and reconnaissance patrol operations.[145]

The Brigade administrative officer's section of the weekly tactical and situational report for this time period notes the difficulties in supplying the troops in these areas. Apparently the weather was dry so that the making the long marches was not as difficult as it was in the muddy and very wet conditions in the swamps, but the lack of vehicles posed special problems. As a result of this vehicle shortage, the supply troops had to cover their long routes as many as three times in what

---

[140] ibid.

[141] ibid.

[142] ibid.

[143] "Kriegstagebuch Nr. 1 des Kommandostabs 'Reichsführer-SS.'"

[144] "Tätigkeitsbericht für die Zeit vom 20. - 26. 9. 1941." an den Kommandostab "Reichsführer-SS" Abt. Ia in Arys, dated September 26, 1941 and signed by SS-Hauptsturmführer Karl Gesele and "Kriegstagebuch Nr. 1 des Kommandostabs 'Reichsführer-SS.' "

[145] "Tätigkeitsbericht für die Zeit vom 20. - 26. 9. 1941."

Left: A bridge across the Dnjepr river destroyed by the retreating Russians in early September 1941. After the initial panic of the German offensive, the Russians became adept at controlled retreat. Barges, such as the one on the water, helped the German advance but it was the work of combat engineers that was most responsible for continuing the advance despite such obstacles. (Yerger Archives) Right: Brigade troops unloading at the Pripet marshes. (Yerger Archives)

should have been single trips. These poor conditions forced the supply office to request a 30 ton truck column or their ability to supply the Brigade would be severely reduced.[146]

Corps order No. 55 arrived on September 29th and included a special directive for the Brigade to move to Toropez, some 200 kilometers north of Smolensk. There they were to meet up with the 403.Sicherheits Division (Security Division) to which they would be subordinated. The Brigade's Reconnaissance Detachment was ordered removed and attached to Kampfgruppe "von Roedern," a special strengthened regiment of the 403.Sicherheits Division that was to be subordinated to Army Group "Center." Orders also indicated that the upon the arrival of the Brigade in Toropez, Kampfgruppe "von Roedern" would be dissolved and replaced with the SS-Kavallerie-Brigade. Thereafter, the Brigade was to receive orders for a security operation, the details of which were not known at that time.

The Gomel area was the site for the Brigade's departure on October 1. The transport began by marching to Rogatschev where they loaded onto trains and rode to Orscha. After unloading they continued marching through Witebsk and on to Newel, a 180 kilometer journey. At Newel the Brigade, with the exception of its Reconnaissance Detachment that had already arrived, departed by train to Toropez. Due to the poor condition of the roads and lack of equipment for the transport and supply troops, the absence of the 30 ton trucks the Brigade had requested was especially felt. The transport operation was not to proceed without incident and on October 3rd the regimental physician of SS-Kavallerie-Regiment 1, SS-Obersturmführer Dr. Willy Nieswandt, was accidentally killed during train transport. All arrivals were to conclude on October 12th, at which time the Brigade was to be placed in reserve and subordinated to the Commander of Army Group "Center."[147] Contact with the XXIII.Armeekorps (a component of 9.Armee, Army Group "Center") had been established on October 6th. On September 29th the headquarters of the Brigade began its move to Witebsk which completed October 3rd when the HQ was fully operational. A few days later several trucks belonging to the Brigade staff, situated some 50 kilometers north of their headquarters, were fired upon by partisans and two wounded were reported. Brigade elements continued on towards Toropez on October 6.[148]

---

[146] ibid.

[147] Not to be confused with the rear area commander of Army Group "Center," this was the front line combat command.

[148] "Tätigkeitsbericht für die Zeit vom 27. 9. - 4. 10. 41." an den Kommandostab "Reichsführer-SS" Abt. Ia in Arys, dated October 5, 1941 and signed by SS-Standartenführer Hermann Fegelein, "Beitrag zum Tätigkeitsbericht v. 27. 9. - 4. 10. 41, Anlage 2." an den Abteilung Ia, dated October 4, 1941, "Tätigkeitsbericht für die Zeit vom 5. - 11. 10. 1941." an den Kommandostab "Reichsführer-SS" Abt. Ia in Arys, dated October 11, 1941 and signed by SS-Hauptsturmführer Karl Gesele and the "Kriegstagebuch des Kommandostabs der 'Reichsführer-SS' Nr. 1."

Left: A partial view of Gomel. (Yerger Archives) Right: Horses and men of the Brigade crossing the Dnjepr river on September 26, 1941, after the bridge to be used was destroyed. (Yerger Archives)

On October 7th 28 Iron Crosses of the 2nd class were awarded to men of the Brigade for the Pripet marshes actions.[149] SS-Hauptsturmführer Willi Plänk, now commanding 1st Squardon in the Reconnaissance Detachment, was awarded the Iron Cross 1st class.

In other rear area sectors of Army Group "Center" on October 7th the Bicycle Reconnaissance Detachment was assigned to secure the rail line between Weliki-Luki and Toropez while SS-Kavallerie-Regiment 2 was assigned to pacify the area on both sides of the road between Weliki-Luki and Toropez. During heavy fighting they killed 60 partisans, three of which were female. No German casualties were reported while several heavy machine guns and over 40 rifles were captured.[150]

On October 10th the Brigade established its new headquarters in Toropez. Two days later SS-Kavallerie-Regiment 2 departed for operations in the Newel area. By the 14th SS-Kavallerie-Regiment 1 and the Reconnaissance Detachment were located in Toropez while SS-Kavallerie-Regiment 2 was 30 kilometers northeast of Newel.[151]

A weekly situational and tactical report filed on October 18th reported that the Russians were situated on the entire front of the 9.Armee and had retreated from the forests and field positions east of Toropez and west of Rshev. In these areas small groups of troops were left behind and formed fighting groups which harassed supply lines passing through the forests around Toropez.[152]

The 500 kilometer transport operation to Toropez was finally concluded on October 15th, three days later than originally planned. Shortly afterwards the Brigade received orders from 9.Armee to pacify an area encompassing the rail line between Weliki-Luki and Rshev and a 9.Armee area border line connecting the towns of Luschnida (located 30 kilometers northwest of Toropez) and the southern point of Lake Ochwat. The area of responsibility extended as far as the road connecting Rshev and Lukowojkowa.

Contact was again established with XXIII.Armeekorps for the pacification operation which began after normal measures secured the rail line between Weliki-Luki and Rshev and the road connecting Toropez and Rshev. To commence these operations, the Brigade dispatched several reconnaissance patrols to confirm strong Russian forces which were assumed to be positioned between the north flank of 9.Armee in the Jeltzy area and the southern flank of the II.Armee in the

---

[149] "Tätigkeitsbericht für die Zeit vom 5. - 11. 10. 1941."

[150] "Tätigkeitsbericht für die Zeit v. 18.10. - 18.11.1941." an den Befehlshaber des Rückw. Heeresgebietes Mitte, dated November 21, 1941 and signed by SS-Standartenführer Hermann Fegelein. Even though the activities reported to do not fall within the report time frame, there are included in that report.

[151] "Kriegstagebuch des Kommandostabs der 'Reichsführer-SS' Nr. 1."

[152] "Tätigkeitsbericht für die Zeit vom 12. - 17. 10. 1941." an den Kommandostab "Reichsführer-SS" Abt. Ia in Arys, dated October 18, 1941 and signed by SS-Standartenführer Fegelein.

Loading Brigade vehicles at Rogatschev in the first week of October, 1941. (Yerger Archives)

vicinity of Lake Ochwat. While several patrols were reconnoitering their assigned areas, the main strength of the Brigade, its two Kavallerie-Regimenter, were positioned in the northern sector. The Bicycle Reconnaissance Detachment and the Army's partly motorized Wach Bataillon 705 were handed the task of securing the rail line and the road that ran in the direction of Rshev.[153]

Another partisan attack on a truck belonging to the Brigade staff was also reported. This time the truck was located 20 kilometers west of Toropez. The partisans managed to kill one man and wound four others. Several patrols were dispatched to protect the survivors and assure their safe return to headquarters.[154]

On October 18th the Brigade was spread out in the area of Toropez and formed a wide reaching front. Since no more partisan activity was reported, the Brigade resumed its trek to the east. Their new task was pacification of the northern rear area sector of 9.Armee. Due to favorable weather and resulting transport conditions, progress was reported as good until the 22nd when it began to rain heavily. After this date the Brigade was not unable to report any forward progress as the unpaved roads turned to mud and strained supply lines.[155]

When the rain began to fall SS-Kavallerie-Regiment 2 had reached the area north of Schatry and had just completed reconnoitering the entire area. SS-Kavallerie-Regiment 1 had passed through Dubno and Lugi while combing through the area south of Lake Ochwat. Due to problems with communication lines SS-Kavallerie-Regiment 1 received the order to stop some 18 hours too late. Because of this the Regiment had advanced into a completely uninhabited area with very difficult terrain. By this time the horses were exhausted and the Regiment had run out of rations and feed

[153] ibid.

[154] ibid.

[155] "Tätigkeitsbericht für die Zeit vom 18. - 24. 10. 1941." an den Kommandostab "Reichsführer-SS" Abt. Ia in Arys, dated October 18, 1941 and signed by SS-Hauptsturmführer Karl Gesele and "Tätigkeitsbericht für die Zeit v. 18.10. - 18.11.1941."

Although taken during the 1943 period of the later SS-Kavallerie-Division, this important photo shows two officers also connected to the Brigade during a significant event. On the right is SS-Standartenführer Fritz Freitag, former Ia of the Kommandostab "Reichsführer-SS" and then commanding the SS-Kavallerie-Division. On the left, just presented with the Knight's Cross, is long time commander of SS-Kavallerie-Regiment 1, SS-Standartenführer Gustav Lombard. (Photo: Jost Schneider)

making a return impossible. Because of this the staff of the Brigade decided to permit SS-Kavallerie-Regiment 1 to continue its march to the east in the hopes that it could reach the area west of Okowtzy where it was believed the road conditions were better and the Regiment would also have the possibility of obtaining food and water.[156]

A few days after the rain had done its damage, the supply conditions worsened considerably and the absence of the requested transport column was again noticeable. Supply lines were moved and after a transport lasting some twelve days, a shipment of rations and feed arrived, but only enough to last for some three days. Because the Brigade had not traveled as far east as projected, it was still supplied through Toropez and not Rshev as planned. Occupying Army troops were not set up in Rshev according to schedule as only three of fifty vehicles were capable of arriving in Rshev up to this time. The weather was very poor in this sector of the front and all operations were slowed considerably. Fortunately, reconnaissance patrols revealed no organized resistance in the surrounding area and the Brigade was forced to stop and wait for better weather or frost to set in.[157]

On or about October 25th, the Brigade was ordered by the Army Group "Center" rear area commander to cooperate with the 9.Armee to secure the road between Toropez and Rshev as a supply line. The Brigade ordered the Bicycle Reconnaissance Detachment to work alongside units of Wachbataillon 705 to complete this task. The order to secure the supply lines served little purpose because no transports were possible. Weather conditions had halted all forward progress of the Brigade since October 21st. It was viewed, however, that after the frost had arrived that the supply lines would again be opened for regular transport.[158]

The bad weather did not halt ongoing patrols by all three of the main components of the Brigade and several successful operations were recorded. SS-Kavallerie-Regiment 1, having been given the primary task of securing the supply line utilized by the XXIII.Armeekorps (the 102. and 253.Infanterie Division) connecting Rshev, Molodoy Tud and Szjelisharowo, was also given the secondary task of preventing partisan activity. To blunt this possibility, SS-Kavallerie-Regiment 1

---

[156] ibid.

[157] ibid.

[158] "Tätigkeitsbericht für die Zeit vom 25. - 31. 10. 1941." an den Kommandostab "Reichsführer-SS" Abt. Ia in Arys, dated November 1, 1941 and signed by SS-Hauptsturmführer Karl Gesele.

conducted 54 reconnaissance patrols in this area during the last weeks of October. SS-Kavallerie-Regiment 2 completed 20 anti-partisan patrols between October 21st and October 29th. These probes revealed a partisan group that was using a former Russian bunker as their headquarters which SS-Kavallerie-Regiment 2 later destroyed.

During the same period the Bicycle Reconnaissance Detachment was responsible for securing the road between Toropez and Jetkino. It conducted some 60 patrols south of the road to the rail line between Weliki-Luki and Rshev and several to the north.[159] During these patrols a combined total of 2,120 partisans and suspicious people were taken prisoner. Fegelein reported that these prisoners were "handled in the general way," although that was not elaborated upon.[160] Casualties in the Brigade were light and during the same period there was only one incident in which an exploding mine injured three men.[161] On October 28, 1941 the SS-Kavallerie-Brigade was officially subordinated to the rear area commander of Army Group "Center."[162]

Units of the Kommandostab "Reichsführer-SS"
Direct assigned units and field post (Feldpost) numbers in October 1941[163]

Chief: SS-Brigadeführer Kurt Knoblauch
First Staff Officer: SS-Sturmbannführer Ernst-August Rode[164]

Kommandostab[165]	40 600
Kradmeldezug (motorcycle dispatch platoon	"
Kartenstelle (cartographic section)	"
Nachrichtenkompanie (signals company)	31 757
Feldpost beim Kommandostab (postal section)	08 801
Polizei Nachrichtenkompanie 10[166]	33 243
SS-Kavallerie-Brigade	
Stab	17 771

---

[159] ibid.

[160] "Tätigkeitsbericht für die Zeit v. 18.10. - 18.11.1941." It is generally assumed they were executed. Actions of that type were often referred to in such superficial language during communications.

[161] "Kriegstagebuch des Kommandostabs der 'Reichsführer-SS' Nr. 1."

[162] ibid.

[163] SS-Führungshauptamt, Kommandoamt der Waffen-SS, Ic Tgb.Nr. 180/42 geh., dated January 10, 1942 as well as previous reports dated June, August and October 1941. Printed in Berlin, this list would have incorporated data received until late October 1941 but the reconnaissance detachment data for the Kavallerie-Brigade is missing and not added in the next list addendum of March 1942 (by which time it was completely destroyed), despite the fact it existed for several months previously by order of the SS-Führungshauptamt. Likewise SS-Infanterie-Regiment 14 is not listed. While these lists give a good overall indication of the units and composition assigned to the Kommandostab "Reichsführer-SS," as seen, Feldpost numbers are not always an accurate indication of the exact structure of a unit, especially since the number assigned was retained even if the unit was destroyed, until officially incorporated into another unit, dissolved or recorded as created (which was often long after the fact such as the reconnaissance detachment of the Kavallerie-Brigade). A unit retained an assigned number that often did not reflect the actual situation in the field.

[164] He took Freitag's place as Ia of the Kommandostab "Reichsführer SS" early in the campaign. Born August 9, 1894, he had a lengthy career in the Schutzpolizei and won both Iron Crosses in WWI when he served as an Army officer. He was a Major der Schutzpolizei when assigned to the Kommandostab and was promoted SS-Sturmbannführer on July 1, 1941. Rode eventually replaced Knoblauch as Chief of the Kommandostab "Reichsführer-SS" and was later assigned to von dem Bach's anti-partisan command and became his Chief of Staff. He was awarded the German Cross in Silver, on von dem Bach's recommendation, on February 20, 1945 with the rank of SS-Brigadeführer und Generalmajor der Polizei.

[165] This is the staff of the Kommandostab "Reichsführer-SS" and controlled all units. It subordinated other Kommandostab combat and support units when needed to the four largest combat elements: the three Brigades and the Begleit Bataillon "Reichsführer-SS." As seen in the officer and unit listing for the SS-Kavallerie-Brigade in December 1941, some elements and officers with the SS-Kavallerie-Brigade were portions of other Kommandostab "Reichsführer-SS" units attached to it on a temporary basis.

[166] An Ordnungspolizei unit created in 1941 and dissolved by 1943. The Orpo provided numerous armed regiments and battalions to various second-line commands with a number attached to each HSSPF.

Sanitäts Zug (medical platoon)	17 771A
Krankenkraftwagenzug (ambulance platoon)	17 771B
Nachrichtenkompanie	47 253

SS-Kavallerie-Regiment 1
Stab	22 711
Kradmeldezug	"
Musikzug (band)	"
1.Schwadron	18 364
2.Schwadron	18 650
3.Schwadron	19 320
4.Schwadron	19 555
5.Schwadron	19 660
6.Schwadron	20 497
7.Schwadron[167]	20 903
reitende Batterie	21 753
leichte Kavallerie Kolonne	22 549

SS-Kavallerie-Regiment 2
Stab	40 144
Nachrichtenzug	"
Kradmeldezug	"
Musikzug	"
1.Schwadron	40 610
2.Schwadron	41 255
3.Schwadron	41 928
4.Schwadron	42 014
5.Schwadron	42 572
6.Schwadron	43 008
7.Schwadron	43 441
reitend Artillerie Abteilung Stab[168]	44 880
reitende Batterie	43 755
leichte Kavallerie Kolonne	44 101

1.SS-Infanterie-Brigade (mot)[169]
Stab	16 441
Feldgendarmerie (field police)Trupp	05 913
Feldpostamt	09 144

SS-Infanterie-Regiment 8
Regiment Stab	18 830
Nachrichtenzug	"
Kradmeldezug	"
Musikzug	"

[167] At that time already incorporated into the bicycle reconnaissance detachment as was the same unit from SS-Kavallerie-Regiment 2, as well as portions of 6th Squadron.

[168] The detachment staff being attached to a regiment and a single battery with SS-Kavallerie-Regiment 1 confirms the conclusion of later combat reports that the detachment did not operate as an independent unit as was normally the case for an Artillerie Abteilung.

[169] According to later Feldpost addendum, SS-Infanterie-Brigade 1 received its final support unit in 1942. This is the 15.Kompanie, a motorcycle unit. 13.Kompanie was infantry gun, 14.Kompanie anti-aircraft and 16.Kompanie engineers in the case of both units.

Stab I.Bataillon	19 087A
1.Kompanie	19 087B
2.Kompanie	19 087C
3.Kompanie	19 087D
4.Kompanie	19 087E
Stab II.Bataillon	19 644A
5.Kompanie	19 644B
6.Kompanie	19 644C
7.Kompanie	19 644D
8.Kompanie	19 644E
Stab III.Bataillon	20 387A
9.Kompanie	20 387B
10.Kompanie	20 387C
11.Kompanie	20 387D
12.Kompanie	20 387E
13.Kompanie	20 926
14.Kompanie	21 135
16.Kompanie	37 552
leichte Infanterie Kolonne	21 799
Sanitäts Kompanie (medical company)	17 166
Krankenkraftwagenzug (ambulance platoon)	44 650
Nachrichtenkompanie	18 610
Werkstattkompanie	45 431

SS-Infanterie-Regiment 10

Stab	22 110
Nachrichtenzug	"
Kradmeldzug	"
I.Bataillon Stab	22 782A
1.Kompanie	22 782B
2.Kompanie	22 782C
3.Kompanie	22 782D
4.Kompanie	22 782E
II.Bataillon Stab	22 948A
5.Kompanie	22 948B
6.Kompanie	22 948C
7.Kompanie	22 948D
8.Kompanie	22 948E
III.Bataillon Stab	23 331A
9.Kompanie	22 331B
10.Kompanie	22 331C
11.Kompanie	22 331D
12.Kompanie	22 331E

13.Kompanie	73 719
14.Kompanie	23 846
16.Kompanie	39 394
leichte Infanterie Kolonne	16 504

2.SS-Infanterie-Brigade (mot)[170]

Stab	43 500
Feldgendarmerie Trupp	47 836
Feldpostamt (postal section)	10 512

SS-Infanterie-Regiment 4

Stab	26 292
Nachrichtenzug	"
Musikzug	"
I.Bataillon Stab	27 795
1.Kompanie	29 621
2.Kompanie	30 232
3.Kompanie	30 795
4.Kompanie	31 474
II.Bataillon Stab	32 215A
5.Kompanie	32 215B
6.Kompanie	32 215C
7.Kompanie	32 215D
8.Kompanie	32 215D
III.Bataillon Stab	08 042
9.Kompanie	08 690
10.Kompanie	09 239
11.Kompanie	10 176
12.Kompanie	11 677
13.Kompanie	26 292A
14.Kompanie	26 292B
15.Kompanie	26 292C
16.Kompanie	40 146
leichte Infanterie Kolonne	35 152
Sanitäts Kompanie	46 742
Krankenkraftwagenzug (ambulance platoon)	47 122
Nachrichtenkompanie	46 594
Werkstattkompanie	47 466

Begleit Bataillon "Reichsführer-SS"

Stab	41 104A
1.Kompanie	41 104B

[170] At this time the Brigade was split with SS-Infanterie-Regiment 4 in Krakau undergoing rebuild and the two regiments fought independently. The SS-Führungshauptamt Feldpost list does not list SS-Infanterie Regiment 10 as a component of the Kommandostab "Reichsführer-SS" at this time though the unit was still in existence per published sources. Though in Poland, SS-Infanterie-Regiment 4 was still listed as a subordinate of the Kommandostab "Reichsführer-SS." It returned to Russia and earned the honor title "Langemarck."

2.Kompanie	41 104C
3.Kompanie	41 104D
4.Kompanie	41 104E
Genesungsbatterie (convalescence) Batterie[171]	41 104F

SS-Flak Abteilung "Ost"[172]

Stab	35 595
1.Batterie	35 741
2.Batterie	36 853
3.Batterie	36 949
4.Batterie	37 497

Flak Abteilung Kommandostab "Reichsführer-SS"[173]

1.Batterie	38 183
2.Batterie	39 840
3.Batterie	36 949
4.Batterie	45 606

Nachrichtenabteilung[174] (Signals Detachment)

Stab	45 215
1.Kompanie	45 648
2.Kompanie	46 239
leichte Nachrichten Kolonne	47 338

Nachschub-Dienste (supply troops)

Nachschubführer (supply officer)	37 569
1.Kraftwagenkolonne (supply column)	37 831
2.Kraftwagenkolonne	38 005
3.Kraftwagenkolonne	38 997
4.Kraftwagenkolonne	39 241
5.Kraftwagenkolonne	40 328
6.Kraftwagenkolonne	40 815
Nachschubkompanie	40 304

Verwaltungsdienste (administration service)

Verpflegungsamt (food rations office)	42 301
Bäckerei Kompanie (backery company)	41 094
Schlächterei Zug (butchering platoon)	41 516

---

[171] Personnel wounded or ill but able to perform some limited duties were assigned to this battery.

[172] Formed during May 1941 in Weimar under the command of SS-Obersturmbannführer Karl Burk who won the German Cross in Gold on November 5, 1942, for his command of the unit. Composed of light, medium and heavy batteries (one each) with a light anti-aircraft column, it was assigned to the Kommandostab "Reichsführer-SS" in September 1941 and initially attached to the 2.SS-Infanterie-Brigade (mot). When it was withdrawn from the front in the spring of 1942 its remaining personnel were, along with the single anti-aircraft battery then attached to the SS-Kavallerie-Brigade, used to form the basis of the Flak Abteilung of the SS-Kavallerie-Division. The remnants of "Ost" arrived after Ewald Keyk's original battery in late September 1942.

[173] The four batteries were divided among other Kommandostab elements (see footnote 52). Later, two other anti-aircraft units were created and attached to the Kommandostab. Flak Abteilung Kommandostab "Reichsführer-SS" I (formed mid-1942 with four batteries) and II (formed mid-1943) became components and fought attached to the various elements of the Kommandostab for the balance of their existence.

[174] Expanded from the original signals company assigned to the Kommandostab when formed.

Field conference with Karl Gesele (right), Hermann Fegelein (center) and the commander of the Brigade Field Police unit Franz Rinner (left). (Yerger Archives)

Veterinärdienste (veterinary section)

1.Veterinärkompanie	43 864
Veterinär-Park (veterinary depot)	35 707
Pferdelazarett (horse hospital)	36 868

Until the beginning of November 1941 the 9.Armee along with its XXIII.Armeekorps were advancing along both sides of Rshev and had turned to the north to repel attacks by Russian forces moving south. The Russians initiated strikes from their positions along the general line between Kalinin and the Lake Seliger. The Germans noticed that their enemy was fighting tenaciously but that they were disorganized, as if fighting without leadership. In a report to the Kommandostab "Reichsführer-SS" Ia in Arys, SS-Hauptsturmführer Karl Gesele reported he believed that it was the intent of 9.Armee to prevent the Russian forces from the northern front from pulling off their attack and retreating to Moscow. Hermann Fegelein also noted that attacks on the Russians had to take place without artillery preparation as no stocks of ammunition or fuel were available due to poor conditions of the supply lines.[175]

SS-Kavallerie-Regiment 1, due to its lack of supplies, left its position in the forest east of Lugi and traveled east towards the Okowtzy area. The main components of the Regiment were in Okowtzy on November 5th where they were to receive necessary supplies. Afterwards they would travel on the road between Toropez and Rshev and then prepare to pacify the area east of Jetkino.[176]

During this period several components of SS-Kavallerie-Regiment 1 were ordered to stand as a security check for the left flank of 9.Armee. However, while the Regiment was assuming its positions they were put on alert by the 102.Infanterie Division. The left flank of this division, positioned on the large bend in the Volga river (Volga Bend) was being severely threatened by Russian forces. The regimental commander, SS-Sturmbannführer Gustav Lombard, decided that he should block these enemy units by ordering several groups from the 102.Infanterie Division in battalion

---

[175] "Tätigkeitsbericht für die Zeit vom 25. - 31. 10. 1941."

[176] "Taetigkeitsbericht fur die Zeit vom 1. - 7. 11. 1941." an den Kommandostab "Reichsführer-SS" Abt. Ia in Arys, dated November 1, 1941 and signed by SS-Hauptsturmführer Karl Gesele and "Kriegstagebuch des Kommandostabs der 'Reichsführer-SS' Nr. 1."

strength to intercept these forces west of Jeltzy in the area of the Volga Bend. Another urgent request of the 253.Infanterie Division for help was received soon after this and Lombard determined that the dispatched intercepting forces of the 102.Infanterie Division, heavily depleted by casualties, would not be able to stop the approaching Russians. Lombard decided, in agreement of the Brigade staff, that he should send some of his own troops to strengthen the line. An added benefit of this decision was that such a move would prevent the partisan groups in the area assigned to the Brigade from receiving reinforcements.[177]

A battle with the approaching Russian troops ensued resulting in 141 casualties and 112 taken prisoner for the Russians as well as a destroyed enemy bunker. On November 6th the commander of 253.Infanterie Division, Generalleutnant Schellert, thanked SS-Kavallerie-Regiment 1 and especially SS-Standartenoberjunker Joachim Boosfeld and gave them special recognition for protecting his left flank.[178]

Having completed the operations protecting the left flank of the 253.Infanterie Division, the commanders of the rear area of Army Group "Center" and 9.Armee ordered SS-Kavallerie-Regiment 1 to Cholmjetzy where they arrived on November 6th. The Regiment was to secure the area of Cholmjetzy which would serve to protect the supply point of Jetkino to the west. The following day the Regiment set up positions 15 kilometers north and south of the Jetkino road. Several intercepted Russian radio messages revealed that partisans planned to attack Jetkino from the south. On November 8th several elements the Regiment were attacked on the road between Cholmjetzy and Jetkino. Other partisan groups were reported moving north and approaching Jetkino. Soon after it was reported to the Army Group rear area commander that the field hospital in Jetkino was overrun by partisans. Several fighting groups of the Regiment were immediately dispatched and managed to take over the newly formed partisan stronghold. In reaction to the partisan attack, several squadrons of the Regiment dispatched reconnaissance patrols southeast of Jetkino where they reported strong partisan groups were disrupting the area east and southeast of the town. The strongpoint in Berjosa Tal was later destroyed on November 11th and 85 prisoners taken. Patrols in Berjosa Tal took 20 more prisoners. On November 14th the pacification operations in Berjosa Tal were registered in the Kommandostab "Reichsführer-SS" war diary as having concluded. The fighting had resulted in 842 enemy dead including one Russian officer dressed in a paratrooper uniform and six partisan leaders. The Germans also took 48 rifles, a large amount of ammunition and rations. At the conclusion of these operations the Regiment had covered approximately 4600 kilometers since the beginning of November 1941.[179]

Elsewhere in this sector of Russia SS-Kavallerie-Regiment 2 was anticipating better weather which would mean opening of the supply lines. At this time (the end of October) the Brigade was made responsible for securing the entire rear of 9.Armee north of the rail line running between Weliki-Luki and Rshev. As a secondary assignment, the Brigade was expected to pacify the area between Toropez and Cholm where large partisan groups as well as Russian paratroopers were reported. For this assignment, the Regiment broke camp on October 28th, was reinforced with an engineer platoon, and then sent in the direction of Cholm. Next, they were to pacify the area between the Lake Nagobje and the road between Toropez and Cholm. On October 31st the Regiment performed pacification operations in the area northwest of Toropez and on the road connecting Toropez and Rshev. The Regiment was on route to Cholm and situated 20 kilometers northwest of Toropez where they engaged partisan forces. During the battle, 71 partisans were captured while one SS man was killed by a mine. On November 4th the Regiment continued regular patrols in a

---

[177] "Tätigkeitsbericht für die Zeit v. 18.10. - 18.11.1941."

[178] "Tätigkeitsbericht für die Zeit v. 18.10. - 18.11.1941," "Tätigkeitsbericht für die Zeit vom 1. - 7. 11. 1941" and "Kriegstagebuch des Kommandostabs der 'Reichsführer-SS' Nr. 1."

[179] "Tätigkeitsbericht für die Zeit v. 18.10. - 18.11.1941," "Tätigkeitsbericht für die Zeit vom 1. - 7. 11. 1941," "Tätigkeitsbericht für die Zeit vom 8. - 14. 11. 1941." an den Kommandostab "Reichsführer-SS" Abt. Ia in Arys, dated November 14, 1941 and signed by SS-Obersturmführer Erich Streubel and "Kriegstagebuch des Kommandostabs der 'Reichsführer-SS' Nr. 1."

village situated 36 kilometers northwest of Toropez. Several units brought in 92 partisan prisoners during operations. November 7th the Regiment performed patrolling actions in the direction of Cholm and the following week reconnoitered the area of Lake Nagobje. Since no partisans were reported in this area, patrols were sent east and west of the road between Toropez and Cholm. On November 11th the Regiment was situated in Toropez. Two days later the entire Regiment took over security operations of the rail line running through Toropez, Dubno and Shitowo. 105 prisoners were taken during these operations.[180]

Since the beginning of November, the Bicycle Reconnaissance Detachment, in conjunction with several companies of Army Wach Bataillon 705, were assigned operations south of the road between Toropez and Jetkino as well as the road connecting Schatry and Jetkino. It was intended that these carrying out of these actions would free enough troops to form an attack group to pursue a unit of 1,000 regular Russian soldiers reported in the area east of Jetkino. During the second week of November several elements of the Reconnaissance Detachment secured the road between Schatry and Jetkino and guarded the Duna Bridge while patrols were also dispatched to the area northeast of Butaki. In other sectors of the area assigned to the Reconnaissance Detachment in the second week of November, several units working with the Brigade's engineer unit destroyed 26 enemy bunkers. They also conducted patrols north of the road between Toropez and Rshev. During the patrols an additional 24 partisan bunkers were destroyed and several mines the enemy had laid detonated. Other enemy groups placed several street obstacles which were dismantled. Some reconnaissance units engaged partisans in a brief battle that brought in 44 prisoners and captured five rifles as well as 15 grenades. Late in the week the Detachment took command of a POW camp in Butaki and supervised the transfer of 342 prisoners to Toropez.[181]

Casualties for the time period between the latter half of October and the first half of November were light for the Brigade and seemingly heavy for the opposition. Summarizing the weekly tactical and situational reports for the time period between October 18th and November 14th as well as the monthly tactical and situational report written by Hermann Fegelein, the Brigade suffered seven dead and nine wounded while reporting that 281 partisans were killed while another 3018 were taken prisoner including six officers. Another 141 regular Russian soldiers were killed and 112 taken prisoner during fighting in this period.[182]

The pace of the offensive was fast, with German units spreading out over vast regions of Russia. Demands were made of material and men not experienced in Poland or the Western campaign. While many types of equipment wore and broke down, the horses of the SS-Kavallerie-Brigade managed fairly well. The Brigade possessed a strength of 3,138 mounts and in the period between the 25th and the 31st of October only four horses died of exhaustion while 51 were reported sick and unfit for service. This report is typical for the time period: during the first week of November the Brigade lost another three horses dead while the Brigade's veterinarians treated 102 horses for sickness or wounds.[183]

During the week of November 15th, SS-Kavallerie-Regiment 1 was sent southwest between Jetkino and Berjosa Tal based on reports of partisan activity in that area. There the Regiment fought several stubborn battles and on November 16th took 176 prisoners north of Jetkino. After this fighting the Regiment was sent on to Rshev. At this time there was no partisan activity reported on the road between Toropez and Rshev.

---

[180] "Tätigkeitsbericht für die Zeit vom 25. - 31. 10. 1941," "Tätigkeitsbericht für die Zeit vom 1. - 7. 11. 1941," "Tätigkeitsbericht für die Zeit vom 8. - 14. 11. 1941" and "Kriegstagebuch des Kommandostabs der 'Reichsführer-SS' Nr. 1."

[181] "Tätigkeitsbericht für die Zeit vom 1. - 7. 11. 1941," "Taetigkeitsbericht fuer die Zeit vom 8. - 14. 11. 1941," and "Kriegstagebuch des Kommandostabs der 'Reichsführer-SS' Nr. 1."

[182] It is difficult to differentiate between partisans killed in action and those that were executed, although references are made to both. Sources: Weekly tactical and situational reports filed between October 25 and November 14, 1941 and the monthly tactical and situational report filed by Hermann Fegelein on November 21, 1941.

[183] "Tätigkeitsbericht für die Zeit vom 25. - 31. 10. 1941" and "Taetigkeitsbericht fuer die Zeit vom 1. - 7. 11. 1941."

Early the next week SS-Kavallerie Regiment 1 departed from Toropez. After passing Jetkino, the Regiment dispatched patrols near the train station in Semtzy in conjunction with the Bicycle Reconnaissance Detachment. During the week of November 22nd a platoon of the Regiment was loaded on trucks and conducted a punitive expedition along with the Brigade's Motorcycle Reconnaissance Platoon in the Tschistowa area. During that excursion a partisan camp was uncovered and destroyed. On November 23rd strong partisan activity was reported south of the rail line between Rshev and Jetkino but reconnaissance patrols only managed to capture two of the enemy. The next day fighting erupted between the Regiment and partisans 31 kilometers east of Jetkino during patrols of the rail line. On November 25th the Regiment conducted patrols on the road between Jetkino and Rshev where enemy activity was observed the following day. Several operations in the area of Semtzy were conducted on November 30. During fighting with partisans the Regiment suffered one wounded and claimed four partisans killed while other units of the Regiment prepared for a larger-scale operation to be carried out southwest of Semtzy.[184] Since mid-November repeated references to preparations for SS-Kavallerie-Regiment 1 to be relieved and return to Warsaw were highlighted in weekly tactical and situational reports.[185]

The majority of SS-Kavallerie-Regiment 2 was situated in the area around Pog. Potschen during the week of November 15th while other portions secured parts of the rail line between Toropez and Dubno. On November 21st elements of the Regiment were dispatched to acquire the strongpoints in Basary and the rail line west of the Rayon border that reached as far east as Shishiza. During reconnaissance operations along the rail line between Dubno and Toropez an area of track damaged by sabotage was discovered near Dubno in time to be repaired without incident.[186]

Partisan activity surfaced in the middle of November within the sectors assigned to the Brigade containing the village of Butaki. Several patrols of the Bicycle Reconnaissance Detachment were sent out to thwart this action. Afterwards, reports to the Brigade stated that this area could again be considered secure. The Detachment then traveled to the area of northwest of Suwarewo. At the train station in Olenino they found a munitions dump that had been reported by the civil population. The cache housed 400 kilograms of explosives, several cases of detonators, 950,000 rounds of infantry ammunition and 1,200 rounds of rifle grenades. The Detachment was then assigned to secure the line between Toropez and Jetkino while guarding the captured munitions. Besides security tasks they conducted patrols north and south of the area between Toropez and Jetkino up to the rail line between Weliki-Luki and Rshev. During the third week of November XXIII.Armeekorps reported enemy activity in the eastern sector of the area assigned to the Brigade and the Bicycle Reconnaissance Detachment dispatched platoon-strength patrols in response.[187]

In the "General Status" section of the weekly tactical and situational report written by the SS-Kavallerie-Brigade Ia, SS-Hauptsturmführer Karl Gesele, to the Kommandostab "Reichsführer-SS" Ia, SS-Sturmbannführer Ernst-August Rode, dated November 29, 1941, the Brigade reported increased partisan raids on supply lines due to the recent departure of the 255.Sicherheits Division. The war diary of the Kommandostab "Reichsführer-SS" reports one such incident occurring on November 27th near Bibjerevo.[188] During this attack 16 partisans were killed while three rifles and one heavy machine gun were captured. In another section, Gesele reported that several statements made by captured partisans referred to a Jewish partisan leader by the name of Eselssohn

[184] "Tätigkeitsbericht für die Zeit vom 15. - 21. 11. 1941" an den Kommandostab "Reichsführer-SS" Abt. Ia in Arys, dated November 22, 1941 and signed by SS-Standartenführer Hermann Fegelein, "Tätigkeitsbericht für die Zeit vom 22. - 28. 11. 1941" an den Kommandostab "Reichsführer-SS" Abt. Ia in Arys, dated November 29, 1941 and signed by SS-Hauptsturmführer Karl Gesele and "Kriegstagebuch des Kommandostabs der 'Reichsführer-SS' Nr. 1."

[185] "Tätigkeitsbericht für die Zeit vom 15. - 21. 11. 1941" and "Tätigkeitsbericht für die Zeit vom 22. - 28. 11. 1941."

[186] ibid.

[187] " Tätigkeitsbericht für die Zeit vom 15. - 21. 11. 1941" and "Kriegstagebuch des Kommandostabs der 'Reichsführer-SS' Nr. 1."

[188] Although not confirmed, most probably the Bicycle Reconnaissance Detachment as they were situated in this area at the time.

Joachim Boosfeld, platoon leader in 5th Squadron, SS-Kavallerie-Regiment 1, shown here as an SS-Hauptsturmführer and commander of 4th Squadron, SS-Kavallerie-Regiment 16, SS-Kavallerie-Division. Born in Aachen on June 1, 1922, Boosfeld came to the Brigade after graduating from SS officer school Bad Tölz. As a platoon leader he was acknowledged by Army headquarters for bravery on November 6, 1941 and won the Iron Cross 1st class on March 30, 1942. Promoted to SS-Untersturmführer on December 1, 1941, and to SS-Obersturmführer on November 9, 1943, he remained with the SS-Kavallerie-Division until 1945 when he transferred to the SS Kavallerie Schule Göttingen. He won the German Cross in Gold on December 30, 1944, the Knight's Cross on February 21, 1945 as well as the rare Close Combat Clasp in Gold. (Photo: Jakob Tiefenthäler)

who controlled several partisan groups. Eselssohn had apparently been wounded during a recent skirmish with the Brigade in Berjosa Tal[189] and retreated east with a 300 man unit of partisans.[190]

The casualty sections of the weekly tactical and situational reports for November 15-28 reported that one officer died as the result of an unspecified accident while three were wounded. During the same time period no partisans were reported killed but 400 were taken prisoner.[191]

Even though this book concentrates on the fighting aspects of the SS-Kavallerie-Brigade, it is interesting to note reports regarding other aspects as they paint a true picture of the occurrences in this area of Russia. A good example is supplied in the weekly tactical and situational report written by Hermann Fegelein concerning the Sanitätsdienst (Medical Detachment) of the Brigade. This is translated verbatim for the reader's interest showing one aspect of SS and Army cooperation:[192]

"The medical section of the SS-Kavallerie-Brigade, besides caring for its own troops, also took part in taking care of units of the Wehrmacht during all actions in the east. While the medical unit

[189] Although not confirmed, most probably SS-Kavallerie-Regiment 1 as they were situated in this area at the time.

[190] "Tätigkeitsbericht für die Zeit vom 22. - 28. 11. 1941" and "Kriegstagebuch des Kommandostabs der 'Reichsführer-SS' Nr. 1."

[191] "Tätigkeitsbericht für die Zeit vom 15. - 21. 11. 1941" and "Tätigkeitsbericht für die Zeit vom 22. - 28. 11. 1941."

[192] "Tätigkeitsbericht für die Zeit vom 15. - 21. 11. 1941."

was in Toropez they took over the local doctor and dentist offices. Besides taking over its work, they also cared for the troops from these offices.

'The dentist's office has two chairs at this time, used uninterrupted by three dentists and four men as helpers. The approximate performance of this office is as follows: 70 patients per day, from which 85% are members of the Wehrmacht-Heer. The work accomplished is as follows:

35% fillings
15% extractions
25% dental plate replacement (couldn't be completed, since the necessary technical equipment is not available)
25% gum disease problems and other similar problems.

'It should especially be emphasized that there is an extreme lack of functioning dentures for the older reservists and with that there is a danger that these men will not be suitable for action and worse will not be able eat properly causing their health to suffer.

'The ambulance platoon, besides being used for its usual purposes, was used for transporting off 705 cases of badly wounded and extremely sick patients that were staying in local field hospitals and needed to be transported to larger field hospitals. The following numbers were transported:

Members of the Waffen-SS (over an eight-week period)   *276*
and members of the Wehrmacht (Heer and Luftwaffe)   *429*

'The medical company of the SS-Kavallerie-Brigade will set up a local SS hospital after the Army Field Hospital 3/532 returns to this area. In this hospital there will be surgeons and interns and all the necessary equipment including an X-Ray machine."

In early December, 1941 the absence of the 255.Sicherheits Division continued to be felt in the area south of the Toropez /Rshev rail line. Although it seemed the partisan groups were wandering aimlessly, they concentrated operations on the road between Toropez, Jetkino and Rshev and the rail line between Weliki-Luki and Rshev. Enemy raids on larger transport columns were conducted on the road between Toropez and Rshev. To halt these attacks, the Brigade cleared all bushes and shrubs from both sides of the road which removed cover that could be used in surprise attacks. A schedule for transports was also developed so that the Brigade could accompany them through their area assigned area and this helped to further deter attacks.[193]

On December 1st, the Brigade reported that a group of partisans with a strength of between 100 and 150 men was observed 21 kilometers southwest of Siminnovka in a strongly built up area. 40 partisans were killed during an engagement with this group. The enemy groups north of Trubschevsk and Pogav were captured while 68 armed partisans south of Gremjatsch were surprised and taken prisoner, one of which was a partisan leader. Another thirteen were captured in the area of Pogorelzy and a reconnaissance operation reported a partisan cavalry patrol west of the town. An operation against the enemy center northwest of Putivl came up against strong resistance. That enemy unit possessed a medium sized German tank which was still operational. Casualties during this engagement: SS-Kavallerie-Brigade, three dead, eight wounded (two officers), partisans: 73 dead and 93 captured.[194]

[193] "Tätigkeitsbericht für die Zeit vom 29. 11 -5.12. 1941" an den Kommandostab "Reichsführer-SS" Abt. Ia in Arys, dated December 6 and signed by SS-Hauptsturmführer Karl Gesele.

[194] "Kriegstagebuch des Kommandostabs der 'Reichsführer-SS' Nr. 1."

Johannes Göhler shown (left) as an SS-Obersturmführer and (right) as an SS-Hauptsturmführer after his award of the Knight's Cross on September 17, 1943. Born September 15, 1918, in Bischofswerder, he was assigned to SS-Totenkopfstandarte "Oberbayern" after joining the SS in November 1936. When the war began he served with SS-Infanterie-Ersatz-Bataillon "Ost" until attending SS-Junkerschule Braunschweig beginning in August 1940. Leaving Braunschweig at the end of February 1941, he was assigned to 3rd Squadron of Kavallerie-Regiment 1 as a platoon leader and was commissioned an SS-Untersturmführer on April 20, 1941. In January 1942 he became adjutant of SS-Kavallerie-Regiment 1 (awarded the Iron Cross 1st class on January 18, 1942) followed by promotion to SS-Obersturmführer on March 16, 1942. With formation of the SS-Kavallerie-Division in May 1942 he took command of 3rd Squadron of SS-Kavallerie-Regiment 1 and later moved to command 4th Squadron. At this latter assignment he won the Knight's Cross on September 17, 1943. Awarded the German Cross in Gold on September 26, 1943, he was promoted to SS-Hauptsturmführer on November 9, 1943, to SS-Sturmbannführer on December 21, 1944, and ended the war as an SS liaison officer at Hitler's headquarters. (Photo: Jakob Tiefenthäler)

During the second week of December, continuing patrols as well as statements by the general population determined that partisans had concentrated in a large forest southwest of Jetkino. The Brigade sent out patrols to this area and the fighting resulted in several winter camps being destroyed. The partisans suffered 50 wounded and 385 dead, two of which were female and one of whom was the long sought after partisan leader Frohmenkoff. 46 were also taken prisoner and later shot. A large amount of material was captured including several heavy machine guns, 150 rifles and over 350 grenades.[195] One of the partisan camps consisted of 19 barracks and two well-built transit camps which were taken in close-combat and subsequently destroyed along with four munitions dumps and five underground shelters. There were six houses and a small nearby village that likewise served the partisans and these facilities were also put to the torch. The Brigade, recognizing the sophistication of these camps, and also because they could not bring up heavy weapons due to the poor road conditions, decided to recall all patrols for this attack during which three SS men were wounded.[196]

[195] "Tätigkeitsbericht für die Zeit vom 6. 12 -12.12. 1941" an den Kommandostab "Reichsführer-SS" Abt. Ia in Arys, dated December 13 and signed by SS-Hauptsturmführer Karl Gesele.

[196] ibid.

Hans Ertl, platoon leader in 5th Squadron, SS-Kavallerie-Regiment 2, shown here as an SS-Untersturmführer. Born on January 29, 1920, he joined the SS in May 1938 with SS-Totenkopfstandarte "Brandenburg." After attending SS-Junkerschule Bad Tölz he was assigned to the Brigade in September 1941 and commissioned an SS-Untersturmführer on April 20, 1942. He remained with the later SS-Kavallerie-Division except when wounded and was then assigned to SS-Junkerschule Braunschweig (June to December 1943) and the SS-Kavallerie-Schule Göttigen (October 1944 to January 1945). Promoted to SS-Obersturmführer on April 20, 1944 he was awarded the German Cross in Gold on April 17, 1943 with the later divisional Kampfgruppe "Z." His last command was the 6th Squadron of SS-Kavallerie-Regiment 2. (Photo: BDC)

During the first week of December all elements of SS-Kavallerie-Regiment 1 gathered in Toropez and prepared for their awaited departure to Warsaw. It was then decided that due to an action planned for the vicinity of Rshev, SS-Kavallerie-Regiment 1 would have to take over security operations for the Bicycle Reconnaissance Detachment between Toropez and Jetkino since the Detachment would soon be departing to take part in the action. Since SS-Kavallerie-Regiment 2 needed several replacement units to bring it up to strength, these were transferred from SS-Kavallerie-Regiment 1. This weakened SS-Kavallerie-Regiment 1 enough that it was given several days to prepare for departure to its assigned positions along the transport lines between Toropez and Jetkino. It should also be noted that due to the poor supply conditions, feed for the horses had not arrived. Because of this the mounts were in no condition to take part in the transport operation and were left behind. On December 12th SS-Kavallerie-Regiment 1 made preparations to take over the operations assigned to the Bicycle Reconnaissance Detachment even though Himmler had forbidden front-line action. Instead they were reassigned to the area east of Cholmjetzy and were later brought up for action on the front in the area of 9.Armee around Rshev during which 21 partisans were killed.[197]

SS-Kavallerie-Regiment 2 secured the road between Toropez and Jetkino and the rail line between Toropez and Dubno during the first week of December. Several patrols in the area led to the destruction of a large number of partisans and their camps. The following week elements of the Regiment took part in the attacks on the partisan camps described previously. On December 9th, other units of the Regiment departed to attack an enemy camp near Boroj (40 kilometers south of

---

[197] "Tätigkeitsbericht für die Zeit vom 29. 11 -5.12. 1941," "Tätigkeitsbericht für die Zeit vom 6. 12 -12.12. 1941" and "Kriegstagebuch des Kommandostabs der 'Reichsführer-SS' Nr. 1."

Semtzy). The partisans were reinforced during the fight by others arriving on sleds from the road to the north. SS-Kavallerie-Regiment 2 won this battle and counted 74 partisans killed. On December 13th the Regiment pursued a band of partisans 10 kilometers northeast of Dubno and after several engagements they were destroyed. 15 partisans were killed during the combat while ten escaped. Dudina (ten kilometers northwest of Dubno) was enemy occupied but was taken in close combat during which 21 of the adversaries were killed.[198]

The Bicycle Reconnaissance Detachment spent the first week of December guarding Brigade positions and sending out patrols along the line area between Jetkino and Rshev. One of the patrols destroyed a small partisan group reported by local residents. Also during the first week of December, the Detachment was subordinated the Kommandostab "Reichsführer-SS" 2cm anti-aircraft gun battery as a support unit after it was deployed strengthening Jetkino on December 1st. Two days later a supply column of the Reconnaissance Detachment was attacked by partisans in the area of Bibjerevo during which three trucks were destroyed. One NCO was killed and two men wounded. December 7th the Detachment attacked partisan groups south of the area rail line which the enemy defended bitterly utilizing several fortifications complete with heavy weapons set up in the forests. The Detachment, which was split into two Kampfgruppen, called off the attack because of cold and symptoms of frostbite. During the engagement the Detachment suffered eight wounded. The next day preparations were made for a renewed attack on the fortifications. The attack proved difficult, since the ground of the area in front of the forest where the partisans were was not suitable for transporting heavy weapons. In spite of this, the partisans lost 140 dead while numerous weapons were captured.[199]

During the second week of December the Brigade received word from the rear area commander of Army Group "Center" that the Bicycle Reconnaissance Detachment as well as the Kommandostab "Reichsführer-SS" Flak Batterie would shortly be receiving orders to depart in the direction of Rshev. There they would be subordinated to 9.Armee for action on the front, supposedly south of Kaljnin. The Brigade had already initiated plans for the Reconnaissance Detachment to conduct an operation against a strong band of regular Russian troops which had been overrun and left stranded south and southwest of Jetkino. Preparations for this engagement, which was to last some five days, continued as no time frame for future orders was available. Not knowing whether to continue with their strategy, the Brigade staff sent a message to the rear area commander of Army Group "Center" on December 12th explaining the situation and requesting further information regarding the transfer orders to the front. This message was not answered.[200]

The weekly Ia tactical and situational report filed for the time period between December 13 and 19, 1941, reports that the Brigade continued its security operations along the rail lines between Weliki-Luki/Rshev and Weliki-Luki/Dubno. The Bicycle Reconnaissance Detachment along with the Brigade's attached Flak-Batterie engaged in fighting bypassed regular Russian troops while at the same time continued to organize themselves in anticipation of concrete orders for deployment at the front. During this period it is noted that 98 partisans, three of which were officers, were taken prisoner and shot.[201]

In the third week in December 1941 SS-Kavallerie-Regiment 1 took over operations in the sector between Jetkino and Basary (mainly at the train station in Nelidova) and the rail line between Weliki-Luki and Rshev. On December 14th, the Regiment also assumed responsibility for the area previously assigned to the Bicycle Reconnaissance Detachment. By order of Army, operations southwest of Jetkino were to be conducted in spite of recent successes by the partisans. While

[198] ibid.

[199] "Tätigkeitsbericht für die Zeit vom 29. 11 -5.12. 1941" and "Tätigkeitsbericht für die Zeit vom 6. 12 -12.12. 1941."

[200] "Tätigkeitsbericht für die Zeit vom 6. 12 -12.12. 1941," "Tätigkeitsbericht für die Zeit vom 29. 11 -5.12. 1941" and "Kriegstagebuch des Kommandostabs der 'Reichsführer-SS' Nr. 1."

[201] "Tätigkeitsbericht für die Zeit vom 13. -19.12. 1941" an den Kommandostab "Reichsführer-SS" Abt. Ia in Arys, dated December 23 and signed by SS-Standartenführer Hermann Fegelein.

Karl Weeke, platoon leader in 7th Squadron, SS-Kavallerie-Regiment 1 and later platoon commander in the 1st Squadron of the Reconnaissance Detachment, shown here as an SS-Hauptsturmführer. Awarded the German Cross in Gold on May 26, 1943 with the later Kampfgruppe "Z" of the SS-Kavallerie-Division, he remained with the reconnaissance elements of the SS-Kavallerie-Division and as commander of its 1st Company and was killed in Budapest on February 11, 1945. (Photo: BDC)

traveling to their newly assigned sector on December 18th, the Regiment discovered a bomb on the train tracks 17 kilometers west of Basary which was removed before any harm could be done. The following day the Regiment was situated in the area of Jetkino-Toropez-Basary.[202]

On December 13th SS-Kavallerie-Regiment 2 pursued and destroyed a small partisan group. Later that day the Regiment took the enemy-occupied village of Dudina (11 kilometers northwest of Dubno) in close combat. Three days later the Regiment captured 35 partisans, two of whom were officers. Interrogation of the latter revealed information about other groups located southwest and the Regiment immediately dispatched several patrols to intercept and destroyed these groups along with their camps. On December 17th the regimental headquarters in Dubno were attacked by a Russian fighter plane. A total of ten bombs were dropped and several rounds of machine gun fire were fired from the plane but without inflicting damage. It was later reported the plane was shot down by machine-gunners of 253.Infanterie Division. On December 18th the strongpoint in Dubno was also attacked by Russian aircraft. The following day the Regiment was officially assigned to secure the area between the villages of Toropez, Bibjerevo and Dubno. Also that day a Regimental Jagdkommando (hunting command), equipped with two artillery pieces departed from Bibjerevo to attack a partisan group of about 30 men. The enemy was intercepted 28 kilometers northeast of Dubno and destroyed in the ensuing battle. On December 21st a Wachkommando (guard command) of the Regiment destroyed two bands of partisans in two actions in Dovrez, a village situated 25 kilometers north of Dubno.[203]

On December 13th the Brigade received orders from the rear area commander of Army Group "Center" that the Bicycle Reconnaissance Detachment was to depart immediately to the left (northern) flank of 9.Armee in the area of XXIII.Armeekorps. There they would be subordinated to the

---

[202] "Tätigkeitsbericht für die Zeit vom 13. -19.12. 1941" and "Kriegstagebuch des Kommandostabs der 'Reichsführer-SS' Nr. 1."

[203] "Tätigkeitsbericht für die Zeit vom 13. -19.12. 1941," "Tätigkeitsbericht für die Zeit vom 20. -26.12. 1941" an den Kommandostab "Reichsführer-SS" Abt. Ia in Arys, dated December 29 and signed by SS-Standartenführer Hermann Fegelein and "Kriegstagebuch des Kommandostabs der 'Reichsführer-SS' Nr. 1."

SS-Untersturmführer Kurt Portugall, platoon leader in the Flak Batterie. He would remain with the Flak Abteilung of the later SS-Kavallerie-Division and was adjutant in 1942. Portugall ended the war as an SS-Hauptsturmführer and was awarded the German Cross in Gold on January 6, 1945 as Batterie Chef of 3./Flak Abteilung. He died on September 26, 1992. (Photo: Private U.S. collection)

253.Infanterie Division. The Brigade staff immediately responded by repeating the message it had previously sent explaining the current situation, but on December 14th the rear area commander called off the transfer to the front so that the Bicycle Reconnaissance Detachment could continue its preparations for relocation. He also changed his previous orders and subordination of the Bicycle Reconnaissance Detachment was transferred not to the 253.Infanterie Division but directly to the rear area commander of Army Group "Center" himself. The Reconnaissance Detachment was still to relocate to the area of the 9.Armee and its commander, SS-Sturmbannführer Albert Faßbender, was to report to XXIII.Armeekorps headquarters. The action against the band of regular Russian soldier that had been overrun was postponed. The Reconnaissance Detachment continued their normal activities and on December 15th caught a partisan group consisting of 16 men and one officer preparing to destroy the train tracks west of Jetkino. New orders for the Detachment arrived on the 16th from its commander who radioed from XXIII.Armeekorps headquarters that they were to wait for further instructions before departing. He also sent orders from XXIII.Armeekorps that SS-Kavallerie-Regimenter 1 and 2 were to take over security operations along the important supply lines of 9.Armee. Two days later new orders arrived from XXIII.Armeekorps in the form of a directive to renew pursuit of the band of straggling regular Russian troops. The Reconnaissance Detachment was ordered to remain in the captured areas while initiating engagement preparations. This enemy group of two regiments was reported to be south and southwest of Jetkino in the forest areas between Basary and Jetkino. Further information retrieved by reconnaissance patrols indicated that the enemy consisted primarily of fully equipped soldiers in contact with front line Russian units by communicating with airplanes. In a number of encounters it was determined that the partisans were spread out and set up in many different areas. They had built various barracks to house their troops and several bunkers and stalls for their horses. Since they were equipped with winter clothing and received excellent supplies, the partisans proved that their general staff was operating toward a tactical goal. Prisoners brought in by SS-Kavallerie-Regiment 1 stated that it was not their assignment to conduct partisan raids and acts of sabotage, but to wait for the day of "freedom from the terror" and link up with the returning mass of the Russian army. The ensuing attack went well and four Russian 7.5 cm artillery pieces, which were left ignored during the attack so that they could later be taken intact, were captured undamaged. On December 19th the Reconnaissance Detachment was situated in the area between Jetkino, Chotmietzyimol and Molodoy Tud.[204]

On December 19th the Brigade headquarters moved to Toropez. The following day command of the entire Brigade was placed under the direct control of 9.Armee which allocated the Brigade to its XXIII.Armeekorps.[205] The XXIII.Armeekorps then subordinated the Bicycle Reconnaissance Detachment to the 253.Infanterie Division and sent them to Szjelisharov where that division was situated.[206] Because of this new front line situation, the Kavallerie Pionier Kompanie (Cavalry Engineer Company) as well as the Veterinär-Kompanie (Veterinary Company) were called from Warsaw and sent to Toropez.[207]

SS-Kavallerie-Brigade
December 20, 1941

Brigade Commander: SS-Standartenführer Hermann Fegelein

Brigade Staff

Ia (First Staff Officer):	SS-Hauptsturmführer Karl Gesele
Ib (Quartermaster):	SS-Obersturmführer Erich Strebel
Ic (Intelligence Officer):	SS-Obersturmführer Franz Rehbein
adjutant (officers and enlisted men):	SS-Hauptsturmführer Karl Richter
1st ordnance officer:	SS-Obersturmführer Toni Ameiser
2nd ordnance officer:	unknown
3rd ordnance officer:	SS-Obersturmführer Kurt Becher
administration:	SS-Obersturmbannführer Wilhelm Jeppe
regimental physician:	SS-Sturmbannführer Dr. Fritz Baader
assistant physician:	SS-Obersturmführer Dr. Helmuth Urbainski
dentist:	SS-Hauptsturmführer Dr. Albert Kurth
administrative officer:	SS-Hauptsturmführer Gerhard Held
veterinary officer:	SS-Untersturmführer Johann Kramer
brigade engineer:	SS-Sturmbannführer Hans Fierlein
2nd engineer:	SS-Hauptsturmführer Hans Harder[208]
special duties officer:	SS-Obersturmführer Walter Schädler
weapons and munitions officer:	SS-Hauptscharführer Karl Hildgardt
food/rationed supplies officer:	SS-Obersturmführer Franz Konrad
reserve officer:	SS-Hauptsturmführer Walter Dunsch
motorcycle platoon commander:	SS-Untersturmführer Albert Tonak[209]

---

[204] "Tätigkeitsbericht für die Zeit vom 13. -19.12. 1941," "Tätigkeitsbericht für die Zeit vom 20. -26.12. 1941," Kriegstagebuch des Kommandostabs der 'Reichsführer-SS' Nr.1," and "Bericht über den Einsatz der SS-Kav. Brigade Winter 1941/1942," dated February 11, 1942 and signed by SS-Sturmbannführer Gustav Lombard.

[205] The front-line situation required all available mobile units this nullifying Himmler's demand the Brigade remain under his direct control via the Kommandostab "Reichsführer-SS." The 1942 reversals on the entire front would see a similar transfer of command authority for other elements of the Kommandostab. From this date the Army directed all operational use of the SS-Kavallerie Brigade.

[206] "Tätigkeitsbericht für die Zeit vom 13. -19.12. 1941," "Tätigkeitsbericht für die Zeit vom 20. -26.12. 1941" an den Kommandostab "Reichsführer-SS" Abt. Ia in Arys, dated December 29 and signed by SS-Standartenführer Hermann Fegelein and "Kriegstagebuch des Kommandostabs der 'Reichsführer-SS' Nr. 1."

[207] "Tätigkeitsbericht für die Zeit vom 13. -19.12. 1941."

[208] Ended the war as an SS-Obersturmbannführer and divisional engineer of the 7.SS-Gebirgs-Division "Prinz Eugen."

[209] Killed on April 15, 1942.

commandant brigade staff quarters:	SS-Untersturmführer Heinrich Diekmann[210]
field police platoon:	SS-Hauptsturmführer Franz Rinner
motorcycle dispatch platoon:	SS-Untersturmführer Hermann Ahlborn[211]
trumpet corps:	SS-Untersturmführer Albert Hellmann
postal unit:	SS-Obersturmführer Gerhard Hille[212]

SS-Kavallerie-Regiment 1

commander:	SS-Sturmbannführer Gustav Lombard
adjutant:	SS-Obersturmführer Hans-Georg von Charpentier
ordnance officer:	SS-Untersturmführer Dr. Wilhelm Heyd
food/rationed supplies:	SS-Untersturmführer Wilhelm Mevis[213]
regimental physician:	SS-Hauptsturmführer Dr. Max Grüter
assistant physician:	SS-Untersturmführer Dr. Hermann Reichart
dentist:	SS-Hauptsturmführer Siegfried Bock
signals officer:	SS-Untersturmführer Georg Reuther
regimental veterinarian:	SS-Untersturmführer Dr. Otto Hubseck
veterinary officer:	SS-Untersturmführer Dr. August Franz[214]
administrative officer:	SS-Obersturmführer Fritz Mayer-Schmid
1st Squadron:	SS-Obersturmführer Rudolf Maeker
car platoon:	SS-Standartenoberjunker Hans Müller
1.platoon:	SS-Untersturmführer Willi Brutkuhl[215]
2.platoon:	SS-Oberscharführer August Schulte-Uffelage
3.platoon:	SS-Standartenoberjunker Wilhelm Bingel[216]
2nd Squadron:	SS-Hauptsturmführer Ulrich Görtz[217]
car platoon:	SS-Untersturmführer Georg Veith
1.platoon:	SS-Obersturmführer Erich Krell[218]
2.platoon:	SS-Untersturmführer Richard Nakat
3.platoon:	SS-Oberscharführer Fritz Jettkand
3rd Squadron:	SS-Hauptsturmführer Johann Schmid
car platoon:	SS-Untersturmführer Horst-Günther Jüngling[219]
1.platoon:	SS-Untersturmführer Johannes Göhler

[210] Took command of 2nd Squadron, SS-Kavallerie Regiment 1 in January 1942 and awarded the Iron Cross 1st class on March 21, 1942.

[211] In early 1942 moved to 3rd Squadron, SS-Kavallerie Regiment 1 as a platoon leader and won the Iron Cross 1st class on February 28, 1942.

[212] Killed on August 20, 1944 while assigned to the postal section of II.SS-Panzer-Korps.

[213] Died on July 10, 1981.

[214] Killed on February 12, 1942.

[215] Killed on February 11, 1942 and posthumously awarded the Iron Cross 1st class on February 15, 1942.

[216] Killed on February 27, 1942.

[217] Awarded the Iron Cross 1st class on January 15, 1942 and killed on March 18, 1942. He was replaced by SS-Obersturmführer Heinrich Diekmann.

[218] Awarded the Iron Cross 1st class on February 4, 1942.

[219] Awarded the Iron Cross 2nd class on January 18, 1942 and killed on January 25, 1945 as an SS-Hauptsturmführer with SS-Kavallerie-Regiment 16.

2.platoon:	SS-Untersturmführer Heinz Keller[220]
3.platoon:	SS-Standartenoberjunker Hermann Sanner
4th Squadron:	SS-Hauptsturmführer Hermann Gadischke
1.platoon:	SS-Obersturmführer Erich Brockmann
2.platoon:	SS-Obersturmführer Willi Geier
3.platoon:	SS-Obersturmführer Karl Braunstein[221]
5th Squadron:[222]	SS-Obersturmführer Hermann Schneider[223]
1.platoon:	SS-Untersturmführer Anton Vandieken
2.platoon:	SS-Untersturmführer Gerhard Südekum[224]
3.platoon:	SS-Standartenoberjunker Joachim Boosfeld
4.platoon:	SS-Standartenoberjunker Hans Ries[225]

SS-Kavallerie-Regiment 2

commander:	SS-Sturmbannführer Hermann Schliefenbaum
adjutant:	SS-Hauptsturmführer Walter Bornscheuer[226]
ordnance officer:	SS-Hauptsturmführer Hermann Lindemann
administrative officer:	SS-Hauptsturmführer Walter Meyer
food/rationed supplies officer:	SS-Obersturmführer Friedrich Butz[227]
regimental physician:	SS-Obersturmführer Dr. Dominik Romani[228]
assistant physician:	SS-Untersturmführer Dr. Franz Fischer[229]
dentist:	SS-Untersturmführer Richard Schreider
veterinarian:	SS-Obersturmführer Dr. Erich Butt
veterinary officer:	SS-Untersturmführer Josef Schmidt
signals platoon:	SS-Untersturmführer Johann Stahl
1st Squadron:	SS-Hauptsturmführer Stefan Charwat[230]
car platoon:	SS-Standartenoberjunker Friedrich Conrad[231]
1.platoon:	SS-Untersturmführer Rudolf Wappler[232]

[220] Killed February 14, 1942.

[221] Awarded the Iron Cross 2nd class on January 19, 1942 and the Iron Cross 1st class on February 8, 1942.

[222] The heavy squadron, it is now expanded from the dissolved 6th squadron.

[223] Awarded the Iron Cross 1st class on February 2, 1942 and killed on February 14, 1942. He was replaced by 1st Platoon Leader Anton Vandieken.

[224] Killed January 15, 1945 as an SS-Hauptsturmführer and commander 5th Squadron of SS-Kavallerie-Regiment 52, 22.SS-Freiwilligen-Kavallerie-Division "Maria Theresia."

[225] Killed on August 29, 1943 as an ordnance officer on the SS-Kavallerie-Division staff.

[226] As an SS-Sturmbannführer he commanded SS-Kavallerie-Regiment 54, 22.SS-Freiwilligen-Kavallerie-Division Maria Theresia" and ended the war as Divisionsadjutant (IIa) of the 37.SS-Freiwilligen-Kavallerie-Division "Lützow."

[227] Killed on November 8, 1944 with the 14.Waffen-Grenadier-Division der SS.

[228] Awarded the Iron Cross 1st class on February 8, 1942.

[229] Missing in action during mid-January 1942.

[230] Killed on March 7, 1942 and replaced by SS-Untersturmführer Wilhelm Schmidt.

[231] Moved to 2nd Squadron of the same regiment in 1942 and as a platoon leader won the Iron Cross 1st class on February 28, 1942.

[232] Killed in January 1942.

2.platoon:	SS-Untersturmführer Willi Hammann[233]
3.platoon:	unassigned
2nd Squadron:	SS-Obersturmführer Heinz Wowerat[234]
car platoon:	SS-Oberscharführer Hans Zech-Nentwich
1.platoon:	SS-Obersturmführer Helmuth Guggolz[235]
2.platoon:	SS-Untersturmführer Heinrich Weissplock[236]
3.platoon:	SS-Standartenoberjunker Karl Jacobson[237]
3rd Squadron:	SS-Hauptsturmführer Hans-Viktor von Zastrow
car platoon:	SS-Standartenoberjunker Wolfgang Flügel[238]
1.platoon:	SS-Untersturmführer Werner Geissler[239]
2.platoon:	SS-Hauptscharführer Emil Pittermann
3.platoon:	unassigned
4th Squadron:	SS-Hauptsturmführer Kurt Wegener
1.platoon:	SS-Obersturmführer Hans Essl[240]
2.platoon:	SS-Standartenoberjunker Fritz Trösken[241]
3.platoon:	SS-Untersturmführer Wilhelm Schmidt
5th Squadron:[242]	SS-Hauptsturmführer Herbert Schönfeldt
1.platoon:	SS-Standartenoberjunker Hans Ertl
2.platoon:	SS-Untersturmführer Bodo Radmann[243]
3.platoon:	SS-Untersturmführer Ulrich Schönberg
4.platoon:	SS-Oberscharführer Alfred Luyken
5.platoon:	SS-Oberscharführer Cassilo Streicher
light calvary column:	SS-Obersturmführer Paul Hoppe

---

[233] Killed on March 7, 1942.

[234] Killed on February 11, 1945 as an SS-Hauptsturmführer commanding 4th Squadron of SS-Kavallerie-Regiment 54, 22.SS-Freiwilligen-Kavallerie-Division "Maria Theresia."

[235] Became commander of 2nd Squadron and died on September 10, 1987.

[236] Killed on January 23, 1942.

[237] Killed on February 22, 1942.

[238] Killed in January 1945 assigned to SS-Kavallerie-Regiment 53, 22.SS-Freiwilligen-Kavallerie-Division "Maria Theresia."

[239] Severely wounded in January 1942, during 1945 in Budapest he commanded 3rd Squadron of SS-Kavallerie-Regiment 16 (later designation of SS-Kavallerie-Regiment 2).

[240] Took command of the squadron when Wegener went to the SS-Führungshauptamt, awarded the Iron Cross 1st class on January 18, 1942 and was killed on March 17, 1942.

[241] Killed on March 3, 1945.

[242] Enlarged with troops of the dissolved 6th Squadron, its composition as the heavy weapons unit was stronger than 5th Squadron of SS-Kavallerie-Regiment 1 as that regiment's 6th Squadron went primarily to the Radfahr-Aufklärungsabteilung.

[243] Killed January 1942.

Bicycle Reconnaissance Detachment (Radfahr-Aufklärungsabteilung)

commander:	SS-Sturmbannführer Günther Temme[244]
adjutant:	SS-Untersturmführer Heinz Rebholz[245]
ordnance officer:	SS-Obersturmführer Walter Schmitt
detachment physician:	SS-Obersturmführer Dr. Sepp Spitzy
1st Squadron:	SS-Hauptsturmführer Willi Plänk
car platoon:	SS-Untersturmführer Karl Weeke
ordnance officer:	SS-Untersturmführer Walter Aust
1.platoon:	SS-Standartenoberjunker Erich Schaub
2.platoon:	SS-Oberscharführer Wolfgang Reinhardt
3.platoon:	SS-Standartenoberjunker Gerd Bauer
2nd Squadron:	SS-Obersturmführer Anton Koppenwallner[246]
car platoon:	SS-Standartenoberjunker Erhard Mösslacher[247]
1.platoon:	SS-Untersturmführer Walter von Scholz[248]
2.platoon:	SS-Standartenoberjunker Karl Schwarzmaier[249]
3.platoon:	SS-Untersturmführer Hans-Hermann Loy
3rd Squadron:	SS-Untersturmführer Rudi Schweinberger[250]
1.platoon:	(squadron commander)
2.platoon:	SS-Untersturmführer Artur Kessler
3.platoon:	SS-Obersturmführer Fritz Höhenberger[251]

Artillery Detachment (Artillerie Abteilung)

commander:	SS-Hauptsturmführer Arno Paul
administrative officer:	SS-Untersturmführer Werner Siemann[252]
physician:	SS-Hauptscharführer Dr. Hans Handrick
dentist:	SS-Untersturmführer Dr. Georg Grief
veterinarian:	SS-Untersturmführer Dr. Georg Leitner

---

[244] The exact date Temme replaced Albert Faßbender as commander of the Reconnaissance Detachment is as yet unclear. Temme was commanding the unit during the January 1942 operations and Faßbender is listed with several documents in December 1941 so the period of this list is as close as can be determined. Faßbender remained with the Brigade per award data for his Iron Cross and may have been serving as Army/SS liaison officer, a position which he had experience at previously. Temme probably arrived when the additional Brigade elements were summoned from Warsaw.

[245] Killed on January 28, 1942.

[246] Killed on January 10, 1942 and replaced by SS-Untersturmführer Hans Kleinlogel.

[247] Awarded the German Cross in Gold on September 26, 1943 as an SS-Obersturmführer in command of 6th Squadron of SS-Kavallerie-Regiment 2 (8.SS-Kavallerie-Division "Florian Geyer") and the Knight's Cross at the same command on February 9, 1945. He was killed in Budapest on February 11, 1945.

[248] Killed February 14, 1942.

[249] Later commanded SS-Kavallerie-Regiment 17 which formed in the summer of 1942 as the third regiment of the SS-Kavallerie-Division. Its numerical designation changed in October 1943 and was retained when a component of the second SS cavalry division was formed in order to perpetuate it.

[250] Killed on November 13, 1943 with the SS-Kavallerie-Division.

[251] In June 1944 commanded the reconnaissance detachment of the 8.SS-Kavallerie-Division "Florian Geyer."

[252] Became the first administrative officer of SS-Kavallerie-Regiment 3 of the SS-Kavallerie-Division in 1942.

1.battery commander: (detachment commander)
observation officer: SS-Obersturmführer Franz Spiehorn

2.battery commander: SS-Hauptsturmführer Friedrich Meyer[253]
observation officer: SS-Obersturmführer Johann Billerbeck

Anti-aircraft Battery (Flak Batterie)

commander: SS-Obersturmführer Ewald Keyk
ordnance officer: SS-Untersturmführer Friedrich Greger[254]
1.platoon: SS-Untersturmführer Hugo Riegger[255]
2.platoon: SS-Untersturmführer Kurt Portugall

Engineer Company (Pionier Kompanie)

commander: SS-Hauptsturmführer Karl Fritsche
1.platoon: (company commander)
2.platoon: SS-Obersturmführer Friedrich Maletta

Veterinary Company (Veterinär Kompanie)

commander: SS-Obersturmführer Dr. Fritz Eichlin
animal hospital section: SS-Oberscharführer Dietrich Schubert
administrative officer: SS-Untersturmführer Friedrich Kübler

Signals Company (Nachrichtenkompanie)

commander and platoon leader: SS-Obersturmführer Wilhelm Wiersch[256]
platoon leader: SS-Untersturmführer Herbert Wende

Medical Company (Sanitäts-Kompanie)

commander: SS-Hauptsturmführer Dr. Otto Mittelberger[257]
1.platoon: SS-Obersturmführer Dr. Friedrich Alteneder[258]
2.platoon: SS-Obersturmführer Dr. Karl Liesau
pharmacist: SS-Obersturmführer Dr. Karl Müller

[253] Awarded the Iron Cross 1st class on January 21, 1942 and killed on January 31, 1942. The remnants of this battery were absorbed by 1.Batterie.

[254] Awarded the German Cross in Gold on December 30, 1944 in command of 3.Batterie, SS-Flak Abteilung 8 which he led from 1942 to 1944. He became the last commander of the Flak Abteilung of the 8.SS-Kavallerie-Division "Florian Geyer."

[255] Later commander 14.(Flak)/SS-Panzer-Grenadier-Regiment 38, 17.SS-Panzer-Grenadier-Division "Götz von Berlichingen."

[256] Awarded the Iron Cross 1st class on February 12, 1942.

[257] Became divisional medical officer of the 8.SS-Kavallerie-Division "Florian Geyer" in 1944 and while holding the same position with the 9.SS-Panzer-Division "Hohenstaufen" was killed in January 1945 with the rank of SS-Obersturmbannführer.

[258] Died on January 12, 1987.

1st surgeon:	SS-Untersturmführer Dr. Hans-Georg Buddee[259]
2nd surgeon:	SS-Untersturmführer Dr. Hermann Hölscher
ambulance platoon:	SS-Obersturmführer Alfred Becker

As the situation became critical in other sectors of Army Group "Center," the potency of second-line units decreased as these were used to reinforce the front line. Almost simultaneously, an increasing number of partisan groups began forming and making their presence felt. Statements from captured partisans, regular Russian soldiers and local residents began to flood in from all over the rear area of Army Group "Center."[260] The enemy was becoming active both in front of and behind the German units.

These statements revealed several discouraging developments for the Germans. First, large groups of organized partisans led by military officers were located south of Basary where they were reconnoitering positions abandoned by SS-Kavallerie-Regiment 1 which was then marching toward the front. Another report told of a 100 man group of partisans, led by a Russian colonel, located 30 kilometers south of Jetkino. In the area 30 kilometers north-northeast of Jetkino a group of 200 to 300 partisans equipped with artillery was assembling. Northeast of Bolshcaja there were supposedly cut-off Siberian troops with a strength of 600 men moving in the direction of Szjelisharovo. All of these groups were in a position to directly effect 9.Armee. Another statement by a prisoner told of a larger partisan camp on the rail line between Weliki-Luki and Leningrad that intended to meet up with cut-off Russian troops in the October Forests along the rail line connecting Moscow and Leningrad. The last report, made on December 19th, claimed that an enemy transport plane with a crew of partisans was observed 30 kilometers south of Jetkino.[261] Any rumor of aircraft support understandably worried Army intelligence.

Fighting against partisans as well as accelerated preparations for mobility in the quickly approaching winter could only be continued until December 23rd, and then with only limited success. At this time SS-Kavallerie-Regiment 2 was fighting partisans 25 kilometers north of Dubno. Only one small anti-partisan operation was registered during this period. This occurred on December 22 and was of limited success considering the situation at hand. During a patrol, SS-Kavallerie-Regiment 2 managed to uncover a partisan camp 16 kilometers west of Bibjerevo equipped with eight bunkers which they later destroyed. Later that day the Regiment engaged in combat in Lunovka, a village situated 12 kilometers north of Bibjerevo. The Regiment suffered only one man wounded while the partisans lost two dead. A small amount of material was also confiscated: one light machine gun, five rifles, ten grenades and a number of Molotov-Cocktails as well as seven sacks of meal for the horses.[262]

After December 20th, communication was taken up with the XXIII.Armeekorps which reported that the Bicycle Reconnaissance Detachment would remain in its current position guarding the railway between Weliki-Luki and Rshev until at least the new year due its strategic importance. In spite of these orders, the Bicycle Reconnaissance Detachment, strengthened by the Flak-Batterie, was ordered by the XXIII.Armeekorps on December 22nd to march to Szjelisharovo (on the Volga river) and report to the 253.Infanterie Division. The transport of the motorized portions of the unit had to be canceled due to poor road conditions. The Bicycle Reconnaissance Detachment had to depend on sleds and the first units reached Nishnyja Goritzy on December 28 from where they conducted several reconnaissance probes.[263]

---

[259] Later served with the medical section of the 22.SS-Freiwilligen-Kavallerie-Division "Maria Theresia" as an SS-Hauptsturmführer.

[260] "Tätigkeitsbericht für die Zeit vom 20. -26.12. 1941."

[261] ibid.

[262] ibid.

[263] ibid.

Between December 24th and 28th, SS-Kavallerie-Regiment 1 and 2 were busy relocating to their newly assigned positions where they were to secure the rail lines between Weliki-Luki and Rshev and the line between Toropez and Dubno while also constructing fortified positions. While relocating they were ordered by SS-Standartenführer Hermann Fegelein (who had been stationed at the headquarters of 9.Armee since December 24th) to halt their march and equip themselves with sleds to regain mobility in view of the worsening winter weather conditions.[264]

According to an order issued by 9.Armee later that week, all available elements of the Brigade were to abandon their current positions guarding their respective rail lines and be put into action on the front south and southwest of Szjelisharovo. The fact that the Brigade was removed from guarding the supply lines of 9.Armee reflected the seriousness of the front line situation. SS-Kavallerie-Regiment 1 departed for the front from its position along the Basary/Rshev rail line with its forward most units reaching Nelidovo on December 28. The next day SS-Kavallerie-Regiment 1 secured strongpoints and the railway between Bary and Jetkino. Two days later they were traveling east along the rail line between Weliki-Luki and Rshev. The Regiment was able to use the sleds they had constructed under Fegelein's orders for this transport. SS-Kavallerie-Regiment 2 was relieved from its duties guarding the rail line between Shitovo and Dubno by parts of Army Wach-Bataillon 705 and left for the front from Dubno on December 28. Two days later the Regiment had reached an area 40 kilometers northeast of Dubno. The Bicycle Reconnaissance Detachment was already on its way to the front line and conducted reconnaissance patrols on route. On December 31st the Detachment reached the village of Pjenno on the Volga river.[265]

Elsewhere behind Army Group "Center," the loading of the Brigade's Mounted Artillery Batteries onto sleds was to be expedited so that they too could be transferred to the front. The Brigade even considered forming guard and horse care elements using prisoners with the support of former Czarist officers. Skis and winter clothing were to be supplied to the troops. Every available replacement from the SS-Kavallerie-Ersatz-Abteilung (cavalry replacement detachment) was ordered to report for duty. The rest of the report submitted by Hermann Fegelein was copied from the war diary of 9.Armee and reads as follows:[266]

"The enemy is attacking along the entire front as never before with strong forces. The condition on the front lines is serious since not enough reserves are available. The troops are fighting without winter clothing and the result is that they are freezing and only able to fight in localized strongpoint formations. The situation at this time requires only 'defense' and strong nerves to withstand the incredible fighting. By shortening the front, much equipment, including artillery and armored cars, had to be left behind. The Brigade with its equipment, weapons and strength in numbers has a fighting value of between one and two divisions and has been positioned in the furthermost line. The spirit of our troops is first rate."

---

[264] ibid.

[265] "Tätigkeitsbericht für die Zeit vom 20. -26.12. 1941" and "Kriegstagebuch des Kommandostabs der 'Reichsführer-SS' Nr. 1."

[266] "Tätigkeitsbericht für die Zeit vom 20. -26.12. 1941."

6

1942

In late December 1941 the situation along the German front was critical. The lines were spread thin and many months of fast-paced Blitzkrieg offensive operations had worn down both men and equipment. To make matters worse, the harsh Russian Winter caught the Germans totally unprepared to withstand the climatic change: there was a profound lack of winter clothing and equipment was not engineered to withstand the harsh change with temperatures plummeted on occasion to less than -35C. Vehicles were immobilized and men suffered from frostbite. To compound these problems, communication lines became increasingly difficult to maintain. All movement was grinding to a halt and orders quickly changed from *"advance!"* to *"hold at all costs!"*

The Russians, on the other hand, were accustomed to winter warfare and planned to take advantage of this favorable situation by mounting an offensive spearheaded with their elite Siberian troops. These units were well-equipped for the cold and even possessed several tank brigades. The offensive would serve to blunt the German Blitzkrieg and hopefully for the Russians reverse the front line situation.

In the front sector where the SS-Kavallerie-Brigade was positioned the Russians mounted an attack against the area of 9.Armee with numerous units aiming to surround this portion of Army Group "Center" that was generally centered in Rshev. Soviet forces, including the 1st, 3rd and 4th Strike Armies as well as the 22nd, 39th, 29th, 30th and 31st Armies blasted through the German lines of 9.Armee and the tangent flank of Army Group "North." Three German corps bore the brunt of the onslaught as Russian forces headed for the main road to Moscow situated south of 9.Armee, in hopes of encircling these German forces and destroying them. Due to their situation, the German units were initially unprepared to repulse such a massive attack. Directly in the path of the Soviet offensive was XXIII.Armeekorps and among the unfortunate units that were subordinated to it was the SS-Kavallerie-Brigade. In fact, the Brigade's Bicycle Reconnaissance Detachment found itself standing in front of the direct attack by the 4th Soviet Strike Army and other Russian units. The result of the attack would be the almost total destruction of the Detachment.

It was during this time period that the Brigade's status as a rear-area anti-partisan unit changed completely to that of a full-fledged front-line combat formation. Despite the fact that the Brigade gained its initial combat experience fighting poorly organized partisan forces while taking its orders from higher SS rear area commanders, the Brigade performed well operating under the command of critical Army generals. They more than held their own in this arena of experienced Wehrmacht troops, troops which maintained organizational and leadership methods which had thus far remained foreign to Fegelein's units. The success of the SS-Kavallerie-Brigade was evidenced by the continuous praise offered by Army leaders and by the award of the Knight's Cross to Hermann Fegelein. Numerous Iron Crosses were awarded to his troops as well. Despite the Brigade's relative success, the difficult operations on the Eastern Front gradually consumed all of its reserves and by the end of March the Brigade was reduced in size to that of a battle group consisting of some 700 men.[1]

---

[1] These battles were extremely difficult for all units situated on the Eastern Front during this time period. The severe conditions under which the soldiers were fighting is illustrated in an article titled "SS-Kavallerie-Brigade im Osten" in the February 1955 issue of the Waffen-SS veteran's magazine "Wiking Ruf." This article includes a report written by a war-reporter of the Brigade's Kriegsberichter unit.

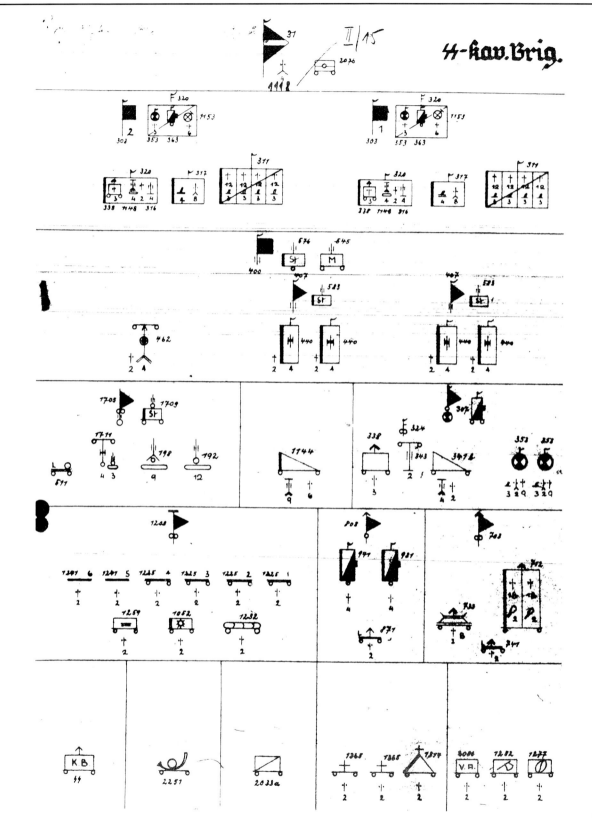

Order of Battle chart for the Brigade dated February 23, 1942. Many of the illustrated units, especially the reconnaissance detachment, were non-existent at this point after the massive Soviet offensive in January 1942. The anti-tank unit is shown as a separate Kompanie (it never was) and the artillery and anti-aircraft units are combined. These charts are often inaccurate and were revised often, both in the field and in Berlin, as new information was received. (National Archives)

Late in December 1941 the Brigade was officially subordinated to 9.Armee and received orders to gather in the area southwest of Lake Volga. The troops were scheduled to assemble after completing their winter movements which were to be carried out as soon as possible. The Bicycle Reconnaissance Detachment had already concluded its operations and was immediately dispatched from the area of Jetkino where it was ordered to report to the 253.Infanterie Division in Szjelisharov. SS-Kavallerie-Regiment 1 continued its security operations along the railway between Weliki-Luki and Rshev in the section due west of Basary (east of Jetkino). This involved relieving several security operations along the railway which had been endangered by partisans. SS-Kavallerie-Regiment 2 prepared to be sent by train to Dubno where they would embark on a march to Lugi.[2]

The Annihilation of the Bicycle Reconnaissance Detachment

During late December 1941 the Reconnaissance Detachment was subordinated to the 253.Infantrie Division which came under the command of the XXIII.Armeekorps led by General der Infanterie Albrecht Schubert.[3] At this time the Detachment had other units of the Brigade attached to it including portions of both SS-Kavallerie-Regimenter, the staff quarters of the Brigade's commander, an artillery battery, a light cavalry column, a motor vehicle platoon, the vehicle repair platoon, the veterinary element, portions of the Brigade communications unit and additional communications personnel attached from the Kommandostab "Reichsführer-SS." On December 25, 1941 the first parts of the Bicycle Reconnaissance Detachment were arriving in Selisharovo, located on the left flank of the 253.Infanterie Division, to which unit the Detachment was to be subordinated in the coming weeks. The first element to arrive consisted of one officer and 35 men and by the end of the following day the entire Detachment had arrived. Continuing its march east after a short pause to rest, the Detachment reached Goritzy by December 28th. Elsewhere, the 253.Infanterie Division was actively conducting reconnaissance patrols around Lake Volga and the villages of Koscheljeva and Postchinck where on December 30th a large enemy movement was reported. Further reconnaissance patrols were sent to Inssinkoje and Gorodischtzche which later revealed that these villages were occupied by Russian troops, while another patrol sent to Peno ascertained that this village was not occupied. Since Peno was situated on the open left flank of 253.Infanterie Division, the Bicycle Reconnaissance Detachment was sent to this village to protect the flank. Shortly after arriving there the Division ordered the Reconnaissance Detachment to reconnoiter Lake Volga in the direction of Kusstynja and Pokrovskaja. Later the same day, several of the Division's returning reconnaissance patrols reported increasing enemy activity in the area of their left flank.

In the early hours of December 31st some fighting was noted as the Division was attacked by a Russian patrol plane which flew from Momonovo to Boykovo. At 1115 hours 9.Armee sent a message to the 253.Infanterie Division informing them that SS-Kavallerie-Brigade[4] would not be subordinated to them on their left flank as originally intended, but instead would be put on the right flank. The Division was promised that they would be subordinated a different unit, most probably the 189.Infanterie Regiment[5] which was to be transported to the front from Dubno. The 253.Infanterie Division continued to feel the pressure on its left flank but events were relatively calm in this sector of the front and the Division only reported receiving light shelling by heavy Soviet artillery. This occurred in the section of the front occupied by the 473.Infanterie Regiment.[6] It was a brief pause before the storm.

---

[2] "Bericht über den Einsatz der SS-Kav.Brigade Winter 1941/42."

[3] Awarded the Knight's Cross on September 17, 1941 as commander of XXIII.Armeekorps.

[4] Not to be confused with the Bicycle Reconnaissance Detachment, this is a reference to the SS-Kavallerie-Regimenter 1 and 2.

[5] The 189. (Silesian) Infanterie Regiment was originally subordinated to the 81.Infanterie Regiment and had been called in from southern France to strengthen the critical situation developing on the Eastern Front.

[6] "Kriegstagebuch Nr. 9, XXIII.Armeekorps, Abt. Ia, 1.11-1941-31.1.42."

Albert Faßbender during formation of the SS-Kavallerie-Division as an SS-Sturmbannführer while commanding SS-Kavallerie-Regiment 3. He is on the right shaking hands with the Division Medical Officer SS-Obersturmbannführer Dr. Edwin Jung. His WWI Iron Crosses have clasps attached to show his being awarded both decorations in WWII as well (with the SS-Kavallerie Brigade). Faßbender was commanding the SS-Kavallerie-Brigade Reconnaissance Detachment prior to the Russian offensive and in January returned to Debica, Poland with some survivors. Commander of the Reconnaissance Detachment in Russia during the Soviet offensive was Günther Temme who arrived from the Berlin based replacement unit in late December 1941. (Photo: Jost Schneider)

Light fireworks brought in the New Year for the Germans as shelling continued early on the morning of January 1, 1942 in the villages of Koslovo and Schachvorostovo. At 1600 hours that afternoon, the Division reported it had been attacked. The Russians first attempted to soften up the Germans by barraging them with heavy artillery fire from heavy and light artillery pieces as well as grenade launchers followed by a battalion strength attack at 0900 hours. This was repulsed but the Russians attacked again twice. These assaults were also repelled. Multiple battalion-strength attacks were also held back between the Sselisharov-Otherkov road and Kokoschino.[7]

At 1120 hours on January 2nd the men of the 253.Infanterie Division and all their components (which included at that time the 189.Infanterie Regiment and the Bicycle Reconnaissance Detachment) were read the latest order from the Führer: *"9.Armee will not take one more step back!"* Later that day the 253.Infanterie Division sent a message to the XXIII.Armeekorps stating that 189.Infanterie Regiment was in transport to Dubno and was then to be sent on to Okovtzy. Massive confusion followed as multiple commands claimed operational jurisdiction over this Army regiment until it was decided that for the moment it would be under the command of 16.Armee (Army Group "North").[8]

---

[7] ibid.

[8] ibid.

Meanwhile, the Bicycle Reconnaissance Detachment was busy patrolling the surrounding areas of their position and setting up defensive positions as ordered by the 253.Infanterie Division. The village of Peno was practically abandoned before the German offensive had run through the town. This made it easier for the men of the Detachment to build their defensive positions, consisting of several bunkers made of snow. Reconnaissance operations revealed that the Russians were situated in the area of Polrovakoje (25 kilometers southwest of Osztaschkov). The Bicycle Reconnaissance Detachment's nearest enemy neighbors on both flanks were only 12 kilometers away. In order to at least reduce the size of the gap to their left neighbor, a platoon was positioned 4 1/2 kilometers north of Peno in the village of Potschinck. During this time the Detachment urgently reminded the 253rd Division of the threatening situation and reported that due to the Detachment's complete lack of heavy weapons and the fact that the Detachment reconnaissance operations were revealing the increasing strength of the enemy, the situation in the area of Peno is to be considered dangerous." Commander SS-Sturmbannführer Günther Temme also complained about the supply situation. Instead of receiving supplies from the forward depots, as did the rest of XXIII.Armeekorps, the Detachment was forced to receive theirs from the rear area facilities in Dubno. The weather, along with the long distances required to receive these supplies, made matters even more difficult. In spite of the difficult resupply situation, Temme reported his satisfaction with the morale and reliability of his troops. The men of the Detachment performed their duties with enthusiasm, continuing to conduct patrol operations and build defensive positions as ordered by 253.Infanterie Division. They also made the necessary supply runs to Dubno and assisted in the transportation of the wounded to Dubrovski.[9]

The 253.Infanterie Division reported what they thought the enemy situation in their area was. Their intelligence determined in Osstaschkov there was a collection of strong Russian forces and it is possible that they could be planning an offensive against Szjelisharovo (the open left flank) or drive a wedge over Peno into the gap between Army Group "Center" and Army Group "North." On January 3rd a unit of the Bicycle Reconnaissance Detachment captured a Russian messenger. The runner was searched and a message to a partisan staff located behind the German lines was found. This message gave the Germans the impression that the two groups *"would see each other again in Peno in about ten days."* The Reconnaissance Detachment reported this critical information to the Division, but they had already convinced themselves that an attack would most likely come against Szjelisharovo.[10]

During the next few days, the situation in the sector of the 253.Infanterie Division remained relatively calm. On January 4th the Division reported to XXIII.Armeekorps that their front had stretched to a length of 60 kilometers. The Division reported on January 5th that Russian patrols had mined the road between Sasykov and Trofimkov while heavy partisan activity was reported four kilometers north of Peno. In the minds of the Detachment's personnel, this information reinforced their conviction that Peno and not Szjelisharovo would be the center of an attack. No fighting erupted, however, and on January 6th, the situation remained calm on the left flank of the Division while several patrols reconnoitering the surrounding area produced no results. Reconnaissance operations continued the next day and the Division requested that the triangular area, formed by the cities of Sselcharov, Osstaschkovo and the train station in Peno, be reconnoitered. The Bicycle Reconnaissance Detachment took part in these operations. Elsewhere, the Division defeated enemy artillery battery positions and several fighting groups in the area around Ssorokino, the villages north of the Lake Volga and in Jassenskoe.

[9] "Bericht über den Einsatz der SS-Kav. Brigade Winter 1941/42," dated February 11, 1942 and signed by SS-Sturmbannführer Gustav Lombard and "SS-Kavallerie-Brigade im Osten," Wiking-Ruf, 4. Jahrgang, Nr. 2, Februar 1955.

[10] "Bericht über den Einsatz der SS-Kav. Brigade Winter 1941/42," dated February 11, 1942 and signed by SS-Sturmbannführer Gustav Lombard.

Field Marshal Walter Model, one of the best commanders of the Army. As commander of 9.Armee after mid-January 1942, the SS-Kavallerie-Brigade was under his command during the 1942 Soviet winter offensive. He was awarded the Knight's Cross on July 9, 1941 as commander of 3.Panzer-Division, the Oakleaves on February 13, 1942 for command of XLI.Panzerkorps, the Swords on April 2, 1943 as commander of 9.Armee and the Diamonds on August 17, 1944 while commanding Army Group "Center." Model committed suicide on April 21, 1945 while commanding Army Group "B." (Photo: Jess Lukens)

At 1030 hours on the morning on January 9th the feared Russian offensive began on the left flank of the 253.Infanterie Division,[11] and just as the Detachment had feared, the offensive headed right in their direction and not towards Szjelisharovo as predicted by the Army. At 1115 hours the Reconnaissance Detachment received an order from 253.Infanterie Division to hold the village at all costs. At 1215 hours the Detachment reported that the situation at its outpost situated in Postchink was becoming critical. The Russians attacked hard there and the platoon situated there was forced to retreat to Peno, which concurred with orders given by 253.Infanterie Division. After softening up the Reconnaissance Detachment's positions in Peno with light infantry artillery fire, the brunt of the enemy attack began at 1650 hours that evening. Wave upon wave of Russian troops attacked the north end of the small village. The attacking Russian forces were well-equipped Siberian units, outfitted with snow-shoes for better mobility. The attacking units recognized the gaps left open by the thinly distributed German troops and took full advantage of the situation, forcing the Germans to change positions several times. Then came the first attack by Soviet tanks. Several T-34s began blasting the Germans out of their positions and by 1755 hours the enemy surrounded the village from three sides and succeeded in penetrating and holding the northern part of the village. After the fighting continued for two more hours, the commander of the 2nd Squadron, SS-Obersturmführer Anton Koppenwallner, saluted a "Sieg Heil!" to the Führer and led a thrown together group of veterans back into the northern part of the city for a counterattack. After over an hour of close

---

[11] The Russian units attacking in the sector held by the Bicycle Reconnaissance Detachment were from the 249th Soviet Rifle Division under Major-General Terassov. This unit, of which half were members of the Russian Communist Party, was viewed as an elite unit of politically motivated soldiers. Their ultimate goal was to reach Toropez, the German supply center, in the hopes to capture much needed supplies.

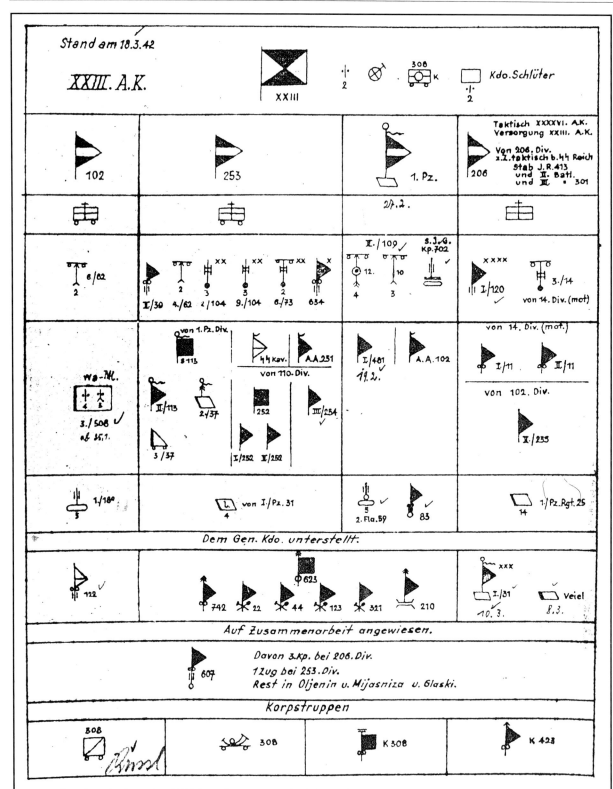

Two Order of Battle charts for XXIII.Armeekorps in March 1942 with both showing attachment of the SS-Kavallerie-Brigade. Though only separated by a week, the number of units attached or changed varied considerably. The two primary divisions, 102. and 253., are seen in both while one shows 1.Panzer Division which fought in conjunction with the Korps often during the opening months of 1942. Numerous smaller Army units were attached independently as was the remnants of the SS-Kavallerie-Brigade. (National Archives)

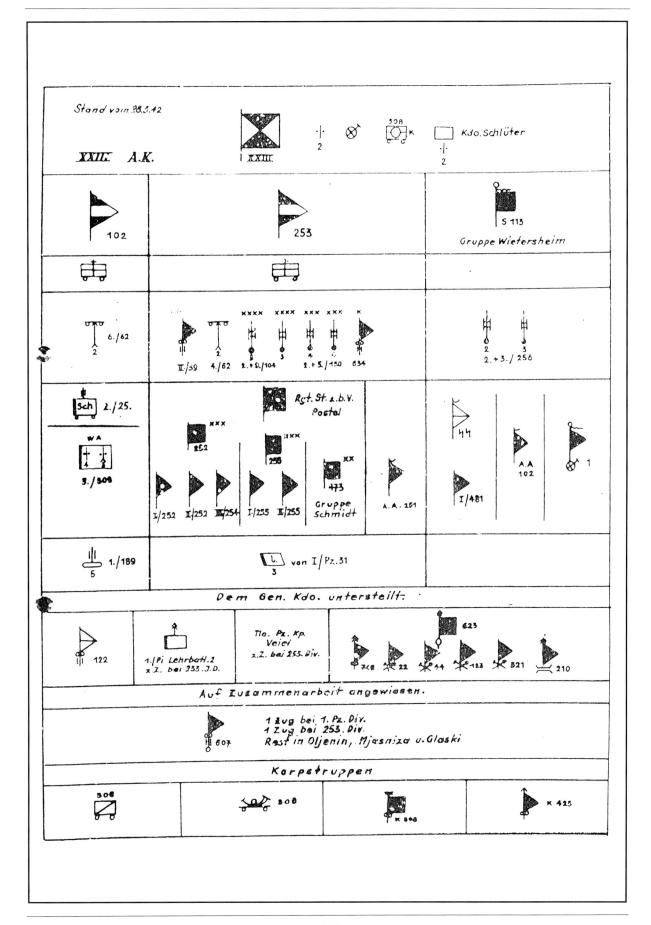

combat, Koppenwallner's group managed to throw the Russians out of the village and at 2115 hours Peno was again in the hands of the Bicycle Reconnaissance Detachment.[12] SS-Obersturmführer Koppenwallner was killed during this fight and the remaining officers badly wounded. According to statements made by prisoners, the attack was led by the 917th and the 925th Russian Rifle Regiments and two more Russian regiments were on their way from the northwest. During subsequent communication with the 253.Infanterie Division, the divisional commander expressed special recognition for the defensive fighting against a more than superior enemy force, due to a large extent from the actions of Koppenwallner and his men. Praise being of little value at that point, the Detachment did not lose any chance to inform 253.Infanterie Division of the high casualties they had suffered and the urgent need to receive reserves and at the very least to be re-supplied with ammunition. Their requests to be supplied through air-drops continued until 2300 hours, but to no avail. The Division promised to do what was in its power. As it later tuned out it was not in any position to help the Reconnaissance Detachment.[13]

Meanwhile the Russians tried to destroy the positions of the 253.Infanterie Division on the southern shore of Lake Volga with continuous waves of air attacks. The Russians led bomber attacks on the villages of Bor, Ssossnovatka, Juschino and Volga, but only light casualties were suffered. In the middle of the day the XXIII.Armeekorps lost all radio contact with the 253.Infanterie Division and could only rely on wire communication lines to try and receive status information. The Division strongpoint in Devitschje was overrun by the Soviets and it appeared that the attack was carried out further by planes in a wide attack formation between Gorodischtsche and Baranaja Gora. In consideration of this situation, the Division requested the XXIII.Armeekorps to reconnoiter the area north of Lake Volga. The Division also pleaded with the Korps to somehow bring in the 189.Infanterie Regiment. Another message which was sent to the Korps arrived at 1940 hours and reiterated the critical condition on the left flank of the 253.Infanterie Division. In a sector that was 35 kilometers wide, the strengthened 453.Infanterie Regiment as well as the Bicycle Reconnaissance Detachment were fighting dogged defensive battles, but were surrounded. 253.Infanterie Division itself was attacked at 1855 hours. The details of this fighting were unclear to Korps headquarters, but they predicted that the enemy would continue to attack in a southeast and southwest direction.[14]

On January 10th more Russians arrived for the battle against the Bicycle Reconnaissance Detachment around Peno. The pressure on the Detachment grew stronger by the hour and it began to form new defensive positions in the southern part of the village. This was the only area of the village open to the Russians and permission to establish new positions was granted by 253.Infanterie Division. After fighting for over 20 continuous hours, the Detachment had run out of grenades for its heavy grenade launchers and ammunition for its 7.5 cm infantry cannons. Almost all light and heavy weapons had frozen solid and the ammunition supply for the remaining machine guns and rifles was running dangerously low. Low on firepower and completely surrounded, the fate of the Detachment was sealed. The remaining elements, realizing this, gathered around commander Temme to plan a breakout attempt. Temme ordered any weapon heavier than a light machine gun and all horses to be left behind. The troops broke out at 1500 hours and managed to escape the village in a southwesterly direction. After a 22 kilometer march over incredibly difficult terrain, the surviving remnants of the Bicycle Reconnaissance Detachment reached the village of Orlina.[15]

[12] Although this book is based almost exclusively on period documentation while avoiding the input of opinion, Koppenwallner's bravery and tenacity in this critical situation were undoubtedly worthy of the award of a decoration for valor. As happened often in pressing situations, there was neither time or ability to write such a recommendation.

[13] "Bericht über den Einsatz der SS-Kav. Brigade Winter 1941/42," "SS-Kavallerie-Brigade im Osten" and "Bericht über die R.A.A. der SS-Kav.-Brig. während der Unterstellungszeit unter 253. I.D. vom 26.12.1941 bis Mitte Januar 1942," written by the commander of the XXIII.Armeekorps General der Infanterie Albrecht Schubert.

[14] "Kriegstagebuch Nr. 9, XXIII.Armeekorps, Abt. Ia, 1.11-1941-31.1.42."

[15] "Bericht über den Einsatz der SS-Kav. Brigade Winter 1941/42," dated February 11, 1942 and signed by SS-Sturmbannführer Gustav Lombard.

By this time significant losses had greatly depleted the strength of the Detachment. Aside from losing the majority of their equipment and all of their mobility, a large number of men were killed in the battle for Peno. The last weekly tactical and situational report in December listed the Detachment with a strength of 20 officers, 76 NCOs and 518 enlisted ranks, a combined total of 614 men.[16] It can be assumed that the Detachment began the battle in Peno with approximately the same number of men, since no real fighting took place between the time the report was written and the battle. The report written later by SS-Hauptsturmführer Gustav Lombard lists the strength of the Detachment at the end of the Peno battle as 11 officers, 55 NCOs and 352 men, a combined total of 418 men, bringing their losses to a total of almost 200 or 30% of their pre-engagement strength.[17]

On January 10th the 253.Infanterie Division reported to the XXIII.Armeekorps that all contact with the Bicycle Reconnaissance Detachment had been lost since sometime before noon. The Division stated that based on this situation, it had assumed that Peno was no longer in German hands. The Division also reported that they had determined that one of the Detachment's strongpoints, located five kilometers southeast of Peno in the village of Shukopa, had been overrun and was now in the hands of the enemy. Russian forces were then dispatching reconnaissance patrols to Gorovastiza and the Division itself had to break off an attack against the Russians in the forest east of Bor since it was getting dark.[18]

On January 11th the 253.Infanterie Division reported light enemy reconnaissance activity in the sector of 464.Infanterie Regiment. Contact with the Bicycle Reconnaissance Detachment had not yet been reestablished. The Luftwaffe was requested to conduct aerial reconnaissance in the area between the Lake Volga and Peno to hopefully determine where the Detachment was located. Elsewhere the 253.Infanterie Division continued to be attacked. Fierce assaults were carried out on Bor and in the direction of Chorevo while the Russians had managed to penetrate through the line connecting the villages of Frolovo, Schyvaevo and Gorovastiza. The Division also received a transmission that the 189.Infanterie Regiment had arrived in Lugi with two battalions, one artillery battery, two light infantry cannon platoons and an anti-tank gun. 253.Infanterie Division also reported that 189.Infanterie Regiment was to be sent on to Peno through Ochvat and Lauga and was to arrive in Szoblago on January 12th. The Regiment at this time was still under the direct command of the Army High Command (Oberkommando des Heeres). This report was confirmed by the II.Armeekorps at 1700 hours. The Division briefed the II.Armeekorps (positioned on the southern or right flank of Army Group "North") of the situation in Peno and informed them that they would shortly be requesting the Regiment be sent to Peno. The whereabouts of the Bicycle Reconnaissance Detachment was finally reported to XXIII.Armeekorps at 1800 hours. They were reportedly retreating to the southwest and were in Volok on their way to the village of Lugi. The 253.Infanterie Division also reported continued heavy combat taking place in and around Bor. Between Bor and Paschutina there was a large gap and it was unknown at this time as to whether the remaining forces of the Division could close it in time to halt another Russian assault.[19]

As the Bicycle Reconnaissance Detachment was retreating on January 11th, the Soviets were in hot pursuit. Several Soviet units were reportedly on the road between Peno and Lugi with a 50 man portion of an advance unit in Volok. These units immediately proceeded to attack the Detachment, but the 1st Squadron managed to repulse their attack and throw them out of the village. This attack cost the Detachment considerably, but exact numbers of casualties were not reported. Lack of information about these battles in reports is a good indication that casualties were high. Later that day the Detachment arrived in Lugi where it met up with elements of the 189.Infanterie Regiment.

---

[16] "Tätigkeitbericht für die Zeit vom 20. - 26. 12. 1941," dated December 29, 1941 and "Bericht über die R.A.A. der SS-Kav.-Brig. während der Unterstellungszeit unter 253. I.D. vom 26.12.1941 bis Mitte Januar 1942."

[17] "Bericht über den Einsatz der SS-Kav. Brigade Winter 1941/42."

[18] "Kriegstagebuch Nr. 9, XXIII.Armeekorps, Abt. Ia, 1.11-1941-31.1.42."

[19] ibid.

The commander of 3rd Squadron, SS-Kavallerie-Regiment 1 in early 1942, SS-Obersturmführer Hans-Georg von Charpentier. Shown here (left) as an SS-Hauptsturmführer in the autumn of 1942 and (below) with SS-Obersturmbannführer Gustav Lombard after being awarded the Knight's Cross. Born in Strassburg on July 16, 1902, he served in an Army cavalry unit during 1919. Joining SS-Reiterstandarte 6 in March 1935, he served with the SS-Totenkopf-Reiterstandarte in 1st Squadron as an NCO from the beginning. Commissioned an SS-Untersturmführer d.R. on October 29, 1940, he served with 3rd Squadron, SS-Kavallerie-Regiment 1 and later commanded a car platoon before becoming regimental adjutant in August 1941. Promoted to SS-Obersturmführer d.R. July 15, 1941, he took over 1st Squadron briefly after the Soviet offensive started in 1942 and then took command of 3rd Squadron. He was awarded the Iron Cross 1st class on January 26, 1942. Promoted to SS-Hauptsturmführer d.R. on March 16, 1942 he was given command of the new third regiment of the SS-Kavallerie-Division in December 1943 (which became SS-Kavallerie-Regiment 18) and held command until killed in Budapest on February 11, 1945. He was awarded the Knight's Cross on December 29, 1942 and received a final promotion to SS-Sturmbannführer d.R. on October 11, 1944. (Photo: National Archives and Jost Schneider)

SS-Sturmbannführer Temme informed the Regiment that the Detachment was no longer fit for action and demanded that they be allowed quarter in the Dubno area.[20]

At noon the next day (January 12th) the 189.Infanterie Regiment reported to the 253.Infanterie Division that during their march to Peno that they had observed the Bicycle Reconnaissance Detachment fleeing from fights in several villages including Ochvat on its retreat to Weliki-Luki. The Division then sent requests as to the exact whereabouts of the Detachment so it could issue orders. In agreement with XXIII.Armeekorps, the 253.Infanterie Division subordinated the Reconnaissance Detachment to the 189.Infanterie Regiment and ordered the Regiment to absorb the Detachment under any circumstance at 1730 hours. If the Reconnaissance Detachment refused, the Division instructed the 189.Infanterie Regiment to make an immediate report to this effect.[21]

In other sectors of the 253.Infanterie Division January 12th began with continued strong Russian attacks on its left flank in the sector of Lake Volga but these were repulsed. Two Russian regiments were pushed in the direction of the train station in Peno while the furthermost troops of the 189.Infanterie Regiment were engaged in defensive fighting near the train station in Ochvat.[22]

On January 13th, the 253.Infanterie Division was busy holding out in a ring of defensive fighting that had thus far lasted for five days. They had continued to hold back continuous breakthrough attempts, but now the front was ripped open near the area Peno where the Bicycle Reconnaissance Detachment had been defeated earlier that day. II.Armeekorps was also retreating to the east. The Russians were deploying strong forces along the front of the 253.Infanterie Division near Peno and were also sending troops located in the south in a westerly direction towards Dubno. There the Russians reached the train station in Ochvat and it was questionable as to whether or not 189.Infanterie Regiment could hold out. Later that day a further advance of the Russians from Peno to the southeast into the back of the 253.Infanterie Division had just reached Gorowastiza and the Division, lacking any reserves, was forced to call back the now weak companies that it had positioned north of the line between Ramenje and Mal. Lochovo. Attacks by the Russians near Schywaevo, which penetrated through the gaps in front of the 253.Infanterie Division, forced them to send units to the south to relieve other units of the Division as well as portions of the 206.Infanterie Division. The Army units were being given a clearer view of the attack intensity the Reconnaissance Detachment withstood without being properly supplied. Later that day the 253.Infanterie Division reported receiving the following message from the Reconnaissance Detachment:[23]

"1.) Bicycle Reconnaissance Detachment has packed up in Dubno with the purpose of regrouping and re-equipping in Toropez.
2.) We have just received the order that we are subordinated to the 189.Infanterie Regiment.
3.) Strength: 5 Officers, 20 NCOs and 165 enlisted men. Weapons: 8 light machine guns, otherwise the Detachment is without any equipment whatsoever.
4.) I will report to the advanced command post of the 189.Infanterie Regiment. Immediate answer urgently requested.

signed Temme
Commander, SS-R.A.A."

---

[20] "Bericht über den Einsatz der SS-Kav. Brigade Winter 1941/42" and "Bericht über den Einsatz der SS-Kav. Brigade Winter 1941/42,"

[21] "Bericht über die R.A.A. der SS-Kav.-Brig. während der Unterstellungszeit unter 253. I.D. vom 26.12.1941 bis Mitte Januar 1942."

[22] "Kriegstagebuch Nr. 9, XXIII.Armeekorps, Abt. Ia, 1.11-1941-31.1.42."

[23] "Kriegstagebuch Nr. 9, XXIII.Armeekorps, Abt. Ia, 1.11-1941-31.1.42." and "Bericht über die R.A.A. der SS-Kav.-Brig. während der Unterstellungszeit unter 253. I.D. vom 26.12.1941 bis Mitte Januar 1942."

Temme's unit had suffered casualties amounting to 70%. On January 14th the enemy continued its advance and took Lugi. The city of Dubno was then put on alarm and the Reconnaissance Detachment, still without any weapons, was ordered to build a defense system. After finally being re-equipped with weapons received from the 189.Infanterie Regiment, the Detachment took position in the neighboring village of Rochov. During mid-day on January 15th the Russians attacked the Detachment with infantry supported by tanks. The battle raged for seven hours and, despite losing all of their heavy machine guns and a complete lack of heavy weapons of any type, the Detachment held the Russians back. By 0430 hours next day the Detachment had lost all contact with the 189.Infanterie Regiment. After the command to give up Dubno was given, the Detachment slowly pulled back to the railway while continuing to fight and was the last unit to be evacuated, covering the withdrawal of the Army troops despite it being the most battle damaged unit. After escaping the village by train, the Reconnaissance Detachment set out by foot and marched for sixteen hours before finally reaching the village of Toropez early the morning of January 17th. The defensive fighting in Dubno cost the unit a further 3 officers and 41 men.[24] On January 18, 1942 the Brigade was awarded 60 2nd class Iron Crosses (one was a clasp to a WWI award) and one Iron Cross 1st class. On January 16th the following order was received by 9.Armee:[25]

"Commander of the rear area Army Group 'Center' takes over the command of all troops in the area of Lugi, Toropez and Dubno. Seperational line of 9.Armee (XXIII.Armeekorps) is the Basary railway to the train station in Semzy to Schankareva to Jassinakoje. All deployed forces north and west of this border are to be subordinated to the 403. Sicherheits Division."

With this order both the remnants of 189.Infanterie Regiment and the Bicycle Reconnaissance Detachment departed from the command of the XXIII.Armeekorps. Unfortunately for the Detachment, the fight was not over. The Russian offensive did not cease and on January 19th the Russians attacked Toropez with tanks and strong infantry forces. Two companies of a police regiment situated there suffered heavy casualties immediately. The police regiment, in possession of three anti-tank guns, managed several direct hits on the attacking tanks with absolutely no effect whatsoever. As the battle continued, two of the anti-tank guns were knocked out of action. Despite heavy casualties and lack of weapons, the constant Russian attacks were beaten back until 0200 hours on January 20th. Two infantry platoons of the Wach Bataillon 705 (Guard Battalion 705), which had arrived as reinforcements, managed to slightly lighten the burden of the fighting troops. Casualties totaling more than 75% and six newly arrived Russian tanks make it necessary to pull back the remaining men of the Reconnaissance Detachment along the railway to Weliki-Luki at 1700 hours. During this fighting the Detachment lost another nine dead, seventeen missing and 22 wounded, leaving it with a collective strength of some 109 men. Of these 109 men, 91 had mild to severe frostbite by the time they arrived in Weliki-Luki. On January 22nd SS-Sturmbannführer Temme, his adjutant and the 1a of the Brigade[26] reported to the commander of Army Group "Center," Field Marshal Günther von Kluge, at his headquarters in Smolensk. There they discovered there were no forces available to improve the situation in Toropez and that the poor supply conditions, which were rendering the German troops almost ineffective, could not be improved. After this depressing conversation, the three officers set out for SS-Kavallerie-Brigade headquarters while the rest of the men were subordinated to the 189.Infanterie Regiment. The last known reference to the Bicycle Reconnaissance Detachment refers to the battle for Nelidova, another supply center near Toropez, during which several men of the Detachment's heavy squadron under the leadership

[24] "Bericht über den Einsatz der SS-Kav. Brigade Winter 1941/42."

[25] "Kriegstagebuch Nr. 9, XXIII.Armeekorps, Abt. Ia, 1.11-1941-31.1.42."

[26] The Brigade administration officer, SS-Sturmbannführer Wilhelm Jeppe, is listed in one document during this period as Ia, most probably as a temporary position when Karl Gesele was situated with other elements of the Brigade due to the fluid nature of the fighting. Gesele remained official Ia of the SS-Kavallerie-Brigade throughout the fighting in Russia and held that position with Kampfgruppe "Zehender" as well.

of SS-Obersturmführer Fritz Höhenberger were holding the village during a Russian attack on January 24th.[27]

Most of these few remaining men were eventually evacuated from the front and returned to Poland where they sent to the Debica training grounds for rest and refit. The rebuilt Reconnaissance Detachment remained there and was deployed to fight partisan groups for the remaining existence of the Brigade before the 8.SS-Kavallerie-Division was officially formed.[28] The conflicting reports about the Reconnaissance Detachment and observations by Army officers about the unit initially insinuated the Detachment ran from the fighting, as explained by Gustav Lombard in his report. It was eventually (correctly) seen that Temme and his men fought bravely against impossible odds in a deadly situation, a situation partly caused by the Army's inability to supply the Detachment. On March 25, 1942 General der Infanterie Albrecht Schubert, the commander of XXIII.Armeekorps, approved the following awards of the Iron Cross 1st class to the men of the Detachment.[29]

SS-Sturmbannführer Günther Temme:	Detachment Commander
SS-Untersturmführer Hans Kleinlogel:	Commander 2nd Squadron
SS-Untersturmführer Rudi Schweinberger:	Commander 3rd Squadron
SS-Untersturmführer Dr. Sepp Spitzy:	Detachment Physician
SS-Untersturmführer Artur Kessler:	2nd Platoon Leader, 3rd Squadron
SS-Standartenoberjunker Karl Schwarzmeier:	2nd Platoon Leader, 2nd Squadron
SS-Standartenoberjunker Erhard Möslacher:	Car Platoon Leader, 2nd Squadron
SS-Hauptscharführer Wolfgang Reinhardt	
SS-Unterscharführer Hans Arthuber	
SS-Sturmann Anton Rüdgers	

With the almost total destruction of the Bicycle Reconnaissance Detachment the Brigade lost one of its three primary units. It was now reduced to the two Kavallerie Regimenter (including the artillery batteries), Brigade Staff, Engineer Company, a light cavalry column, the Anti-aircraft Battery from the Kommandostab "Reichsführer-SS," most of the Signals Company and the surviving medical personnel and their support components.

SS-Kavallerie-Regimenter 1 and 2 in the Battle for Rshev

The ongoing security operations assigned to SS-Kavallerie-Regiment 1 in late December 1941 along the railway to Rshev were assumed from German police units. These formations did not possess the necessary strength to protect this area effectively as they were better suited for guard operations. The Regiment was also assigned to take over guard duties at a local prison which held approximately 500 inmates.[30]

The operations in these areas, the occupied sectors closest to the front, allowed SS-Kavallerie-Regiment 1 to maintain occupation operations within the towns of their former quarters. In correspondence with a Korps order these towns were used as strongpoints. This not only retained the towns under German rule, but also provided a secure place to keep the reserve horses. Deployment at the front required great mobility of troops assigned to the stables, a mobility which the worsening winter weather had all but completely eliminated. Rear area strongpoints also served as checks against threatening situations at the front.[31]

---

[27] "Bericht über den Einsatz der SS-Kav. Brigade Winter 1941/42."

[28] "Schlacht- u.Gefechtsbezeichnungen für das 1.Halbjahr 1942," dated February 28, 1943 and signed by SS-Standartenführer Fritz Freitag.

[29] Generalkommando XXIII.A.K., Abt. IIa Brb. Nr./42 "Verleihungsliste Nr. 67,"Dated February 25, 1942 and signed by Schubert. The commander of 1st Squadron , Willi Plänk, had already won the decoration on October 27, 1941 for command of his unit.

[30] "Bericht über den Einsatz der SS-Kav.Brigade Winter 1941/42."

[31] ibid.

Due to these reasons, the Brigade's staff was under the impression that while being subordinated to the XXIII.Armeekorps they would only be temporarily deployed to strengthen the winter defense line and only long enough for the situation to be stabilized. The increasingly critical situation at the front placed special emphasis on the one-track railway between Weliki-Luki, Toropez and Dubno which would have to remain open for supply operations to continue. Army Group "Center" was also aware that the Brigade was very familiar with the rear areas from both a terrain and geographical point of view, since SS-Kavallerie-Regiment 1 had only recently (October) been subordinated to the 253.Infanterie Division. Should any threat cause front-line units to retreat, the Army Group could depend on the Brigade to stabilize the situation. But on the other hand, the Brigade's staff also sensed the increasingly difficult and unpredictable situation in the east. It was clear to them that Army Group "Center" had calculated the Russians would make strong attempts to break through from the general direction of Osstaschkov. They knew that the strength of the Army troops in the area south of the Lake Volga had been greatly depleted after months of maintaining the extreme left flank of Army Group "Center." [32]

By December 31st the Brigade reached Gorovasstizy with SS-Kavallerie-Regiment 1 while SS-Kavallerie-Regiment 2 was on a train to Dubno. After arriving in Dubno, SS-Kavallerie-Regiment 2 was given march orders to Lugi. The remaining portions of SS-Kavallerie-Regiment 1 were ordered to depart from Jetkino for Cholmjetzy. The Regimenter were forced to leave the majority of their horses behind with the bulk of the troops continuing their transport on sleds. Only combat troops were sent to the front, the rest of the personnel remained stationed at the rear. 9.Armee reiterated their demand that the Brigade be brought to the front immediately as the XXIII.Armeekorps desperately needed to put it into action as soon as possible. The situation remained confusing when again at 1115 hours the Brigade was informed it would not be engaged on the left flank of the corps as was originally intended, but instead would be sent from Selisharowo through Jeltzy on to support the right flank of the XXIII.Armeekorps. [33]

As it turned out, however, the Brigade could not depart as planned and SS-Kavallerie-Regiment 1 did not begin marching to the front until January 3, 1942 with the last squadron joining the trek on January 5th. XXIII.Armeekorps was notified of this delay and expected the Brigade to arrive in Okovtzy on January 5th. Early in the morning of January 4th 9.Armee informed the XXIII.Armeekorps that SS-Kavallerie-Regiment 1 had reached the area north of Cholmjetzy and SS-Kavallerie-Regiment 2 the area around Okovtzy. The Korps had not established contact with the Brigade due to the poor weather and communication had to take place through 9.Armee. [34]

Until January 4th continuous Russian attacks against the 206.Infanterie Division and the 102.Infanterie Division were repulsed. But that evening the Soviets stormed over the frozen Volga river, broke through the thin lines of the 256.Infanterie Division commanded by Generalleutnant Gerhard Kaufmann[35] and advanced to the forest areas southwest of Rshev. The Russians even managed to penetrate the city itself. This breakthrough meant that there was now a 15 kilometer gap in the lines and even worse, XXIII.Armeekorps was now cut off from its supply lines. The Korps would have to be supplied by air.

On January 5th a new order for the Brigade, which voided the previous directive, instructed the Regimenter to reach the area south of Molodoy-Tud and the road between Molodoy-Tud and Rshev by January 6th. The Brigade Staff was to set up headquarters in Truschkova and the Ia of the Brigade arrived there that evening. Later that night XXIII.Armeekorps received a message that SS-Kavallerie-Regiment 2 could not continue its march in the direction of Molodoy-Tud due to ex-

---

[32] ibid.

[33] "Bericht über den Einsatz der SS-Kav.Brigade Winter 1941/42." and "Kriegstagebuch Nr. 9, XXIII.Armeekorps, Abt. Ia, 1.11-1941-31.1.42."

[34] ibid.

[35] Awarded the Knight's Cross on July 9, 1941 for his command of this division.

haustion and poor transport conditions. Since the Brigade was urgently needed, SS-Kavallerie-Regiment 2 received the following message from the Ib of the 102.Infanterie Division:[36]

"SS-Kavallerie-Regiment 2 must carry out the order to arrive in Molodoy-Tud. If the Regiment disobeys this order, a court martial will be issued."

At about 2000 hours SS-Standartenführer Fegelein reported this message had been received by SS-Kavallerie-Regiment 2. The order from XXIII.Armeekorps stated that the Russians had widened their new penetration into the German lines west of Bachmatova and patrols were reaching the railway between Olenino and Rshev. The Brigade was ordered to advance along the road between Truschkova and Rshev to make contact with a Kampfgruppe from the VI.Armeekorps approaching from the east. The purpose of this attack was to close the gap between the XXIII. and VI.Armeekorps and end the threat of a Soviet breakthrough. The Brigade arrived for the attack and was to be supported by XXIII.Armeekorps. During the battle, command of the Brigade was transferred to VI.Armeekorps to improve tactical supervision. This was to be only temporary and command of the Brigade would eventually return to XXIII.Armeekorps.[37]

The attack was successful and closed the gap between the units, at the same time enabling the Brigade to perform reconnaissance operations in a north and northeasterly direction. On January 6th XXIII.Armeekorps was of the firm opinion (before the results of reconnaissance patrols in these areas were submitted) that strengthening the thin closure was only a question of moving the rest of the Brigade troops to the area and from then on the Brigade could be supplied from the Rshev rear area.[38]

The High Command of the Soviet Army didn't give up its offensive goals. New orders on January 7th called for its armies to cut off all German forces in the north and south of the roads to Moscow, break through the open flanks of Army Group "Center" and completely destroy it. The Russian command gave the task of cutting through the seam of Army Group "North" (in the sector of VI.Armeekorps) and Army Group "Center" (in the sector of XXIII.Armeekorps) to the 3rd and 4th Soviet Strike Armies.

The march to the Brigade's assigned positions began on January 7th with SS-Kavallerie-Regiment 2 in the lead followed by SS-Kavallerie-Regiment 1. The march was to proceed in a northerly direction to Solomino and over the Volga river until they were in the specified area where the Brigade was to begin performing reconnaissance operations. After passing through the village of Gliadova, an unimaginable picture appeared: the remnants of a chaotic German retreat. Cannons, machine guns, ammunition of all types, vehicles, several of which were complete with desks and file cabinets filled with secret documents, were all left completely abandoned and intact. This proved the German troops had fled from here without suffering any type of enemy attack. Since the Brigade gathered in the area to collect the abandoned materials without receiving any enemy fire, these items could not have been set up by the Soviets as bait. There were no booby-traps and everything appeared completely undisturbed as if it had not been touched by anyone.[39]

There were still Wehrmacht soldiers in the neighboring village of Pogorelki, a few of whom had tried to stop the fleeing troops with limited success. These men reported that the last attack had not consisted of more than a few grenade-launcher barrages in the villages near Mantorova. The troops, for the most part a battalion of the 481.Infanterie Regiment which was positioned on the left flank of the 256.Infanterie Division, were at the end of their strength just before the beginning of the extreme winter conditions and had never received any sort of winter clothing. The effects of

---

[36] "Bericht über den Einsatz der SS-Kav.Brigade Winter 1941/42." and "Kriegstagebuch Nr. 9, XXIII.Armeekorps, Abt. Ia, 1.11-1941-31.1.42."

[37] ibid.

[38] "Bericht über den Einsatz der SS-Kav.Brigade Winter 1941/42."

[39] ibid.

continuous tank attacks, which came despite the high snow drifts, and effective fighter plane attacks, which took place without a single German plane coming to the defense, were just too much for these troops. The catastrophe apparently began on January 6th after fighter planes with German insignia attacked the troops with bombs and machine gun fire.[40]

Before noon Major Robert Kaestner,[41] a detachment commander from the 256.Artillerie Regiment, reported to the SS-Kavallerie-Brigade command post. He had collected 300 men from a collapsing infantry battalion and presented himself, the men and two artillery batteries from his regiment to the Brigade. After SS-Standartenführer Fegelein personally inspected his troops and was sufficiently convinced they had recovered adequately enough to be taken in by the Brigade, permission was obtained from Korps headquarters for the strengthened battalion, under the leadership of Major Kaestner, to be officially subordinated to the Brigade. This group was given the title Kampfgruppe "Kaestner." [42]

At 1400 hours on January 7th the SS-Kavallerie-Brigade reported that the cities of Solomino, Efimova and Antipoa were occupied by the enemy. The furthermost portions of the SS-Kavallerie-Brigade took up position before Solomino and reported that they were going to attack the village. Kampfguppe "Kaestner" was to hold the positions south of Solomino.[43]

In the late afternoon of January 7th the first sign of the enemy appeared. The 3rd Squadron of SS-Kavallerie-Regiment 2 confronted a Russian field guard unit in Gusevo which was quickly destroyed. The Squadron wanted to immediately advance on Solomino, but during their approach found themselves engulfed in fire. Since the unit received heavy casualties during the first attack, it remained in its position between Solomino and Gusevo. During the battle one officer was killed while the commander, SS-Hauptsturmführer Hans-Viktor von Zastrow, 1st Platoon Leader SS-Hauptsturmführer Werner Geissler and SS-Untersturmführer Rudolf Wappler (1st Platoon Leader from 1st Squadron) were badly wounded. All the other platoon leaders were killed. During an attempt by 1st Squadron to support 3rd Squadron from their flank through the village of Letsino, it was recognized that the Russians had built up defensive positions on the Volga river in the area between Solomino and Kokoschino. The positions had been used during previous defensive battles against the advancing Wehrmacht. Meanwhile, the lead Squadron of SS-Kavallerie-Regiment 1 was advancing in a westerly direction from Mantorova towards Gusevo and triggered strong fire from Russian positions on the northern edge of the Volga river from a location north and northwest of Solomino. It was realized that any attack on these positions would be futile without artillery support. A second squadron of SS-Kavallerie-Regiment 1 then approached the Volga river crossing on the road between Ploty and Charino. The Squadron's task was reconnoitering this area where the Regiment planned on crossing the river and in the general direction of Miaszova, while at the same time protecting the flank of SS-Kavallerie Regiment 1. As the Squadron crossed the river reports arrived that villages in the area Miaszova and south of Miaszova to the Volga were occupied with strong enemy forces. Meanwhile, in the villages south of Letsino, several patrols engaged in light confrontations with the enemy.[44]

During the evening of January 7th the Brigade's staff was of the opinion that the Russians had shielded the road between Bachmatova and Kokoschino (west of the Volga river). This served the purpose of strengthening the just reported breakthrough which was occurring in the direction of the railway.[45]

---

[40] ibid.

[41] Awarded the Knight's Cross on December 11, 1943 as commander of Grenadier Regiment 105 and the Oakleaves on February 21, 1944 while commanding the same unit.

[42] "Bericht über den Einsatz der SS-Kav.Brigade Winter 1941/42."

[43] "Kriegstagebuch Nr. 9, XXIII.Armeekorps, Abt. Ia, 1.11-1941-31.1.42."

[44] "Bericht über den Einsatz der SS-Kav.Brigade Winter 1941/42."

[45] ibid.

During the night of January 7th/8th a battery of Kampfgruppe "Kaestner" positioned itself near Gusevo. The strengthened 1st Squadron of SS-Kavallerie-Regiment 2 was placed on the flank in Letsino. Shortly after 0300 hours on January 8th the Russians attacked Letsino from three sides with strong forces during a massive snowstorm. In spite of heavy casualties, the Russians continued to bring up new reserves. Their last attempt to break into the village was carried out by a battalion equipped with snow shoes. The Squadron had up to this time suffered a casualty rate of 60% and was forced to break off its defense, retreating from the village.[46]

The attack that the Brigade had planned to carry out on the strongly fortified Russian positions in Solowino could not take place on January 9th as intended, since the XXIII.Armeekorps could not supply either Kampfgruppe "Kaestner" or the artillery batteries attached to SS-Kavallerie-Regimenter 1 and 2. The Artillery Detachment only had a few rounds, which they used to give the Russians the impression the Brigade was stronger than it actually was. During the day of January 9th it became increasingly apparent that the Brigade was acting independently and could not depend on any support from the Wehrmacht. The right flank was completely open and there was no help to be found to the left either, since the closest neighbor, a single infantry platoon, was located 10 kilometers north of Charino. The situation in front of the Brigade was just as bleak. An army Kampfgruppe, which had been dispatched from the east by VI.Armeekorps, was nowhere in sight. The Brigade's staff feared they had run into strong enemy forces and must not have been able to proceed further. A battle group patrol of SS-Kavallerie-Regiment 1 was removed from the Brigade and given the assignment to advance towards Rshev by swinging through the south. This battle group was reportedly withdrawn according to reports from the area of Savino since the general line connecting the villages of Karpova, Slobyrevo, Brodnikova and Kokoschino was held by the Russians. In these villages were between 100 and 300 Russians supported with artillery. The most disturbing news arrived late in the day as several prisoners were in the possession of messages reporting the position of the Brigade north of the Volga river.[47]

Later that evening the Brigade reported to XXIII.Armeekorps it had been forced to retreat due to attacks by superior Russian forces from the north and south. The Brigade was at this time positioned in Truschkova and maintained contact with the 206.Infanterie Division. At 1855 hours 9.Armee reported the threatening situation developing for the units of the 206.Infanterie Division, situated east of Molodoy-Tud. These elements were in danger of being surrounded and to avoid this XXIII.Armeekorps ordered the Division to attack. To support the assault, the SS-Kavallerie-Brigade in Truschkova was subordinated to the 206.Infanterie Division.[48]

On January 10th the right flank of the 206.Infanterie Division was completely isolated in the Itomlja sector. Even worse was the fact that the forces on the Volga river were weak and that the Division was no longer in contact with the SS-Kavallerie-Brigade. It was decided that the right flank on the Volga was to be brought back in order to re-establish contact with the Brigade. The official order to push back the date of the attack to the January 13th arrived during the evening of the January 10th. Later that day the 206.Infanterie Division reported that the village of Truschkova (where the Brigade was situated) and the area occupied by the Division had received artillery fire of all calibers.[49]

Meanwhile, the Brigade was busy assessing the tactical situation from its point of view. Report intelligence gained from the reconnaissance operations conducted by SS-Kavallerie-Regiment 1 south and southwest of the Brigade's position during the nights of January 10th and 11th resulted in conclusive proof that the Russians were approaching from the area between Gusevo and Slobyrevo. From the general direction of Pogorelki the Russians intended to surround the Brigade. Also, the

[46] "Kriegstagebuch Nr. 9, XXIII.Armeekorps, Abt. Ia, 1.11-1941-31.1.42." and "Bericht über den Einsatz der SS-Kav.Brigade Winter 1941/42."

[47] "Bericht über den Einsatz der SS-Kav.Brigade Winter 1941/42."

[48] This order returned the subordination of the SS-Kavallerie Brigade to the XXIII.Armeekorps from the VI.Armeekorps.

[49] "Kriegstagebuch Nr. 9, XXIII.Armeekorps, Abt. Ia, 1.11-1941-31.1.42."

Russians were applying pressure from the north on a squadron of SS-Kavallerie-Regiment 1 located on the northern edge of the Volga River between Saborki and Anzyferova, forcing that unit's retreat to Saborki.[50]

Based on this information the Brigade developed two plans to relieve the impending situation. It was their intention to consider the situation of the entire XXIII.Armeekorps and choose the plan that would bring the Army's leadership the best tactical advantage. The plan decided on was for the Brigade to retreat about 7 kilometers in a westerly direction. Positive arguments for the adopted plan were as follows. The flank of the XXIII.Armeekorps, made up of the very weak 206.Infanterie Division right flank, was completely open. Since the Russians had made a move to completely encircle the SS-Kavallerie-Brigade, this flank was no longer just open, it was now endangered. Furthermore, the life supporting fork in the supply line road formed by the highways between Truschkova, Urdom and Molodoy-Tud and Truschkova, Kurkino and Olenino was not occupied. If the Russians were successful in encircling the Brigade, other enemy forces could quickly reach Olenino without encountering any resistance. The Russians would then be able to continue their advance on Molodoy-Tud.[51]

The arguments that spoke for their adopted plan made the most sense to the Brigade's staff. It was decided to secure this fork in the road by erecting a defense line between the villages of Ploty, Truschkova and Askewo with SS-Kavallerie-Regiment 1 and by gathering the forces of SS-Kavallerie-Regiment 2 in an area southwest of Saizevo.[52]

This decision did not meet the approval of VI.Armeekorps, but the Brigade stuck with its decision based on the fact that it was the judgment that would best benefit the Brigade itself as well as XXIII.Armeekorps. The Brigade would be in a better position for obvious reasons while securing of the defensive line between Ploty, Truschkova and Askewo would protect XXIII.Armeekorps. As it turned out, the Brigade made a move which was a decisive measure of the greatest magnitude.[53]

After the Brigade retreated to its new defensive line, it quickly became apparent what the Russian intentions for it were. During the day the enemy barraged their former positions from the opposite side of the Volga and south of the street with heavy weapons. The Russians did not attack on the strong side obstacles which had been placed on side streets and led to the main street from the south, even though they just had occupied the towns of Ovsjanikovo and Usovo. Instead they moved up the advance street slowly. A row of trees forming a small forest patch was stormed by the Russians early on the morning of January 12th after scrupulous attack preparations which gave away the fact they were under the impression it was occupied. A rider platoon which was left behind to screen the rest of the troops knew how to simulate a forward post line. They deceived the enemy by spreading out their men into eighteen double posts while cleverly changing positions of their machine guns to give the Russians the impression that their strength was much greater than it actually was. In reality the forest was not suitable for a defense, since it was impassable due to the high snow which covered every street except the main highway.[54]

Since the Russians were busy attacking empty positions and being held down by mere platoons, SS-Kavallerie-Regiment 1 was able to work on building its defensive line the evening of January 12th without being harassed by the enemy. An anti-aircraft battery, subordinated to the Regiment, arrived during the night of January 11th/12th. Shortly thereafter a battery from Kampfgruppe

---

[50] "Bericht über den Einsatz der SS-Kav.Brigade Winter 1941/42."

[51] "Bericht über den Einsatz der SS-Kav.Brigade Winter 1941/42." and "SS-Kavallerie-Brigade im Osten," <u>Wiking-Ruf</u>, 4. Jahrgang, Nr. 2, Februar 1955.

[52] ibid.

[53] In early February the commander of the 206.Infanterie Division (XXIII.Armeekorps) as well as the commander of the 256.Infanterie Division (VI.Armeekorps) concluded that the Brigade's decision to evacuate the area of Mantorowa was tactically the only correct decision and had prevented significant damage.

[54] "Bericht über den Einsatz der SS-Kav.Brigade Winter 1941/42." and "SS-Kavallerie-Brigade im Osten," <u>Wiking-Ruf</u>, 4. Jahrgang, Nr. 2, Februar 1955.

Alfred Luyken (here an SS-Untersturmführer) was a platoon leader in 5th Squadron, SS-Kavallerie-Regiment 2 by the end of 1941. As an SS-Obersturmführer he was adjutant of SS-Kavallerie-Regiment 2 in 1943 and won the German Cross in Gold on May 17, 1943 in command of the anti-tank unit of Kampfgruppe "Z" (for Zehender) with the SS-Kavallerie-Division. (Photo: BDC)

"Kaestner" which had received 100 rounds of ammunition from Olenino was also attached. During the night of January 12th/13th the Russians sent out many patrols which executed one attack after another between 0200 and 0830 hours on the 13th. The Russians suffered heavy casualties amounting to over 100 dead while German casualties were light. This engagement served to lift the spirits of the Wehrmacht soldiers who had earlier witnessed the panicked retreat resulting from the Russian breakthrough. At the same time, however, the Germans found the effect of the strong Russian defense sobering as later that day the Russians sent three more battle group patrols to attack different positions. Two of these patrols were completely destroyed.[55]

Meanwhile, in the sector of the 206.Infanterie Division, the Russians attacked the center of the Division with strong forces west of Klimova during the day and succeded with a deep penetration in the direction of Erajewo. The Division defended this attack with all available troops and were forced to bring up their last reserves. Also, a message arrived at 2000 hours from the commander of 9.Armee, Generaloberst Adolf Strauss: *"Pulling back the front will not be permitted. The Führer has ordered us to hold our current positions."* Shortly thereafter Strauss added the following: *"In case the enemy movements cannot be stopped, the XXIII.Armeekorps must hold the Volga-Line under any circumstances. A movement by the 206.Infanterie Division or the Brigade Fegelein is completely out of question."*[56]

Late in the evening of January 13th the Brigade received an order from 9.Armee instructing them to pull out a squadron and sent it to Meschkovo (7 kilometers southwest of Ashevo). Their orders stated that they were to send out as many patrols as possible to reconnoiter the area up to the

---

[55] ibid.

[56] "Kriegstagebuch Nr. 9, XXIII.Armeekorps, Abt. Ia, 1.11-1941-31.1.42." The SS-Kavallerie-Brigade was sometimes referred to unofficially as the Brigade "Fegelein" after its commander.

railway while fending off enemy forces that were breaking through in a westerly direction. The Brigade also reported they had suffered another 22 dead and 84 wounded during the previous battles.[57]

On January 14th several Russian soldiers, dressed in German uniforms, waved to one of the Brigade's patrols, signaling them to come over. As the Germans approached, the Russians opened fire, killing almost all of them. A few survivors managed to escape and make their way back to the Brigade.[58]

In other sectors of the front, a message was sent to Army Group "Center" reporting that enemy forces with a strength of 500 men were in the area of Oserki (6 kilometers north of the XXIII.Armeekorps supply route) and were attacking in Lugi from the east. Supplying the Korps from Dubno was then deemed impossible. The VI.Armeekorps were therefore urgently requested to attack Rshev from the northwest, otherwise XXIII.Armeekorps would be lost.[59]

Later that evening the enemy breakthrough in the area of the 206.Infanterie Division halted. The Division reported that it intended to mop up the area with night counterattacks. Soon after Army Group "Center" requested XXIII.Armeekorps to inform it as to the whereabouts of the forward line of the 206.Infanterie Division as well as the current position of the SS-Kavallerie-Brigade in order to ascertain how deeply the enemy had penetrated. In response to this the Brigade reported it was located in the section between Ashev and Ploty. The right flank of the 206.Infanterie Division began in Volgakni near Sukonzev, extending to the eastern edge of Orjechovo and further to the eastern edge of Ovtschiniki, Botscharovo and Drosdy. The strength of the enemy that had penetrated south of the Ovtschiniki was two regiments while the breakthrough east of Jarajev had been beaten back.[60]

On January 15th the 206.Infanterie Division was ordered to retreat west to an area east of Molodoy-Tud. By retreating, the eastern flank was left open and the SS-Kavallerie-Brigade was ordered to hold its position to the last man. However, on January 16th the Brigade was ordered to come to the rescue in Rshev and relieve Generalmajor Albrecht Baler's 102.Infanterie Division. The Brigade was to be supported by portions of the 206. and 256.Infanterie Divisionen. On a positive note, a large transport of oats arrived for the horses that day, in spite of the incredibly difficult weather conditions. The Brigade was also deservedly awarded twelve 1st class Iron Crosses and 90 2nd class Iron Crosses by General der Infanterie Albrecht Schubert, the commander of XXIII.Armeekorps.[61]

Although recent breakthrough attempts by the Russians had been futile, they were not about to abandon their objectives. On January 18th the enemy renewed its effort to forge a gap between VI. and XXIII.Armeekorps by advancing against the flank positions over Charino and Schpalevo. To prevent this, the 206.Infanterie Division decided to close the gap between Ploty and its right flank by inserting a battalion of the 301.Infanterie Regiment. But the Soviets were too quick and reached Schpalevo before even a company of the 301.Infanterie Regiment could arrive. Apparently the indescribable weather conditions were to blame once again and the lead company became bogged down during the march. The Korps was immediately informed of this situation. The XXIII.Armeekorps had foreseen deployment of the SS-Kavallerie-Brigade for these operations. Soon after the arriving situation report from the 301.Infanterie Regiment had been received, the Brigade was ordered by the 9.Armee through the XXIII.Armeekorps to help close the gap. The Brigade immediately took the villages of Schpalevo and Charino to hold the area free until the battalion could arrive. Schpalevo was mopped up by the strengthened 2nd Squadron of SS-Kavallerie-

[57] "Kriegstagebuch Nr. 9, XXIII.Armeekorps, Abt. Ia, 1.11-1941-31.1.42."

[58] "SS-Kavallerie-Brigade im Osten," Wiking-Ruf," 4. Jahrgang, Nr. 2, Februar 1955.

[59] "Kriegstagebuch Nr. 9, XXIII.Armeekorps, Abt. Ia, 1.11-1941-31.1.42."

[60] ibid.

[61] "Wiking Ruf," February 1955 and "Bericht über den Einsatz der SS-Kav.Brigade Winter 1941/42."

Regiment 1 after difficult street fighting which lasted for several hours. The same was required for Charino, although the defense of the Soviets was not quite as determined here.[62]

The Brigade's staff was also under the impression that the German troops positioned furthest east were not of the opinion that the Russians had broken through to the railway with considerably stronger forces than originally assumed. But then on January 18th the truth arrived in the form of a message from Kampfgruppe "Meyer" led by SS-Hauptsturmführer Friedrich Meyer, 2nd Battery commander of the Brigade's artillery unit. Meyer's group reported the Russians were now marching south of the railway in the direction of Olenino. As a result of this observation the defensive lines were ordered to be thinned out and extended in a southerly direction. The next day (January 19th) the Brigade was ordered to attack the enemy across from the right flank of the XXIII.Armeekorps on both sides of the road leading to Rshev. The Brigade was ordered to come from the area northeast of Olenino and advance along the line between Nikolskoje and Manturovo. To protect the southern flank of the Brigade, a company was to be deployed east of Olenino. For this operation SS-Kavallerie-Regiment 1 was to be relieved from their current position on January 21st and sent to Fetinino. On January 20th the 206.Infanterie Division received the order that one Regiment of the Brigade is to mop up and strengthen the positions in Olenino. During the early afternoon hours the Brigade made the following report about what was happening in their area in Olenino:[63]

"Two enemy battalions are attacking along the railway to Olenino. The attack of a third battalion is expected. In case that condition in Olenino becomes threatened, the 2nd Regiment of the Brigade will be put into action."

Shortly after 1500 hours, SS-Sturmbannführer Fegelein reported that Olenino was being attacked by two enemy divisions. On January 21st the enemy pushed forward with new forces near Olenino and the SS-Kavallerie-Brigade received the order to hold and throw the enemy back to the east. In the center sector enemy movements from Antipov to the southeast were barraged with artillery fire. This counterattack on Olenino forced the Brigade to divide its forces. SS-Kavallerie-Regiment 2, strengthened by Kampfgruppe "Meyer" and later an infantry regiment of the Army, was thrown into the battle for Olenino. Here they managed to do considerable damage to the Soviet troops, but at the same time were also forced into a few defensive combats. The result was that Olenino was mostly controlled by German units.[64]

Elsewhere on January 21st, two Russian battalions tried to retake Schpalevo and Charino by launching a strong counterattack. The enemy attacked the two towns which had been taken over by German army troops. During the battle the troops in Charino retreated to Schpalevo and the town was again in the hands of the Soviets. The Army company that had occupied Schpalevo suffered high casualties before the 2nd Squadron of SS-Kavallerie-Regiment 1 could counterattack from Ploty. The Russians were then beaten badly and suffered extremely high casualties. An entire Russian company was completely destroyed after which the Russians fled and in the area south of Schpalevo 160 dead Russians were counted.[65]

By this time the situation on the Eastern Front was approaching critical. The staff at 9.Armee felt as if they were confronting a catastrophe. The Russians had broken through along the seam of the VI. and XXIII.Armeekorps just as was feared, and their advance was continuing. Gathered in the headquarters of the 9.Armee were several divisional commanders, waiting for the arrival of Oberbefehlshaber of 9.Armee, Generaloberst Adolf Strauss. As the generals were arguing the cur-

[62] "Kriegstagebuch Nr. 9, XXIII.Armeekorps, Abt. Ia, 1.11-1941-31.1.42." and "Bericht über den Einsatz der SS-Kav.Brigade Winter 1941/42."

[63] ibid.

[64] ibid.

[65] ibid.

rent situation, the Ia of 9.Armee arrived to inform them that their leader was too sick to carry on any longer and would have to be evacuated from the front. The Army was to wait for their new Oberbefehlshaber, General Walter Model, who just three months before was commanding the famous 3.Panzer Division.[66] When Model arrived, he entered a room full of depressed faces. Despite this, he was extremely optimistic and gathered the commanders together and devised a plan to stabilize the very threatening situation at hand. When asked by the assembled officers what he had brought in the way of reinforcements, Model replied "myself." The resulting laughter eased the tension of the situation and it would in fact be Model himself who would stabilize the precarious front line status.[67] His eventual success in this critical situation made him among Hitler's favorite and most trusted commanders, earning him the nickname "Fireman" to reflect his ability in hot combat scenarios.

The plan basically called for cutting off the advancing Soviet troops and forcing them into a pocket of their own. On January 22nd Model recalled VI.Armeekorps from their area west of Rshev. Leading the advance would be 256.Infanterie Division strengthened by components from four other divisions including artillery, anti-tank and anti-aircraft units. The Division was to proceed in an westerly direction against the Russian breakthrough points. From the west would come the cut off XXIII.Armeekorps with the 206.Infanterie Division, the SS-Kavallerie-Brigade and Sturmgeschützabteilung 189. This would serve to close the gap between the VI. and XXIII.Armeekorps and re-establish the supply lines for 9.Armee while cutting off both Soviet Armies from their supply base. [68]

On January 22nd parts of the 206.Infanterie Division and strong forces of the VI.Armeekorps were dispatched to attack the Russians positioned along the road between Molodoy-Tud and Rshev. It was their assignment to close this gap. The strengthened SS-Kavallerie-Regiment 1 attacked from its positions in the area of Fetinino and dislodged the Russians from their positions in Volkov, Jagodino, Ljutjagino, Kustaschka, Reschelalovo and Usova. With these successes they secured the flank of the attacking 206.Infanterie Division. During that evening SS-Standartenführer Fegelein reported that the travel conditions were catastrophic and required every bit of energy that the Brigade had left. Despite this poor state of affairs and a bitter temperature of -45° C, the Germans attacked the Russians on January 23rd from two directions. Despite the poor condition of the Brigade, the Russians were not able to defend against an attack fought on two fronts. The goal of the assault, the closing of the gap in the front, was accomplished and during the night a battle group patrol from SS-Kavallerie-Regiment 1 shook hands with members of the 6th Company of Regiment "Der Führer" from the motorized SS-Infanterie Division "Reich" in Solomino.[69] The remnants of the destroyed Russian forces were positioned on a narrow bridge and were completely cut off. After a German attack they surrendered.[70]

The road between Truschkova and Solomino which crossed the Volga in a northwesterly direction, now served as the northern front for VI. and XXIII.Armeekorps. The 403.Infanterie Regiment and SS-Kavallerie-Regiment 1 made up the southern front on the road between Reschelalovo, Usovo and Schalgino which advanced to reach a general line between the villages of Morosovo, Tschermolino, Saizevo, Dmitrova, and Stany.[71] The Commanding General of XXIII.Armeekorps sent the following message to his troops:

---

[66] Model was assigned command of 9.Armee on January 15, 1942 but did not arrive to assume command until the following week.

[67] Carrel, Paul: "Unternehmen Barbarossa," page 353.

[68] ibid.

[69] This unit was a component of VI.Armeekorps.

[70] "Bericht über den Einsatz der SS-Kav.Brigade Winter 1941/42." and "Kriegstagebuch Nr. 9, XXIII.Armeekorps, Abt. Ia, 1.11-1941-31.1.42."

[71] "Bericht über den Einsatz der SS-Kav.Brigade Winter 1941/42."

"The Korps has been attacking successfully since early on January 22nd with the 206.Infanterie Division and the SS-Kavallerie-Brigade. The gap west of Rshev has been closed. The time of Russian superiority, which only made itself felt due to their masses and not their fighting ability, has passed. The superiority of the German Soldier is proven. On no position on the front where cold-bloodedness was the way was there a danger of the enemy infiltrating the front. It is now true, that the old trust, the old proven feeling of superiority of the German Soldier, has been felt by every fighter. The commanding general requests all divisional commanders to re-establish order and fighting spirit within our troops during combat with everything available. The Korps has four weeks of difficult defensive fighting against a vastly superior enemy behind it. The Korps has cut off the enemy in every direction and despite the Russian Winter has fought a heroic battle in rare form. The only thing left is to completely win this battle."

A few days later a message arrived at Brigade headquarters from Generalleutnant Hoevel, commander of the 206.Infanterie Division:

"Dear Fegelein! The 'Special Daily Order' which gave special recognition to the leaders and men of the Division was also meant for the SS-Kavallerie-Brigade, which was tactically subordinated to the Division during these battles. Over and above this order, I would like to express to you and your brave soldiers my special thanks and give you my high recognition. Your part and your service during the successful combats of these difficult operations is proven, since you were able to protect the supply base in Olenino while at the same time carrying out repeated attacks which protected the right flank of the Division. Your ability to carry out these operations successfully contributed greatly to the overall success of the Division."

SS-Obersturmführer Rudolf Maeker, then commanding a squadron of SS-Kavallerie-Regiment 1, performed to such an extent that his actions partly resulted in his eventual award of the German Cross in Gold.

"On January 23, 1942 Squadron Chief Maeker took a strongly-built and well-defended enemy fortification in Karpova while fighting at the lead of his men. Maeker pulled his men continually forwards through special dash. With this, Maeker had carried-out his order, after which the intended attack, initiated from our defensive positions, was completed. This attack served the purpose of enabling us to occupy the no-mans land near Karpova and resulted in the capture of six artillery pieces, four light machine guns and various light and heavy grenade launchers, as well as producing a high percentage of enemy dead and wounded."[72]

On January 24th the Brigade reported that it intended to send a patrol from SS-Kavallerie-Regiment 1 east from Usovo. Further reconnaissance operations were to take place in Kokoschino. Later the Brigade reported to the XXIII.Armeekorps that SS-Kavallerie-Regiment 1 was holding the line between Pustoschka, Reschetalovo, Tarutiono, Ovsjanikovo, and Usovo and had met a battalion of the 253.Infanterie Division to defend the front to the south. SS-Kavallerie-Regiment 2 threw the enemy out of his positions and held the line between Glaski, Mjasnitza, Velovaschki and Sady. The Brigade also reported that it intended to dispatch strengthened reconnaissance formations from SS-Kavallerie-Regiment 1 to the south while SS-Kavallerie-Regiment 2 would conduct further attacks in a southwesterly direction, reaching the road between the villages of Terechovka, Alferovo and Uliki. On January 25th the Brigade, along with the 413.Infanterie Regiment, supported the 206.Infanterie Division to reach the general line between the villages of Nachartovo, Saizevo and Stany. The units overcame tough enemy resistance during this advance.[73]

---

[72] Quotation from Maeker's recommendation for the German Cross in Gold, the only one found to date for those awarded that decoration for bravery while attached to the SS-Kavallerie-Brigade. See photographs of Maeker for biographical information.

On January 26th the enemy had reorganized their troops and once again went on the offensive. The attack began in a small section of the front and by the next day the entire line north of Rshev was active. The Russians attacked with tank supported infantry covered by fighter aircraft and it appeared they wanted desperately to blow the bridge the Germans had just taken. These attacks reached their climax between the 28th and the 30th when the Russians were on the verge of breaking through the German lines in several locations.[74]

On January 27th the SS-Kavallerie-Brigade took the town of Sagrebino and the next day the Russians attacked Gusevo, while on the southern front the Brigade took Kokoschino. SS-Kavallerie-Regiment 2 then reconnoitered the area south of Olenino with battle group patrols and came upon weak enemy forces in the area between Ivanovka and Vssokoje. Late that evening the threat of an enemy breakout emerged. To reduce the chances of this happening XXIII.Armeekorps planned on placing Battle Group "Raesfeld" at the train station in Tschertolino as quickly as possible. An attack was to be carried out in accordance with the advance of the VI.Armeekorps and the SS-Kavallerie-Brigade from the north with the intention of surrounding the enemy from the north to the south. Shortly afterwards the 102.Infanterie Division, along with the SS-Kavallerie-Brigade, received the order to approach along the railway and build a southern defense line with Battle Group "Raesfeld." The 102.Infanterie Division observed enemy reconnaissance activity on the front in Molodoy-Tud. Battle Group "Raesfeld" broke to the south while attacking enemy forces near Grischino and Macherovo, passed over the railway between Tschertolino and Olenino and surrounded an enemy group south of Terechova. Battle Group "Raesfeld" and the SS-Kavallerie-Brigade then stood on the general line connecting Voronivo, Ivanovka, Vysokoje, Selenovka, Bereski, Osninki, Kamenzy and Sobolevo.[75]

In Olenino Kampfgruppe "Meyer" was busy holding off the Russians in bitter close combat. During the course of the fighting on January 29th, the leader of this Kampfgruppe, SS-Hauptsturmführer Friedrich Meyer, was killed along with two platoon leaders. The message reporting his death stated that despite facing a superior opponent, many times the strength of the Kampfgruppe, Meyer and his men were able to hold Olenino. Meyer was from then on referred to as "The Defender of Olenino."[76]

During the morning of January 30th the Brigade was ordered by 206.Infanterie Division to follow the advance of the 251.Infanterie Division and secure the railway behind them. Located in the sector of Ljunino, Stany, Podschinki were three battle groups from the 413.Infanterie Regiment. Situated on the line between Dmitrovo and Apajevo was SS-Kavallerie-Regiment 1, while a Brigade reconnaissance squadron was located in Kashino. During the night of January 30th/31st, SS-Kavallerie-Regiment 2 was relieved from the command of Battle Group "Raesfeld" and again subordinated to the Brigade. The section of the front assigned to the Brigade was extended to Choldejevo. A gap between the Brigade and the left flank of the 102.Infanterie Division was closed by the reconnaissance squadron. The command post of the SS-Kavallerie-Brigade, which controlled the entire southern flank, was now located in Gusino. The XXIII.Armeekorps also reported that the 102.Infanterie Division was not in any condition to attack.[77]

During the battles in January the Brigade reported that it had been adequately supplied with rations, although at times deliveries were sparse. Supplies of air dropped infantry ammunition were also deemed as sufficient, although it was noted that obtaining artillery ammunition had proven difficult as the Brigade and its subordinated troops were forced to receive these supplies from the

---

[73] "Kriegstagebuch Nr. 9, XXIII.Armeekorps, Abt. Ia, 1.11-1941-31.1.42."

[74] "SS-Kavallerie-Brigade im Osten," Wiking-Ruf, 4. Jahrgang, Nr. 2, Februar 1955.

[75] "Kriegstagebuch Nr. 9, XXIII.Armeekorps, Abt. Ia, 1.11-1941-31.1.42."

[76] "SS-Kavallerie-Brigade im Osten," Wiking-Ruf, 4. Jahrgang, Nr. 2, Februar 1955.

[77] "Kriegstagebuch Nr. 9, XXIII.Armeekorps, Abt. Ia, 1.11-1941-31.1.42."

Hermann Maringgele (left) as an SS-Oberscharführer and right as an SS-Untersturmführer. As an SS-Unterscharführer with 2nd Squadron, SS-Kavallerie Regiment 1 he was awrded the Iron Cross 1st class on March 30, 1942 along with fellow future Knight's Cross holder Joachim Boosfeld. Both awards were recorded in the war diary of XXIII.Armeekorps. Born on November 29, 1911, he served briefly in the Italian armed forces before joining the SS in February 1940. He was assigned to the SS-Totenkopf-Reiterstandarte in March, 1940 and stayed with SS-Kavallerie Regiment 1 until Budapest. Awarded the German Cross in Gold on January 27, 1945 as a platoon leader in 2nd Squadron, on February 21, 1945 he won the Knight's Cross as well as the Close Combat Clasp in Gold (for 84 combats) while at the same position. He ended the war as an SS-Untersturmführer. (Photos: BDC and Otto Weidinger)

Wehrmacht. Unfortunately the Wehrmacht's supply lines were already greatly overburdened and their first priority had been to supply their own troops.[78]

The casualties of the two cavalry regiments, which had a strength of 1500 men (including the Flak-Batterie) reached 370 men on February 1st, but additional cases of frostbite increased this number to approximately 500, which served to reduce the strength of the Brigade (not including the Bicycle Reconnaissance Detachment) to two-thirds of its original strength. The casualties suffered by the horses of the Regiments were just as serious, and many of them that survived the battles were in poor shape and were no longer fit for service. These horses were shipped to secure areas far behind the lines where they were to be nurtured back to health by SS veterinarians. Fortunately for the Brigade, there were enough healthy horses kept on reserve so that the Brigade could be completely refitted with its requirements.[79]

On February 4, 1942 a message sent to XXIII.Armeekorps from the 206.Infanterie Division mentioned that the SS-Kavallerie-Brigade had taken Tarasovo and Upyri on the southern front during the course of the day. In Upyri there was still on-going house-to-house combat. Battle Group "Raesfeld" was still engaged in battle around Stupenka where the Russians continued in attack mode. Later that day the Brigade was busy mopping up the newly conquered villages and took

---

[78] "Bericht über den Einsatz der SS-Kav.Brigade Winter 1941/42."

[79] ibid.

Pogorelki. Four 1st class Iron Crosses were awarded to the Brigade including one to SS-Unterscharführer Willi Hartmann.[80] At noon on February 5th, Oberst Raesfeld was assigned to take control of the entire southern front which, besides his own battle group, consisted of the SS-Kavallerie-Brigade and the special advance elements of the 1.Panzer-Division, until the Panzer Division itself had arrived. Tschertolino was to be mopped up, before any further operations could be undertaken. The 102.Infanterie Division and the Ia of the SS-Kavallerie-Brigade were then informed of this new directive while the Brigade was to inform the advanced detachment of 1.Panzer Division of the situation. During this time the staff of the XXIII.Armeekorps was planning a possible attack for these units which was to proceed to the south and commence after operations in Tschertolino had concluded. At 1530 hours SS-Standartenführer Fegelein reported that the SS-Kavallerie-Brigade and Kampfgruppe "Kaestner," still subordinated to the Brigade, took Siminy and were engaged in house-to-house combat in Tschertolino. The 481.Infanterie Regiment, also engaged in the fight for Tschertolino, was to be returned to the 206.Infanterie Division after the fighting concluded.[81] Later that day a Korps order arrived that mentioned the SS-Kavallerie-Brigade:

"Strengthening enemy resistance against the successfully progressing attack of the SS-Kavallerie-Brigade near Tschertolino as well as break-out attempts of the surrounded strong enemy east of Tschertolino to the west or northwest is to be predicted."

At 1700 hours the SS-Kavallerie-Brigade reported that Tschertolino was taken after eight hours of fighting. The commander of XXIII.Armeekorps, General der Infanterie Albrecht Schubert, gave the SS-Kavallerie-Brigade special official recognition during reports for the successful fighting during the day. Schubert later recommended the Brigade's Commander, SS-Standartenführer Hermann Fegelein, for the Knight's Cross to the Iron Cross. The recommendation was approved and Fegelein was awarded the decoration on March 4, 1942.[82] The Brigade reported over 100 prisoners and captured one 7.5 cm cannon, two grenade launchers and one heavy machine gun during the fighting in Tschertolino and Siminy. They also counted over 200 dead Russian soldiers.[83]

On the morning of February 6th communication had still not yet been established between the 1.Panzer Division and the SS-Kavallerie-Brigade so it was left to XXIII.Armeekorps to explain the Brigade's plans to 1.Panzer Division. The Brigade intended on attacking the dug-in enemy positions at the train station north of Tschertolino and on both sides of Semenovo. After re-evaluating the situation, the Brigade decided to first take Svistuny. Bacharevo was later reported to occupied by the enemy. At 1055 hours a report made by the Brigade stated that the enemy had retreated to the south from the area between Svjagino and Svistuny. The XXXXVI.Armeekorps was informed of the situation and requested to quickly move the advanced detachment of 1.Panzer Division to the north and instruct them to make contact with the Brigade. By mid-afternoon the Brigade had set out according to plan and was to hold a 20 kilometer front which would make it difficult for them to make any quick movement. At 1715 hours the Brigade reported it had beaten off an attack during the evening that came from Svistuny to Tschertolino. Since the SS-Kavallerie-Brigade was bogged down fighting the enemy near Bacharevo, the 1.Panzer Division was ordered to advance from Swistuny to Laptevo. The Korps then received a message from the Ia of 9.Armee:[84]

---

[80] "Verleihungsliste Nr. 60" signed by Albrecht Schubert, commander XXIII.Armeekorps. Those awarded officers are listed with the December 1941 officer list in Chapter 5.

[81] "Kriegstagebuch Nr. 10, XXIII.Armeekorps, Abt. Ia, 1.2.42-31.3.42."

[82] For the details of the award recommendation, which also included praise from Generaloberst Walter Model, commander of 9.Armee, see Chapter 2.

[83] "Kriegstagebuch Nr. 10, XXIII.Armeekorps, Abt. Ia, 1.2.42-31.3.42."

[84] ibid.

"XXIII.Armeekorps will attack with the SS-Kavallerie-Brigade to the east until reaching Bykovo, and then will annihilate the enemy surrounded to the west and then will turn to the north and advance to Brechovo. XXXXVI.Armeekorps[85] will join in the attack to the north after mopping up the area south of the railway and will reach the railway connecting the train station in Mantschalovo, Ortmantschalovo, Bykovo, and the barracks southeast of Tschertolino."

XXIII.Armeekorps responded to this message by stating that both the SS-Kavallerie-Brigade and XXXXVI.Armeekorps were positioned next to a battalion of VI.Armeekorps and were undertaking mopping up actions to the northeast. This response indicated that the XXIII.Armeekorps did not want to relieve them from their current duties. 9.Armee responded they required the services of the SS-Kavallerie-Brigade because they did not possess the necessary reserves, and even if they did that it would require too much time to position them for the attack. If the Brigade ran into difficulties 9.Armee promised to deploy the "Bataillon Guppenberger" which would fight its way through to the Brigade and support the attack. 9.Armee closed its message by stating that the order given to the Brigade was to be carried out under any circumstances.[86]

Later on February 6th the Advance Detachment of the 1.Panzer Division took Rubeshnoje and Svjagino and was reportedly advancing to Svistuny while stronger enemy forces were still located in the area northeast of Tschertolino. Also, enemy movements were sighted from Bacharevo to the south. In other sectors the SS-Kavallerie-Brigade prevented an enemy breakout to the west from the general line between the villages of Tschertolino and Karpovo and was taking measures to occupy the village of Barygino (northeast of Tschertolino). At this time there was still no contact between the Brigade and the Advanced Detachment of the 1.Panzer Division. Still later on February 6th the 102.Infanterie Division reported that they had successfully carried out a patrol operation on the northern front to Schagovko (8 Kilometers west of Molodoy-Tud), during which the enemy lost 50 dead. On the southern front the SS-Kavallerie-Brigade remained engaged in battle in Barygino and the Advanced Detachment of 1.Panzer Division was advancing to Svistuny. The Brigade and the Advanced Detachment were still unable to establish any contact and enemy movements from Bacharevo in a westerly direction were observed. According to statements made by local residents, large number of Russians troops were fleeing in retreat from the northeast through Petroskije. The villages of Vysokje and Komisarovo, located 9 kilometers south of Olenino, were determined to be occupied by the enemy. The command post of the SS-Kavallerie-Brigade was now situated at Tjusino (Gusina).[87]

Early on the morning of February 7th, the Brigade reported it had finally managed to make contact with the Advanced Detachment of 1.Panzer Division. 9.Armee headquarters, thinking several steps ahead of the current situation, requested that the Brigade initiate an attack directed from Tschertolino and Svistuny together with parts of 1.Panzer Division to Laptevo. A second advance was to begin northwest of Pgorelki and Savino then proceed to Morsowo. The Brigade was still engaged in battle, however, and their advance remained stalled due to strong enemy forces coming from the east approaching their positions in Barygino and Semenovo. Proceeding with the attack would only be possible after the attack of 1.Panzer Division on Ovsjaniki and Svinina concluded. Unfortunately, Barygino and Semenovo, which were now occupied by parts of the 206.Infanterie Division and the Brigade, were immediately counter-attacked by the Russians. Despite tough defensive fighting, the troops could not hold the villages. At 1230 hours the Russians penetrated Barygino and Semenovo with tank support and were in complete possession of the villages by the afternoon.[88]

---

[85] All period documents make reference to the "XXXXVI" Army Corps, when in reality the correct Roman numeral designation for the number 46 is "XLVI." The former is used within the text to avoid confusion and match the documentation utilized.

[86] "Kriegstagebuch Nr. 10, XXIII.Armeekorps, Abt. Ia, 1.2.42-31.3.42."

[87] ibid.

[88] ibid.

After retreating from their old positions in Barygino and Semenovo (these positions were located along the general line connecting the villages of Svistuny and Tschertolino) the SS-Kavallerie-Brigade met up with the Advanced Detachment of 1.Panzer Division. The group then proceeded to attack towards the north after which they planned on next assaulting the villages of Laptevo, Ovsinaiki and back to Semenovo. Later that day a message was received from the Oberbefehlshaber der 9.Armee (Supreme commander of the 9th Army) Generaloberst Walter Model,[89] in which he gave the leader of the SS-Kavallerie-Brigade, SS-Standartenführer Hermann Fegelein, special recognition.[90]

"The enemy around Mantschalovo is still fighting tough and is surrounded. Parts of 1.Panzer Division[91] were successful in taking the railway near Tschertolino after repeated attacks. These attacks were supported by 86.Infanterie Division and parts of the SS-Brigade-Fegelein. I speak my special recognition to the leadership and the troops for their excellent performance. The attack will continue and the surrounded opponent will be annihilated."

Model then issued instructions for February 8th, which ordered several strongpoints to be formed in the positions north of Tschertolino and south and southeast of Pogorelki by 1000 hours. These moves were to support the 1.Panzer Division which was advancing from Svistuny in the direction of Pogorelki. After the Brigade had again met up with these troops, Fegelein was to take orders from the commander of 1.Panzer Division. Later on the 7th the Brigade reported that their attack, which began in Semenovo, was still unsuccessful. However, they still planned on attacking from their positions in Tschertolino, Pogorelki, Ovsinaiki and Semenovo while other parts of the Brigade were to meet up with the Advanced Detachment of 1.Panzer Division in Svistuny and continue on to Laptevo.[92]

Early in the morning of February 8th the Advanced Detachment of 1.Panzer Division reported they were now successfully advancing and that SS-Kavallerie-Regiment 2 was situated to the east and ready to initiate an attack northwest of Tschertolino. Orders later arrived from 9.Armee which officially subordinated the SS-Kavallerie-Brigade to the Advanced Detachment of 1.Panzer Division.[93]

"On February 8, 1942, after the break-in and capture of the village of Svinino, SS-Obersturmführer Rudolf Maeker mopped-up the village. After he completed this assignment he embarked on a lightening advance to the land northeast of Sivino upon his own decision. This advance served to greatly lighten the burden of the infantry unit of 1.Panzer Division. For this unheard-of dash, Maeker was given the personal recognition of the commander of 1.Panzer Division, Generalleutnant Eugen Krüger."[94]

On February 9th an attack by VI.Armeekorps and XXXXVI.Armeekorps on the surrounded Russian forces was planned. The two Armeekorps were to attack the pocket from both sides and annihilate the surrounded enemy forces. The SS-Kavallerie-Brigade was to follow behind the advancing forces and mop up the villages of the Brechovo, Kopytovo and Savino while a one regi-

---

[89] Model was promoted to Generaloberst on February 1, 1942.

[90] "Kriegstagebuch Nr. 10, XXIII.Armeekorps, Abt. Ia, 1.2.42-31.3.42."

[91] Model is referring to the Advanced Detachment of 1.Panzer Division.

[92] "Kriegstagebuch Nr. 10, XXIII.Armeekorps, Abt. Ia, 1.2.42-31.3.42."

[93] "Kriegstagebuch Nr. 10, XXIII.Armeekorps, Abt. Ia, 1.2.42-31.3.42." Both units at that moment were under the command of VI.Armeekorps.

[94] See footnote 72.

ment was to hold the area of Stany and make preparations to join the attack by advancing to the northeast and the southeast.[95]

On February 10th the attack initiated as planned. XXXXVI.Armeekorps proceeded to smash the surrounded enemy forces with support from artillery and aircraft. Parts of the Advanced Detachment of 1.Panzer Division took Bacharevo while combined forces of the Advanced Detachment and the SS-Kavallerie-Brigade took Kopytovo and the forest southeast of this village. Plans for February 11th were for a breakthrough on both sides of the roads between Morusovo and Montschalovo to the east. SS-Kavallerie-Regiment 1 was to advance from Sokulovo through Brechovo to Jersovo. SS-Kavallerie-Regiment 2 was to be held in reserve in Saizevo and remain under command of the Brigade. The Brigade command post was located in Stany on February 11th. On February 12th XXIII.Armeekorps received a report from the Brigade stating after it had been attacking Russian positions on a hill for over 20 hours and that the hill could not be taken. The Brigade broke off the attack to regroup and wait for more forces to arrive but no reports of a subsequent counter-attack were registered.[96] Fifteen 2nd class Iron Crosses and two awards of the 1st class were given to the Brigade. Thirteen of the 2nd class awards went to the artillery battery attached to SS-Kavallerie Regiment 2.[97]

In the report filed by Lombard on February 11, 1942 which characterized the operations of the SS-Kavallerie-Brigade from the beginning of January to the middle of February, Lombard felt that the Brigade could have operated more effectively and blunted many of the Russian breakthroughs. This would have been possible if the Brigade had been adequately supplied with heavy ammunition and given more freedom to make its own decisions, considering its own actions instead of being subject to often incorrect decisions made by the leading officers of VI. and XXIII.Armeekorps.[98]

On February 15th Oberst Edmund Blaurock was notified that 102.Infanterie Division had succeeded in taking Schentropalovka and the enemy forces located near Savidovo were two thirds surrounded. The Division reported that a complete encirclement of these strong forces would only be possible if they were sent some help. XXXXII.Armeekorps offered the Brigade to the Division to assist in these operations, but on February 16th a message from 9.Armee stated that the SS-Kavallerie-Brigade would remain a reserve unit for the XXIII.Armeekorps for an attack planned for the 17th. The Brigade was to remain in the area of Stany and would subsequently be positioned so that it could break into the areas to the southeast and northeast. 9.Armee headquarters also mentioned other attacks by the Brigade were planned to take place on the 18th.[99]

"On February 15, 1942, SS-Obersturmführer Rudolf Maeker was at the lead of his Squadron, of which only 30 men remained.[100] Maeker fought with weapon in hand and with extreme bravery during close-combat. After they were done fighting, he and his squadron had blown nine enemy forest bunkers. Through this action the left flank bordering Ersovo (where the Brigade was engaged) was freed from enemy fire."[101]

On the 16th the Brigade also reported the following enemy casualties and captured material from the fighting around Jeresovo: 1150 dead, 178 captured, seven cannons, three heavy machine

[95] "Kriegstagebuch Nr. 10, XXIII.Armeekorps, Abt. Ia, 1.2.42-31.3.42."

[96] ibid.

[97] "Verleihungsliste Nr. 206" signed by Albrecht Schubert, commander XXIII.Armeekorps.

[98] "Bericht über den Einsatz der SS-Kav.Brigade Winter 1941/42."

[99] "Kriegstagebuch Nr. 10, XXIII.Armeekorps, Abt. Ia, 1.2.42-31.3.42."

[100] At normal strength a squadron contained more than 150 men.

[101] See footnote 72.

guns, twelve light machine guns, thirteen grenade launchers, 635 rifles, two machine pistols and a field kitchen along with large amounts of equipment for men and horses.[102] 33 2nd class Iron Crosses were awarded the Brigade on February 17th with awards of the Iron Cross 1st class going to SS-Oberreiter Ferdinand Tietz, SS-Unterscharführer Alfred Wacker and SS-Unterscharführer Edwin Benndorf, all of SS-Kavallerie Regiment 2.[103]

On February 18th the Brigade received orders for an attack which was to commence on February 21st. The Brigade was to fight along with Battle Group "Raesfeldt," consisting mostly of remnants of I./Infanterie Regiment 35 that were subordinated to 102.Infanterie Division, and attack enemy forces located in the villages around Savidovo. The units were to attack from both sides and annihilate the surrounded enemy forces. The next day the Brigade was officially re-subordinated to the XXXXII.Armeekorps. On February 20th the Brigade arrived in the staging zone, ready to fight along with Battle Group "Raesfeldt" and surround the enemy in the Savidovo area. On February 21st potentially bad situations were brewing in other sectors of the front. In order to free forces for warding off an enemy attack, the 102.Infanterie Division spread out the regiment positioned on its right section and then ordered Battle Group "Raesfeldt" from Olenino to the north to occupy the area around Pasksovo, located 5 kilometers east of Cholmjetzy. It doesn't appear as if the battle group carried out these orders immediately since the it was busy taking the villages of Kulakova and Medvediza from the southwest and advancing further west to Sagrebeno and Scheltavez. A strong enemy counter-attack on the village of Medvediza began at 1100 hours and was subsequently repulsed. The battle group also managed to dislodge enemy positions in Poldenka during this battle and was in possession of the village by the time the battle had concluded. Meanwhile, the SS-Kavallerie-Brigade attacked Mantrovski, but the attack was stopped due to difficult snow conditions and several mine fields positioned directly in the path of their advance.[104]

During the early evening of February 21st 9.Armee was informed of the threatening situation in the area of 102.Infanterie Division. The Division feared that enemy forces could still regroup in the area of Cholmjetzy which would threaten their unit. Model responded by ordering the area of Cholmjetzy to be mopped up. If this was to prove too difficult a task, the Division was given permission to call up portions of Battle Group "Raesfeldt" to assist. The SS-Kavallerie-Brigade and the remainder of the battle group were to remain in their current position and proceed as planned. At 1700 hours the Brigade reported it had seized the village of Mantrovskje and was preparing for further attacks on the villages of Kotschereschki and Visokoje. Early during the day of February 22nd the 102.Infanterie Division reported that the Brigade was continuing to make progress, but messages concerning their exact location and the details of the battles were unavailable. Later, the Brigade, supported by all the heavy weapons of the Battle Group "Raesfeldt," was able to report it had taken the village of Kotschereschki after difficult fighting. The Brigade was still fighting to the northwest at this time.[105]

"February 21, 1942 attack on Mantrovkie: By enabling the attack and resulting break-in of SS-Kavallerie-Regimenter 1 and 2 into the village over a considerable stretch of land, SS-Obersturmführer Rudolf Maeker brought his unit to the attack in such a way that the opponent must have expected a strong German assault. Through this aversion, which was executed with considerable bravery, the charge of the remaining mass of the Brigade was considerably successful."[106]

---

[102] "Kriegstagebuch Nr. 10, XXIII.Armeekorps, Abt. Ia, 1.2.42-31.3.42."

[103] "Vorschlagsliste Nr. 65" issued by XXIII.Armeekorps and signed by General der Infanterie Albrecht Schubert.

[104] "Kriegstagebuch Nr. 10, XXIII.Armeekorps, Abt. Ia, 1.2.42-31.3.42."

[105] ibid.

[106] See footnote 72.

By February 22nd the situation in the sector of the 102.Infanterie Division became too critical and plans for deployment of called-up forces near Olenino were taking place. Instead of removing only portions of Battle Group "Raesfeldt" as originally planned, the situation now required the assistance of the entire battle group as well as the SS-Kavallerie-Brigade. XXIII.Armeekorps ordered the two groups to conclude their attacks after darkness at which time they were to be rushed to the area around Olenino and be deployed in the direction of Gravino. For these operations, the Brigade was to be directly subordinated to the 102.Infanterie Division. Meanwhile, on the southern front, the Brigade was busy taking the village of Saborino. By taking this village it had succeeded in closing the ring around Russian forces located near the village of Savidovo. Two cannons and two grenade launchers were captured during the fighting. At 1900 hours Battle Group "Raesfeldt" and the Brigade were removed from their positions according to plan. The Brigade collected itself at the train station in Macherevo while Battle Group "Raesfeldt" was located in the area of Aleksino. Another group was put on the alert for the upcoming battles, Aufklärungsabteilung 102, which was collecting in the area of Repki (ten kilometers southwest of Olenino).[107]

As the 102.Infanterie Division had predicted, the Russians had indeed recognized the weakness of the German troops in the Olenino area. Not willing to waste such an opportunity, the Russians went on the offensive at 2200 hours on the evening of February 22nd and the village of Padsosennicki was immediately taken. At this time Battle Group "Raesfeldt" and the SS-Kavallerie-Brigade were in transit to this sector. The next day the Brigade was located six kilometers southwest of Olenino in Siderovo and was to proceed further southwest in the direction of Gusevo and Gluchovo. XXIII.Armeekorps was in the middle of forming a new southwestern front on the general line of the northern bank of the Beresina river. On February 24th command of the Brigade was removed from 102.Infanterie Division and was directly subordinated to the XXIII.Armeekorps. Later, the Chief of Staff of 9.Armee, General Hans Krebs, ordered parts of 1.Panzer Division and the SS-Kavallerie-Brigade to mop up the area south of the railway leading to Bjeloj. XXIII.Armeekorps expected more specific orders to arrive the next day. During mid-morning on February 25th, SS-Standartenführer Hermann Fegelein received instructions pertaining to how the upcoming battle was to be led. Later that morning SS-Kavallerie-Regiment 1, positioned near Gusevo, was attacked by a battalion strength Russian force. SS-Kavallerie-Regiment 2 was busy fighting enemy troops which attacked their positions near Kommissarova from Aleksino. The Brigade informed their nearest neighbor, 1.Panzer Division, of their current situation and requested they push their southern front further to the south and take Aleksino. The strength of the Russians was later estimated at about 500 men and they were attacking Brigade positions in Gusevo from the south, southwest and southeast. The enemy was supported by weak artillery from their positions in the south. The Brigade reported heavy casualties for the Russians during these battles but at the same time the Brigade itself was forced to call in several reserve units to assist in the fighting. At the end of the day the Brigade held a line between Gusevo and Polilejevo with SS-Kavallerie-Regiment 1 and a line between Polilejevo and Borki with SS-Kavallerie-Regiment 2. During the night of February 25th/26th the Brigade repulsed a Soviet attack on Gusevo. Early the next day they reported that they were ready to initiate an attack on enemy positions directly south. The 102.Infanterie Division was ordered to assist this assault by securing the right flank of the Brigade. The Division was to accomplish this by pulling security troops positioned along the northern bank of the Berjosa river to Tatjeva and Deidova along the southern bank. These troops were also to dispatch several reconnaissance patrols deep into the forest areas south and southwest of the villages. At 1100 hours the Brigade made the following report:[108]

---

[107] "Kriegstagebuch Nr. 10, XXIII.Armeekorps, Abt. Ia, 1.2.42-31.3.42."

[108] ibid.

August Zehender, probably the best combat leader assigned to the Brigade during its existence and certainly one of the bravest. On the left he is shown as an SS-Obersturmbannführer and commander of SS-Kavallerie Regiment 2 in 1942 and on the right in a 1943 formal portrait as an SS-Standartenführer after being awarded the Knight's Cross. He did not arrive until the Russian offensive so did not participate in any of the Brigade's previous second line operations. Born April 28, 1903 in Aalen, he served in the Army before joining the SS/VT in November 1935 as an SS-Obersturmführer with Regiment "Deutschland." After serving as a platoon leader and company chief with 12th, 8th and 4th Companies, he took command of the anti-aircraft unit of the SS/VT in September 1939 and retained command when this was incorporated into the first field division of the Waffen-SS (eventually titled "Das Reich"). Promoted to SS-Hauptsturmführer on April 20, 1937, and to SS-Sturmbannführer on December 13, 1940, he won both Iron Crosses in 1940. In December 1940 he took command of I./SS-Infanterie-Regiment 11 and in February 1941 led the Kradschützen (motorcycle) Bataillon of "Reich." Wounded in late June 1941 he led II./Deutschland after his recovery until September that year. Again wounded, after his recovery he transferred to the SS-Kavallerie-Brigade in 1942. He may have briefly commanded the remnants of SS-Kavallerie-Regiment 1 when Gustav Lombard assumed command of the Brigade remnants in March 1942. He then led the Battle Group named after him until its personnel were incorporated into the SS-Kavallerie-Division after withdrawl from the front in late June, 1942. Zehender then commanded SS-Kavallerie-Regiment 2 until February 1944 when he was placed in reserve. He was promoted to SS-Obersturmbannführer November 9, 1942 and to SS-Standartenführer April 20, 1943. In early May 1944 he took command of the 22.SS-Freiwilligen-Kavallerie-Division "Maria Theresia" and led it until killed in Budapest on February 11, 1945. He was promoted SS-Oberführer on October 16, 1944 and to SS-Brigadeführer January 15, 1945. His German Cross in Gold awarded October 16, 1942, was probably for his leadership of the two Battle Groups named for him. Awarded the Knight's Cross on March 8, 1943 for leadership of Kavallerie Regiment 2 and the Oakleaves on February 4, 1945 for his divisional command, he was among the best Waffen-SS cavalry commanders. He competed often in the pre-war years for the SS Main Riding School in Munich. (Photos: Jakob Tiefenthäler and Jost Schneider)

"The fighting in Gusevo was hard. The Russians attacked during the night with continuous assaults and managed to break into the southern portion of the village. The battle cost the Russians many casualties. We managed to count at least 300 dead soldiers in the village alone. The prisoners that we took belonged to the 380th Division. The Brigade is ready to attack to the south and will initiate the attack with SS-Kavallerie-Regiment 1 departing from Gusevo. The goal of the Regiment is to take Lutschessa."

A further indication of the fighting is seen in a portion of the award recommendation for one of the Brigade's officers.

"On February 25, 1942, SS-Obersturmführer Rudolf Maeker, along with a strengthened squadron, was ordered to defend against an attack on the village of Gusevo by a strong superior enemy. Gusevo was occupied by a only a company of the 102.Infanterie Division. After nine hours of continuous fighting, the enemy, at a strength approximately 6 times as strong as our forces, was able to break into the first houses of the village. By this time the men positioned most forward were strongly shaken and attempted to give up the village. Without any regard for himself, Maeker put a halt to this attempt to retreat. Through his actions, the village remained in our possession. Maeker was shot through the shoulder during these combats."[109]

By mid-day the Brigade's attack proceeded against heavy enemy resistance and only managed minimal progress in a southwesterly direction. SS-Kavallerie-Regiment 1 was fighting in Aleksandrovka at this time. The Brigade reported many Russian casualties and 600 men were counted thus far. These men belonged to the Rifle Regiment 1262 of the 380th Division. At this time the Brigade reached a general line north of Gusevo, Polilejevo, Korotnja, Kommissarovo and Nevaja. Later on February 26th the Brigade reported that its attempts to take Aleksandrovka during the evening had failed. The attack continued into the next day at 0830 hours the Brigade reported that the village was now in German hands. This offensive move screamed forwards after enemy resistance was broken and at 1030 hours the village of Schalbilovk (northwest of Gusevo) has been taken.[110]

At the command post of XXIII.Armeekorps, the staff was contemplating the threat to the very existence of their Korps. They determined survival was based on their ability to hold their northern and northwestern front as well as the success of the attacks south of the Korps in the area between the villages of Nelidovo, Bjeloj, Szytschevka and Olenino. To improve their current situation, the Korps devised a large scale plan which included the SS-Kavallerie-Brigade.[111]

1.Panzer Division, now subordinated to the XXIII.Armeekorps was to break enemy resistance near Gravino and then secure the road between Nelidovo and Bjeloj and advance to the village of Monino. This would give them the opportunity to annihilate the opposing enemy forces (their 380th Division) located south of the railway between Nelidovo and Mostovajo. For this task, the following units were subordinated to 1.Panzer Division:[112]

a) SS-Kavallerie-Brigade
b) Kampfgruppe "Schell" which consisted of the following units:
    II.Bataillon, Schutzen Regiment 1
    2.Batterie of Flak Abteilung 59
    3.Kompanie of Panzerjäger Abteilung 37
    Parts of I.Abteilung, Artillerie Regiment 73

The Korps viewed quickly securing the village of Monino as decisive since the road running through this village (which connected Nelidovo and Bjeloj) was used by the Soviets as a supply line. For clearing the roads from Olenino through Gravino to Monino of debris and snow, some 450 men from several companies of Construction Battalion 321 and the Bridge Building Battalion 210 were obtained from Korps Pionier Führer 623.[113] The 253. and 102.Infanterie Divisionen were to prevent the enemy from advancing to the north from their southern positions. They were also to

---

[109] See footnote 72.

[110] "Kriegstagebuch Nr. 10, XXIII.Armeekorps, Abt. Ia, 1.2.42-31.3.42."

[111] ibid.

[112] ibid.

[113] The Korps Pionier Führer (Stopi) controlled engineer units attached as support units to the Korps and was the senior staff engineer of the Korps staff.

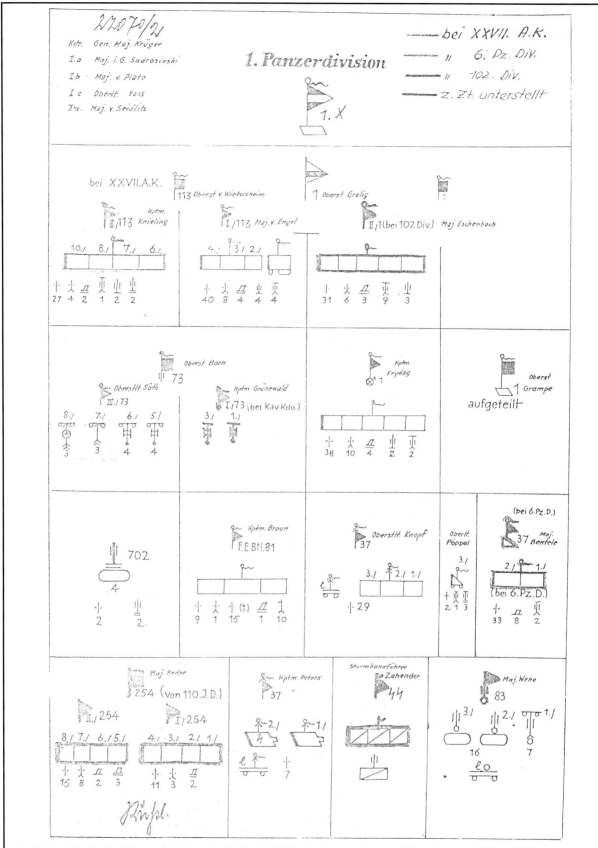

An Order of Battle for 1.Panzer Division dated May 14, 1942 showing attachment of Kampfgruppe "Zehender" consisting of the SS-Kavallerie-Brigade remnants.

protect the railway that was of significant meaning to the overall outcome of the operation. Generalleutnant Scheller's 253.Infanterie Division also received the order to fill the gap formed between the advancing 1.Panzer Division and the rest of the troops during their approach of Monino.[114]

By 1100 hours on February 27th the SS-Kavallerie-Brigade had advanced from Aleksandrovo and reached Partenovo. The attack continued in the direction of Gluchovo, northwest of Gusevo, and Schalpilovka was taken. The Brigade reported that they had been fighting Soviet Rifle Regiment 298 of the 186th Division and Rifle Regiment 419 of the 119th Division. These units had been thrown out of their positions in Aleksandrovka, Gluchovo, Partenovo, and Schapilovka. The forest southwest of Gusevo had been mopped up and an attack on the forest edge was repulsed. During the fighting the Brigade captured two cannons, eight grenade launchers and nine machine guns. The Brigade then continued their advance taking Gluchovo.[115]

According to a message from 1.Panzer Division, the engineer and anti-aircraft companies of II./Schutzen Regiment 1 from Battle Group "Schell" reached the area around Kommissarovo. At that time an order arrived from Model: *"Take Gravino!"* For this task the 253.Infanterie Division was dispatched to be supported by the SS-Kavallerie-Brigade and 1.Panzer Division. The SS-Kavallerie-Brigade was then removed from the command of XXIII.Armeekorps and subordinated to 1.Panzer Division along with the two companies and the column of the Building Bataillon 321 and the two companies and a platoon of Bridging Bataillon 210. In reality the command of Brigade was indirectly subordinated to the Korps, because 1.Panzer Division was still subordinated to XXIII.Armeekorps.[116]

On February 28th 23 2nd class Iron Crosses were awarded to the Brigade. The same day the Chief of Staff of 9.Armee, General Hans Krebs,[117] called the Chief of Staff XXIII.Armeekorps and informed him that Generaloberst Model placed incredible value on the securing of the situation near Mostovaja and that the forces of 1.Panzer Division or its attached components would have to be put into action there. The order forbidding deployment of the few tanks left to the Division was lifted for this operation. The 1.Panzer Division then sent artillery and engineer units to Mostaovaja since units of the Soviet 155th Rifle Division were sighted there. Later, SS-Kavallerie-Regimenter 1 and 2, now a part of 1.Panzer Division, continued their advance with SS-Kavallerie-Regiment 1 taking Gordejovo and Kusovlevo and SS-Kavallerie-Regiment 2 capturing Vaskovo. The Brigade later also managed to take Kletischtsche. After three days of continuous fighting the Brigade counted 1,200 enemy dead and captured several artillery pieces as well as a relatively large number of machine guns. The village of Gravino would be attacked by Battle Group "Schell" which was to pass through the area held by the SS-Kavallerie-Brigade and attack there. The command post of the Brigade as well as Battle Group "Schell" was moved to Komissarovo.[118]

While 1.Panzer Division prepared for its attack on Gravino, the SS-Kavallerie-Brigade took Marinovo, Tschernosekovo, Gorovatka and Merusohi, fighting weak enemy forces and Battle Group "Schell" took Bogorodizkoje after encountering tough enemy resistance. Then 1.Panzer Division made its way through those villages taken by the SS-Kavallerie-Brigade and Battle Group "Schell" while the Brigade was busy pursuing weak Russian forces fleeing to the northwest. In the afternoon a Ju 88 captured by the Russians was used to drop bombs on Olenino. The bombs shut down all communication with the Korps, killing 12 and wounding 50. The heavy anti-aircraft battery that was supposed to be in Olenino had not yet arrived. At 1600 hours the SS-Kavallerie-Brigade re-

---

[114] "Kriegstagebuch Nr. 10, XXIII.Armeekorps, Abt. Ia, 1.2.42-31.3.42."

[115] ibid.

[116] "Kriegstagebuch Nr. 10, XXIII.Armeekorps, Abt. Ia, 1.2.42-31.3.42." This transfer of subordination allowed 1.Panzer Division to direct the SS-Kavallerie Brigade tactically without going through Korps headquarters first.

[117] Awarded the Knight's Cross as Chief of Staff on March 26, 1944 and the Oakleaves on February 19, 1945 as Chief of Staff, Army Group "B."

[118] "Kriegstagebuch Nr. 10, XXIII.Armeekorps, Abt. Ia, 1.2.42-31.3.42."

A spring 1942 photo after Fegelein was awarded the Knight's Cross (March 2, 1942) for bravery in action as the commander of the SS-Kavallerie-Brigade. At this time he was in Poland with portions of the Brigade for formation of the SS-Kavallerie-Division. Gustav Lombard was then commanding the 700 man remnant of the Brigade still in Russia. (Photo: National Archives)

ported the northern battle group of 1.Panzer Division reached Bojewka and the southern group reached Merkuschi. The villages north and south of the road connecting Gusevo and Gravino were now in German hands. The enemy still occupied the villages of Voronino (north of Gravino), Lutschessa-Tal (south of the river in Smolkovo) and Nikolskoje. In Koniliva Kampfgruppe "Schell" established contact between the German forces located between Kletischtsche and Mal. Ivanovka while at 1725 hours 1.Panzer Division took Gravino. After these operations concluded, the Commanding General of the Korps expressed his special recognition to the Division and the SS-Kavallerie-Brigade. At the end of the day, the Brigade established contact with the 253.Infanterie Division.[119]

On March 2nd the Russians surprise attacked troops of the 1.Panzer Division located in Vissokoje and took the village but elements won back the village at 1315 hours. The tanks that were to be supplied to the 1st Panzer Division were stuck in Gusevo due to poor street conditions. 1.Panzer Division was getting bogged down in the mud and putting the tanks into action became virtually impossible. The absence of tank support for Battle Group "Schell" that afternoon made it difficult for them to take Potschinov while fighting against strong enemy forces. Elsewhere, the SS-Kavallerie-Brigade took Smolkovo in bitter house-to-house fighting at 1030 hours and overran the troops securing the village of Nikolskoje. Later the Brigade was engaged in combat at the strongly fortified village of Noviki and took the village after encountering tough Russian resistance. They then advanced in the direction of Ladyschino, Kaversnovo and Tolkatschi during which they encountered only light enemy resistance. By the end of the day the Brigade had secured the general line connecting Kaversnevo, Noviki, Smolkovo, Schernoskevo Gordejevo and Partenovo along with the I./481.Infanterie Regiment. The command post of the SS-Kavallerie-Brigade was situated in Aleksandrowka early in the day but had moved to Merkuschi before night. Battle Group "Schell"

---

[119] ibid.

was marching with the bulk of the troops in a westerly direction and later was on its way to Griva for an attack.[120]

During the morning of March 3rd 1.Panzer Division reported only light enemy patrol activity in the section of the SS-Kavallerie-Brigade, otherwise the night had been relatively calm. Later, a section of the railroad tracks on the rail line between Rshev and Olenino was destroyed by the Russians which strained the supply situation for XXIII.Armeekorps, already short of ammunition. A train which was still on the tracks had reached the village of Bulachi (six kilometers east of Olenino) during the evening of March 2nd and was now stuck there. Instead of waiting for track repairs which could not be completed until late in the day, the supply troops used all available means to transport the material which reached Bulachi and was then used to resupply 1.Panzer Division and the SS-Kavallerie-Brigade. Later that day Kampfgruppe "Grolig" of 1.Panzer Division attacked Dunino and Griva but could not report any success in spite of the fact that all available infantry and artillery forces were deployed. The losses of the battle group were substantial and the casualties included a battalion commander as well as three platoon leaders. In other sectors an attack of the SS-Kavallerie-Brigade, which was not intended to secure the area, remained stagnant even after they had overcome very difficult terrain. Due to the difficult topography the Brigade was unable to deploy its heavy weapons and was stuck on the edge of the forest southwest of Schopotovo. The Russians offered strong resistance and called in several reserve units from Djakovo.[121]

On March 4th the Russian troops positioned in front of 1.Panzer Division were observed building defensive positions along the line connecting the villages of Griva, Schopotovo and Starosselje. At the same time 1.Panzer Division prepared its attack which was to commence the next day. The plan of attack situated Battle Group "Grolig" on the right flank and the SS-Kavallerie-Brigade on the left flank. The Division possessed only six tanks and six artillery pieces. The goal for the attack was the village of Redanovo. At 1230 hours on March 5th Generaloberst Walter Model showed up at Korps headquarters to review the attack plan. After much discussion the original plans were altered. The attack of 1.Panzer Division was to take place as planned, but the Division was only to advance until reaching Monino. The SS-Kavallerie-Brigade was to follow the Division and maintain the rearward positions until the 206.Infanterie Division, attacking to the north, could relieve the Brigade which would subsequently be assigned to secure the southern front. The 1.Panzer Division was then to attack the enemy bridgehead located at Molodoy-Tud while the 102. and 253.Infanterie Divisionen were to advance in a northwesterly direction, then cut due west and approach Nelidovo along with the 110.Infanterie Division. The advance was then to proceed to Osztaschkovo.[122]

On March 6th the 1.Panzer Division took Sjabriki and Griva. The SS-Kavallerie-Brigade took the village of Schitiki after winning the river crossing near Sagorje and claimed 350 enemy killed. The river crossing was not adequate for tanks and so a bridge near Poschinok was under construction. Shortly later the supply conditions and a general lack of reserve forces for the engaged units forced attack plans to be altered. The staff of XXIII.Armeekorps reported to 9.Armee that since they could not supply reserves, they were forced to request that 1.Panzer Division be allowed to turn to the north. 9.Armee replied that Generaloberst Model was of the opinion that the Korps would be allowed to mop up the area between and near the villages of Karpovo and Mostovaja and was generally in agreement with the assessment of the situation. However 9.Armee did not grant them their wish to turn 1.Panzer Division to the north. Model was of the opinion that the sleds of the SS-Kavallerie-Brigade would be adequate for these mopping up operations. The Chief of Staff of XXIII.Armeekorps then pointed to the fact that the Brigade was not adequate for such an operation and asked once again that the 1.Panzer Division be allowed to be brought up to strengthen the northern sectors but 9.Armee still did not agree. The SS-Kavallerie-Brigade was then informed of

[120] ibid.

[121] ibid.

[122] ibid.

the new directives supplied by 9.Armee and received the order to advance by deploying SS-Kavallerie-Regiment 2 to the west and north. According to a message from SS-Standartenführer Fegelein, heavy weapons and munitions could only be brought up during the day since the supply routes from Olenino were long and the horses were already completely worn out. Furthermore, the Brigade could promise the success of the planned operations only if they were to be supplied with tank support since their heavy weapons were no longer mobile (again due to the exhausted horses). This message reached 9.Armee headquarters by radio at 2245 hours. They responded that Model was in agreement with the original order and the SS-Kavallerie-Brigade was to proceed north to Mostovaja while destroying all enemy forces along the way. Elements of 1.Panzer Division were only to be brought up if the Brigade could not accomplish its tasks with its current forces and if the weather and road conditions were adequate.[123]

Early on March 7th more tanks were supplied to 1.Panzer Division. The SS-Kavallerie-Brigade got its wish. The tanks were immediately subordinated to the Brigade which had set out to the north at 0000 hours and was engaged in fighting since 0600 hours. SS-Kavallerie-Regiment 1 and a company of Pionier Regiment 37, equipped with four Panzer IIIs as well as two light field guns, reached Kornilovka with advance elements. By 0640 hours SS-Kavallerie-Regiment 2 had advanced as far as Griva and by 0815 hours had defeated enemy forces in Dubki. I./Schutzen Regiment 113 followed behind SS-Kavallerie-Regiment 2. Forces of 1.Panzer Division, also following behind, passed through Dubki and went on to Mevidki where they encountered well-built enemy fortifications. Only after very bitter fighting did the Division manage to take this village and casualties ran high. A second attack on Russian forces located in Ploskoje was not successful due to a heated Russian counterattack. Kampfgruppe "Grolig" took Sagorje and reached Schitiki at 2000 hours.[124]

With the attack to the north, the Germans had seemingly surprised the Soviets. In Medvediki the Brigade overran a Russian battle group with a battalion staff from Russian Rifle Regiment 786 of the 155th Russian Rifle Division. In Medvediki the enemy had lost between 100 and 120 killed and 80 prisoners while captured Russian supplies were found to be well-organized and of high quality. The Brigade also captured several anti-tank guns and other light artillery pieces as well as a few machine guns and a large number of rifles. More importantly the Brigade captured a Russian map which gave away the enemy attack plan. According to a captured map, the 155th Russian Rifle Division began their attack with three regiments situated in different villages in the area.[125]

On March 8th XXIII.Armeekorps complained bitterly that 1.Panzer Division was becoming too weak because 9.Armee would not supply them with reserves. The Russians, recognizing this, attacked their positions continuously. The Korps was under the impression that 9.Armee did not really understand how many men they were losing daily nor how desperately they need reinforcements. At this time the Panzer Division was split up, half of it was advancing to the north with other units while the other half was situated in Griva, tied down by continuous Russian attacks supported by heavy artillery. Model was of the opinion that the enemy forces in Mostovaja would have to be defeated, but the XXIII.Armeekorps staff knew that 1.Panzer Division was too weak for such an undertaking. Later, the SS-Kavallerie-Brigade, together with forces of 1.Panzer Division under the Brigade's command, left Medvediki at 1330 hours for an attack. During the early afternoon they fought tough enemy forces in Dubrovka and managed to gain contact with the 253.Infanterie Division. The enemy forces surrounded near Kljasty were annihilated. In Luschessa-Tal enemy patrols attacked German security forces near Karsskaja but were repulsed. At 1625 hours the SS-Kavallerie-Brigade, together with their troops from 1.Panzer Division, were tactically subordinated to the

---

[123] ibid.

[124] ibid.

[125] "Kriegstagebuch Nr. 10, XXIII.Armeekorps, Abt. Ia, 1.2.42-31.3.42." in which the identity of the specific regiments is not given.

253.Infanterie Division and were to be supplied by them as well. The four tanks, however, were to remain at the disposal of 1.Panzer Division.

On March 9th, Model visited XXIII.Armeekorps command post. There he was informed of the situation and ordered that the cleansing operations planned for Mostovaja were to be carried out by 252.Infanterie Regiment and the SS-Kavallerie-Brigade. The Brigade set out from Ploskoje and advanced towards Oserki. The attack was initially successful but bogged down as enemy resistance stiffened. After one of their four tanks was taken out during a strong enemy counter-attack, the Brigade retreated back to Ploskoje.[126]

On March 10th an order arrived from 9.Armee instructing the SS-Kavallerie-Brigade be sent to Gravino and subordinated to the XXXXVI.Armeekorps after defeating enemy forces in Mostovaja. Based on later reports, it can be assumed that the Brigade was successful in taking Mostovaja. No mention of the Brigade surfaced in the war diary of XXIII.Armeekorps until March 14th. An order from 9.Armee arrived stating that the Brigade, as well as the remaining units of XXIII.Armeekorps, were to hold the northern front, take Berjosa Tal and retain the area around Gravino. After these operations, the remaining parts of 1.Panzer Division were to be subordinated to XXXXVI. Armeekorps. The operational strength of the Brigade was some 1,500 after they received reinforcements of ethnic Germans during March.[127]

No more reports about the Brigade surfaced until March 18th during which the Ia of XXIII.Armeekorps noted that there was generally no change in the status of enemy positions. In Berjossa Tal the enemy attacked with two tanks supported by infantry at 1630 hours and advanced on to Toropino and Sukina. The attack on Sukina was beaten back by German artillery but the Russian tanks were still active. The enemy also reconnoitered the area east of Oserki and near Perchirevo (three kilometers south of Medvediki) the results of which led the enemy to move the spearhead of their attacks further east. Later, Perchirevo was occupied by stronger German forces. Elements of the SS-Kavallerie-Brigade were then to be brought up to Dubki and Perchievo.[128] SS-Sturmbannführer Gustav Lombard took command of the Brigade remnants in mid-March and commander Fegelein returned to Debica to initiate rebuilding of those units undergoing refit in Poland.[129] On March 21, 1942, the Brigade was awarded 48 2nd class and three 1st class Iron Crosses.

On March 23rd the SS-Kavallerie-Brigade was ordered by 9.Armee to relieve 1.Panzer Division commanded by Generalleutnant Eugen Krüger which was positioned in the area around Griva. The command of those troops subordinated to the Division (Aufklärungsabteilung 102 and 481.Infanterie Regiment) were transferred to the Brigade. 9.Armee noted that these operations were to be carried out quickly since future operations depended on it. The SS-Kavallerie-Brigade was to be replaced by 255.Infanterie Regiment (110.Infanterie Division) which was to arrive in the Brigade's former positions on March 25th. The staff of 255.Infanterie Regiment was to arrive in Mostovaja on the 25th. The SS-Kavallerie-Brigade had completed relieving 1.Panzer Division by the evening of March 27th and the Division was in its new positions to begin their assigned security operations. At this time the command of the Brigade transferred back to XXIII.Armeekorps. A reluctant spring was surfacing in late March and by noon on the 27th the snow on the roads was beginning to thaw, but by that evening another snow storm had arrived. On March 28th the Brigade's last units of 1.Panzer Division departed. Since the Brigade's strength was weak, they were only to

---

[126] "Kriegstagebuch Nr. 10, XXIII.Armeekorps, Abt. Ia, 1.2.42-31.3.42."

[127] "Kriegstagebuch Nr. 10, XXIII.Armeekorps, Abt. Ia, 1.2.42-31.3.42" and Bender/Taylor, "Uniforms, Organization and History of the Waffen-SS," volume 3, page 29.

[128] "Kriegstagebuch Nr. 10, XXIII.Armeekorps, Abt. Ia, 1.2.42-31.3.42."

[129] The exact date of the command transfer is unknown. Bayer gives "the first days of March" while the only dated document found thus far is the statistics page of Lombard's Knight's Cross recommendation which gives March 18, 1942. It is possible that SS-Sturmbannführer August Zehender assumed command of the remnants of Lombard's former regiment at this time for the two or three weeks until the formation of Kampfgruppe "Zehender."

Two views of SS-Standartenführer Hermann Fegelein with SS-Brigadeführer Wilhelm Bittrich during Bittrich's formal assumption of command of the SS-Kavallerie-Division which he was assigned to as its first divisional commander. Fegelein turned over command of the Brigade units already at the Debica training area at that time while remants of the Brigade in the form of Kampfrguppe "Zehender" were still in Russia. The photos are from very late May 1942. (Photos: Jess Lukens)

remain in their current positions until the 253.Infanterie Division arrived. Until then the Brigade was to send out several reconnaissance patrols to monitor the surrounding area. At this time the Brigade had a cumulative strength that amounted to approximately five squadrons and was equipped with seven heavy machine guns, four light infantry artillery pieces, three anti-tank guns, three heavy grenade launchers and seven heavy anti-aircraft guns.[130] XXIII.Armeekorps awarded the men of the Brigade 19 2nd class and two 1st class Iron Crosses on March 30th. The 1st class awards went to SS-Untersturmführer Joachim Boosfeld and SS-Unterscharführer Hermann Maringgele, both from SS-Kavallerie-Regiment 1.[131]

On April 2, 1942, several Russian attacks in the area of Gravino forced the leadership of 9.Armee to construct their own attack plan. This attack strategy did not include the SS-Kavallerie-Brigade, but when the battle orders came to XXIII.Armeekorps, a special order for the Brigade accompanied them. Apparently, the temporary Brigade commander, SS-Sturmbannführer Gustav Lombard, had reported to XXIII.Armeekorps that the condition of the Brigade was very poor. The men were completely exhausted and the unit's fighting ability had dwindled to a fraction of its original strength. This was true for many of the units subordinated to XXIII.Armeekorps as well as 9.Armee itself. All formations were almost completely depleted of equipment and men during the recent incredibly harsh and non-stop battles. Therefore, in agreement with 9.Armee, the staff recommended to the Reichsführer-SS that the unit change its official status from a "brigade" to that of a "weak rider regiment." 9.Armee intended on conducting an exchange of officers between the Brigade and a new cavalry regiment, termed "Kavallerie-Regiment 3,"[132] which was to consist of strengthened units of Aufklärungsabteilung 102.[133]

Meanwhile, Generaloberst Walter Model and his staff planned an operation codenamed "Nordpol," devised to win back the villages of Karpovo and Nelidovo from the Russians. The details of this operation began arriving at XXIII.Armeekorps on April 4th. The planning and execution of such operations on the Eastern Front were now difficult and very slow-paced, generally due to the weak strength and lack of equipment of the units. Orders for the preparation of this relatively large operation were only "possibly" to include units of the SS-Kavallerie-Brigade operating under the command of the "Kavallerie-Kommando z.b.V." (Special Purpose Cavalry Commando), a thrown-together unit that included Armee-Kavallerie-Regimenter 1,2 and 3 as well as the "SS-Reiter-Regiment."[134] On April 8th, more specific plans arrived for the deployment of the Kavallerie-Kommando z.b.V. for Operation "Nordpol." The unit would attack from the area south between Nishe and Federovsskije. The unit would assist the 102.Infanterie Division in their attack on the enemy groups in Karpovo and south of Karpovo while being subordinated to this unit. Their contribution included attacking along the railway in a westerly direction. After the successful conclusion of the attack, the unit was to continue on and mop-up the area around Ch.Sstrutschje. The forested area on both sides of the railway was also to be mopped-up. After those operations were completed, the Kavallerie-Kommando z.b.V. was to depart from the line between Ch.Mal.Rjabinovk and Mal.Tolstucha where they were to have been protecting the railway there, and prepare for an attack along the railway from Ch.Sstrutschje to the south until reaching Popovzeva. If enemy troops were found on the Mosstovaja Front, they were to be defeated. If required, the unit was to continue its advance to the southern bank of the Beresa River, to the area between Sselo and Baruli, and secure the enemy supply line in this area. These orders were not final, however, and the unit was to wait for specific "special orders," to be received from 9.Armee.[135]

---

[130] "Kriegstagebuch Nr. 10, XXIII.Armeekorps, Abt. Ia, 1.2.42-31.3.42."

[131] "Vorschlagsliste Nr. 75" signed by Albrecht Schubert, commander XXIII.Armeekorps.

[132] This was an Army not an SS cavalry regiment.

[133] "Kriegstagebuch Nr. 11, XXIII.Armeekorps, Abt. Ia, 1.4.42-31.7.42."

[134] The term used for the now depleted SS-Kavallerie-Brigade.

[135] "Kriegstagebuch Nr. 11, XXIII.Armeekorps, Abt. Ia, 1.4.42-31.7.42."

SS-Obersturmbannführer August Zehender, shown here (left) with Oakleaves winner General der Panzertruppe Joachim Lemelsen in Russia with the SS-Kavallerie-Division during November/December 1942, and (right) as an SS-Brigadeführer in command of the 22.SS-Freiwilligen-Kavallerie-Division "Maria Theresia" in 1945. He led Kampfgruppe "Zehender" with the SS-Kavallerie-Brigade and the larger Kampfgruppe "Z" named for him with the SS-Kavallerie-Division in late 1942. His German Cross in Gold was probably, by its award date, for leadership of these two independent battle groups. When Zehender returned to Poland in June, 1942 with the surviving 500 men of the Brigade Kampfgruppe, they were incorporated into the SS-Kavallerie-Division during August and September. (Photos: Ott collection and BDC)

On April 9th a special order from Generaloberst Model arrived, specifying plans for refurbishing the SS-Kavallerie-Brigade and to supply them with better-condition horses from Warsaw. After several discussions with SS-Sturmbannführer Gustav Lombard, the Brigade was reorganized as follows:[136]

1) Regiment staff including a signals platoon of 30 men.
2) Three rider squadrons, each with 70 men and five light machine guns. (This would be increased to 100 men if possible)
3) One heavy squadron with 120 men, six heavy machine guns, two heavy grenade launchers and one light infantry cannon platoon.
4) An artillery platoon with three field pieces and a strength of 59 men.
5) An anti-aircraft platoon with five 2cm guns and 72 men.

This reorganization was to be proposed to the Reichsführer-SS. Later, however, the intended reformation was impossible too carry-out at the front, since all vehicles, saddles and spurs were

---

[136] ibid.

captured by the enemy in Toropez in January. Also, the reformation of the mounted units was impossible due to the complete lack of adequately trained riders.[137]

Because of this SS-Sturmbannführer Lombard personally made a request to Model himself, that the Brigade be relieved from duties at the front so that it could reform in the area around Warsaw. The Brigade would be relieved gradually until April 15th, so that all elements of the Brigade could take part in the reformation. To assist in the rebuilding, 45 to 50 men from the 110.Infanterie Division were placed at the disposal of the Brigade to serve as instructors for up-coming training operations.[138]

During April the Brigade was subordinated to the 110.Infanterie Division and reports about their activity included light skirmishes with Russian troops during patrol operations. On April 18th the Brigade sent out a strong patrol to the village of Krivuscha and independently defeated weak Soviet troops there (twenty men) and mopped up the surrounding area. The Russians lost four dead during this battle.[139]

Battle Group "Zehender"

It is unclear from the records of XXIII.Armeekorps or those available from the Brigade exactly how the Brigade was relieved. It appears that the relief operations took place gradually. To replace the Brigade at the front during its reformation period in Warsaw, a special Battle Group (Kampfgruppe) officially formed in mid-April 1942 and given the title Kampfgruppe "Zehender," named after its commander, SS-Sturmbannführer August Zehender. Zehender would lead the Kampfgruppe while SS-Sturmbannführer Gustav Lombard accompanied those men returning to Warsaw. A war diary from one of the units of the Kampfgruppe begins on April 15th. As to exactly when the Kampfgruppe became officially registered, a document written by Fritz Freitag indicates that the unit officially formed on April 19, 1942, but no mention of it is in the war diary of XXIII.Armeekorps.[140] The structure of Kampfgruppe "Zehender" is outlined in this document and is very similar to the earlier plan envisioned by Lombard and Model. Kampfgruppe "Zehender" consisted of the most battle worthy remnants of the depleted SS-Kavallerie-Brigade.[141]

1st Squadron came from the mounted squadrons (1-3) of SS-Kavallerie-Regiment 1 and led by SS-Hauptsturmführer Karl Braunstein. 2nd Squadron came from the mounted squadrons (1-3) of SS-Kavallerie-Regiment 2 and led by SS-Obersturmführer Heinz Wowerat. 3rd Squadron formed from the Brigade's Engineer Company and led by SS-Hauptsturmführer Karl Fritsche. 4th Squadron was the heavy weapons unit[142] and combined the remnants of the 4th and 5th Squadrons of both SS-Kavallerie-Regimenter and commanded by SS-Obersturmführer Erich Brockmann. The Brigade anti-aircraft battery became a component, commanded by SS-Obersturmführer Ewald Keyk. The single remaining artillery battery led by SS-Hauptsturmführer Arno Paul was a supporting unit as were the Signals Company remnants led by SS-Obersturmführer Wilhelm Wiersch. Ia of the Kampfgruppe was SS-Hauptsturmführer Karl Gesele and physician was SS-Untersturmführer Dr. Hermann Reichart.

On April 16th several members of the Kampfgruppe were awarded the Iron Cross and the following day several other men were awarded the War Merit Cross 2nd Class with Swords. Also a patrol of the Heavy Squadron went from Aleksandrovka at 0400 hours to engage a Russian patrol.

---

[137] ibid.

[138] ibid.

[139] ibid.

[140] The compilation of the Brigade's record written by Freitag was done in 1943 when he commanded the SS-Kavallerie-Division. Due to its later date it was only used for confirmation of other documentation.

[141] "Schlacht- u.Gefechtsbezeichnungen für das 1.Halbjahr 1942."

[142] Although no reference designating 4th Squadron as the heavy weapons unit is in Freitag's report, the existence of the war diary for the Kampfgruppe heavy unit confirms the units used to form it as well as its commander and designation.

SS-Sturmbannführer Karl Gesele stands here in the center during late summer 1942 wearing the German Cross in Gold awarded him for his service as Ia of the SS-Kavallerie-Brigade. Gesele stayed in Russia as Ia of Kampfgruppe "Zehender" and then continued as Ia for the SS-Kavallerie-Division. Third from left of this 1942 training photo is Wilhelm Bittrich, commander of the SS-Kavallerie-Division. To the right of Gesele is the new commander of the artillery unit, Joachim Rumohr. He was later awarded the Knight's Cross on January 16, 1944 in command of the artillery unit and the Oakleaves on February 4, 1945 as the last commander of the 8.SS-Kavallerie-Division "Florian Geyer." As an SS-Brigadeführer, Rumohr led the Division from April 1, 1944 until February 11, 1945. (Photo: Private U.S. collection)

No casualties were reported when the patrol returned. Later that day SS-Obersturmführer Erich Brockmann issued instruction for some replacements who had arrived. On April 18th a Kampfgruppe patrol spotted stronger Russian forces. The Kampfgruppe Ia, SS-Sturmbannführer Karl Gesele, ordered Brockmann to put together a patrol to confront the Russians. The patrol engaged the enemy positions with heavy machine guns and defeated them. There were several Russian casualties but none were suffered by the Kampfgruppe. SS-Untersturmführer Arnold Tofahrn arrived later that day from Warsaw, bringing a number of replacements with him.[143]

On April 19th 110.Infanterie Division reported to XXIII.Armeekorps that Kampfgruppe "Zehender"[144] dispatched reconnaissance patrols from their left flank to the enemy-occupied villages of Pustlschka, Kischkino and Reischtsche. Kampfgruppe "Zehender" was subordinated to the 110.Infanterie Division and for the rest of April the 110.Infanterie Division reported various skirmishes between their forces and enemy units, but no major battles resulted.[145]

On April 22nd plans for Operation "Nordpol," the taking the village of Karpovo, resumed and this was to commence on April 25th.[146] The next day Kampfgruppe "Zehender" sent out several strong patrols towards Dubki. These troops engaged several weak Russian patrols and defeated them.[147]

On April 24th SS-Sturmbannführer Zehender ordered SS-Obersturmführer Günther Boigs[148] and SS-Obersturmführer Hans Stapenhorst[149] to capture three Russians for interrogation. The two men, accompanied by an enlisted man who volunteered for the operation, set out at 1500 hours. Later that day a Russian patrol attacked the Kampfgruppe but was beaten back. The Kampfgruppe

[143] "Kriegstagebuch Schwere Schwadron SS-Kavallerie-Brigade, vom 15.4.42 bis 23.6.42." Tofahm stayed with the SS-Kavallerie-Division and in 1944 was an SS-Hauptsturmführer with SS-Kavallerie-Regiment 16.

[144] Referred to as the SS-Kavallerie-Brigade in the war diary of XXIII.Armeekorps, but hereafter referred to as Kampfgruppe "Zehender."

[145] "Kriegstagebuch Nr. 11, XXIII.Armeekorps, Abt. Ia, 1.4.42-31.7.42."

[146] ibid.

[147] ibid.

[148] Killed October 14, 1944 while serving with the 7.SS-Freiwilligen-Gebirgs-Division "Prinz Eugen."

[149] Born on July 30, 1903, he went on to serve as commander of 4th Squadron, SS-Kavallerie-Regiment 1 in the 8.SS-Kavallerie Division, ending the war serving in the SS-Führungshauptamt as an SS-Hauptsturmführer.

A rare photo showing some of the primary Brigade officers during transfer of command from Hermann Fegelein to Wilhelm Bittrich in 1942 when the Division began formation. From left are Albert Faßbender, Dr. Edwin Jung (Divisional Physician), Hermann Fegelein, unknown, Wilhelm Bittrich (Divisional Commander), unknown, August Zehender and Franz Rehbein. (Photo: Jess Lukens)

lost a man in this battle. That evening the Russians continued to attack Kampfgruppe positions, supported by artillery. On April 25th Boigs, Stapenhorst and the volunteer returned with three prisoners they had captured in Krivuscha and handed them over to the Kampfgruppe staff. During the morning of April 26th the Russians barraged Kampfgruppe positions in Partenovo with artillery fire. Nothing was damaged, although some of the shots were close. Later, a Russian messenger was intercepted and a message reporting a planned attack on Alexandrovka found on him. Because of this several patrols were dispatched to assess the situation.[150]

On April 26th new orders for Operation "Nordpol" arrived, delaying it until further notice. On April 27th Oberst Walter Fries, commander of Kampfgruppe "Fries,"[151] arrived in Alexandrovka to inspected Kampfgruppe "Zehender" positions there. The planned Russian attack on Alexandrovka never developed. On April 30th more patrols were dispatched to observe Russian movements.[152] On May 1st an award ceremony was held and SS-Sturmbannführer Zehender awarded 100 Infantry Assault Badges (Infanterie Sturmabzeichen) to the men of the Kampfgruppe. On May 2nd the observation patrols returned and were not able to report any enemy movements. Two days later the

---

[150] "Kriegstagebuch Nr. 11, XXIII.Armeekorps, Abt. Ia, 1.4.42-31.7.42." and "Kriegstagebuch Schwere Schwadron SS-Kavallerie-Brigade, vom 15.4.42 bis 23.6.42."

[151] Kampfgruppe "Fries" consisted mainly of remnants of Panzer-Pionier-Bataillon 89 and was subordinated to the 110.Infanterie Division. This unit was dissolved on May 7, 1942 and its components were relieved from the front to return to their previous units which were rebuilding in the rearward areas. Fries was awarded the Knight's Cross on December 14, 1941 as commander of 87.Infanterie Regiment and ended the war in command of the 29.Infanterie Division. He was awarded the Swords for his divisional command on August 11, 1944 as a Generalleutnant.

[152] "Kriegstagebuch Nr. 11, XXIII.Armeekorps, Abt. Ia, 1.4.42-31.6.42" and "Kriegstagebuch Schwere Schwadron SS-Kavallerie-Brigade, vom 15.4.42 bis 23.6.42."

Russians were attacking in several sectors close to the Kampfgruppe and the unit put on alarm. On May 5th the Heavy Squadron received a message that the Kampfgruppe was being attacked in the sector held by SS-Hauptsturmführer Ernst Imhof and that they should send troops to assist. By the time the units arrived from the heavy Squadron, however, the Russians had already been defeated. On May 6th, the Kampfgruppe received a special treat: a sauna. It was set up near the staff headquarters and all the units of the Kampfgruppe took turns using it. The men were very pleased and the war diary of the Heavy Squadron noted that this was the first chance that the men had to correctly bathe in several months.[153]

On May 7th the 1.Panzer Division was subordinated to XXIII.Armeekorps from the VI.Armeekorps. The Division was to take over operations in various sectors of the 110.Infanterie Division. After these operations had concluded, plans for the retaking of the town of Cholm, termed Operation "Caesar," were to be carried out. Besides 1.Panzer Division, 254.Infanterie Regiment and Kampfgruppe "Zehender" were to take part so it was unclear whether they would take part in Operation "Nordpol." It was at about this time that the command of the Kampfgruppe changed from 110.Infanterie Division to 1.Panzer Division. Operation "Caesar" would be conducted as soon as physically possible, since both 254.Infanterie Regiment and Kampfgruppe "Zehender" were to be relieved from their duties at the front so that they could return to the rear areas for rest and refit. The assignment of Kampfgruppe "Zehender" in the attack required them to win back the area between Partenovo and Andresjevskoje. 1.Panzer Division was requested to have the plans for the attack completed by May 14th. On a lighter note, one of the cooks from the Kampfgruppe celebrated his birthday by baking cookies for the entire Kampfgruppe.[154]

On May 9th 1.Panzer Division reported to XXIII.Armeekorps that Operation "Caesar" could commence on May 18th at the earliest. They cited the following reasons: The enemy occupation near Cholm and Repischtsche, with the strength of at least a reinforced company in each village, protected by well-built field positions, required a well thought-out plan that would deploy strong forces. The Russians maintained a battalion command post in Subovka and a regimental command post in Nareski, so an immediate counter-attack was expected. Therefore, the attack was to take place utilizing two assault groups, one from the area of Korotnja and the other from Komissarovo. Each group required battalion strength. These forces could prepare for the attack only after several other operations had taken place.[155]

To illustrate the weakness of the German forces in the area, it is interesting to note that the 110.Infanterie Division consisted of only nine weak battalions, two cannons, three heavy and ten light artillery guns and a single tank company, the latter only to be used in the event of a Russian attack. This was typical of all divisions on the Eastern Front during this time period and the 253. and 102. Divisionen were operating under the same conditions.[156]

On May 11th the Kampfgruppe troops reconnoitering the village of Parfenovo ran into a Russian patrol after they had reported the village was empty. During the ensuing battle, two members of the Kampfgruppe were killed while others were wounded.[157]

On May 11th, mention of Operation "Nordpol," which was originally to be initiated on April 25th, surfaced once again. Reports cited equipment being brought to the front for the operation, not the desired weapons, but trucks and similar equipment. The operation was now to commence on May 14th. On May 12th 9.Armee reported that Generaloberst Model agreed with initiating Operation "Caesar" as planned. He added that the occupational duty areas recaptured by Kampfgruppe

[153] "Kriegstagebuch Schwere Schwadron SS-Kavallerie-Brigade, vom 15.4.42 bis 23.6.42."

[154] "Kriegstagebuch Nr. 11, XXIII.Armeekorps, Abt. Ia, 1.4.42-31.7.42." and "Kriegstagebuch Schwere Schwadron SS-Kavallerie-Brigade, vom 15.4.42 bis 23.6.42."

[155] "Kriegstagebuch Nr. 11, XXIII.Armeekorps, Abt. Ia, 1.4.42-31.6.42"

[156] ibid.

[157] "Kriegstagebuch Schwere Schwadron SS-Kavallerie-Brigade, vom 15.4.42 bis 23.6.42."

Group photo showing several decorated officers while with the SS-Kavallerie-Division, most of whom served with the Brigade. From left SS-Untersturmführer Siegfried Korth who did not serve with the Brigade (German Cross in Gold September 22, 1943 and Knight's Cross February 9, 1945, the latter with the 22.SS-Freiwilligen-Kavallerie-Division "Maria Theresia"), SS-Hauptsturmführer Hans-Georg von Charpentier, SS-Sturmbannführer Gustav Lombard, SS-Hauptsturmführer Johannes Göhler and SS-Hauptsturmführer Anton Vandiecken (German Cross in Gold September 22, 1943 and Knight's Cross December 26, 1944) who served as a platoon leader in 5th Squadron, SS-Kavallerie-Regiment 1 at the end of 1941. (Photo: Jess Lukens)

"Zehender" and 254.Infanterie Regiment would be taken over by 1.Panzer Division after the conclusion of the operation, since these units were to be relieved from their duties at the front.[158]

On May 15th positions held by the Kampfgruppe were again attacked by Russian patrols. All the attacks were beat back and no casualties for the Kampfgruppe recorded. The engineer troops continued to lay mines in the outlying areas in front of Kampfgruppe positions.[159]

Meanwhile, at the command post of XXIII.Armeekorps, the initiation of Operation "Caesar" was set back to at least May 20th, since 1.Panzer Division was waiting for the arrival of two infantry battalions that were to be relieved from their current duties and report to the Division for the operation. On May 13th, the commencement of Operation "Nordpol" was set back another day to May 15th. On May 15th it was set back to May 20th. Delays are attributed to poor weather and the lack of mobility (very muddy road conditions due to weather) which hindered supply operations.[160]

On May 16th the 1.Panzer Division altered the original plan of Operation "Caesar" so that it could be conducted on May 18th, two days earlier than the last report cited. In preparation for the attack, Kampfgruppe "Zehender" and Schüchützen Regiment 113 assumed their new positions along the line between Vaskovo, Kusovleva (Schützen Regiment 113) and Tschernosvkovo (Kampfgruppe "Zehender"). On May 17th 1.Panzer Division received three tanks from II./Panzer Regiment 1 and three assault guns from Sturmgeschützabteilung 209 for the upcoming operation. Several Stukas from the Luftwaffe were also to play a role in this operation.[161]

[158] "Kriegstagebuch Nr. 11, XXIII.Armeekorps, Abt. Ia, 1.4.42-31.6.42"

[159] "Kriegstagebuch Schwere Schwadron SS-Kavallerie-Brigade, vom 15.4.42 bis 23.6.42."

[160] "Kriegstagebuch Nr. 11, XXIII.Armeekorps, Abt. Ia, 1.4.42-31.6.42"

[161] ibid.

Operation "Caesar" commenced at dawn on May 18th. The operation ran as planned and concluded at 1645 hours. A strong patrol of Kampfgruppe "Zehender" was responsible for destroying enemy bunkers in Pußtoschka and Gavritschki for their part of this operation. The Germans then built new positions along the new front line and sent out patrols in several directions to determine the enemy situation. For their part of the operation, the Heavy Squadron, with a strength of two officers, one NCO and 13 enlisted men, was equipped with several machine pistols and four plate mines for the engineers. The battle in Pußtoschka took place as planned and the Heavy Squadron returned having suffered no casualties after having completing their assignments at 1000 hours. Unfortunately, Russian fighter planes attacked Kampfgruppe positions in Parfenevo and Alexandrovka and several men wounded. Worse still, several German Stukas shot up some of the men from the Kampfgruppe and they had to be evacuated to the nearest field hospital, though nobody was killed.[162]

On May 19th the Russians counter-attacked Cholm with a strength of 150 men on three separate occasions. These assaults were repulsed and 20 Russians soldiers killed. Several men of the Kampfgruppe took part in an attack on Stepanovka supported by Army assault guns. SS-Obersturmführer Erich Brockmann and SS-Obersturmführer Friedrich Maletta rode with SS-Sturmbannführer Karl Gesele to observe the fighting. During the battles one of the men from the Kampfgruppe was killed. After the combat had concluded, Generaloberst Model awarded ten second class War Merit Crosses with Swords to the men of the Kampfgruppe. Awards of the Iron Cross 2nd class were awarded later to the men by SS-Sturmbannführer Zehender for this battle on May 30th.[163]

Plans for Operation "Nordpol" originally to require Kampfgruppe "Zehender" would have to be altered as the Kampfgruppe was soon to be relieved. The password "Krüger" was the signal that the Kavallerie-Kommando z.b.V. (which no longer contained Kampfgruppe "Zehender") was to be removed from the command of 102.Infanterie Division and placed in the area of 1.Panzer Division. There it was to relieve Kampfgruppe "Zehender" and 254.Infanterie Regiment. Kampfgruppe "Zehender" was to be relieved no later than May 24th and this began being on May 21st. Command of the Kampfgruppe was officially removed from the XXIII.Armeekorps on May 23rd.[164] After a short preparation period the men of Zehender's command returned to the Debica area in Poland and conducted some security operations before being distributed among the newly forming SS-Kavallerie-Division.

The End of the SS-Kavallerie-Brigade and creation of the SS-Kavallerie-Division
The Russian winter offensive decimated all the Brigade elements, especially the Reconnaissance Detachment. Portions of Fegelein's command withdrew from the front in January 1942 followed by others in late March and April. The strongest remnants remained in Russia under August Zehender's command until those 500 men returned to Poland and formed the primary cadre of the new SS-Kavallerie-Division. Portions of the SS-Kavallerie-Division conducted anti-partisan operations throughout the summer 1942 formation and training period.

By March 1942 plans were already being formulated by the SS Main Operational Office for rebuilding of the Brigade, starting with the reconnaissance unit ordered in mid-March to be rebuilt in Warsaw.[165] The reforming was to start April 1st and Albert Faßbender undertook the initial two months of this task. In April 1943 it became a fully motorized reconnaissance unit.[166]

[162] "Kriegstagebuch Nr. 11, XXIII.Armeekorps, Abt. Ia, 1.4.42-31.6.42" and "Kriegstagebuch Schwere Schwadron SS-Kavallerie-Brigade, vom 15.4.42 bis 23.6.42."

[163] ibid.

[164] "Kriegstagebuch Nr. 11, XXIII.Armeekorps, Abt. Ia, 1.4.42-31.7.42."

[165] SS-Führungshauptamt, Org.Tgb. Nr.90/42 g. Kdos., "Gliederung der SS-Kav.Brg." dated March 13, 1942.

[166] SS-Kavallerie-Division Ia, (heading title illegible) dated April 27, 1943. At that time it was to have one each motorcycle, reconnaissance and heavy squadrons.

Relaxing in Berlin with an unidentified Army General are (from left) Karl Maas (Ia, SS-Kavallerie-Division), Günther Temme and August Zehender. The latter two officers were primary contributors to the Brigade, especially in 1942. On the right is Hitler's adjutant Otto Günsche so the photo may have been during a visit to Hitler's headquarters. The photo scene is sometime after April 1943 when Zehender was promoted to SS-Standartenführer. (Yerger Archives)

It was soon evident the remaining personnel were insufficient for the task and the decision made instead to form a new unit as a division. The SS-Kavallerie-Division became established on June 21, 1942, at the Debica training area in Poland with SS-Oberführer Wilhelm Bittrich appointed commander and head of the formation staff on May 1, 1942. He later won the German Cross in Gold for his command of the SS-Kavallerie-Division.

Some former Brigade units already started rebuilding, prior to formal establishment of the Division being ordered, in various locations. The unit contained primarily ethnic Germans from Hungary and as expected there were linguistic problems that had to be overcome.

As partial training assistance the SS Cavalry School in Zamosc formed in Poland during mid-June 1942.[167] It assisted with both riding and cavalry related vehicle training. The composition of the SS-Kavallerie-Division was much larger and fully complete compared to the field forming of the original Brigade.

SS-Kavallerie-Regiment 1 reformed in Kielce and along with SS-Kavallerie-Regiment 2 another regiment formed. On June 24, 1942, SS-Kavallerie-Regiment 3 was ordered established at the training area in Debica.[168] The three regiments were strengthened with additional platoons added to their staffs in addition to the four mounted, one machine gun and heavy squadrons. By the time the units were again operational Gustav Lombard (Regiment 1), August Zehender (Regiment 2) and Hans-Viktor von Zastrow (Regiment 3) were the regimental commanders. All three had been with the SS-Kavallerie-Brigade. When von Zastrow was killed in 1942, command of SS-Kavallerie-Regiment 3 went to Hans-Georg von Charpentier who commanded for the remainder of

---

[167] SS-Führungshauptamt, Org.Tgn.Nr. 3331/42 g.Kdos, "Aufstellung der SS-Reit und Fahrschule Zamosc," dated June 2, 1942.

[168] SS-Führungshauptamt, Org.Tgb.Nr. 209/42 g. Kdos., "Aufstellung des 3.SS-Kav.Regiments," dated June 24, 1942

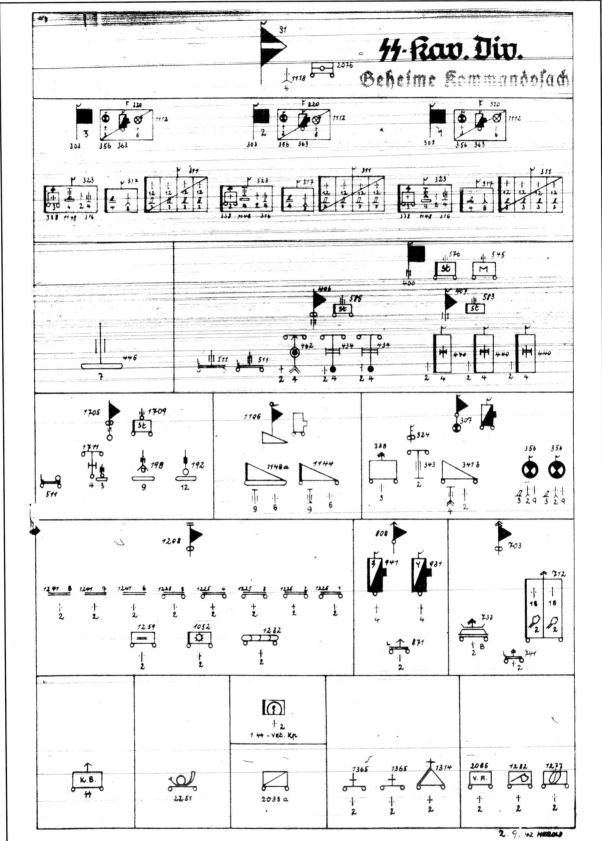

A September 1942 Order of Battle showing the newly created and much larger SS-Kavallerie-Division, especially the expansion to three (later four) Kavallerie Regimenter. (National Archives).

its existence. In August 1943 a fourth regiment was added. The four regiments were renumbered in October 1943 as 15, 16, 17 and 18.[169] SS-Kavallerie-Regiment 3 was later detached and eventually used to form the 22.SS-Freiwilligen-Kavallerie-Division "Maria Theresia" in 1944.

The artillery component was ordered rebuilt in June 1942, first as a detachment with three batteries and in July ordered expanded to a regiment containing two detachments.[170] During formation SS-Sturmbannführer Joachim Rumohr arrived as regimental commander. He would become the last commander of the SS-Kavallerie-Division and win the Oakleaves to the Knight's Cross. The regiment later expanded to three detachments, one of which equipped with self-propelled artillery.

The engineer component expanded to a Pionier Bataillon but was detached from the Division in April 1943. Its personnel later formed part of the 37.SS-Freiwilligen-Kavallerie-Division "Lützow."

An assault gun battery (Sturmgeschützbatterie) formed in Weimar-Buchenwald in September and in Debica an anti-tank detachment (Panzerjäger Abteilung) added.[171] The assault gun unit later expanded to detachment strength and then dissolved with portions going to the anti-tank unit. Supply and support units expanded in relation to a division sized unit. The division underwent almost constant unit changes during its existence and, like the Brigade, its elements often fought independently or assigned to other formations on a temporary basis.

The SS-Kavallerie-Division became the 8.SS-Kavallerie-Division in on October 22, 1943, and on March 12, 1944, received its final designation and honor title: 8.SS-Kavallerie-Division "Florian Geyer." It became the sixth most decorated unit of the Waffen-SS for awards of the Knight's Cross. With an eventual strength of some 15,000 men, the Division fought almost continuously in the East until trapped and destroyed in Budapest, along with its sister division "Maria Theresia," on February 11, 1945. Less than 200 men between the two divisions survived the breakout attempt from the Hungarian city to become cadre for the 37.SS-Freiwilligen-Kavallerie-Division "Lützow" that formed in the final months of the war. However, the SS-Kavallerie-Division is a story for another volume.

---

[169] Regiments were numbered consecutively starting with the "Leibstandarte" for multiple units of the same type in each division. The 17th regiment held that designation when with "Maria Theresia" following a decision to perpetuate the number.

[170] SS-Führungshauptamt, Org.Tgb.Nr. 208/42 g. Kdos, "Neugliederung der SS-Kav.Brigade," dated June 24, 1942.

[171] SS-Führungshauptamt, Org.Tgb.Nr. 355/42 g. Kdos., "Gliederung der SS-Kavallerie-Division," dated September 9, 1942.

MAPS

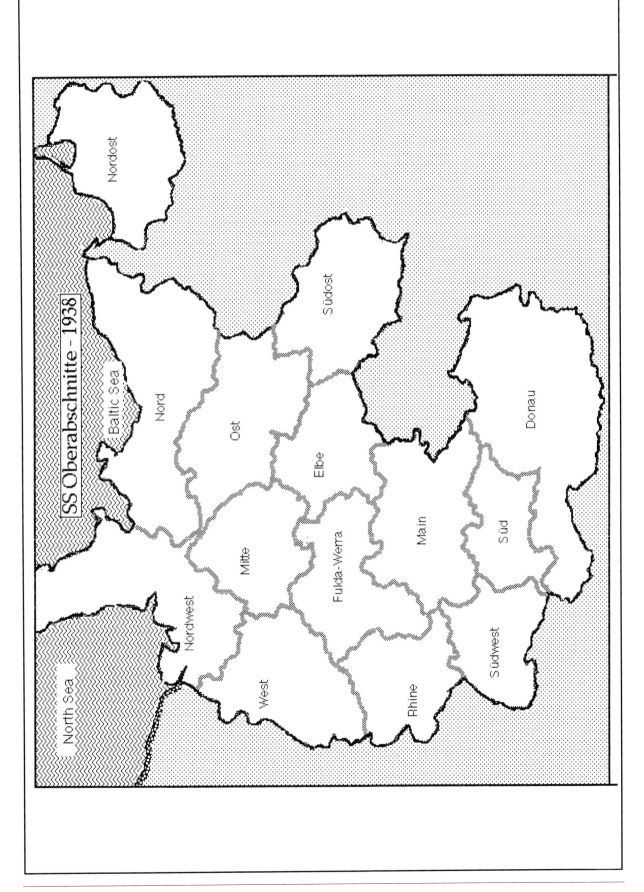

SS Oberabschnitte - 1938

North Sea

Baltic Sea

Nordost

Nord

Nordwest

West

Ost

Mitte

Elbe

Fulda-Werra

Rhine

Südost

Main

Süd

Südwest

Donau

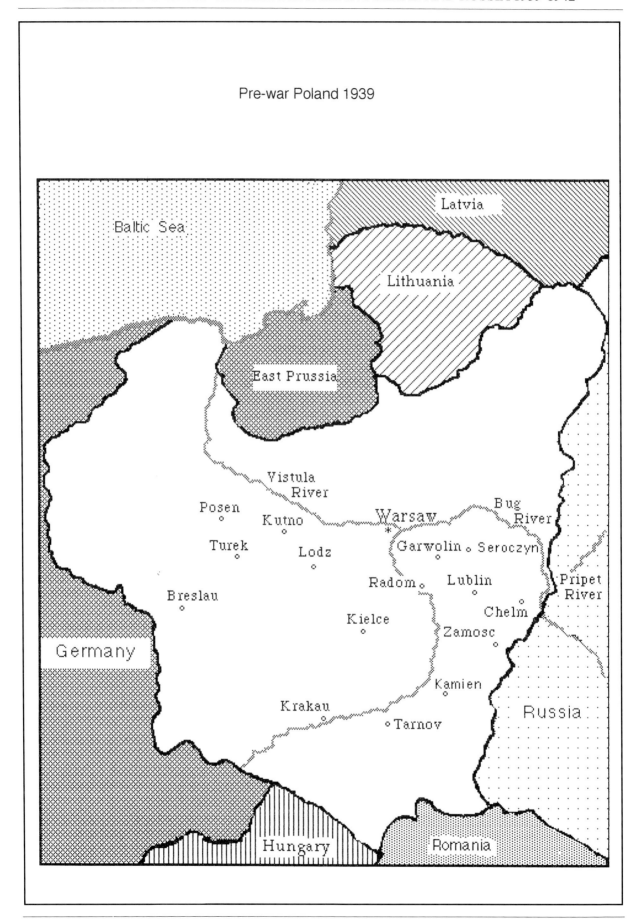

Pre-war Poland 1939

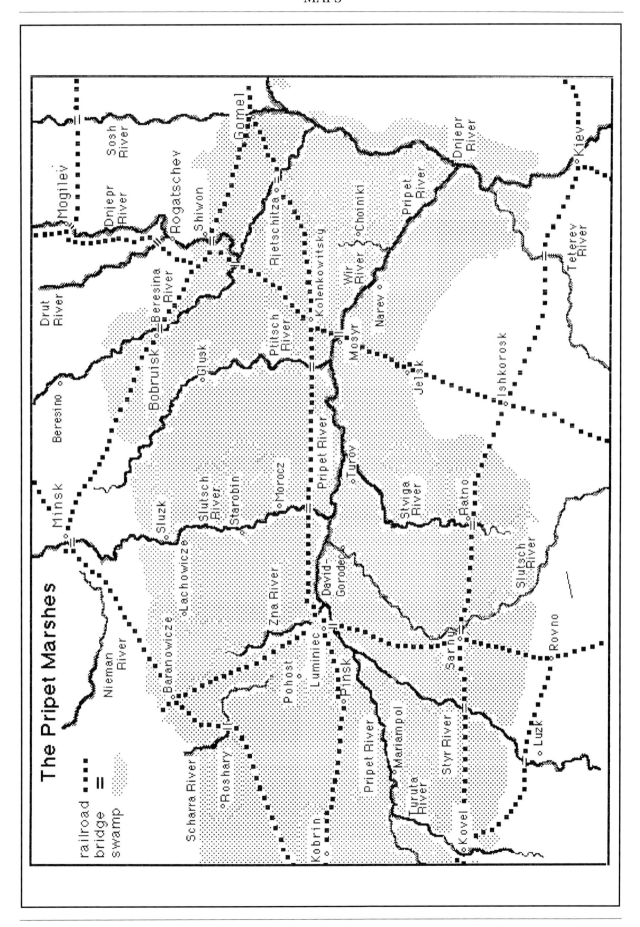

The Pripet Marshes

railroad ▪▪▪▪
bridge ╪
swamp

Mogilev
Dnjepr River
Sosh River
Gomel
Rogatschev
Shiwon
Rietschitza
Kolenkowitsky
Wir River
Choinki
Narev
Dnjepr River
Pripet River
Kiev
Teterev River
Drut River
Beresina River
Bobruisk
Glusk
Piltsch River
Mosyr
Jelsk
Ishkorosk
Beresino
Slutsch River
Starobin
Morocz
Pripet River
Turov
Stviga River
Ratno
Slutsch River
Minsk
Sluzk
Lachowicze
Zna River
David-Gorodec
Luminiec
Pinsk
Sarny
Rovno
Baranowicze
Nieman River
Pohost
Mariampol
Styr River
Luzk
Scharra River
Roshary
Kobrin
Pripet River
Turula River
Kovel

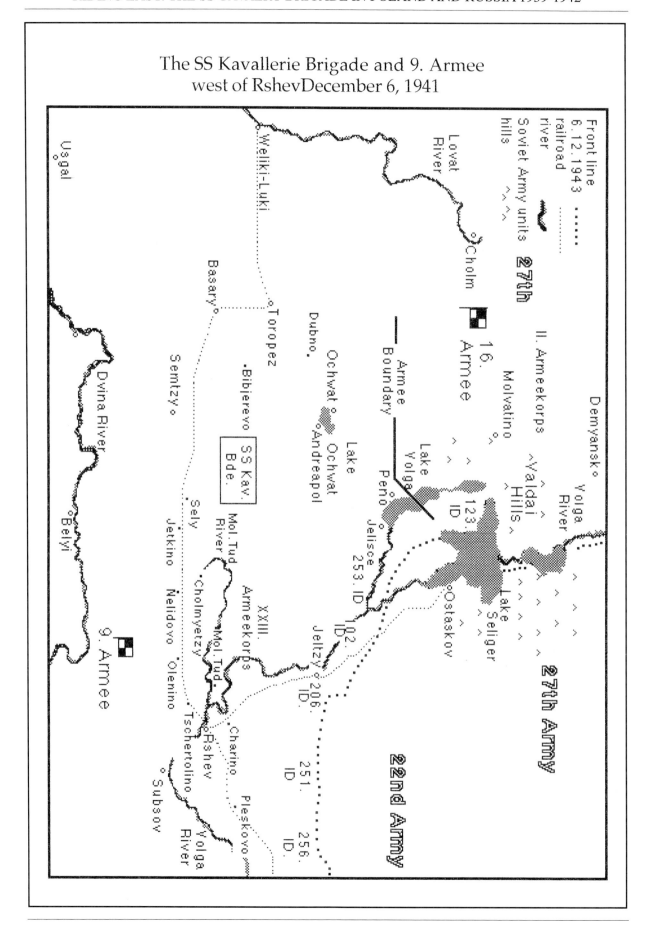

The SS Kavallerie Brigade and 9. Armee
west of Rshev December 6, 1941

The Deployment of SS Kavallerie Brigade - January 9, 1942

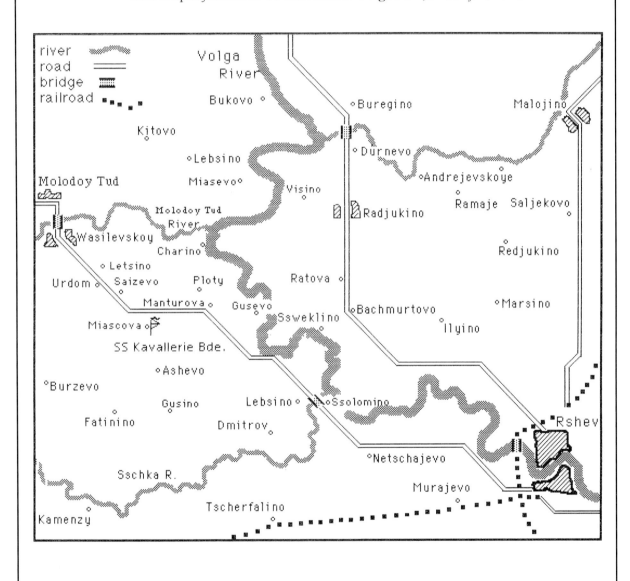

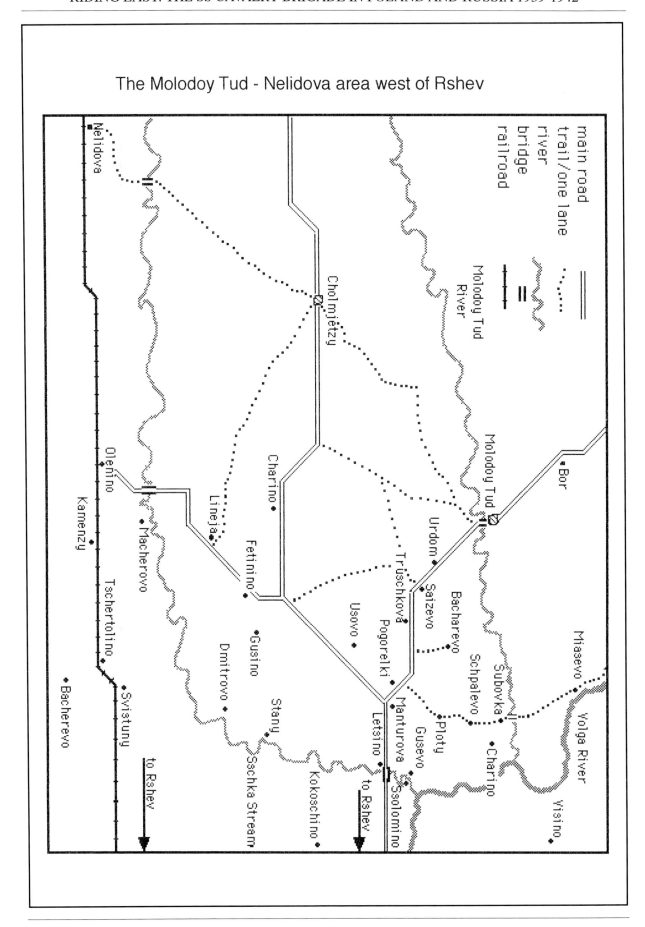

The Molodoy Tud - Nelidova area west of Rshev

APPENDIX: SS RANKS

Reichsführer-SS (Heinrich Himmler)	General of the Army
Oberst-Gruppenführer	Colonel General
Obergruppenführer	General
Gruppenführer	Lieutenant General
Brigadeführer	Major General
Oberführer	Brigadier General
Standartenführer	Colonel
Obersturmbannführer	Lieutenant Colonel
Sturmbannführer	Major
Hauptsturmführer	Captain
Obersturmführer	First Lieutenant
Untersturmführer	Second Lieutenant
Sturmscharführer (primarily Waffen-SS)	Sergeant Major
Stabsscharführer	Sergeant Major
Hauptscharführer	Master Sergeant
Oberscharführer	Technical Sergeant
Scharführer	Staff Sergeant
Unterscharführer	Sergeant
Rottenführer	Corporal
Sturmmann	Private First Class
SS-Mann, for cavalry SS Reiter (rider)	Private

BIBLIOGRAPHY

The primary reference materials used were individual records, reports and orders of the SS-Totenkopf-Reiterstandarte/SS-Kavallerie Brigade and its component sub-elements. Specific references are footnoted in the case of noteworthy facts or actions in the case of these numerous individual documents. These include all the Brigade weekly situation and tactical reports from August 1941 (when actual Brigade formation began) to late December 1941 as well as monthly operational reports during the period the units were deployed in Poland. The number of documents examined are too voluminous to list individually. All these individual documents and collections were from holdings in the National Archives, Washington D.C. and the Vojensky historicky archiv, Prague. The vast aray of superior command and control documents were primarily from the SS-Führungshauptamt and Kommandoamt der Waffen-SS materials deposited in the National Archives on microcopy T-175. Biographical information contained in photographic or footnote information is based for the most part on individual personnel files of the Berlin Document Center.

Primary sources

SS-Führungshauptamt, "Feldpostübersicht," 1940, 1941, 1942, 1943, 1944

SS-Personalkanzlei & SS-Personalhauptamt, "Dienstalterliste der Schutzstaffel der NSDAP,"
Stand vom: 1 Dezember 1937,
1 Juli 1935
1 Dezember 1936
1 Dezember 1937
1 Dezember 1938
30 Januar 1942
20 April 1942
1 Oktober 1942
9 November 1942
15 Mai 1943
1 Oktober 1943
30 Januar 1944
1 Juli 1944
1 Oktober 1944
9 November 1944

SS-Personalkanzlei, (title page missing in original, compilation of early Allgemeine-SS unit facts), Berlin, 21.Dezember 1938.

SS-Verordnungsblatt & SS-Personalveränderungsblatt, 1932-1945

Kriegstagebuch der 1.SS-Totenkopf-Reiterstandarte

Kriegstagebuch Nr. 1, Kommandostab "Reichsführer-SS," 16.6.41 - 31.12.1941

Kriegstagebuch, schwere Schwadron/SS-Kavallerie-Brigade, 15.4.1942 - 23.6.1942

Kriegstagebuch Nr.9, XXIII.Armeekorps, 1.11.1941-31.1.1942

Kriegstagebuch Nr.10, XXIII.Armeekorps, 1.2.1942-31.3.1942

Kriegstagebuch Nr.11, XXIII.Armeekorps, 1.4.1942-31.7.1942

Secondary sources

Angolia, John: "Cloth Insignia of the SS," R.James Bender Publishing, 1983.

Bayer, Hans: "Die Kavallerie der Waffen-SS," Truppenkameradschaft 8., 22., 37.SS-Kavallerie-Divisionen, Gailberg/Heidelburg, 1980.

Bayer, Hans: "Kavallerie Divisionen der Waffen-SS,", Munin Verlag, Osnabrück, 1982.

Bender, Roger James and Taylor, Hugh Page: "Uniforms, Organization and History of the Waffen-SS", 5 volumes, R. James Bender Publishing, San Jose CA, 1969-1982.

Birn, Ruth Bettina: "Die Höheren SS und Polizeiführer, Himmlers Vertreter im Reich und in den besetzten Gebieten," Droste Verlag.

Browder, George Clark: "SIPO and SD, 1931-1940: Formation of an Instrument of Power," University of Wisconsin Ph.D. thesis, 1968.

Carell, Paul: "Hitler Moves East, 1941-1943," Fedorowicz Publishing, 1991.

"Der Freiwillige"/"Wiking Ruf", Munin Verlag, Osnabrück, 1951-1995.

Gelwick, R.A.: "Personnel Policies and Procedures of the Waffen-SS," unpublished Phd dissertation, 1971.

Hausser, Paul: "Soldaten wie andere auch," Munin Verlag, Osnabrück, 1966.

Höhne, Heinz: "The Order of the Death's Head," Coward-McCann, 1970.

Husemann, Friedrich: "Die Guten Glaubens Warren," 2 volumes, Munin Verlag, Osnabrück, 1971 and 1972.

Kannapin, Norbert: "Die deutsche Feldpostübersicht 1939-1945," 3 volumes, Biblio Verlag, 1981.

Klietmann, Dr. E.-G., "Die Waffen-SS, eine Dokumentation," Verlag "Der Freiwillige" G.m.b.H., Osnabrück, 1965.

Koehl, Robert Lewis: "The Black Corps, The Structure and Power Struggles of the Nazi SS," University of Wisconsin Press, 1983.

Krätschmer, Ernst-Günther, "Die Ritterkreuzträger der Waffen-SS," Schütz Verlag, 1982.

Krausnick, Helmut: "Anatomy of the SS State," William Collins Sons, 1968.

Krausnick, Helmut: "Hitlers Einsatzgruppen, Die Truppe des Weltanschauungskriegs 1938-1942,"Fischer Verlag, 1993.

Lucas, James: "Battle Group," Arms and Armor, 1993.

Lumans, Valdis O.: "Himmler's Auxiliaries, The Volksdeutsche Mittelstelle and the German National Minorities of Europe 1933-1945," University of North Carolina Press, 1993.

Mollo, Andrew: "Uniforms of the SS, volume 4 SS-Totenkopfverbände 1933-1945," Windrow and Green, 1991.

Reitlinger, Gerhard: "The SS, Alibi of a Nation 1922-1945," Prentice Hall, 1981.

Scheibert, Horst: "Die Träger des Deutschen Kreuzes in Gold," Podzun Pallas Verlag.

Von Seemen, Gerhard: "Die Ritterkreuzträger 1939-45," Verlag Hans-Henning Podzun, Bad Nauheim, 1955.

Stein, George H.: "The Waffen-SS, Hitler's Elite Guard at War," Cornell University Press, 1966.

Stöber, Hans: "Die Flugabwehrverbände der Waffen-SS," Schütz Verlag, 1984.

Tessin, Georg: "Die Stäbe und Truppeneinheiten der Ordnungspolizei," Teil II of "Zur Geschichte der Ordnungspolizei 1936-1945," Bundesarchiv, Koblenz, 1957.

Tessin, Georg: "Verbände und Truppen der Deutschen Wehrmacht und Waffen-SS 1939-45," 13 volumes, Verlag Mittler & Sohn, Frankfurt/Main.

Wagner, Bernd: "The Waffen-SS," Blackwell Publishing, 1990.

Yerger, Mark C.: "Knights of Steel, The Structure, Development and Personalities of the 2.SS-Panzer-Division 'Das Reich,'" Volume 2, Mark C. Yerger, P.O. Box 4485, Lancaster, PA, 17604, USA, 1994.

Ziegler, Herbert: "Nazi Germany's New Aristocracy, The SS Leadership 1925-1939," Princeton University, 1989.

NAME INDEX

Ahlborn, Hermann: 89, 151
Alteneder, Dr. Friedrich: 155
Ameiser, Toni: 87, 150
Arthuber, Hans: 171
Aust, Walter: 154

Baader, Dr. Fritz: 76, 88, 150
Bach, Erich von dem: 97-98, 104, 107, 110, 117, 126, 128
Baler, Albrecht: 178
Bauer, Gerd: 154
Baumgardt, Hans: 14
Becher, Kurt: 89, 92, 150
Becher, Rolf: 15, 42, 51, 79
Becker, Alfred: 156
Becker, Herbert: 33-34
Bene, Otto: 69
Benndorf, Edwin: 188
Berg, Hans: 51
Berndt, Walter: 41, 52, 90
Beutel, Lothar: 34
Bieter, Rolf: 42, 51
Billerbeck, Johann: 51, 91, 155
Bingel, Wilhelm: 89, 151
Birkigt, Egon: 79
Bittrich, Wilhelm: 198, 202-203
Blaurock, Edmund: 187
Bock, Fedor von: 83
Bock, Dr. Siegfried: 88, 151
Bock und Polach, Carl von: 14
Boigs, Günther: 76, 202
Boosfeld, Joachim: 143, 152, 199
Bornscheuer, Walter: 90, 152
Bösel, Rudolf: 15
Brantenaar, Paul: 13-14
Braune, Martin: 76
Braunstein, Karl: 152, 201
Brenner, Karl: 33, 37
Brockmann, Erich: 89, 152, 201
Brutkuhl, Willi: 89, 108, 151
Buddee, Dr. Hans-Georg: 156
Bug, Anton: 89, 106
Busch, Ernst: 83
Butt, Dr. Erich: 77, 90, 152
Butz, Friedrich: 41, 50, 91, 152

Charpentier, Hans-Georg von: 89, 151, 168, 205, 207
Charwat, Stefan: 78, 90, 152
Christoph, Hans: 90
Claussen, Günther: 21
Conrad, Franz: 76
Conrad, Fritz: 88
Craas, Wolfgang: 13, 41, 51, 77

Daluege, Kurt: 45-46
Deinhard, Carl: 14, 16
Demelhuber, Carl-Maria: 68-69, 84
Diebitsch, Karl: 36
Dieckmann, Heinrich: 42, 50, 57, 62, 67-69, 89, 113, 151

Dietrich, Josef: 83
Dorne, Otto: 14
Dunsch, Walter: 42, 72, 77, 91, 150

Eichlin, Dr. Fritz: 93, 155
Eicke, Theodor: 83, 86
Ertl, Hans: 146, 153
Essl, Hans: 78, 91, 153
Etzler, Gustav: 91

Faßbender, Albert: 40, 43, 50, 77, 85, 90, 92, 119, 125, 161, 203
Fegelein, Hermann: 15, 16, 19-29, 40, 45, 49, 52, 57, 62, 64, 68, 71, 75-76, 81-82, 92, 98, 104, 105-106, 107, 109, 115, 117, 119, 123, 126-127, 141, 143, 157-158, 173, 184, 186, 194, 196-198, 203
Fegelein, Waldemar: 50, 56, 77, 89, 106-107, 110, 112, 115
Findeisen, Richard: 90
Fircks, Karl von: 15
Fischer, Dr. Franz: 77, 152
Floto, Dr. Hans: 16
Flügel, Wolfgang: 153
Frank, August: 66
Frank, Dr. Hans: 30, 33, 53, 65-66
Franz, Dr. August: 151
Freitag, Fritz: 85, 94, 133
Friedrich, Franz: 49, 79
Fries, Walter: 203
Fritsche, Karl: 51, 71, 90, 93, 101, 120-121, 155, 201
Fritz, Josef: 14, 15, 18, 67
Fritzel, Dr. Otto: 14, 16, 18

Gadischke, Hermann: 41-42, 50, 71, 77, 89, 115, 152
Geier, Willi: 89, 108, 111, 152
Geissler, Werner: 77, 91, 102, 153, 174
Gervers, Wilhelm: 15
Gesele, Karl: 87, 119, 127, 139, 142, 150, 201-202
Geyr, Rudolf von: 16
Gilhofer, Herbert: 16
Göhler, Johannes: 89, 145, 113, 151, 205
Görtz, Ulrich: 68-69, 71, 75, 77, 89, 151
Götz, Dr. Arthur: 89
Globocnik, Odilio: 34, 37, 38, 65
Grabsch, Ernst: 50
Greger, Friedrich: 155
Grief, Dr. Georg: 154
Grothe, Alexander: 88
Grothmann, Werner: 95
Grüter, Dr. Max: 151
Guderian, Heinz: 83
Guggloz, Helmuth: 42, 50, 91, 153
Gunst, Walter: 35

Hadlich, Dr. Rudolf: 77, 90
Hahn, Philipp: 12
Hammann, Willi: 90, 153
Hampel, Otto: 12, 40, 49, 78
Handrick, Dr. Hans: 154

Pohl, Ortwin: 66
Portugall, Kurt: 149, 155
Poth, Heinrich: 50
Prager, Friedrich: 18
Prützmann, Hans-Adolf: 26

Queckenstedt, Günther: 77

Rademacher, Ernst: 18
Radmann, Bodo: 91, 153
Rebholz, Heinz: 154
Rehbein, Franz: 49, 78, 89, 119, 150, 203
Rehfeldt, Emil: 23
Reichart, Dr. Hermann: 151, 201
Reichenwallner, Wilhelm: 41, 50, 53, 60-61, 72, 78
Reinhardt, Christian: 76, 88, 92, 98
Reinhardt, Wolfgang: 88, 154, 171
Reinsch, Dr. Karl: 50
Reuther, Georg: 151
Ribbentrop, Joachim von: 83
Richter, Karl: 76, 88, 92, 150
Riege, Paul: 33
Rieger, Hugo: 155
Riehm, Dr.Walter: 50
Riehn, Dr. Kurt: 77
Ries, Hans: 152
Rinner, Franz: 17, 51, 77, 90, 139, 151
Rode, Ernst-August: 134, 142
Roloff, Thorvald: 41
Romani, Dr. Dominik: 77, 90, 152
Rüdgers, Anton: 171
Ruge: 42, 50, 67-68
Rumanof, Michael: 129
Rumohr, Joachim: 202, 209
Rundstedt, Gerd von: 83

Sack, Dr. Albert: 12
Saffert, Karl: 91
Salviati, Hans von: 14
Sanner, Hermann: 152
Schadendorf, Walter: 14
Schädler, Walter: 90, 150
Schaub, Erich: 154
Schiefer, Dr. Hans: 89
Schlaefke, Arthur: 50
Schleifenbaum, Hermann: 92, 112, 152
Schmid, Johann: 77, 89, 107, 112, 151
Schmidt, Josef: 152
Schmidt, Wilhelm: 91, 153
Schmitt, Walter: 53, 154
Schneider, Hermann: 89, 152
Schnerr, Karl: 16
Scholz, Walter von: 77, 91, 154
Schonberg, Ulrich: 153
Schönfeldt, Herbert: 41, 51, 77-78, 91, 153
Schöngarth, Eberhard: 34, 36
Schottes, Michael: 88
Schubert, Albrecht: 171, 178
Schubert, Dietrich: 155
Schulte-Uffelage, August: 111, 151
Schuster, Karl: 35
Schützek, Ernst: 87
Schwarzmaier, Karl: 154, 171
Schwedler, Dr. August: 14
Schwedler, Hans: 37, 55, 64

Schweinberger, Rudi: 154, 171
Seelig, Werner: 90
Senne, Wilhelm: 70
Sessler-Herzinger, Viktor: 78
Sickel, Dr. Kurt: 50
Siemann, Werner: 154
Skepsgardh, Horst von: 12
Skudlarek, Erdmann: 16
Spichern, Franz: 90
Spiehorn, Franz: 155
Spitzy, Dr. Sepp: 77, 89, 154, 171
Stahl, Johann: 90, 152
Stapenhorst, Hans: 202
Stebani, Anton: 18
Stolle, Gustav: 35
Strauss, Albert: 83, 177
Streckenbach, Bruno: 34-35
Streicher, Cassilo: 153
Streubel, Erich: 90
Strohschneider, Dr. Harald: 40, 49
Struve, Karl: 14, 16
Stülpnagel, Carl von: 83
Südekum, Gerhard: 152

Täger, Heinrich: 51
Temme, Günther: 17, 27, 28, 40, 45, 49, 79, 154, 169-171, 207
Tietz, Ferdinand: 188
Tofahrn, Arnold: 202
Tonak, Albert: 150
Trösken, Fritz: 153
Truchsess, Veith: 51, 90
Truenfeld, Karl von: 87

Urbanski, Dr. Helmuth: 76, 88, 150

Vandieken, Anton: 89, 113, 152, 205
Veith, Georg: 89, 109, 114, 151
Vessen, Peter van: 120

Wacker, Alfred: 188
Wappler, Rudolf: 90, 120, 152, 174
Warth, Karl: 51
Weeke, Karl: 90, 100, 148, 154
Wegener, Kurt: 72, 91, 153
Wein, Jakob: 16
Weisspflock, Hein: 90
Wende, Herbert: 93, 155
Wendt, Walter: 103-104
Weyhe, Dotharbus von: 14
Wexel, Peter: 14, 18
Wiersch, Wilhelm: 52, 70, 76, 88, 93, 155, 201
Woikowski-Biedau, Wilhelm von: 14, 15
Wolff, Günther von: 14
Wolff, Karl: 107
Wowerat, Heinz: 78, 92, 153, 201
Wuthenau, Hubert von: 18

Zaika, Danilo: 111
Zapp, Ewald: 14
Zastrow, Hans-Viktor von: 41, 50, 72, 78, 91, 116, 122-123, 153, 174
Zech, Karl: 37, 38
Zehender, August: 190, 200-201, 203-207
Zilling, Karl: 72
Zimmermann, Kurt: 40, 76, 90

The Author

Mark C. Yerger has been researching the SS for more than 15 years. His previous books include the first two volumes of *Knights of Steel*, a multi-volume photographic and documentary history of the 2.SS-Panzer-Division "Das Reich." His most recently published release is an authorized biography of Oakleaves to the Knight's Cross winner Ernst August Krag. With a primary interest centered on Waffen-SS related topics, he has contributed research and material to more than a dozen books by American and European authors. Among the several projects he is currently researching is the biography of a Waffen-SS divisional commander.

AUTHOR'S REQUEST

The creation of this volume and previous books has been possible with the help of numerous individuals. Research continues on a variety of SS related themes and further material is needed in response to reader requests for subject topics. Particularly sought are photographs of any personalities (especially German Cross holders), ceremonies and weapons. Books and periodicals related to the SS and tangent topics are sought as well. Photocopies of award documents (all types) are also particularly needed. Readers wishing to loan, trade or sell material for use in future volumes are asked to contact the author. Materials used will be credited and a copy of the volume containing the material will be provided to the contributor by the author. Correspondence with other historians, researchers and authors for the exchange of material is welcome.

Mark C. Yerger
P.O. Box 4485
Lancaster, PA 17604
U.S.A.

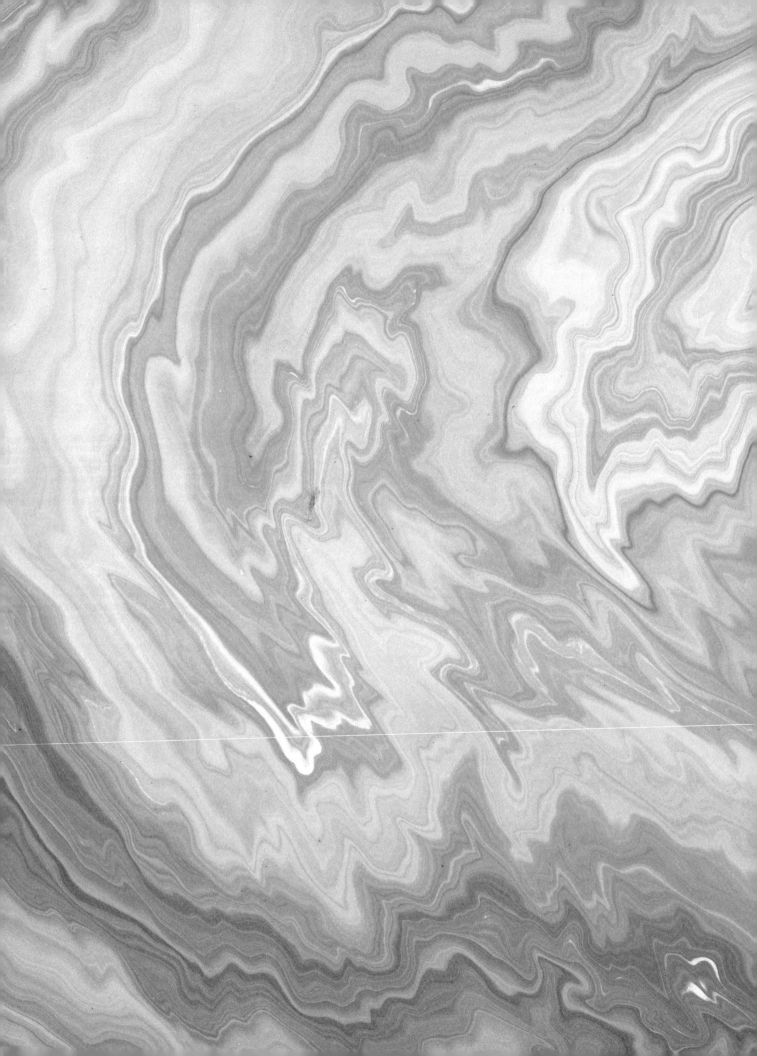